Dr LEO RUICKBIE, PhD (Lond), MA, BA (Hons), Associate of King's College, is a professional writer, editor, social scientist and historian, specialising in controversial areas of human belief and experience.

His PhD is from King's College, London, for his thesis on contemporary witchcraft and magic use, building on research on the theory of re-enchantment that won him an MA with distinction from Lancaster University. He is the author of several books – *Witchcraft Out of the Shadows* (2004 and 2011), *Faustus: The Life and Times of a Renaissance Magician* (2009), *A Brief Guide to the Supernatural* (2012), *A Brief Guide to Ghost Hunting* (2013) and *The Impossible Zoo* (2016) – as well as numerous publications in scholarly journals, magazines, such as *Fortean Times*, and newspapers, including the *Daily Express*. He is also the co-editor with Dr Simon Bacon of *Little Horrors: Interdisciplinary Perspectives on Anomalous Children and the Construction of Monstrosity* (2016), and with Dr Antje Bosselmann-Ruickbie of *The Material Culture of Magic* (forthcoming).

As well as writing, he is the editor of the *Paranormal Review*, the magazine of the Society for Psychical Research, established in 1882 for the scientific study of what we now call the 'paranormal', and has worked on several editorial projects for the Römisch-Germanisches Zentralmuseum (Romano-German Central Museum) in Mainz, Germany. In addition, he is an elected member of the Royal Historical Society, a council member of the Society for Psychical Research, a committee member of the Gesellschaft für Anomalistik (Society for Anomalistics), as well as a member of the Parapsychological Association and the Royal Anthropological Institute.

He has appeared several times on the Travel Channel series *Mysteries at the Castle* and his work has been mentioned in the media from the *Guardian* to Radio Jamaica. Not only has his expertise been sought by film companies, museums and charities, but he is also cited in the current student book for A-Level Sociology in the UK. He can be found on the web at www.ruickbie.com.

Angels in the Trenches

Spiritualism, Superstition and the
Supernatural during the First World War

DR LEO RUICKBIE

ROBINSON

ROBINSON

First published in Great Britain in 2018 by Robinson

13 5 7 9 10 8 6 4 2

Copyright © L. P. Ruickbie, 2018

The moral right of the author has been asserted.

A CIP catalogue record for this book
is available from the British Library.

Research for this book was partly funded by the Society for Psychical Research.

ISBN: 978-1-47213-959-7

Typeset in Scala by Hewer Text UK Ltd, Edinburgh

Printed and bound in Great Britain by CPI Group (UK) Ltd, Croydon CR0 4YY

Papers used by Robinson are from well-managed forests and other responsible sources.

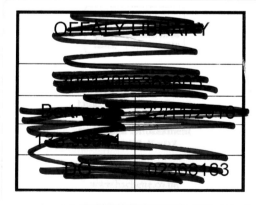

www.littlebrown.co.uk

To
My Mother
Bernice Ruickbie (1949–2017)
The angel in all my battles
and
My Great-Grandfather
Walter Ruickbie (1893–1966)
The Royal Scots, and The Cameronians (Scottish Rifles)
Who was there

Contents

But man, proud man,
Drest in a little brief authority,
Most ignorant of what he's most assured,
His glassy essence, like an angry ape,
Plays such fantastic tricks before high heaven
As make the angels weep [. . .]

William Shakespeare,
Measure for Measure, Sc. II

When the war came it brought earnestness into all our souls and made us look more closely at our own beliefs and reassess their values. In the presence of an agonized world, hearing every day of the deaths of the flower of our race in the first promise of their unfulfilled youth, seeing around one the wives and mothers who had no clear conception whither their loved ones had gone, I seemed suddenly to see that this subject was really something tremendous, a call of hope and of guidance to the human race at the time of its deepest affliction.

Sir Arthur Conan Doyle, *Metropolitan Magazine* (January 1918), p. 10.

Sonnet
(Suggested by some of the *Proceedings
of the Society for Psychical Research*)

Not with vain tears, when we're beyond the sun,
We'll beat on the substantial doors, nor tread
Those dusty high-roads of the aimless dead
Plaintive for Earth; but rather turn and run
Down some close-covered by-way of the air,
Some low sweet alley between wind and wind,
Stoop under faint gleams, thread the shadows, find
Some whispering ghost-forgotten nook, and there

Spend in pure converse our eternal day;
Think each in each, immediately wise;
Learn all we lacked before; hear, know, and say
What this tumultuous body now denies;
And feel, who have laid our groping hands away;
And see, no longer blinded by our eyes.

Rupert Brooke, 1913
(*1914 and Other Poems*)

1914

Mars Ascendant

Before 1914 even began, its terrible course had already been seen in the stars. Mars, the Roman god of war and a twinkling red spark in the night sky, had laid claim to 1914. Each year, beginning about 1827, a book of astrological forecasts appeared called *Raphael's Almanac*, then being published by Robert Thomas Cross, one of a long line of Raphaels, and in 1913 this latest Raphael duly printed his prognosis for the next year. Under the title of 'The Crowned Heads of Europe' a surprisingly accurate prediction was made:

> The Kaiser of Germany is under very adverse directions, and danger both to health and person is indicated. The year opens with Mars in square to the radical Sun, and with Uranus transiting the Sun's place at birth, and Mars passing over the Ascendant, the indications of war and disaster are strongly marked. The Moon is opposed to Uranus in January, a further indication of trouble. A crisis is apparent in the history of the German Empire.[1]

A crisis would, of course, be apparent in the histories of all the European Empires. A certain Madame de Thèbes – in reality Anne Victorine Savigny, a noted French clairvoyant and palmist – also published a yearly *Almanac*. She was said to have already predicted the death of the French General George Ernest Boulanger – nicknamed Général Revanche – in 1891, the Boer War (1899–1902), the death of Queen Victoria (1901), the Russo-Japanese War (1904–1905), the death of the French poet Catulle Mendès in 1909, the death of the influential journalist and Spiritualist William Thomas Stead, who lost his life aboard the *Titanic* in 1912 – the list goes on. When she read Stead's hand she

1 Reprinted under 'Some Prophecies Recalled' in *Light*, No. 1,754, Vol. XXXIV (22 August 1914), p. 406.

saw that 'water was his enemy' – Stead apparently replied by telling her that his familiar spirits would save him from drowning. Such predictions had already brought her international fame – in 1913 she was 'the world's most renowned seeress' in the words of one US newspaper – her words for 1914 would only add to it.[2]

As early as 1903, she had published the prediction that 'the future of Belgium is extraordinarily sad'. Despite 'an impression of peace and happiness', Belgium 'will set all Europe in flames'.[3]

In 1912, she had forecast that 'Germany menaces Europe in general and France in particular.' It took little in the way of clairvoyance to see that, but Madame de Thèbes added 'the days of the Emperor are numbered, and after him all will be changed in Germany'. In her 1913 *Almanac* she prophesied that 'In Austria, he who expects to reign will not come to the throne, and a young man who should not come to the throne will reign.' On 28 June 1914 it became clear what she meant: the heir presumptive to the Austro-Hungarian Empire, Archduke Franz Ferdinand, was assassinated and his nephew Charles became next in line to the throne, reigning as Charles I from 1916. 'We are in the full cycle of Mars,' she later wrote.[4]

As well as publishing her astrological *Almanac*, Madame de Thèbes made her day-to-day living through reading palms. The American writer and poet Ella Wheeler Wilcox – she was the one who wrote 'laugh, and the world laughs with you' – went to see her when in Paris, but such was her popularity that she had to wait two weeks for an appointment. When she did finally get to see her, she noted the many

2 'Famous Prophet Me de Thèbes is Dead', *Los Angeles Herald* (15 January 1917).
3 Quoted in Henry James Forman, *The Story of Prophecy: In the Life of Mankind from Early Times to the Present Day* (New York: Farrar and Rinehart, 1936), p. 6.
4 'Some Prophecies Recalled', *Light*, No. 1,754, Vol. XXXIV (22 August 1914), p. 406; Madame de Thèbes's prophecies relating to the war were also collected and published by Countess Terese Zalinski in *Noted Prophecies, Predictions, Omens and Legends Concerning the Great War and the Great Changes to Follow* (Chicago: Yogi Publishing, 1917), pp. 81–3; additional details from 'Madame de Thèbes: Her Prophecies That Have Come True', *North Otago Times* (26 October 1912).

autographed photographs of European royalty that had been sent as gifts; not to mention photographs of 'almost every celebrity in Europe'. Somewhat to Wilcox's disappointment, de Thèbes predicted the crashing failure of a play she had collaborated on – great things were expected of it, but the Madame's prognostication was correct.[5] According to Countess Zalinski, she had seen 'numerous signs of death and wounds by sword and fire' in the palms of Britons who came to see her before August 1914. 'What,' she had asked herself, 'may signify these signs among so many Englishmen who have no connection or relationship with each other. Can they refer to deaths in war?' It was not just in British hands that she saw sad omens: 'I see in the hands of distinguished Italians,' she wrote in 1913, 'signs of a war of unprecedented violence.' Before the entry of America into the war, she had seen similar signs multiplying in the hands of Americans, or so it was said.[6]

Wilcox had seen the Kaiser reviewing his troops at Mainz in 1906 – the year the Royal Navy launched its first Dreadnought. 'It was a great sight,' she told a friend, 'but made one feel that Universal Peace, so much talked about, is a million miles away.' It was getting further away every day.[7] When she wrote the line 'We have outgrown the need of war' in 1909, it was a desperate appeal against what she had seen rather than a statement of fact.[8]

The *Pittsburgh Press* contacted Madame de Thèbes in 1913 to enquire what the next year would bring for the American people. She was not shy in calling the USA 'the modern Tower of Babel' which had 'reached the crest of her rise'. 'The storm is gathering,' she warned, 'the thunder growls.' There would be 'an explosion as of dynamite turning your New World upside down'. Luckily, through all the 'disasters and upheaval', America 'can rise triumphant'. Lastly, she suggested that American

5 Ella Wheeler Wilcox, *The Worlds and I* (New York: George H. Doran, 1918), p. 318.
6 Zalinski, *Noted Prophecies*, p. 85; Italians quoted in Forman, *The Story of Prophecy*, p. 6.
7 Wilcox, *Worlds and I*, p. 218.
8 'Disarmament' in Ella Wheeler Wilcox, *Poems of Progress* (Chicago: W. B. Conkey, 1909), p. 125.

women should stop wearing pearls and wear diamonds instead, because 'diamonds store up sunshine [...] mankind's first good fortune'. The newspaper printed a photograph of her in her Parisian 'séance studio': we see an elderly woman in a well-appointed library, holding a book in her hand and staring into the distance; around her one can see some of her collection of sixty-two model elephants, apparently 'the best fetich [sic]' (in the sense of magical charm). Nobel Prize winner Maurice Maeterlinck described her 'on her balcony in Paris, peering, listening; waiting at the threshold of the future'.[9]

As European events unfolded, these prophecies would be recalled more than once, but whether American women changed their jewellery fashions we will never know. 'The war was predicted,' Madame de Thèbes later said. 'If the world was not warned, it is because the world paid no attention.'[10]

In 1936, looking back on the years before the First World War, the American writer Henry James Forman made the sweeping statement that 'virtually all astrologers predicted a terrible conflict for Europe and notably for Germany between the years 1913 and 1916'.[11]

'Europe Deluged in Blood': Mrs Foster Turner's Prophecy

Since its beginnings in America in 1848, Spiritualism had had the time and opportunity to spread across the civilised world. What had begun

9 'Madame de Thèbes, World's Most Renowned Seeress, Foretells Great Events of 1914', *The Pittsburgh Press* (28 December 1913), p. 1 – the copy I was able to see was damaged in parts and difficult to read; reference to elephants in 'Madame de Thèbes: Her Prophecies That Have Come True', *North Otago Times* (26 October 1912); Maeterlinck quoted in 'A Prophetess of Paris and the War: Madame de Thèbes Claims to have Predicted Catastrophe', *The Ottawa Journal* (10 June 1916), p. 16.
10 'A Prophetess of Paris'.
11 Forman, *The Story of Prophecy*, p. 277.

as mysterious rapping sounds in a modest house in Hydesville, New York State, was now a world movement. Even Queen Victoria had held a séance after the death of Prince Albert. Death, the only certainty in life, posed the greatest question of all, the question that was at the root and heart of all religion: what happens after we die? After aeons of shamans, mystics and priests – and astrologers and palmists, too – telling us what lay beyond, Spiritualism now offered the possibility to discover it for oneself.[12]

One Spiritualist medium, a Mrs Foster Turner, well known in Australia, was at the Little Theatre on Castlereagh Street in Sydney one Sunday in February 1914. Almost a thousand people were crammed into the theatre to witness her trance communications. Those at the back jostled and strained their necks for a view of the woman.

Sir Arthur Conan Doyle met her some years later and described her as 'a middle-aged lady of commanding and pleasing appearance with a dignified manner and a beautifully modulated voice'. She was, he thought, 'the greatest all-round medium with the highest general level of any sensitive in Australia'. And now, eyes closed, she was speaking in a voice not her own. The famous British Spiritualist W. T. Stead, now dead, was speaking through her from the beyond:

> Now, although there is not at present a whisper of a great European War at hand, yet I want to warn you that before this year 1914 has run its course, Europe will be deluged in blood. Great Britain, our beloved nation, will be drawn into the most awful war the world has ever known. Germany will be the great antagonist, and will draw other nations in her train. Austria will totter to its ruin. Kings and kingdoms will fall. Millions of precious lives will be slaughtered, but Britain will finally triumph and emerge victorious. During the year, also, the Pope of Rome will pass away, and a bomb will be placed in St. Paul's Church,

---

12 For an overview of the history of Spiritualism, see Leo Ruickbie, *A Brief Guide to the Supernatural* (London: Robinson, 2011), pp. 206–35.

but will be discovered in time and removed before damage is done.[13]

Pope Saint Pius X died on 20 August 1914 as German troops marched into Brussels. Since suffering from a heart attack in 1913 he had been in constant ill health. But the bomb went off in St George's Church, Hanover Square, London. Suffragettes planted the device which exploded some minutes after 10 o'clock on 14 June 1914. Firemen forced the doors and found the building filled with dense smoke, and some pews and stained-glass windows damaged. An envelope was found containing the message 'A protest against the torture of women'. Only some shouting was said to have disrupted a service at St Paul's Cathedral. The year before, a bomb had been found in St Paul's and was safely removed – Suffragettes were again to blame.[14]

'Millions Will Die': Sophie's Prophecy

Summer in Athens: sunbeams like lances breaking on the white city. In a shaded room, Dr Antoniou sits in his chair. Across from him a young woman, eighteen years old, lies on a couch. She is in a hypnotic trance.[15]

Dr Antoniou has written 'Sophie, June 19th' across the top of his notebook. He is writing as she speaks.

'The war will begin in about two months.'

13 Sir Arthur Conan Doyle, *The Wanderings of a Spiritualist* (London: Hodder and Stoughton, 1921), pp. 258–9; the prediction was quoted again in Doyle, *The History of Spiritualism*, vol. II (London: Cassell & Co., 1926) p. 328.
14 *The Morning Post* (8 May 1913); *Chicago Tribune* (15 June 1914), p. 1
15 *Revue Metapsychique* (December 1925), pp. 380, 390; A. Campbell Holms, *The Fundamental Facts of Spiritualism* (London: The Psychic Press, 1927), pp. 33–4; Conan Doyle, *History of Spiritualism*, vol. II, p. 234.

What war? He thought. Not the Balkan War, that had already begun.

'The war will be long.'

He wrote it down.

'Millions will die, for this war will be savage.'

He shook his head.

'Unimaginable destruction will take place.'

He was no longer looking at her. She was talking so fast that he only concentrated on her words, watching his pencil moving across the page.

'Thrones will be upset. Ancient states will be dissolved and new ones created. The end of the war will be followed by a long period of negotiations.'

Some new delusion, then, but so matter of fact.

'The Triple Entente will be victorious in the end.'

'Germany will be an Empire no longer. The economic consequences of the war will be terrible for her.'

'The Austrian Empire will be decomposed into its constituent elements.'

When she came out of her trance, he felt like the one who had been mesmerised. He could not get her words out of his head. The ramblings of an hysteric – spoken like an ancient Sybil.

On 28 June he read of the assassination of Archduke Franz Ferdinand in Serbia. Greece had a treaty with Serbia to defend it if ever it were attacked by Bulgaria. Bulgaria mobilised, but the Greek Prime Minister, Eleftherios Venizelos, refused to take his country to war.

As June turned into July, Antoniou told his friends about the case. They raised their eyebrows, asked questions, but he did not have any answers.

The newspaper headlines spoke of escalating tensions. Then on 28 July Austria-Hungary declared war on Serbia and the chain reaction ignited Europe. Greece would not enter the war until 30 June 1917, but Dr Antoniou knew Sophie's prediction had been fulfilled. He sent an account of her prophecies to the Athens' newspaper *To Asty* and they were published from 24 to 27 August 1914.

The Stuff Which Nightmares Are Made Of

There were other private prophecies being made all across Europe. Henry Forman, who wrote a history of prophecy among other things, heard from a Swiss friend of his, the Theosophist Max Gysi, then living in Hampstead, about a Finnish physician, Dr Edvard Wilhelm Lybeck. Lybeck, apparently, for some years prior to 1914 had been having clair-voyant visions of, in his words, 'a great war which would change the map of Europe'. Forman learnt that Lybeck had written to friends in London on 7 February 1914, saying:[16]

> You will remember my speaking of the great war three years ago. Yes! I believe still that there is very near the sudden breaking out of a European war with Germany, Sweden, Austria and Turkey attacking Russia at first and consequently England and France being later drawn into the thing. I believe it is so near that when the summer comes it sees the war in full flame.

Gysi said that Lybeck's wife was also psychic and had herself made predictions of a coming war in January 1914. She told several friends, writing to one of them, a Belgian artist, with instructions to lay up a store of food in anticipation. The Belgian artist replied that there was 'no cloud on the horizon' and rather that it tempted fate to make such pessimistic forecasts.[17]

A certain Mr Lovat Fraser wrote to the *Daily Mail* in July, describing a vivid dream he had had of 'war in the air' and 'a vision of destruction

16 Lybeck quoted in Forman, *The Story of Prophecy*, p. 259. Further informa-tion on Gysi from Crispian Villeneuve, *Rudolf Steiner in Britain*, vol. 1 (Forest Row, East Sussex: Temple Lodge, 2009), p. 199 – he was also closely involved with Steiner.
17 Forman, *The Story of Prophecy*, p. 260.

in Turkey', with airships dropping bombs on what was then still known as Constantinople.

As he lay sleeping, Lovat Fraser saw a building which he took to be a factory with three tall chimneys standing on the Asiatic side of the Bosphorus. Airships approached and reduced it to ruins with their bombs. Lovat Fraser had never before visited the place or seen it 'with his waking eye'. Member of Parliament George Lloyd, 1st Baron Lloyd, wrote the next day to confirm the existence of the place described. He was said to know the country well. As an officer in the Warwickshire Yeomanry, Lord Lloyd was called up in August and found himself sailing for Turkey: he landed with the Australian and New Zealand Army Corps (ANZACs) at Gallipoli.

Under the title 'The Stuff Which Dreams Are Made Of', the *Daily Mail* called Lovat Fraser's dream 'an undoubted case of what has been called telaesthesia, or perception at a distance, by some faculty which is not with man in his waking state'. And, in contrast to our own sceptical and materialistic times, the newspaper stated that 'the incident is not to be explained by the ordinary crude method of ascribing the vision to indigestion or an overdose of lobster, but rather by the existence of some curious power of passing beyond the limitations of space and time'. It was a very public endorsement of premonition.[18]

The Maori Prophecy

One of the factors contributing to the First World War was the naval rivalry between Britain and Germany, and one of the consequences of that rivalry was the construction of HMS *New Zealand*, a ship believed to be under magical protection. The ship was paid for by New Zealand, then a Dominion of the British Empire, in response to the German

18 *Daily Mail* (18 July 1914); 'The Stuff Which Dreams Are Made Of', *Daily Mail* (19 July 1914); both reported in 'Mr Lovat Fraser's Dream', *Light*, vol. XXXIV (27 July 1914), p. 305.

naval programme in 1909. Built in Glasgow, she was launched on 1 July 1911 and commissioned into service on 19 November 1912. She was an Indefatigable-class battlecruiser, packing eight 12-inch guns and sixteen 4-inch guns in an armoured body just short of 600 feet (179.9 m), with a top speed of 25 knots. New Zealanders living in London had commissioned a huge carving of the New Zealand coat of arms to be fixed on the after part of the superstructure, with another, smaller one, attached to the front of the bridge; a silver bell was taken from the old HMS *New Zealand* (renamed *Zealandia*); and another New Zealand Londoner donated the ship's mascot, a bulldog called Pelorus Jack. A great deal of New Zealand pride went into her making.[19]

The new ship was intended to be the flagship of the China Station based in New Zealand, but the growing threat of war changed all that and she was deployed to the North Sea. However, in February 1913, she was despatched on a world cruise, what Commander Cree called 'showing the flag' to the rest of the Empire. Captain Lionel Halsey set out for the other side of the world with his crew of eight hundred. When she arrived in New Zealand, visiting eighteen of her ports, almost half the country's population of 800,000 visited the ship.

Some of those visitors were Maori chiefs. Invited onboard by Lieutenant Jones, a number of chiefs of the Ngatiraukawa tribe, together with Major Ballinger and 250 cadets, visited the warship when she docked in Wellington. One of the chiefs, Rere Nikitini, gave an address (with Kipa Roera interpreting), claiming a spectacular amount of credit for the ship:

19 Cmdr Charles M. Cree, 'Piu-Piu and Tiki', in *True Ghost Stories from WWI and WWII* (London: Bounty Books, 2005), pp. 80–2. This unsourced collection of stories is rather dubious, but there was at least a Cmdr Cree; his name is recorded in *The Navy List*, e.g., in the October 1917 issue (London: His Majesty's Stationery Office, 1917). His account also claims that the ship was captained by Green in 1913 and in 1916, whereas it was captained by Halsey in 1913, then Green from 1915 onwards. Additional information on the case can be found at 'HMS *New Zealand* Piupiu', Royal New Zealand Navy Museum, http://www.navymuseum.co.nz/blog/hms-new-zealand-piupiu/, accessed 11 February 2018.

This ship bears the name of our islands. It was presented on behalf of the people to His Majesty by our Prime Minister, Sir Joseph Ward. We, the Maori people, entirely concurred in the gift, and we realise that some part of its cost has come direct from the land of our ancestors. We are under the mana of England by special treaty – the Treaty of Waitangi. We are under the protection of England, therefore we give her a battleship. As to these garments let them be as sails for your ship, carrying you to distant shores, and even to the presence of war if that should happen. Let there be a further inspiration to you at that awful day – if the day comes – when our ship should clear for action.[20]

The natives then launched into their welcoming song, 'Toia Mai-te waka'. Captain Halsey thanked them for their gifts, the 'garments' referred to in the speech. Described in the newspaper at the time as 'garments of war', these were a *piupiu*, – a skirt made of black and white flax woven together – and what the paper called a '*pois*', a *hei-tiki* or magical amulet (a figure carved in jade – nephrite – and worn around the neck). Halsey was also made an honorary chief of the tribe. There is some debate on who the presenting chief actually was, with other sources giving the names of Te Heuheu Tukino, Paramount Chief of the Ngati-Tuwharetoa tribe, Mana Himiona Te Ataotu, chief of the Ngai Tahu, and Mita Taupopoki, chief of the Tuhourangi (Te Arawa) and Ngati Wahiao.[21]

Whoever the chief was, Commander Cree said that he also made a prophecy. One day, he announced, the ship would be in a great sea battle and would be hit three times – on the conning tower, on the after turret and on the foretop – but casualties would be light. Another legend has it that the chief made three prophecies: the ship would be involved in three battles; that the ship would be hit only once; and that

20 'Maori Chiefs Visit Warship', *Evening Post* (18 April 1913).
21 'HMS *New Zealand* Piupiu', http://www.navymuseum.co.nz/blog/hms-new-zealand-piupiu/, accessed 11 February 2018, cites an exhibition caption for the *piupiu*, an unsourced newspaper clipping, and the diary of Mrs Joan Wood, entry for Monday, 4 December 1933, but not the *Evening Post* article.

no one on-board would be killed. Cree was evidently telling the story second- or third-hand, since he had Green as the captain in 1913, when, in fact, he would only assume command in June 1915; however, there is sufficient documentary evidence to show that a gift of ritual items was made.

The chief requested that Halsey wear the *piupiu* and *hei-tiki* to protect his men in battle. Halsey took careful possession of the gifts and stowed them away for the appointed time, if it should ever come. 'He would keep the gifts,' said the *Evening Post*, 'and preserve them in remembrance of the kindness of the Maoris.' Time would tell whether the prophecies would come true.

The Hand of Kitchener

As the deadline for Britain's ultimatum expired, the country was at war. Field Marshal Horatio Herbert Kitchener, 1st Earl Kitchener – the famous Kitchener of Khartoum, soon to become the even more famous face of British Army recruitment – may well have recalled the prediction of Cheiro all those years ago. 'Cheiro' was the *nom de plume* of a certain individual calling himself Count Louis Hamon, which may or may not have been his real name. Twenty years earlier, the palm reader or cheiromancer, whence the name Cheiro, visited him at the War Office in London with the intention of making an impression of his hand – Cheiro does not relate how he came upon this idea, but he seems to have had quite a collection of these impressions. Kitchener was then (in 1894) Sirdar of the Egyptian Army at the time of the Mahdist War and, according to Cheiro, had returned to Britain to hand in his resignation over 'The Abbas Affair', as Cheiro called it, or 'Frontier Incident' as it was otherwise known. Abbas II was the insufferable teenage Khedive (Viceroy) of Egypt, who disparaged Kitchener's Egyptian Army, and especially its British officers, to Kitchener's face and when Kitchener promptly resigned, begged him not to do so. The British Government rebuked Abbas and he publicly made amends. It was more likely that Kitchener was in London to receive the honour of being created Knight Commander of the Order of St Michael and St George. At any rate, a secretary brought him Cheiro's card and he had him sent in.[22]

'Well,' said Kitchener, 'so you want to have a look at my hand again?'

'Again?' Cheiro was taken aback.

'Years ago,' he said, 'I went to see you like so many others and I can only say you were most singularly accurate in everything you told me.' At least, that is what Kitchener said according to Cheiro's account of their conversation. Elsewhere, Cheiro recorded that their first meeting had been in 1887. Kitchener was a colonel at the time and relatively unknown.[23]

'I had no idea you believed in such studies,' said Cheiro. 'I hardly dared come and ask you to let me have an impression of your hand.'

'Look here,' said Kitchener, turning round. He pointed to a three-inch-high vase on his desk. 'Can you tell me anything about that?'

Cheiro was again taken aback. He took the vase in his hands, looked it over and put it down again. 'I am sorry,' he said, 'but I don't know one vase from another. I never have had the inclination to study such things.'

'Just so,' laughed Kitchener. 'You have answered yourself. I have never studied hands and you have. If a man makes a lifelong study of a thing, I expect him to know more about it than anyone else – so now you know why I went to see you many years ago.'

Cheiro evidently had not told Kitchener everything, as now, leaning back in his chair, he asked him to explain 'the lines in his own clearly marked palms', as well as those of Gladstone, Stanley and others – it turned out that Cheiro had brought impressions of their hands with him. He took the forty-four-year-old's hand.

22 Cheiro, *Confessions: Memoirs of a Modern Seer* (London: Jarrolds, 1932), pp. 97–100; E. S. Grew, *Field-Marshal Lord Kitchener: His Life and Work for the Empire*, vol. I (London: Gresham, 1917), pp. 155–6.

23 Cheiro, *Cheiro's World Predictions*, new and enlarged ed. (London: Herbert Jenkins, 1931), p. xi.

'Tell me what you like,' said Kitchener, 'as long as the end is some distance off.'

'I explained,' said Cheiro, 'the still higher positions and responsibilities that his path of Destiny mapped out before him.' Kitchener might have guessed or wished as much himself. However, that was not all. 'The heaviest and greatest of all,' explained Cheiro, 'would be undertaken in his sixty-fourth year' – 1914. The date meant nothing at the time: 'how little either of us thought that in that year the most terrible war that England has ever engaged in would have broken out'.

Looking at Kitchener's hand, Cheiro drew attention to a line that extended from his Line of Life encircling the ball of the thumb and crossed the Line of Fate and the Line of Success. This was the Line of Voyage. According to Cheiro, this broke the lines of Fate and Success at the point 'where all my books on the subject show to be about the sixty-sixth year of age'.[24]

Cheiro was a numerologist as well as a palmist. He talked of a Law of Periodicity operating in human fate determined by the calculation of 'fadic' numbers – the 'Numbers of Fate'. The important moment for Kitchener was the opening of the Egyptian campaign in 1896. Cheiro took each number from this year and added them together: 1+8+9+6, to get 24, adding the numbers again, 2+4, to get 6; so the fadic number for 1896 was 6. In 1897, Kitchener was victorious at Atbara and Omdurman: fadic number 7. In 1898, Kitchener enjoyed 'rest from labour' and was 'honoured by the nation': fadic number 8. This sequence of fadic numbers again occurred in the next century: 1914, fadic number 6, saw the opening of the war; 1915, fadic number 7, saw the creation of Kitchener's New Army (not quite the same as victory in battle, but Cheiro glossed over this); meaning that 1916, fadic number 8, would again signal rest and honour, but this time, Cheiro saw this as meaning Kitchener's final rest, although he kept that to himself.[25]

Kitchener ran his pencil down the list of Cheiro's figures. Stopping at 1916, he said, 'That then is perhaps "The End." ' According to Cheiro,

24 Cheiro, *Confessions*, p. 100.
25 Cheiro, *Confessions*, p. 98.

he laughed, 'Strange, isn't it? But is there any indication of the kind of death it is likely to be?'

'Yes,' said Cheiro. 'There are certainly indications, but not all perhaps the kind of "end" that one would be likely to imagine would happen to you.'

As well as being a palmist and numerologist, Cheiro was also an astrologer. Now, he proceeded to chart Kitchener's fate as it appeared in the stars:

'Having been born on June 16th, 1850, he was in the First House of Air, in the Sign of Gemini, entering into the First House of Water, the Sign of Cancer, also House of the Moon and detriment of Saturn. Taking these indications, together with the cabbalistic interpretation of the numbers governing his life, the fatal year would be his sixty-sixth year about June, and the death would be by water, probably caused by storm (Air) or disaster at sea (Water), with the attendant chance of some form of capture by an enemy and an exile from which he would never recover.'

Kitchener laughed: 'Thanks, I prefer the first proposition.' But according to Cheiro, he took him seriously.[26]

'I must admit,' said Kitchener, 'that what you tell me about danger at sea makes a serious impression on my mind and I want you to note down among your queer theories, but do not say anything about it unless if some day you hear of my being drowned – that I made myself a good swimmer and I believe I am a fairly good one – for no other reason but that when I first visited you as quite an unknown man many years ago, you told me that water would be my greatest danger. You have now confirmed what you told me then and have even given me the likely date of the danger.'

Cheiro made an impression of Kitchener's hand using paper lying on the great man's desk.[27] Finally, they said their goodbyes.

26 Ala Mana, *The Message: Lord Kitchener Lives*, vol. I (Los Angeles: Grafton, 1922), p. 99.
27 Cheiro, 'What I Read in Kitchener's Hand', *The Strand Magazine*, vol. LII (July–December 1916), p. 196.

'I won't forget,' said Kitchener, 'and as of course you believe in thought transference and that sort of thing, who knows if I won't send you some sign, if it should happen that water claims me at the last.'

With international tensions mounting, Kitchener had been *en route* back to Cairo to resume his post. He got as far as a Channel steamer at Dover before being recalled; the armoured cruiser HMS *Black Prince* had already been despatched to meet him. By late afternoon on the fateful day he was at the Foreign Office in Whitehall. As the chimes of Big Ben marked the expiration of the British ultimatum to Germany at 11 p.m. (midnight in Germany), Tuesday 4 August, did Kitchener, the soon to be appointed Secretary of State for War, look at his hand and, perhaps, think to himself, 'so it was foretold: now it begins'? From along The Mall in the direction of Buckingham Palace a crowd could be heard singing 'God Save the King'. Prime Minister Asquith and his ministers gathered in the Cabinet room were interrupted by the First Lord of the Admiralty, Winston Churchill, bringing the news that he had sent the war telegram – 'Commence hostilities against Germany' – to the fleet.[28]

Lord Kitchener was among those present at an extraordinary Council of War called by Asquith the next day. 'I wonder,' wrote Churchill, who was also present, 'what the twenty politicians round the table would have felt if they had been told that the prosaic British Cabinet was itself to be decimated in the war they had just declared.' If we are to believe Cheiro, Kitchener had already been told.[29]

---

28 Sir George Arthur, *Life of Lord Kitchener*, vol. III (London: Macmillan, 1929), pp. 2–3; 'England [sic] Declares War on Germany', *Manchester Guardian* (5 August 1914); Winston Churchill, *The World Crisis*, vol. I (Toronto: Macmillan, 1923), p. 245. Detail concerning the *Black Prince* from Thomas G. Frothingham, *The Naval History of the World War* (Cambridge, MA: Harvard University Press, 1925), p. 55.

29 Churchill, *World Crisis*, p. 251.

The Sinking of the *Amphion*

On the evening of 6 August 1914, two days after Britain had declared war on Germany, Miss Ann Jones (a pseudonym)[30] was sitting in her room, waiting for some friends to call, when she was overcome by what she described as 'a feeling of great depression and fatigue'. She lay down on the sofa and fell into a trance state, 'a kind of swoon [. . .] between sleeping and waking' as she called it. Her mind filled with the image of a sinking ship. When her friends arrived they found her still in this exhausted condition, talking about a strange dream. That night she wrote in her diary 'had a bad dream of a ship sunk'.

The papers only carried news of a 'ship sunk' on the morning of 7 August: after engaging and sinking the German minelayer, the *Königin Luise*, the light cruiser HMS *Amphion* had struck a mine on the morning of 6 August and gone down, taking with her over a hundred of her crew. It was the first British loss of the war – and the first psychic experience.[31] An account was sent in to the Society for Psychical Research and published in the December issue of the *Journal*.[32]

Psychical Researchers

All of these strange signs and portents did not go unnoticed. The popular press reported some of them, the Spiritualist press almost all of

30 Described as a friend of Helen Verrall (*Journal of the Society for Psychical Research*, vol. 12, December 1912, p. 337) and had a sister called 'L.' (p. 340).
31 Not Private Parr as is usually related.
32 In the account, the only connection made between the dream and a sinking ship is with the *Amphion*, but the *Amphion* had led the destroyer flotilla that sank the *Königin Luise* on 5 August – the first German loss to the British.

them. Nor did they go uninvestigated. At the outbreak of the First World War there already existed an organisation for the investigation of what we would nowadays call the paranormal: the Society for Psychical Research (SPR). Founded in 1882 at the instigation of physicist Professor Sir William Fletcher Barrett and journalist Edmund Dawson Rogers, the Society was now in its thirty-second year. Some of its best and perhaps most important work was already behind it: seminal research into visions of apparitions had resulted in the book *Phantasms of the Living* in 1886 – a landmark publication that was reported in *The Times*.[33]

By the time war was declared, many of the most important original members – Henry Sidgwick (d. 1900), Frederic Myers (d. 1901), Edmund Gurney (d. 1888) and Frank Podmore (d.1910) – were dead, but by no means forgotten. The acute sense of loss for these central personalities among the surviving and subsequent members made something like martyrs out of them and a cult out of their martyrdom. The whole bizarre ensemble of the cross-correspondences – short messages mediumistically received (see below) – was their holy book.

The Society itself had survived that first generation. Not all of the initial wave of investigators had passed beyond the veil that shrouded their research interests, but, more importantly, the Society's scientific approach had found favour among an intellectual, cultural and aristocratic elite that ensured its continued existence.

In 1914, there were 1,212 members of the SPR and we find them engaged in their usual activities. They had voted in the German-born philosopher Dr Ferdinand Canning Scott Schiller to take over from the French philosopher Henri Bergson as President, and had re-elected and co-opted familiar names to the Council.

---

33 Edmund Gurney, Frederic W. H. Myers and Frank Podmore, *Phantasms of the Living*, 2 vols (London: Trübner and Co., 1886). I will occasionally talk of the SPR as a corporate entity. While the Society has always asserted that it holds no corporate opinions, any organisation will tend to be associated with the views of its most active and vociferous members; additionally, editorial opinion and the conclusions reached by its paid research staff tended to represent a distinctive 'voice'.

Eleanor Sidgwick, widow of Henry Sidgwick, former Principal of Newnham College, Cambridge, and former President of the Society, was Honorary Secretary. She shared the position with the Honourable Everard Feilding, second son of the late Rudolph Feilding, 8th Earl of Denbigh. One of Eleanor Sidgwick's brothers, the Right Hon. Gerald Balfour (later 2nd Earl Balfour), was also on the Council and a Vice-President – another of her brothers was the former Prime Minister Arthur Balfour (1st Earl Balfour), who was also a Vice-President of the Society.

For all the Sirs, Professors and Doctors in the Society, it was the charisma of Mrs Sidgwick that held them together. Almost everybody was devoted to her, especially the Society's office staff. She seemed to have an almost hypnotic effect on people. Winifred Coombe Tennant wrote in her diary after their first meeting in 1910 that 'I feel there was nothing she could ever ask of me that I would not do to my very utmost'.[34]

Also on the Council was the physicist Sir Oliver Lodge. He was another dominating figure and much of the history of the Society during the war years revolves around his activities. Coombe Tennant described him as 'wonderfully tall and large, like a lion', although the SPR's Research Officer, Alice Johnson, thought him 'credulous'.[35]

Other members of the Council were equally important and well connected. They included John William Strutt, 3rd Baron Rayleigh, who had been awarded the Nobel Prize for Physics in 1904 for his part in discovering argon; he was also a former President of the Royal Society and member of the Privy Council, amongst many other awards and achievements too numerous to mention. The inventor St George William Lane Fox-Pitt was also a member; he was married to the daughter of the 9th Marquis of Queensberry – the one who gave his name to

34 Winifred Coombe Tennant, *Between Two Worlds: The Diary of Winifred Coombe Tennant, 1909–1924*, edited by Peter Lord (Aberystwyth: The National Library of Wales, 2011), p. 45.
35 Tennant, ibid., p. 46; Johnson's opinion recorded by Tennant, p. 58.

the 'Marquis of Queensberry Rules' in boxing and famously called Oscar Wilde a 'somdomite' (he meant 'sodomite') back in 1895. The Revd Matthew Albert Bayfield, Classical scholar, clergyman and head-master, acted in an unofficial role as the Society's padre – he officiated at the wedding of Helen Verrall (see below) and William Salter, for example. The Right Revd Bishop Boyd Carpenter was also a Vice-President (he had been President in 1912). Sir Lawrence Jones, 4th Baronet of Cranmer Hall, was on the Council, as was the political scientist Goldsworthy Lowes Dickinson – his reaction to the war was to draw up plans for the League of Nations. The writer and politician Ernest Bennett, later Sir (he was knighted in 1930), was then a Fellow of Pembroke College with a dashing past and a still dashing future to come. The Classical scholar Professor Gilbert Murray had been the basis for a character in one of Bernard Shaw's plays: Adolphus Cusins in his 1905 work *Major Barbara* – he would become President of the SPR for 1915 and 1916. The philosopher L. P. Jacks, then a Professor at Manchester College, Oxford, would serve as President in 1917 and 1918.

The Polish medium Stanislawa Tomczyk had been invited to the UK by the Council and a special committee was formed to investigate her claims, involving Everard Feilding, W. W. Baggally, Eleanor Sidgwick, Helen Verrall, Dr Woolley, and two of Feilding's friends, Mr S. Cowper-Coles (photographic expert) and Mark Barr (electrical expert). The medium was in poor health and not all of the séances were successful, despite that the committee witnessed what appeared to be the levita-tion of a small ball. No fraud was detected; however, they decided that the results were inconclusive. Tomczyk had moved more than balls: she had also tugged heartstrings. She married one of the investigators, Feilding, in 1919.[36]

Sir William Barrett was involved in the investigation of a supposedly haunted house in Worcestershire. Eleanor Sidgwick was researching

36 *JSPR* (February 1915), p. 24. A series of eleven sittings were held from 2 June to 13 July 1914.

the medium Mrs Piper's 'trance phenomena'.[37] The Society's Research Officer and Editor, Alice Johnson, began the year by publishing 'A Reconstruction of Some "Concordant Automatisms"', which was as exciting as it sounded.[38] The Society's young Assistant Research Officer, Helen Verrall, was also working on the Icelandic Seer Case (that of so-called 'Dreaming Joe'). There was no particular indication that members of the SPR were any better informed than the general public as to the coming crisis and terrible catastrophe of the Great War. And the question the SPR asked itself at the time was why, given the vast scale of the slaughter, were there not more cases of supposedly supernatural phenomena? The short answer is, there were, if only the Society had cared to look.

It was only after the declaration of war – or even after the end of the war – that pieces of earlier puzzles began to be put together. The more involved members of the Society at that time were much concerned with the so-called cross-correspondences – a series of cryptic psychic messages from different mediums that only made sense when considered as a whole and were taken as possible evidence of communication from deceased members of the SPR. Among these communications there were several that appeared in retrospect to have predicted the war. But the analysis that revealed all this was only published in 1923.[39]

As for the more popular war prophecies that were being touted at the time, Dr Schiller was dismissive: they were symptomatic of what he called 'a recrudescence of many primitive beliefs and practices' brought on by 'war-neurosis'.[40]

---

37 Published *Proceedings of the Society for Psychical Research*, vol. 28 (1915).
38 *Proc. SPR*, vol. 27 (January 1914).
39 J. G. Piddington, 'Forecasts in Scripts Concerning the War', *Proc. SPR*, Part LXXXVII (March 1923).
40 F. C. S. Schiller, 'War Prophecies', *JSPR* (June 1916), pp. 185–92.

Conan Doyle and 'Danger!'

Sir Arthur Conan Doyle was also a member of the Society for Psychical Research. He joined (or applied to join) the SPR in 1893 and had even investigated a haunted house with Dr Sydney Scott and Frank Podmore in 1894.[41] He also contributed his own prophecy, a short story, 'Danger! Being the Log of Captain John Sirius'. Published in *The Strand Magazine* in July 1914, it outlined the threat posed by unrestricted submarine warfare. A panel of naval experts had been invited to contribute their opinions and most of them pooh-poohed the idea. But as Doyle later wrote it turned out to be 'singularly prophetic'.[42]

Conan Doyle had already written 'Great Britain and the Next War' for the *Fortnightly Review* in 1913. He had been thinking about the possibility of war with Germany ever since his participation in the Prince Henry Competition, an amateur motorcar rally from Homburg in Germany to London via Edinburgh. Conan Doyle found the Germans warlike, recalling, 'They were not only sure of the war, but of the date. "It will be on the first pretext after the Kiel Canal is widened." ' Work on the canal was finished in June 1914. 'It was this experience,' said Conan Doyle, 'which first made me take the threat of war seriously.'[43]

'Danger!' was not only prophetic in a metaphorical sense. According to Conan Doyle, 'I have an occasional power of premonition, psychic rather than intellectual, which exercises itself beyond my control, and which when it really comes is never mistaken.' So saying, 'I saw as clearly as possible what the course of a naval war between England and

---

41 Russell Miller, *The Adventures of Arthur Conan Doyle* (London: Harvill Secker, 2008), p. 361.
42 Sir Arthur Conan Doyle, *Memories and Adventures* (London: Hodder & Stoughton, 1924), unpaginated digital edition; John Dickson Carr, *The Life of Sir Arthur Conan Doyle* (London: John Murray, 1949), p. 279.
43 Conan Doyle, *Memories*, unpaginated.

Germany would be'. The nub of the matter was that a small submarine fleet could starve Britain into submission by sinking ships trying to bring in food supplies; and as it happened this is exactly what Germany tried to do.

Sharing the Doyles' home at Windlesham was Lily Loder-Symonds; she had been Jean's bridesmaid at her wedding to Conan Doyle in 1907. At some point she had moved in with them as a companion to Jean and occasional nanny for the children. Her health had always been poor due to a chronic bronchial condition: Jean was looking after her, just as much as she was looking after her children.

It turned out that Lily had a gift for spirit communication using automatic writing. Lily was also deeply attached to Conan Doyle, some say she was in love with him; Conan Doyle for his part seems to have been oblivious to this, although having a medium in the house was of great use to him. It also seems that Jean's conversion to Spiritualism was at least partially due to Lily.[44]

Marching Off to War

Some Society members would fight in the war, some would send their sons – all would be affected. Inevitably, some who sent their sons would not see them alive again, but such tragic loss would lead to some of the most convincing and certainly still controversial demonstrations of an afterlife.

For the Conan Doyles, like many others, it was their last summer of innocence, a final dinner party in Paradise before the Fall. The Doyle household would be deeply affected by the war. Sir Arthur would initially preoccupy himself with his Civilian Volunteers. Lady Conan Doyle would run a home for Belgian refugees at nearby Gorseland. They would turn over a wing of their house to billet soldiers and have a

---

44 Sir Arthur Conan Doyle, *The New Revelation* (London: Hodder & Stoughton, 1918), p. 41.

large group of Canadian officers over for dinner once a week. Doyle's daughter from his first marriage, Mary, would work in the Vickers munitions factory. At the beginning of September, Kingsley, Doyle's son from his first marriage, enlisted as a private in the Royal Army Medical Corps. He had been studying in London to become a doctor and was now posted to Malta, the 'sick bay of the Mediterranean', as an ambulance driver. He had confessed to Mary that he could not reconcile the Hippocratic Oath with the ordinary job of a soldier. It was a secret he kept from his father, who only ever saw him as 'a soldier, first, last, and all the time'.[45]

As well as his eldest son, Doyle's brother Innes, his two brothers-in-law – Malcolm Leckie and Leslie Oldham – and two nephews – Oscar Hornung and Alec Forbes – would serve in the war, as would his private secretary Alfred Herbert 'Woodie' Wood.

All of Lily Loder-Symonds's five brothers were serving in His Majesty's Armed Forces: four with the British Army and one with the Royal Navy. The eldest, John Frederick (b. 1873), was a major in the 1st Battalion, The South Staffordshire Regiment. Frederick Parland (b. 1876) had joined the Navy in 1890 and became a Vice Admiral. Robert 'Bob' Francis (b. 1884) was a captain in the 1st Battalion, The Cheshire Regiment. William 'Willie' Crawshay (b. 1886) was a captain with the 1st Battalion, The Wiltshire Regiment. The youngest, Thomas Lenthall (b. 1892) was a Lieutenant in the 2nd Battalion, The Cameronians (Scottish Rifles). The 1st Battalion, The Cameronians, left Glasgow for Southampton shortly after war was declared. They landed at Le Havre on 15 August.[46]

Conan Doyle tried to go to war and did, in a manner of speaking, but more in the role of war correspondent than combatant. Other SPR members to put on uniform included Francis Deverell, Frank F. J. Ayston, Major Michael Wogan Festing, and Lt Col Henry Glanville Allen Moore.

45 Conan Doyle, *Memories*, unpaginated.
46 Imperial War Museum, Lives of the First World War website, accessed 6 July 2017.

Another member, Frederick John Marrion Stratton, was Assistant Director of the Solar Physics Observatory in 1914. He was also a provisional captain in the Territorial Army and at the outbreak of war was commissioned a temporary captain in the Corps of Royal Engineers (8 September 1914). He was promoted a temporary major and Officer Commanding (Signals) of the 20th Divisional Signal Company, Royal Engineers, going to France in the summer of 1915. He survived the ordeal, showing his mettle by being mentioned in despatches five times, awarded the DSO (1917), made a knight of the Légion d'honneur of France (1919) and appointed an Officer of the Order of the British Empire, Military Division, in 1929. He left the Army with the rank of Lieutenant Colonel. He was a Fellow of Gonville and Caius College, Cambridge, a Fellow of the Royal Society, President of the Royal Astronomical Society (1933–1935) and President of the SPR (1953–1955).

We will follow the adventures of some of those sons who went to war, others we will only have time to mention in passing. Geoffrey, the younger son of Revd Bayfield, was already serving in the Royal Navy when war was declared. Robert and Lewis Palmer, sons of Lord Selborne, were both in the Hampshire Regiment – Robert, 'Bobby', had joined in 1913. Oliver Lyttelton, son of Lord Alfred and Dame Edith Lyttelton, joined up in August 1914, serving first with the Bedfordshire Regiment before being gazetted to the Grenadier Guards. Raymond Lodge, son of Sir Oliver Lodge, joined the South Lancashire Regiment in September 1915. Christopher 'Cruff' Coombe Tennant, son of Charles and Winifred Coombe Tennant, took a commission in the Welsh Guards in May 1917. Others were more difficult to trace, but nonetheless important to mention: L. P. Jacks saw his three sons off to war; Charles Richet had five sons in uniform. These young men, much loved and from good families, were in a sense also 'angels in the trenches'.

The Upstairs Committee

On 30 June 1914, readers of *The Times* may have been somewhat astonished by the revelations of Dr F. C. S. Schiller. He had given his address as the new president of the SPR to an audience at the Royal Society for Medicine on Wimpole Street the evening before.[47]

Schiller began by acknowledging the 'services to psychical research of his philosophic predecessors': Henry Sidgwick, William James and Henri Bergson, all names still known to posterity. With the Society's pedigree established, he sought to establish his own authority by challenging the work that had been done. Beyond some logical and metaphysical niceties, it was the evidence that was found to be lacking, not in quantity, but in quality. Schiller argued that the evidence so far collected by the Society was, he said, 'merely historical and hardly at all experimental' and that this meant that the evidence 'must continually diminish in cogency, owing to mere lapse of time'. He had to acknowledge that 'many sciences, like astronomy and palaeontology, had to reply on historical evidence,' so the approach in itself was not unscientific.

The mysterious occurrences which the Society for Psychical research had for the first time in human history essayed to investigate systematically had never been brought under control, and for this reason had never been able to make good their claim to truth. Unless therefore their alleged knowledge could stand the pragmatic test by becoming applicable to human affairs, psychical researchers could not hope to convince the world, nor perhaps even themselves, that it was genuine knowledge.

47 'A Society of Spirits', *The Times* (30 June 1914), p. 5.

Schiller had proven himself to be something of a sceptic and *The Times* reader would most probably have been nodding happily up until this point. Then, under the subheading 'A Society on the Other Side':

> Success in psychical research, moreover, required not merely systematic and continuous efforts and much larger resources both in men and money than had yet been placed at the society's disposal, but also intelligent co-operation in what, for purposes of reference, might be called the 'spirit' world. Psychical research was far from popular on earth, where everyone had a direct interest in knowing about his future life, if any. There was reason to suppose that in the beyond it must be far more unpopular, because it might well seem unnecessary and degrading to recur to the dreadful past. However, the investigators of the complicated evidence of 'cross-correspondences' seemed to be arriving at a conviction that something like a Society for Psychical Research was beginning to operate from the other side, as more scientifically minded researchers 'joined the majority'.

There was on the side of the living the SPR 'Group of Automatists', the select few who could communicate with the Upstairs Committee. They were: Margaret Verrall, wife of Arthur Verrall, and their daughter Helen Verrall; 'Mrs Holland', Alice Kipling (1868–1948), the sister of Rudyard Kipling, and married to John M. Fleming (1858–1942), a colonel in the British Army; and 'the Macs', two brothers and three sisters of the Mackinnon family; 'Mrs Willett', Winifred Coombe Tennant (1874–1956) – she was to play a central and surprising role in the secret life of the Society; and 'Mrs King', Dame Edith Lyttelton, widow of the politician Alfred Lyttelton.[48]

From the other side came messages from the 'Communicators', particularly a 'Group of Seven': the three principal founders of the SPR,

48 W. H. Salter, 'The Rose of Sharon', *Proc. SPR*, Vol. 54 (May 1963), pp. 1–2; see also Trevor Hamilton, *Arthur Balfour's Ghosts: An Edwardian Elite and the Riddle of the Cross-Correspondences* (Exeter: Imprint Academic, 2017).

Henry Sidgwick (d. 1900), Frederic Myers (d. 1901) and Edmund Gurney (d. 1888); Francis Maitland Balfour (d. 1882); Mary Catherine Lyttelton (d. 1875); Annie Eliza Marshall, known as 'Phyllis' (d. 1876); and Laura Lyttelton, née Tennant, but not related to the Coombe Tennants (d. 1886).[49]

Eyebrows must have been raised by the article in *The Times*, but it ended with a fanfare for science, rather than Spiritualism: 'there was no reason why the methods of science here too should not vanquish difficulties which did not differ in kind from those of all knowing'.

In consequence of Schiller's advocacy of the experimental, the SPR – through its appointed officers and members[50] – would spend most of its time during the war years hunting for what it thought could be 'experimental' evidence and largely ignored a great deal of 'merely' historical evidence – the first-hand accounts of those experiencing these things – that the war produced. I confess that it led me to a kind of exasperation to read continually of SPR members shutting themselves up in darkened séance rooms, trying to contact the spirit world, or tabulating the endless cross-correspondences, when the war was raging outside – a war that uniquely produced such a rich flow of paranormal experience. The defect in Schiller's analysis was that he overlooked the fact that perhaps 'psychical research' was properly more like palaeontology than physics.

As a consequence of its academic founders and its academic presidents, the SPR had an academic reputation. Whilst this brought a measure of acceptability – interestingly, the SPR was more 'acceptable' a hundred years ago than it is today – it also produced a rarefied and rather dry atmosphere. A certain H. A. Dallas wrote to *Light* to complain that the SPR's regular periodical at the time 'usually contains matter only attractive to experts, or, at least to those who have specialised in certain rather difficult phases of this research', in

49 Salter, 'The Rose of Sharon', pp. 1–2.
50 Today, the SPR makes a point of holding no corporate opinions, but any organisation is only the sum of its most productive members' activities.

contrast to the French *Annales Psychiques*, which was, apparently, much more interesting.[51]

20 Hanover Square

In those days, the offices of the Society for Psychical Research were at 20 Hanover Square in London. The square was then little changed from its elegant eighteenth-century design. In contrast to the male-dominated Council, the offices of the SPR were run entirely by women and here fifty-four-year-old Alice Johnson ruled the roost. A graduate of Newnham College with a 'First Class in Natural Science', she was seen by some as 'a rather austere little figure, with an academic manner that alarmed them' or even having a 'love of power' in the words of Isabel Newton, the Society's Secretary. Winifred Coombe Tennant found her kind, even 'splendid', but 'rather New Woman-ish'. Newton conceded that 'her rule was absolute', but described her day-to-day manner as 'gentle and rather shy', although she never failed to be 'exacting to a degree in the matter of accuracy and thoroughness'. It was a paradoxical portrait. She was devoted to the SPR – it, too, could have been described as an austere little society with an academic manner – and Newton observed that 'she sacrificed much for it'.[52]

The Johnsons were a large family, well known in Cambridge, and after graduation, Alice had held the post of first Demonstrator in Animal Morphology at the Balfour Laboratory. She knew the Sidgwicks, of course: Mrs Sidgwick had been instrumental in setting up the laboratory and Johnson went on to become her private secretary when Sidgwick was appointed Principal of Newnham College. She had early shared the Sidgwicks' interest in psychical research, taking part in

51 H. A. Dallas, 'A Case of Lucidity: *Annales Psychique*', *Light*, No. 1,745, Vol. XXXIV (20 June 1914), pp. 290–1.
52 'Obituary: Alice Johnson', *Proc. SPR*, vol. 46 (1940–1941), pp. 16–22; Tennant, *Between Two Worlds*, pp. 45, 46.

séances with Mrs Piper and assisting Eleanor Sidgwick in the 'Brighton Experiments in Thought Transference'; she had also worked with them on the 'Census of Hallucinations', published 1894. It seemed natural that she should take up more official functions for the Society. In 1899 she was appointed Editor of the Society's *Proceedings*. In 1903, she became Organising Secretary. In 1908, she was appointed Research Officer. She was credited as being a factor in holding the Society together after the deaths of Henry Sidgwick in 1900 and Frederic Myers in 1901, and worked with Richard Hodgson in completing Myers's unfinished book *Human Personality*.

One of the SPR's neighbours at 20 Hanover Square was W. B. Yeats's Irish Literary Society. Yeats would sometimes pop in to the SPR's rooms. After talking to Johnson about psychical matters on one occasion, he remarked, in reference to her sceptical attitude, 'It is my belief that if you people had been standing round when the Almighty was creating the world, He couldn't have done it.'[53]

Johnson was first aided by Isabel Newton, who joined in 1903 as Johnson's Assistant. When Johnson became Research Officer, Newton took her place as Secretary, serving in that role for the next thirty years. Unlike most of the rest of the Society, she had no Cambridge connection and no further education, and she had had no previous interest in psychical research before applying for the position as advertised, but on her retirement was made an Honorary Member (a rare accolade) and remembered for 'a practical knowledge of psychical research that few of her contemporaries could rival'; but more than that 'she gained the confidence and affection of all the members with whom she came into contact'. Willie Salter noted that where Alice Johnson was 'small in build, austere in appearance and reserved in manner', Newton was 'in all respects the opposite' – 'she had such beautiful eyes, hair, and skin, and good features, too', said Nea Walker (secretary to Sir Oliver Lodge in later years) – yet, like Johnson, she, too, was devoted to the Society. Like Johnson, she remained unmarried throughout her life, and, like Johnson, her devotion to the Society was perhaps more particularly a

53 'Miss Alice Johnson', *JSPR*, vol. 31 (March–April 1940), p. 161.

devotion to Mrs Sidgwick. Salter did not think her witty, but noted 'a keen sense of humour' often observed in connection with 'the many oddities of mind and temperament with which her daily duties made her familiar'. Salter and others who knew her well were also treated to her gift for mimicry, amusing them with her ability 'to impersonate mutual friends and acquaintances to the life' and 'throw their foibles into sharp relief', but 'always with such warm good humour', as Lydia Allison, Secretary of the American SPR, put it. The artist and psychologist Ina Jephson found that 'she was always good company'.[54]

It was Newton who formulated the general principle of psychical research: 'If ever you have a brilliant new idea, you are almost certain to find out that it has already been said, much better, by Mrs Sidgwick.'[55] Johnson could have said the same thing, perhaps did: both were Sidgwickians through and through.

Shirley Thatcher, probably then in her early to mid-twenties, would join them in the role of Assistant Secretary and when war came her husband would be called up. Even in elegant Hanover Square they could not escape the shadow of the war. In 1915, Johnson would add in a letter to her on Society business, 'I hope that you are getting good news of Mr Thatcher'.[56] This was probably George Robin Thatcher. According to his medal card he had been a Chief Petty Officer (a senior non-commissioned officer) in the Royal Naval Air Service before being promoted to Lieutenant in the Royal Garrison Artillery.[57]

54 [William H. Salter] 'Obituary: Miss Isabel Newton', *Proc. SPR*, 49 (1950), pp. 53–6; with additions from Lydia Allison, Secretary of the American SPR, pp. 56–7, Ina Jephson, p. 57, Nea Walker, pp. 57–8.
55 C. V. C. Herbert, *Proc. SPR*, 49 (1950), p. 59.
56 Letter of Johnson to Thatcher, 30 July 1915, Cambridge University Library, SPR.MS/Journal Vol. XVII 1915–1916.
57 'Medal Card of Thatcher, George Robin', National Archives WO 372/19/197568. The records of the Commonwealth War Graves Commission identify George Robin Thatcher as the husband of Shirley Thatcher.

Daughter of the Regiment

Johnson's Assistant Research Officer was Helen Woollgar de Gaudrion Verrall (1883–1959).[58] Helen was the daughter of the noted Cambridge classicists Arthur and Margaret Verrall, both of whom were also high-profile members of the SPR, leading the philosopher C. D. Broad to call her 'a true daughter of the regiment', the regiment being the Society for Psychical Research, of course. It was no exaggeration. She had grown up surrounded by the great names of the SPR. She had fond memories of childhood games with Frederic Myers and was familiar enough with Richard Hodgson to call him 'Hodge Podge', although she never knew Edmund Gurney and recalled Henry Sidgwick as a 'remote Olympian figure' (it was different with Eleanor Sidgwick). Her mother educated her at home with Aelfrida Tillyard (later to become a poet, mystic and briefly a disciple of Aleister Crowley), before she entered Newnham College, little more than a stone's throw away.

She knew Rupert Brooke, even co-authoring a play with him and the baritone Clive Carey – 'From the Jaws of the Octopus or Cardy' – which they performed at the Hotel Silvretta in Klosters, Switzerland, on 29 December 1908. For his part, Brooke was a great admirer of her father, A. W. Verrall. She was there with a group of Cambridge friends to enjoy the skiing, including Margery and Noel Olivier, daughters of Sydney Olivier, 1st Baron Olivier – Noel was the object of Brooke's amorous attentions; Trinity scholar Jerry Pinsent; Dorothy Osmaston, later Lady Layton; Dolly Rose; Hugh Morgan; Bill Hubback and his fiancé Eva

---

58 She was already well known to the Society as 'H. V.' from the cross-correspondences and when her report on the angels was published it appeared under both her married and maiden names. Because of this, I shall refer to her as Helen throughout.

Spielman – most of them members of an informal group of happy campers dubbed the 'neo-pagans' by Virginia Woolf.[59]

Even before she joined the SPR in 1905, her mother had involved her in psychical experiments – telepathy, table-turning and automatic writing (producing some of the famed cross-correspondences). She started working for the Society in 1908 and in 1910 was appointed Assistant Research Officer. In 1916 she would become Research Officer and Editor of the *Journal*, and from 1921 of the *Proceedings* as well. In 1922 she joined the Council and in 1953 was elected a Vice-President. In life outside the Society, she would hold a number of important public appointments. Broad remembered her for her 'intellectual integrity' and G. W. Lambert commended her 'sound reasoning and good judgement'.[60]

Her friend Aelfrida called her 'the virtuous Helen', meaning to be unkind. When Winifred Coombe Tennant met her in 1910, she described her as 'very charming, with blue eyes that are frank and sympathetic, the head cast upon noble lines, the figure tall and very feminine'. However, as she got to know her better, Winifred found her 'all intellect and no heart, all rather arid science and no imagination' and ultimately 'baffling, chilling and discouraging'.[61]

Helen had recently been given the use of a new room – working in the Library had proven unsuitable due to the continual interruptions. Here, she would decide the fate of the angels in that biggest paranormal mystery of the war years, Mons.[62]

59 'The Papers of Rupert Chawner Brooke', RCB/D/6 and RCB/Ph/62-5, King's College Archive Centre, Cambridge University; Marsh, 'Memoir', p. xxxvi, n. 1. 'Cardy' was the nickname of Lionel Montagu, a son of the Jewish financier Samuel Montagu, 1st Baron Swaythling, see Edward Marsh, 'Memoir', in Rupert Brooke, *The Collected Poems of Rupert Brooke: With a Memoir*, ed. Edward Marsh (London: Sidgwick and Jackson, 1919), p. cxlii.
60 C. D. Broad, 'Obituary: Mrs W. H. Salter', *JSPR*, 40 (September 1959), 129–36; G.W. Lambert, [Untitled], *JSPR*, 40 (September 1959), p. 136.
61 Tennant, *Between Two Worlds*, pp. 44, 78.
62 'Report of the Council for the Year 1914', *JSPR*, 17 (February 1915), p. 22.

The Plan

The Upstairs Committee had what came to be known as 'The Plan', centring on 'Mrs Willett'. Beyond providing proof of the survival of the personality after death – something they had been doing since 1901 – the Committee also wanted to save the world and, as the world raced towards Armageddon, it certainly needed saving.

The identity of 'Mrs Willett', as Winifred Coombe Tennant was known in connection with her mediumistic communications, was a closely guarded secret, known only to a few members of the SPR Council, principally, Sir Oliver Lodge, Eleanor Sidgwick, Gerald and Arthur Balfour, and others, such as Margaret Verrall and Alice Johnson.[63]

Winifred had married into the SPR. Eveleen ('Evie'), the sister of her husband Charles, was married to Frederic Myers and she got to know him well in the 1890s. She was greatly moved when Myers died in 1901, and joined the Society herself. However, the key to Winifred's deeper involvement was the loss of her eighteen-month-old daughter, Daphne, in 1908. Grief-stricken and seeking answers, she had started automatic writing, possibly at the instigation of Margaret Verrall. She was apparently successful in this, but the Upstairs Committee were soon trying experiments with her to achieve more direct communication, which became known as 'Daylight Impressions' (DIs), 'to make you hear without writing' in the supposed words of Myers.[64]

Apparently communicating through Leonora Piper on 23 October 1910, the deceased Edmund Gurney made a series of 'amazing

63 She also sometimes signed herself 'Daphne's Mother' and consequently was sometimes referred to as 'DM'. (See Tennant, *Between Two Worlds*, pp. 59–61, 87, 112.)
64 See Peter Lord in his Introduction to Tennant, *Between Two Worlds*, p. 13; Myers quoted in G. N. M. Tyrrell, *The Nature of Human Personality* (London: George Allen and Unwin, 1954), p. 20.

statements' that were 'incomprehensible and marvellous', as Winifred recorded in her diary. Gurney, it turned out, was in love with her and wanted her to have his child, hence the 'incomprehensible', but even more than that 'the result will be an "Optimus Opus"'. Gurney said that Myers concurred and Sidgwick would also soon send his agreement. She was at the Lodges' home at Mariemont in Birmingham and talked over the matter with Sir Oliver. Birmingham, she found, 'very large and hideous', but Mariemont was 'filled with books and beautiful things'. She was introduced to Mrs Piper as 'Mrs Archer' to disguise both her real name and SPR identity. Winifred had seen Mrs Piper before, on 8 May 1910, when she was in a trance state in the SPR's rooms at 20 Hanover Square, but had not been introduced to her; then, she had thought the thing like 'a live vivisection'. It was quite different in the congenial setting of the Lodges' home.[65]

Winifred had had no intention of having another child – she had already had three (Christopher, Alexander and Daphne) – and confessed that there had been 'no opportunity of any sort of conception'. Myers, communicating through Winifred, on 17 November 1910, stressed the importance of the undertaking: 'Gurney's child that is to come will be a great Incarnation of Divine Effulgence', ending the communication with 'know that this is your destiny'.[66]

Before the year was out, the way became clear. Gerald Balfour expressed a wish to meet her and Winifred was invited to Fisher's Hill, the family home of the Balfours. She arrived on 4 February 1911. She thought Betty, Lady Balfour, 'very charming, clever, natural', etc., but Gerald was 'intensely attractive'. Mrs Sidgwick, Sir Oliver and Arthur Balfour joined them – J. G. Piddington was already there as a live-in cross-correspondences expert – but it was Gerald who made the greatest impression. 'I am *deeply* impressed by Gerald Balfour,' she wrote.[67]

65 Tennant, *Between Two Worlds*, pp. 47, 56–7; statement of Winifred, 12 November 1910, quoted in Archie Roy, *The Eager Dead: A Study in Haunting* (Brighton: Book Guild, 2008), p. 273.
66 Roy, *Eager Dead*, pp. 273–4.
67 Tennant, *Between Two Worlds*, pp. 62, 63, 66.

There would be more meetings with Gerald, more being deeply impressed by him. Communications from Gurney pushed her towards him. She was falling in love with him, fell in love with him and he with her, and, from her point of view, his wife Betty seemed to acquiesce. Winifred's husband Charles, always such a distant figure in her diaries unless she was complaining about him, seemed totally unaware of her growing infidelity. To begin with, it was 'the holiest love', but it eventually became physical as well. The result was Augustus Henry Serocold, born 9 April 1913. Henry was named after Henry Sidgwick and it was as Henry that he was generally known to the world, at least until he changed his name. Privately to Winifred, he was 'the Babe' and, by the beginning of 1914, 'The Wise One'.[68]

As the country went to the war, the SPR was nursing in its bosom the next world saviour. For her part, Winifred launched herself on a public career. Soon after the war began, she was appointed to the Mayor's Committee for Distress, the Prince of Wales's Fund and the Soldiers' and Sailors' Families Association Committee – the Prince of Wales's Fund was the largest of the many private subscription funds that appeared at this time to support the war effort and particularly the needs of families bereft of their breadwinner.[69]

At the time, Winifred was awaiting an operation for either a kidney stone or appendicitis and experiencing intermittently 'fearful pain', as she put it. Her trepidation before the operation mixed with her desperation at the war. She had seen the Kaiser in 1911 during his visit to Britain and remarked then that he was 'the menace to the peace of Europe'; and on 4 August 1914 wrote of 'the awful madness of our joining in this war, slaughtering our brothers for no purpose'.[70]

As she lay recovering from the operation she read the casualty lists printed in the papers and was horrified to see Gerald Balfour's nephew Oswald reported wounded on 19 September. Oswald was the son of Lady Frances and Colonel Eustace James Anthony Balfour. Some days

68 Tennant, *Between Two Worlds*, pp. 117–18, 140.
69 Tennant, *Between Two Worlds*, p. 152.
70 Tennant, *Between Two Worlds*, pp. 70, 150.

Get
So

Do every-
to ge

later she was relieved to learn that he had only been slightly wounded. Others of her acquaintance were not so fortunate. One Captain Mark Haggard of the Welsh Guards and nephew of the writer H. Rider Haggard, only recently married to Betty Vaughan, died of wounds received, possibly in the same action as Oswald. His dying cry had been 'Stick it, the Welsh!' According to Sir Oliver Lodge, it would 'never be forgotten in the Principality'. Soon afterwards, Betty left to become an ambulance driver in France.[71]

Signs of war were not just in the newspapers. She reported seeing armed soldiers guarding bridges and tunnels, stations full of men in uniform (her carriage crammed with them, too), 'the sounds of bugles and firing in the distance' and recruits drilling on the golf links. In October, a family of Belgian refugees arrived to take up residence in the gardener's cottage, just a few of the more than 250,000 fleeing the Kaiser's armies who would arrive in Britain. 'How it brought war home to me,' she wrote, 'looking into their strained faces.'[72]

Psychical Rivals

The SPR did not have the psychical field to itself. For some years an International Club for Psychical Research had met to discuss things paranormal. A note in *The Times* for 30 May 1914 records that they met in Regent Street, with Lady Churchill presiding and Lady Muir-Mackenzie, Miss Lind-af-Hageby, Major General Sir Alfred Turner, the Revd Sir C. J. M. Shaw and Miss Estelle Stead in attendance.

Mrs Annie Besant was giving a talk on 'Common Sense in Psychical Research'. 'There was,' she said, 'nothing really more dangerous in all research into the hidden movements of nature than to suppose miracles where there was nothing but the natural law.' It

71 Tennant, *Between Two Worlds*, p. 153; Sir Oliver Lodge, *Christopher: A Study in Human Personality* (London: Cassell & Co., 1918), p. 232.
72 Tennant, *Between Two Worlds*, pp. 154, 155.

was sensible enough advice, but quite unthinkable that *The Times* of today would report such a talk, reminding us that things were, indeed, different.[73]

The Times article said that they were celebrating their third anniversary, meaning that they were formed in 1911. However, a disclaimer had been printed in the *Journal* of the SPR as early as 1909 distancing itself from the ICPR:

> In consequence of statements that have lately appeared in several newspapers about a club to be called the International Club for Psychical Research, a number of enquiries have reached us. We therefore desire to make it clear that – contrary to the suggestion conveyed by some of the newspaper paragraphs – the proposed Club has no connection of any kind with our Society. It has also been stated that Professor Barrett will be the first President of the Club, but Professor Barrett informs us that this statement is entirely groundless.[74]

Although *The Times* article was not more specific than locating the Club in Regent Street, following the half-erased footprints of the past we are led to the Alchemical Society. In an issue of *Light*, one reads that the Alchemical Society held its meetings at the International Club for Psychical Research and elsewhere that the Alchemical Society held its meetings in Willie Wendt de Kerlor's Occult Library, also home to his Occult Club, in Piccadilly Place, a shabby side street sandwiched in between Regent St and Piccadilly. It was here in this nest of bizarre clubs and societies that Dr Elizabeth Severn – castigated as 'an evil genius' by Freud – turned up to lecture on 'Some Mystical Aspects of Alchemy' in May 1914 at a meeting chaired by the noted Scottish chemist John Ferguson, Regius Professor of Chemistry at Glasgow University and a Fellow of the Royal Society of Edinburgh, as well as the owner of

73 'Mrs Besant on Common-Sense in Psychical Research', *The Times* (30 May 1914), p. 11.
74 *JSPR* (November 1909), p. 148.

one of the most extensive collections of alchemical texts outside the British Library.[75]

De Kerlor was arrested for fortune-telling in April 1915 and, by some 'unfortunate mistake', his lawyer submitted a plea of guilty. He was sentenced to six week's imprisonment and subsequent deportation. An appeal was granted and his friends rallied round to see what could be done. His friends thought that a key factor was the question of de Kerlor's nationality. It seems to have been assumed that he was German, but he had been born in Switzerland to a Russian father and a French mother.[76]

Thunder, Oblivion and Brother Ghosts

Smoke – smoke everywhere – tramping men – high hope – a young face – thunder – oblivion.

On 17 July 1914, the poet William Butler Yeats sat in a darkened room as a medium related a communication from the spirit world. Its meaning would soon become clear and Yeats would later tell this story to the Ghost Club. Yeats's involvement in the Club is known, although largely only among scholars of Yeats; his actual activities there have been almost entirely overlooked.[77]

The Ghost Club was a private, but not quite secret, dining club that met in London to discuss ghosts, naturally. Sir William Crookes, one of the leading lights of the SPR, was President of the Ghost Club throughout the duration of the war. The Ghost Club would also be affected by the

75 *Light*, No. 1,740, Vol. XXIV (16 May 1914); for Severn see Arnold Rachman, *Elizabeth Severn: The 'Evil Genius' of Psychoanalysis* (London: Routledge, 2018).
76 'The Case of Mr W. de Kerlor', *Light* (8 May 1915), p. 224.
77 Minutes for a meeting on 7 October 1914, British Library, Ghost Club Archives, Add MS 52264; the exception is Tara Stubbs, 'W.B. Yeats and the Ghost Club', in *Irish Writing London*, vol. 1, edited by Tom Herron (London: Bloomsbury, 2013), unpaginated digital ed.

war; and some members affected most deeply. They, too, would send their sons and spend the war years on tenterhooks, waiting on every post, for news from the Front. In 1914, the Ghost Club had twenty-two members and, like Crookes, many of them were also members of the SPR. Usually, eight or nine turned up for meetings. All of them were interesting, but few are remembered now, save for W. B. Yeats.

The Ghost Club met once a month on Wednesday evenings at the Maison Jules on Jermyn Street. It was a smart and relatively new establishment with an enviable pedigree. Lieutenant Colonel Nathaniel Newnham-Davis mentioned the restaurant in his *Gourmet's Guide to London*: the Jules in question had been manager at the Berkeley – one of the best places to dine in London – and then the Savoy, before setting up on his own.[78] Jermyn Street had formerly been known for its private hotels, shops and bachelors' rooms, but before the war had been colonised by half a dozen or so restaurants. Jules had taken two houses on the street to offer hotel accommodation and dining. An illuminated globe hung outside the door. Going inside, one entered an ante-room formed by a glazed-glass screen first, leading into a long room that ran the length of the building. It was painted all white, while gilt capitals decorated white pillars and marble. A clock and candelabra of blue china sat on the mantelpiece above the fire. The room ended in a large window – 'almost a wall of glass', according to Newnham-Davis. There was a second room to the back that could be partitioned off and it was probably here that the Ghost Club found the privacy they required. Jules himself – grown rather fuller of figure and whiter of hair – would have met the members as they trooped through the door and led them past the other diners – 'all pleasant and well-to-do, and all the men wear dress clothes' – and taken their orders for the eight-shilling dinner of Creme Americaine (a thick pink soup), Medallion de Boeuf Algerienne and Mousse aux Violettes, and afterwards perhaps a glass of the 1820 Martell brandy from the well-chosen wine-cellar.

78 Nathaniel Newnham-Davis, *The Gourmet's Guide to London* (New York: Brentano's, 1914), pp. 210, 268.

The Lt Col. found that the jovial Jules – 'always so pleased to see me' – did him 'more good than most tonics do', although on one occasion the beans were a little stringy.

Before the declaration of war, the Club listened to Yeats talking about his séance sittings and an investigation of an alleged miracle, along with Everard Feilding and Maude Gonne, of a picture of the Sacred Heart that had dripped blood.

They did not meet in August or September, but when they gathered in October the Hon. Sec. Dr Robert Fielding-Ould recalled that back in 1911 fellow member – they called each other 'Brother Ghost' – Alfred Percy Sinnett had made some 'communications [. . .] in reference to the war'. They regretted that Sinnett had not been able to join them, but Yeats had his own prophecy. A medium he had visited on 17 July 1914 had spoken while in trance of 'smoke – smoke everywhere – tramping men – high hope – a young face – thunder – oblivion.' Yeats believed that a battle scene had been unmistakeably described. Vice-Admiral William Usborne Moore then gave 'an interesting discussion on warfare in general' that sparked a vigorous conversation on the subject, during which Lt Col. Dudley Sampson made frequent warlike declarations. For his part, Alexander Constantine Ionides was concerned about 'the prevalence of these false war rumours' and argued for 'the necessity of carefully distinguishing between subjective and objective phenomena'. Ionides's son, Theodore Alexander, would take a commission in the Oxfordshire and Buckinghamshire Light Infantry.[79]

Sinnett was able to join them the next month and 'gave a short dissertation on war from an occult standpoint'. Sinnett was then seventy-four years old, with a full white beard, a pleasingly domed bald head that was an invitation to knock a spoon against it, and a surprised expression as if someone *had* knocked a spoon against it. He had made a start in life as a journalist, and moving to India, became editor of *The Pioneer*, at the time the leading English-language daily newspaper there. He was courted early by Madame Blavatsky, the bloated, toad-like

79 British Library, Add MS 52264, p. 326.

and hypnotic-eyed charlatan behind the Theosophical Society. Sinnett and his wife, appropriately named Patience, were the recipients of the so-called Mahatma Letters from 1880 to 1884, a series of communications supposedly from the 'Masters of the Ancient Wisdom' Koot Hoomi and Morya, two colourful figments of Blavatsky's imagination conjoined in an elaborate fraud as Richard Hodgson had demonstrated on behalf of the SPR.[80]

According to Sinnett, the physical war taking place was 'a reflection of an equally bitter struggle now taking place on the Astral Plane between the White and Black Lodges'. The German Kaiser was 'obsessed by Black influences' that had suppressed his own personality. Luckily, 'the Germans would be expelled from France next week', which would have been the week beginning Monday, 9 November. The failure of an earlier prediction of a Zeppelin attack on London at the end of October was explained as having been 'side-tracked' by other events and would now occur sometime between 6 and 8 November, 'if no influence intervened in the meantime to prevent it'.

It was the thirty-second anniversary of the Club that night and senior members were asked to reminisce about the old days. Crookes had also brought along two 'psychic' photographs for inspection.

When they met again in December, Sinnett must have been somewhat embarrassed by the non-conformity of worldly events, but, if the minutes are accurate, made no apology. Instead, he extended his occult analysis:

> Sinnett referring to his remarks as given in the minutes of the previous meeting, on the occasion of the war wished to explain that the present war was waged not only on the astral and physical planes, as it had been in the Great Atlantis Struggle, but was now going on on higher planes and that since the Atlantian

80 'Report of the Committee Appointed to Investigate Phenomena Connected with the Theosophical Society', *Proc. SPR*, Part IX (1885), pp. 201–400. The Committee comprised Edmund Gurney, Frederic Myers, Frank Podmore, J. H. Stack, Richard Hodgson, Henry Sidgwick and his wife Eleanor. The report is still the subject of controversy.

period it had been gathering increased potential energy. When the war has ended humanity will enjoy a long cycle of smooth water.[81]

Sinnett, of course, would be proven wrong again. But his tendency to see the war in terms of a simplistic confrontation between good and evil was not his alone.

The Shadow of a Great Calamity

Edmund Rogers was also involved in the creation of the Spiritualist weekly newspaper *Light*. First published in 1881, it had a circulation of several thousand.[82] The Saturday after Britain's declaration of war, its editor David Gow, wrote:

> As we write the shadow of a great calamity hangs over the whole earth. There are ominous marchings and counter-marchings in the great 'armed camp' of Europe, and panic reigns in the money markets of the world.[83]

Even then there was that pious humbug that could see in the impending destruction some wonderful purpose of God. It was 'Mammon' who 'totters on his throne' and 'those who have sown the wind will reap the whirlwind'. Those 'who have realised for themselves the supremacy of the Spirit will find comfort in the darkest hour'. 'Eternal Purpose', it seemed, intended 'to chasten the souls of men, to purge the earth and to purify the air'. Still, Gow was wise enough to see that any 'great

81 Ghost Club Archive, British Library Add Ms 52264, pp. 336, 338 [181–182].
82 Brian Glenney, ' "Light, More Light": The "Light" Newspaper, Spiritualism, and British Society, 1881–1920', unpublished Master's thesis, Clemson University, 2009.
83 'Notes By the Way', *Light*, vol. XXXIV (8 August 1914), p. 373.

purifying of life' – a terrible, misguided phrase – would be 'at a fearful cost of human happiness'.[84]

Elsewhere in that issue, another unsigned item, 'Dark Days: Some Consolations', opined that 'the great affliction that has come upon humanity is a sign that it is still so undeveloped that it has not yet the power to steer itself aright and resist the impulse of the blind brute forces of its lower nature'. Already being called the 'great war', it was the result of 'senseless drifting on the part of senates and peoples'. Dark days, indeed, but the consolation was for the enlightened, those of us 'who have gained a knowledge of the reality of a Higher World'. For them:

> Even if the sun is for a time swathed in the crimson clouds of war, and the stars blotted from our sight, we know that for us and for all nothing can be final, nothing fatal, and that the lights of heaven always are relit.[85]

That week's issue of *Light* was full of discussion of the war and what it would mean; and being a Spiritualist newspaper, the 'spirits' naturally entered into discussion as well. Miss Emily Katharine Bates had been staying with Mrs Alfred Wedgwood in Hogsthorpe, Lincolnshire. Miss Bates regarded Wedgwood highly: she was known to all the 'Old Brigade in Spiritualism' as 'the most remarkable non-professional medium that we have ever had in England'. Bates herself was the author of several Spiritualist books, such as *Seen and Unseen* (1907) and *Do the Dead Depart?* (1908); and would later write *Our Living Dead: Some Talks with Unknown Friends* (1917) and others. Miss Bates was 'greatly upset by the continued grave political news' – for unknown reasons, 'grave as the situation is for all of us, my suffering has seemed almost abnormal during the last three days', something she drew Mrs Wedgwood's attention to several times – and implored the medium to contact the spirit world.[86]

84 'Notes By the Way', p. 373.
85 *Light*, vol. XXXIV (8 August 1914), p. 380.
86 *Light*, vol. XXXIV (8 August 1914), pp. 374–5.

'I suggested asking W. T. Stead,' she said, 'as a very old friend, what he thought as regards England being drawn into the conflict' – *Great Britain* had already declared war by the time this was printed.

Mrs Wedgwood cried out, 'Oh, they are showing me such a huge pair of bellows . . . Now I feel a quantity of soft white wool between my fingers and just a streak of crimson with it.'

'Why, that sounds like the text, "Though your sins . . . be red like crimson, they shall be as wool."' Miss Bates wondered what it could all mean.

The *Daily Mail* had talked about Armageddon, and Bates must have mentioned it, because now Stead replied, presumably through Wedgwood, that:

'The bellows do refer to Armageddon, as I still call it. When the uprising has done its appointed work, the bellows which have fanned the flame will scatter the ashes. You have guessed correctly the meaning of the wool. The soft white wool signifies that England's faults will be forgiven because she loved much and she rules as wisely as she knew how.

'You have seen that the moment danger threatened from outside – when the cloud appeared upon the horizon – all party strife was hushed. The apparently hopeless Irish question was instantly shelved [. . .]'

Stead went on in this vein for some time. All the while Bates was scribbling away, recording the great revelations. From time to time, Mrs Wedgwood would interject, 'There is Lord Salisbury! Gladstone! John Bright! Now I see Disraeli! – and Garibaldi and Mazzini! – and there is Kitchener!' – the latter, of course, not being quite dead yet. 'Finally,' wrote Bates, Wedgwood saw Jon Bunyan 'with the burden dropping off his back' – Bunyan wrote *The Pilgrim's Progress*, an immensely popular Christian allegory: the burden referred to is carried by the book's protagonist called Christian. And so the two old women believed themselves to be in the company of the great and the good, receiving vital communication on the future of the Empire. But that was not the least of it.

Bates and Wedgwood were party to a more profound message. As the clock ticked towards the eleventh hour on 4 August and 'the news had become still more terrible and hope of peace more faint', the ladies sat again, awaiting the spirits.

Wedgwood presently asked, 'Who was that Italian man . . . who had to do with criminals in some way?'

Bates looked vague, then inspiration flashed, 'Lombroso?'

'Yes, that's it.'

Cesare Lombroso (1835–1909) is widely regarded as the founder of criminology, although his theory that criminality was an inherited condition – the 'born criminal' – has been thrown out by modern criminologists, but the belief that physical appearance denotes character remains unassailable in the popular mind. For Lombroso, the criminal inheritance could be diagnosed through physical defects, particularly those giving an apelike appearance, hence indicating a biological reversion to the earlier type. He was also a Spiritualist and had sat with the medium Eusapia Palladino as early as 1891, writing about his beliefs in *After Death – What?*, published the year he died in 1909. Now he had appeared to an elderly lady in Hogsthorpe, Lincolnshire.

'I see him,' continued Wedgwood, 'with a number of skulls. He seems to be examining the heads of various potentates and their Ministers, to see where he could possibly make an entrance mentally.'

Bates and Wedgwood understood this as a symbol. 'It suddenly flashed into my mind,' said Bates, 'that there might be a further intention in showing this to her; i.e., that we on our side of life might also form a bolt of mental thought to help the other side in their splendid work of striving to influence the minds of all those in political authority, towards a peaceful solution of the present situation.'

Bates thought it would be impossible for Britain to remain neutral: war was coming, unless alternative means were tried. Her proposed plan would be 'one of the grandest efforts yet made to become co-workers with God'. She dismissed such attempts as had been made, such as the Peace Meetings in the Hague, as operating at the periphery. Her plan would strike at the centre, at 'the Divine part' of the rulers currently leading their peoples into conflict.

'Let us begin,' she suggested, 'with our own Ministers, strengthening their hands spiritually, and enabling their spirits to reach their outer selves and treat for calmness and wisdom. [. . .] Then let us take Germany, Austria, and Russia as the most important centres just now – the storm centres – and concentrate upon their sovereigns and chief Ministers.'

She claimed to have seen exactly this sort of thing done herself. 'I know by personal experience,' she said, 'what wonders can be effected – have been effected – in this way.' She was vague in the extreme, talking of a 'friend' who had used this method to save a man from a 'ruined life' and called on readers simply to believe that it was possible through her own 'evidence'.

A French Saint and British Prayers

News reached readers of *Light* that Abbé J. A. Petit had received 'mediumistic communications' through 'an almost illiterate woman' purporting to come from the great French heroine of the Hundred Years' War, Joan of Arc. Only officially canonised as a saint in 1920, Joan nonetheless enjoyed a cult of personality and was regarded as a 'folk saint', with serious moves to have her canonised beginning in the nineteenth century – today one cannot enter a church in France without seeing her effigy. So iconic was Joan that she would be the subject of several popular songs during the war, such as Henry Burr's 'Joan of Arc' (1917), Jack Wells's 'Joan of Arc, They Are Calling You' (1917) and J. L. Lavoy's 'Joan of Arc's Answer Song' (1918).

The chief problem for Abbé Petit was that 'there are circulating so many communications alleged to have been transmitted by Joan, but which in many instances are too contradictory to be reliable'. The Abbé was confident that the near illiteracy of the woman meant that she 'in her normal state could not possibly pen such messages' – evidently, they were derived through what is termed automatic writing – leaving only one possible conclusion, or so he thought: 'he frankly admits that if the intervention of an invisible agency were disputed he would be at a loss to account satisfactorily for this phenomenon'. She even signed her messages 'Jehanne d'Arc' – 'Jehanne' was how the original whilst living had signed her name, although she had not used 'd'Arc'. Even so, he thought it best to try and obtain some further proof of the authenticity of this 'Jehanne'. Joan was a little put out by the request, apparently, but finally relented. She swore the Abbé and his medium to secrecy, and so 'gave the desired proof', with the bonus of 'at the same time imparting a communication of such importance that the Abbé declares that even had he not given his word of honour, he would still feel bound not to divulge it'.[87]

As none of these proofs were ever made known to anyone else, we only have the Abbé's word to rely on; and who was this Abbé? Little can be discovered about him. 'Abbé' was used as a courtesy title, meaning 'Father', rather than abbot: he held the post of Chanoine Titulaire of Chambéry, a town in the department of Savoie in the Auvergne-Rhône-Alpes region of south-eastern France. He had written a biography of the Abbé Goddard and published a small pamphlet on Christianity, and was evidently interested in Spiritualism. Beyond that we cannot say more.[88]

The great message that Joan of Arc had brought to the Abbé was news of 'a sudden and unexpected war between France and Germany', with descriptions of the 'principal phases' of this conflict. According to Joan, this war, in the words of *Light*'s correspondent 'F. D.', 'would prove one of the most sanguinary ever recorded in history'. Joan, however, would be on hand to lend invisible guidance to the French Army. They would need it, as Joan forecast a 'severe repulse' before the enemy is finally defeated. In subsequent messages, she characterised

---

87 J. A. Petit published his account in *La Revue Spirite* (no further details given), reported here in 'Notes from Abroad', *Light*, No. 1,752, Vol. XXXIV (15 August 1914), pp. 392–3.

88 J. A. Petit, *Un Homme de Dieu: L'Abbé Goddard, chanoine honoraire de l'Église métropolitaine ... de Chambéry, 1818-1895* (Paris: Currière, 1898); and *Le Christianisme, son Universalite ses Deviations son Avenir* (Paris: Beaudelot, 1908), translated into German 1908.

the coming war as paving the way for 'a great political, social and religious evolution' – this would be a common theme in Spiritualist communications concerning the war – claiming that:

> The ancient religious forms have had their time: they have given all they could, but will now disappear to make room for better enlightenment and higher principles. Providence will raise heralds, or rather mediums, who will be inspired to proclaim the truth to the world at large.[89]

Such 'heralds' did appear and proclaimed what they thought was the truth, but the 'room' that the First World War created led directly to the Second. Platitudes aside, Joan had more particular observations to make: 'the hostile army will try to pass through Belgium'. The Abbé's comment on this was '*Qui vivra verra*' – 'time will tell'. As *Light* went to press, the 1st, 2nd and 3rd German Armies were already fighting their way through Belgium.

Whilst the Abbé entertained a dead saint at the foot of the French Alps, a Belgian Spiritualist facing the onrushing German Armies had placed her castle at the disposal of the Belgian Red Cross Society, for which the Governor of Liège thanked the good Princess Karadja. This was Mary Louise Smith of Sweden (1868–1943), youngest daughter of the distiller and politician Lars Olsson Smith (known as 'The King of Spirits') and second wife (by then widow) of the Ottoman diplomat, the fez-wearing Prince Jean Karadja Pasha; her castle was the Château de Bovigny, Gouvy. She was a poet, writer, medium and esotericist who had founded the White Cross Union and presided over the Universal Gnostic Alliance; and friend of the Spiritualist Lizzy Lind-af-Hageby.[90] She was at the time in London, but 'desires to go there herself as soon as circumstances render it possible, in order personally to assist in

89 'Notes from Abroad', p. 393.
90 Mary Karadja, *Towards the Light* (New York: Dodd, Mead, 1909), and *Esoteric Meaning of the Seven Sacraments* (n.p., 1910); *Encyclopedia of Occultism and Parapsychology* (where her date of death is given incorrectly).

transforming the castle into a hospital' – circumstances, of course, would never allow it. Still, she wanted funds – 'donations will be gratefully acknowledged' – and 'surgeons and nurses with three years' hospital experience who might feel inclined to render aid'.[91] Queen Mary (Mary of Teck, the queen consort), for one, would send her a large quantity of clothing for the wounded.[92]

Light was also interested in the *Daily Chronicle*'s 'Appeal to the People' (5 August), calling on the British populace to pray – not metaphorically, but literally – for victory. According to the British newspaper, 'the Kaiser told a shouting crowd in Berlin' – they could not simply be a 'crowd', but had to appear somewhat unseemly by 'shouting' – 'to go to the churches and pray'. In response the writer made a very British sort of admonition to his readers:

> In this world of unplumbed mysteries, where frail, short-lived, short-sighted humanity gropes amid unmeasured forces, conflicts arise that are past our solving or averting or reconciling. Human wisdom is sorely limited at its best, but we believe that there is a Wisdom beyond it; and to that in the tremendous hour when the resources of human prudence have all been tried and tried in vain, we humbly commit our destiny, our lives, and the lives of our nearest and dearest. We can only make this prayer, as we can only make any that deserves the name, in the spirit of sincere and self-forgetting resignation to duty – the spirit that alone can give honourable victory, alone can found lasting greatness, and alone can ennoble even the darkest defeat.[93]

A frequent contributor calling himself 'Laus Deo' – 'praise be to God' – penned his own prayer for *Light*, what he called his 'Universal Prayer

91 'Princess Karadja and the War', *Light*, No. 1,752, Vol. XXXIV (Saturday, August 15 1914), p. 393.
92 *Light*, No. 1,755, Vol. XXXIV (29 August 1914), p. 416.
93 'Appeal to the People', *Daily Chronicle* (5 August 1914), quoted and commented on by 'D. R.', 'Prayer in War Time', *Light*, No. 1,752, Vol. XXXIV (15 August 1914), p. 390.

Before War', calling on others – 'all thoughtful persons' – to 'formulate in words such a prayer as they conceive utterable with reverence and propriety before proceeding to battle'.[94] Although Laus Deo interpreted 'proceeding to battle' in a spiritual as well as literal sense, the British Expeditionary Force were already digging in at Mons when *Light* published his words.

Apocalypse and a New Napoleon

As the bullets started to fly, there were still more prophecies to consider. There was 'Joanna Southcott and the Year 1914'. Joanna Southcott was a Christian mystic, born in the hamlet of Taleford, Devon, in 1750; she died on 27 December 1814. During her sixty-four years of life she advanced from being a domestic servant with few prospects to a self-proclaimed prophetess with a following believed to number 100,000. She made claims that she was the Woman of the Apocalypse, or Woman of Revelation – in the Book of Revelations (Ch. 12) this woman gives birth to a male Christ-like child who is attacked by a dragon symbolising Satan, leading to War in Heaven – and died of dropsy after a phantom pregnancy. According to *Light*, she left behind a sealed box containing some of her prophecies, which was not to be opened until a hundred years after her death. More worryingly, 'she predicted the end of the world in 1914', which was 'certainly significant in view of current events'. She had said that the last king of Britain would be named George; and indeed George V was on the throne (reigned 1910–1936). *Light* added 'and thus St George overcoming the Dragon will have a new and unexpected meaning', with the observation that in her lifetime 'several of her minor prophecies were fulfilled'.[95]

94 Laos Deo in *Light*, No. 1,754, Vol. XXXIV (22 August 1914), p. 398.
95 'Joanna Southcott and the Year 1914', *Light*, No. 1,754, Vol. XXXIV (22 August 1914), p. 400.

After the Woman of the Apocalypse came the super-Venus. *Light* had already published it; now, suddenly made meaningful, it published it again: Tolstoy's apocalyptic recurrent dream. According to the story, at some point before his death in 1910, Leo Tolstoy's grandniece, Countess Nastasia Tolstoy, took dictation as the old man fell into 'an apparently comatose condition' and started speaking.[96]

'This is a revelation of a universal character,' he began, 'which must shortly come to pass.' He proceeded to describe a vision involving a naked woman floating on 'the sea of human fate': the 'super-Venus' with 'her beauty, her poise, her smile, her jewels', who, 'like an eternal courtesan, flirts with all'. She is an allegory for 'Commercialism' and 'nations rush madly after her'. She has three arms, each holding 'a torch of universal corruption': the 'flame of War'; the 'flame of Bigotry and Hypocrisy'; and the flame of 'the Law'. The flame of war inspires honest patriotism, but ends in 'the roar of guns and musketry'. The flame of bigotry and hypocrisy 'lights the lamp only in temples and on the altars of sacred institutions', inspiring 'falsity and fanaticism'. The flame of the law is the 'dangerous foundation of all unauthentic traditions'. In contrast to Southcott's Woman of the Apocalypse, Tolstoy's super-Venus was the Whore of Babylon. Real commercialism, of course, would have been against the war: dead soldiers and impoverished civilians make poor customers.

Tolstoy was not finished: 'the great conflagration,' he continued, 'will start about 1912, set by the torch of the first arm in the countries of south-eastern Europe'. By 1913, it will have developed into 'a destructive calamity'. In 1913 'I see all Europe in flames and bleeding' and 'I hear the lamentations of huge battlefields'. By 1915, approximately, 'a strange figure from the North – a new Napoleon – enters the stage of bloody drama'. According to the prophecy he would not be the typical military man, but a writer or journalist; nonetheless, he would hold Europe in his grip until 1925.

96 'Tolstoy's Remarkable Prophetic Vision', *Light*, No. 1,754, Vol. XXXIV (22 August 1914), p. 401.

Like most of the other prophecies, all this bloodshed, death and destruction would bring about 'a new political era for the Old World'. Empires and kingdoms would be swept aside and in their place would be 'a federation of the United States of Nations'. After the new Napoleon, a 'great reformer' would arise to renew 'religious sentiments' after the super-Venus's second torch had burnt the old Church to the ground. Monotheism would be replaced by pantheism and 'God, soul, spirit, and immortality will be molten in a new furnace' to inaugurate 'the peaceful beginning of an ethical era'.

The third torch, that of law, was already burning holes in the family, art and morals. Luckily, 'a hero of literature and art' would pop up and purge the world of 'the tedious stuff of the obvious'. All this was given a racial character: the great calamity would leave only 'the Anglo-Saxons, the Latins, the Slavs and the Mongolians'. The man from the north was evidently an Anglo-Saxon, the religious reformer was a 'Mongolian-Slav' and the artistic hero was one of the Latins. There were a few other uninteresting details to the prophecy, as there always are, but the prediction of a great war and close dating of 1913 must have caught the attention of the readers of *Light*. According to the story, the countess forwarded her account to the Czar who had a translation sent to the Kaiser and the Kaiser sent it on to the British monarch. In other versions, Emperor Wilhelm of Germany had asked the Russian Czar to get something new out of Tolstoy and it was the Czar himself who had commanded Tolstoy's grandniece to extract something novel.[97] That Tolstoy had actually made this prophecy is unlikely, but here it was: a prophetic pronouncement verging on accurate posing as having come from a Russian genius – and, whoever wrote it, it was still published before the war.

It was not just readers of *Light* who were exposed to Tolstoy's alleged prophecy; newspapers across the world would print it, and it was not just readers of newspapers who were exposed to prophecies. Anyone walking through Piccadilly Place in August 1914 would be

97 For example, in the account published by *The Day* (13 August 1914).

sure to notice the predictions and omens plastered on the windows of Willie Wendt de Kerlor's Occult Library (also home to the Occult Club and the Alchemical Society), although admittedly it was just a shabby alleyway with an upmarket address mostly frequented by officers of the law and their occasional charges going to and from Vine Street Police Station.

There was, then, a growing sense of an approaching apocalypse and one that the British – for so long the dominant military power – would not necessarily win. The *Daily Chronicle*'s prayerful appeal also reveals a people willing to hear about 'Wisdom' with a capital 'W'. Not only was psychical research more acceptable, but so too was religion – and 'duty' as something almost akin to religion. It created a context for the sorts of experiences and beliefs that we will examine in this book. This is not some catalogue of 'weird things that happened during the Great War' – though weird things were reported to have happened – but an insight into how things were different in the past and, hence, how they are different now.

'The Angel of the Lord' and Mons

'That contemptible little army', the British Expeditionary Force, had crossed the English Channel and made its way with great haste to join the French Fifth Army. Commanded by Field Marshall Sir John French, the BEF consisted of four infantry divisions and one cavalry division, less than 100,000 men in total. It was divided into two groups: I Corps under General Haig and II Corps under General Sir Horace Smith-Dorrien.

Malcolm Leckie, the brother of Conan Doyle's second wife Jean, had been in the Royal Army Medical Corps before the war and now found himself attached to the 1st Battalion, The Northumberland Fusiliers, 9th Infantry Brigade, and on his way to Mons. The Conan Doyles' close friend Lily had two brothers at Mons: Bob and Willie. A third brother, Thomas, a lieutenant with the 2nd Battalion, The

Cameronians, was still trying to reach his regiment, having been on leave. All of them were in II Corps.

Helen's cousin Lt Christopher Francis Verrall was with the 2nd Battalion, Royal Sussex Regiment, in Haig's I Corps. Born in Brighton, he had gone up to Trinity College, Cambridge, and no doubt would have been a visitor, even a frequent one, at Helen's home. He had joined the army after university in 1911 and arrived at Le Havre on 13 August 1914.[98]

As a first-class reservist, Joe Cassells was mobilised the day after war was declared and landed with his regiment, the Black Watch (I Corps), also at Le Havre on 13 August. As they reached Boué, a traffic jam of military transports forced them to stop for a few days. The soldiers went swimming in the canal. Afterwards, an old Frenchman came up to Cassells and his friend and gave them both a half-franc coin, 'saying that it would give us good luck and bring us through alive'. Cassells survived the war and so did his friend, but few 'Old Comtemptibles' did so – a fate he credited to that old Frenchman's lucky coin.[99]

Cassells left Boué at 3 a.m. on 23 August and marched for twenty-four hours, the sound of the German guns pounding the French growing all the while. I Corps were sent east of Mons. The Black Watch were marched south-east of Mons to a location near Grand Reng on the main road to Mons – positioning them adjacent to the French line.

One soldier fixed his lucky coin – a British penny from 1892 – onto a brass shell case and engraved it with 'Mons 23-8-14'. According to the story, his name was S. (believed to be Steven) Adam, Cheshire Regiment, and he carried the coin with him through the war and survived. The shell case was manufactured by Berndorf in 1895, so undoubtedly would have been used early in

98 2nd Battalion, Royal Sussex Regiment, War Diary, National Archives, Kew, WO 95/1269/1; Ray Westlake, *British Battalions in France and Germany, 1914* (London: Leo Cooper, 1997), p. 179.
99 Joe Cassells, *The Black Watch: A Record in Action* (Garden City, NY: Doubleday, Page & Co., 1918), pp. 4–7.

the war, and the 1st Battalion, The Cheshire Regiment, saw action at Mons.[100]

Cassells was not an isolated case of being given luck *en route*. As the 2nd Battalion, the Duke of Wellington's (West Riding Regiment), marched through Hornu near Mons, a young Belgian woman took the rosary from around her neck and gave it to Private Eves. Eves was not a Catholic, but he carried the rosary with him nonetheless and survived the fighting to come. Although told second-hand and at the height of the war, it is still worth quoting the words attributed to him:

> The air was thick with shells and machine-gun bullets, and how I escaped I don't know. A shell burst close to me. A piece of it struck my ammunition band and bent five cartridges out of shape; but I escaped with only a bruise on the chest. I always say this rosary had something to do with it.[101]

As the BEF deployed to meet the advancing Germans, II Corps were stretched along a 20-mile line west of Mons, following the Canal de Centre, with the Eighth and Ninth Infantry Brigades holding the salient formed by the canal as it went north of Mons, turning east again from Nimy to Obourg. Leckie was nearest Mons, stationed along the railway line on the town's left flank. Bob, a captain with the 1st Battalion, The Cheshire Regiment, deployed about 3 miles (5 km) to the left of

100 Roger Bates, personal communication, 7 January 2015. The only soldier I could find with 'Steven' and 'Adam' in his name was 'Adam Steven', a gunner in the Royal Field Artillery (see National Archives, Kew, WO 372/19/41494). The nearest name to this in the Cheshire Regiment was a private called Samuel Adams (see National Archives, Kew, WO 372/1/18484). Their respective army numbers make Samuel Adams a more likely participant at Mons.

101 Michael MacDonagh, *The Irish on the Somme* (London: Hodder & Stoughton, 1917), p. 99. There were three privates called Eves in the West Riding Regiment. William, Reginald and Thomas, according National Archives records – only Reginald is identified as belonging to the 2nd Battalion, see 'Medal card of Eves, Reginald C.', WO 372/7/1039. Hornu was close to the Regiment's position on the front line at Mons.

Mons near Hornu in the rear. Willie, a captain with the 1st Battalion, The Wiltshire Regiment, was in a supporting role behind Mons near the village of Ciply.

Worried relatives at home did not, of course, know the disposition of the troops, or the exact whereabouts of their loved ones. They only knew that they would soon be facing the German advance.

Distant shots and cries had already punctuated the grey dawn on Sunday, 23 August, and, as the old clock tower of Mons chimed 9 a.m., the artillery of General Alexander von Kluck's First Army opened fire on the British soldiers in their hastily dug scrape trenches. The first battle of the First World War between the British and Germans had begun, and the British now found themselves outnumbered almost three to one with the French army they had been sent to support in full retreat. They had to hold the Germans, or France would fall.[102]

The German hammer fell first on the exposed salient. Here, two battalions from the Middlesex and Royal Fusiliers regiments bore the worst of the bombardment. Fast on the heels of the shells came advancing infantry columns of the German IX Corps. The shattered line faced an enemy perhaps ten times as strong. As the casualties mounted the Second Royal Irish were moved up to support. Corporal John Lucy was among them and later recalled his amazement as the rapid rifle fire of the British knocked the Germans down in waves.[103]

Undeterred, the Germans began pushing to the west and east, trying to encircle the exposed salient. Faced with the likelihood of being cut off and wiped out, the British began to pull back. Heavy shelling of

102 David Clarke, *The Angel of Mons: Phantom Soldiers and Ghostly Guardians* (London: John Wiley & Sons, 2005), p. 43; Herbert Arthur Stewart, *From Mons to Loos* (Edinburgh: W. Blackwood, 1916), p. 19; W. Douglas Newton, *The Undying Story* (New York: E.P. Dutton & Co., 1915), p. 12; Sir James E. Edmonds, *Military Operations, France and Belgium, 1914* (London: Macmillan & Co., 1937), p. 76; Lord Ernest Hamilton, *The First Seven Divisions* (New York: E.P. Dutton & Co., 1916), p. 20.
103 John Frederick Lucy, *There's a Devil in the Drum* (London: Faber & Faber, 1938).

their positions along the canal forced Leckie and the 1st Battalion, The Northumberland Fusiliers to fall back and a general withdrawal to Frameries about 2 miles (3 km) south of Mons was ordered.[104]

In the early hours of 24 August, the War Office in London received a telegram from Sir John French:

> My troops have been engaged all day on a line roughly E. and W. through Mons; the attack was renewed after dark, but we hold our ground tenaciously. I have just received message from G.O.C. Fifth Army that his troops have been driven back; that Namur has fallen; and that he is taking up a line from Maubeuge to Rocroy. I have therefore ordered a retirement to the line Valenciennes — Longueville — Maubeuge, which is being carried out now. It will prove a difficult operation if the enemy remain in contact.[105]

The British were between the hammer and the anvil. Everything now hung in the balance. What happened next would seem like a miracle; perhaps it was. Writing a private letter dated 5 September 1914, John Charteris, the Glaswegian aide-de-camp to Lieutenant-General Sir Douglas Haig, noted:

> There is the story of the 'Angels of Mons' going strong through the II Corps of how the angel of the Lord on the traditional white horse, and clad all in white with flaming sword, faced the advancing Germans at Mons and forbade their further progress.[106]

---

104 Westlake, *British Battalions*, p. 43.
105 Quoted in Arthur, *Life of Lord Kitchener*, p. 35.
106 John Charteris, *At GHQ* (London: Cassell and Co., 1931), pp. 25–6.

Or 'St George for Merry England!'

'I seemed to see,' he wrote, 'a furnace of torment and death and agony and terror seven times heated.' The writer Arthur Machen read about Mons in the Sunday newspapers a week later. The account of the battle moved him deeply, so that more than a year later he could still recall the intense vision it evoked. 'And in the midst of the burning,' he continued, 'was the British Army [. . .] so I saw our men with a shining about them.'[107]

Conan Doyle had also been living for the newspapers, presumably his wife Jean, too, as they followed the events of the Battle of Mons and the Great Retirement after it. Somewhere in the hail of bullets and the desperate march, was Jean's brother Malcolm Leckie.

Machen was inspired to write 'The Bowmen', a short story about a soldier who invokes St George's aid at a critical moment in the battle and is astonished to hear England's patron saint rally the ghosts of the bowmen who fought at Agincourt and see 'a long line of shapes, with a shining about them', who, with a cry of 'St George for Merry England', loose a spectral assault upon the Germans. Arrows that strike down, but leave no quivering shaft, to the bafflement of the General Staff's later enquiry. Machen had no idea the impact his story would have when it was printed in the *Evening News* for 29 September 1914.

A few days later he received a letter from Ralph Shirley, the editor of *The Occult Review*, asking whether the story was based on the truth. 'I told him,' he said, 'that it had no foundation in fact of any sort; I forget whether I added that it had no foundation in rumour, but I should think not, since to the best of my belief there were no rumours of heavenly interposition in existence at that time.' Then David Gow, the editor of the Spiritualist periodical *Light*, wrote to him and asked the same

---

107 Arthur Machen, *The Angels of Mons: The Bowmen and Other Legends of the War* (London: Simpkin, Marshall, Hamilton, Kent & Co., 1915), p. 8.

question. Machen gave the same answer, but he would keep being asked the question and it would seem to make no difference that he kept giving the same answer.[108]

Machen claimed to have invented the Angels of Mons, but he overlooked the fact that none of the later 'rumours' involved St George or phantom bowmen. However, the only evidence that there was any sort of rumour of angels before the publication of Machen's story is Charteris's letter. Charteris would later become Chief Intelligence Officer and there was always the lingering suspicion that he had manufactured the evidence to prop up the rumour.[109]

The Conan Doyles had no news of Malcolm until September. He was listed as wounded, missing in action. Jean used her contacts to try and find out more, and was able to get Winston Churchill's wife Clementine to help her – Clementine's sister was working in a field hospital. By the end of the year they learnt the truth. Malcolm had been fatally wounded, but refused to leave his post and continued caring for other wounded soldiers until he himself died of his wounds at Frameries on 28 August. He was posthumously awarded the Distinguished Service Order (DSO).[110]

For those who survived, it seemed like a miracle had happened. The outnumbered and out-manoeuvred BEF had escaped certain destruction. The number of German dead has never been disclosed, but is estimated in the range of five to ten thousand. Against this, the British lost 1,600 men. However, over the course of what was called the Great Retirement as the BEF retreated more than 200 miles (320 km) in thirteen days, British losses rose to 15,000.[111]

108 Machen, *Angels*, p. 13.
109 Clarke, *Angel of Mons*, pp. 63, 215–18.
110 Capt. Malcolm Leckie, DSO, is buried at Frameries Communal Cemetery, plot I, B 1. His name is also inscribed on the Crowborough War Memorial.
111 Alan John Percivale Taylor, *English History, 1914–1945* (Oxford: Oxford University Press, 1965), p. 9.

The *New Zealand* at Heligoland

When war was declared, Captain Halsey no doubt recalled the prophecies of the Maori chief. HMS *New Zealand* had traded the warm
waters of her namesake for the cruel seas of the north. At dawn on 27
August, Halsey received orders to take HMS *New Zealand* out of port
and prepare for battle. With the Germans making rapid advances
across Belgium, breaking the French armies and defeating the British
Expeditionary Force at Mons, the Royal Navy had found itself out-
manoeuvred by submarines and sea mines so that a close blockade of
German naval ports was ruled out. Forced into a patrolling role,
initially to protect British troop transports, an opportunity was nonetheless discovered to take the fight to the German navy, the *Kaiserliche
Marine*.

Commodores Roger Keyes (Head of the Submarine Service) and
Reginald Tyrwhitt (Commander, Harwich Striking Force) had observed
a pattern in German ship movements: cruisers would escort destroyers
to their patrol routes at nightfall, returning to base before meeting
them again in the morning to escort them home. A superior force
could, they reasoned, be sent in under cover of darkness to intercept
the destroyers as they made for home in the morning. Winston
Churchill, then First Lord of the Admiralty, was impressed by the
daring of their plan.

Keyes was to send in his submarines, Tyrwhitt his destroyers, with
support coming from Rear-Admiral Gordon Moore's Cruiser Force K
– HMS *New Zealand* and HMS *Invincible* – and Cruiser Force C's
squadron of five armoured cruisers – HMS *Cressy, Aboukir, Bacchante,
Hogue* and *Euryalus*. When Admiral John Jellicoe, commander of the
Grand Fleet, heard about the plan – the Admiralty only thought to tell
him on 26 August – he sent further reinforcements from Scapa Flow
in Orkney: three battlecruisers and the six ships of 1st Light Cruiser
Squadron.

Commodore Tyrwhitt was onboard the Royal Navy's brand new light cruiser HMS *Arethusa* – commissioned that month – leading the 3rd Flotilla of sixteen L-class destroyers, when the enemy were sighted. At around 07.00 on the morning of 28 August, the *Arethusa* made contact with the German destroyer G-194. Tyrwhitt ordered four destroyers to break formation and attack. They all knew that the Germans' Siemens radios were already calling for reinforcements.

It was after midday when HMS *New Zealand* and the other heavy ships joined the battle. An officer called Chalmers on one of the destroyers recalled seeing the warships arrive:

There straight ahead of us in lovely procession, like elephants walking through a pack of [. . .] dogs came *Lion, Queen Mary, Princess Royal, Invincible* and *New Zealand* [. . .] How solid they looked, how utterly earthquaking. We pointed out our latest aggressor to them [. . .] and we went west while they went east [. . .] and just a little later we heard the thunder of their guns.[112]

Captain Halsey put on the *piupiu* over his uniform and joined his men. Mouths dropped, to say the least. He recalled later:

Officers and men who were in the Conning Tower [. . .] were so startled at seeing me in this extraordinary clothing that they appeared to be quite incapable of carrying on with their very important personal duties and I had quickly to explain why I was thus attired.[113]

The battlecruisers had been intended as a distant support to the lighter destroyer forces, but when the British destroyers failed to end the engagement at 11.35 as per the plan, Admiral David Beatty ordered in his battlecruisers, leading the charge in his flagship HMS *Lion*. As they

112 *The Times History of the War*, vol. II (London: The Times, 1915), p. 12.
113 Letter from Lionel Halsey, 17 February 1939, Object information file for *piupiu* 2007.1.1, The Royal New Zealand Navy Museum.

came out of the mist they found Tyrwhitt's light cruiser *Arethusa* crippled and under fire from the German light cruisers SMS *Strassburg* and *Cöln*. Turrets turned and the British 13.5-inch guns thundered their reply to the 4-inch German guns.

SMS *Strassburg* was able to escape under the mist cover, making smoke for 27.5 knots, but SMS *Cöln* was trapped, taking hit after hit. SMS *Ariadne* now entered the battle, but the elderly light cruiser, sighting the British heavyweights, attempted to flee. HMS *Lion* broke off the attack on *Cöln* to pursue. Three mighty salvoes set *Ariadne* ablaze.

HMS *New Zealand* had been left behind by Beatty's newer and faster battlecruisers – the *Lion* could make 28 knots, compared to *New Zealand*'s 25. Nonetheless, German submarines still posed a threat and a torpedo from one passed her bows. At 13.05, *New Zealand* was within range of *Cöln* to let loose one of her own torpedoes and struck the German amidships. But she was ordered to disengage along with the rest of the Battle Cruiser Fleet and return home.[114]

According to her gunnery record, the *New Zealand* had fired eighty-three shells from her big turret guns during the engagement. Captain Halsey must have been disappointed not to have joined the battle sooner, but as he folded away the *piupiu* he could thank 'the kindness of the Maoris' that his ship had been unscathed and his men unharmed.

The British had run a great risk. Poor communications – Churchill called it 'defective Staff work' – had brought the attacking flotillas into conflict with Jellicoe's reinforcements, mistaking them for Germans. But luck – or Maori magic – had been on their side. Poor visibility had prevented the German shore batteries from providing supporting fire and the low tide meant that the German battleships and battlecruisers were trapped in Wilhelmshafen, waiting until 13.00 before they could cross the bar of the river Jade.

Overall, the Battle of Heligoland had been a notable victory for the British; with only thirty-five killed and no ships sunk they had killed 712 German sailors and sent three of their light cruisers, two torpedo

114 'HMS *New Zealand*', Royal New Zealand Navy Museum, http://navy museum.co.nz/worldwar1/ships/hms-new-zealand/, accessed 12 February 2018.

boats and a destroyer to the bottom of the sea. The Kaiser had been shaken by the defeat and commanded in future that any plans significantly to involve the High Seas Fleet should be first communicated to him directly. Admiral Tirpitz called it a 'muzzling policy'; Churchill agreed.[115] But if the Maoris were right, HMS *New Zealand* still had two sea battles ahead of her.

Raymond Joins Up

Sir Oliver Lodge was already a grandee of the Society when the war broke out. He was a grandee of society in general. In 1898, the Royal Society had awarded him the Rumford Medal. In 1900, the newly established University of Birmingham had invited him to be its Principal. In 1902, King Edward VII had bestowed a knighthood upon him. His portrait photograph by Lafayette Ltd shows the quintessential man of science: a great domed bald head, as if his mighty thoughts had burned away his hair with their sheer energy, but a full and majestic beard to make up for it; hooded eyes, a brooding look, a serious man. Sir George Reid's painting showed much the same, escaping the limitations of black-and-white photography to choose an ochre palette: a beige face above a dark brown suit, a flash of white collar and dull yellow tie, that grey beard floating like ectoplasm about his chin. The painting stills hangs in the National Portrait Gallery, London. He had not long since celebrated his sixty-third birthday. He was still spry, keeping himself in trim by punching a leather ball and assaulting sundry other weights. With his wife of thirty-seven years, Mary Fanny Alexander Marshall, they had had twelve children: six boys and six girls. Even in his marital duties he was an over-achiever. The boys were all engineers, except one, the eldest son, Oliver William Foster Lodge (known as O. W. F. Lodge), who became a poet. Sir Oliver saw little of

---

115 Winston Churchill, *The World Crisis*, vol. I (London: Thornton Butterworth, 1923–1927), pp. 333–4.

his children, being, as he put it, 'so desperately busy all my life'. Of them all, however, he found his youngest son Raymond most like himself, both in appearance (at that age) and character. Sir Oliver frowned at his lack of achievement in mathematics and physics, but conceded that his son was a better engineer and certainly had the keener sense of humour.[116]

At the outbreak of war, Raymond was working with his brothers in their engineering works. A sense of duty compelled him to volunteer for the Army in September 1914 and he would be surprised to find that soldiering came naturally to him. Sir Oliver and his wife were in Australia for a meeting of the British Association for the Advancement of Science (Sir Oliver was its President) and it was some while before they found out.

Sir Oliver and his wife had booked their passage on the *Orvieto*, leaving a Europe at peace, only to find a world at war when they were due to return. They were somewhat inconvenienced to find out that their cabin and indeed every berth in the ship had been turned over to the Army as a troop transport. They found a place on the P&O steamship *Morea*. 'Voyage adventurous, but all well,' he wrote in a note to Arthur Hill, dated 19 October, after they docked at Plymouth.

The 'adventurous' aspect turned out to be more mundane than heroic. A shortage of labour meant that the passengers were drafted in to help swabbing the decks and other menial tasks. Sir Oliver got up at six in the morning with the others in order to help out, but found that there were too few brooms to go round – 'the younger men usually got them first'. Sir Oliver overheard the ladies on board remarking that the effect was superior to the usual job done by the Lascars – the name for the Indian workers who were usually employed to do this. Sir Oliver instead had time to finish Patrick MacGill's autobiographical novel *Children of the Dead End* about his harsh and poverty-stricken life as a navvy in Ireland and Scotland. It was a

116 Sir Oliver Lodge, *Raymond, or Life and Death* (London: Methuen, 1926), p. 9; Sir Oliver Lodge, *Letters from Sir Oliver Lodge: Psychical, Religious, Scientific and Personal* (London: Cassell & Co., 1932), pp. 37, 41–2.

popular book at the time, easily out-selling James Joyce's *Dubliners* (also published in 1914).

There is no mention in his published letters of what he thought of the declaration of war. Later that year, the *Morea* herself would also become a troop transport for the Australian Expeditionary Force.

Like Raymond, MacGill volunteered for Kitchener's New Army and his insight into why he joined is as enlightening of the times as it is unenlightening of the psychology of the recruits.

'Few men,' he wrote, 'could explain why they enlisted.' He knew because he had asked them. One of his new pals, 'a good-humoured Cockney', said, 'Well, matey, I done it to get away from my old gal's jore – now you've got it!' Another said, 'I enlisted because I am an Englishman.' MacGill, of course, was an Irishman in the Irish Rifles – 'rumour has it that the Colonel and I are the only two *real* Irishmen in the battalion'. He gave up asking why people had joined. They had no reasons because they had abandoned reason. Sir Oliver knew it: he had written a pamphlet on *Irrationality and War* in 1912.[117]

Raymond underwent training at Great Crosby, near Liverpool, with the infantry regiment into which he was commissioned, the South Lancashires. His company spent that first winter of the war in Edinburgh, on the banks of the Forth Estuary in Scotland. It would not be until spring next year that he would sail for France and his fate.

A Spiritualist at the War Propaganda Bureau

The Germans had a Propaganda Agency – the British would have one, too. As soon as they found out about it the War Office determined to take action. On 2 September 1914, twenty-five of the foremost writers

117 Patrick MacGill, *The Amateur Army* (London: Herbert Jenkins, 1915), pp. 14–15.

of the day were invited to Wellington House in London's Buckingham Gate. Sir Arthur Conan Doyle, of course, was amongst them. Sitting round the table with him were J. M. Barrie, Arnold Bennett, Ford Maddox Ford, G. K. Chesterton, Thomas Hardy, Rudyard Kipling, H. G. Wells and others. Charles Masterton had been appointed by the Chancellor of the Exchequer, David Lloyd George, to form a War Propaganda Bureau; and as the writers he had summoned seated themselves, he made them swear to secrecy.[118]

They met again two weeks later. This time the writers were joined by publishers, such as John Buchan's company Thomas Nelson, and agents. Conan Doyle and the others signed a declaration of the justness of the war. He was now a fully enrolled propagandist.

Conan Doyle referred to his involvement in his 1924 autobiography as having 'a great deal of literary propaganda work to do'. It was not until 1935 that the wider public learnt of the War Propaganda Bureau.

Masterton himself was only once removed from the SPR circle. He was married to Lucy Blanche Lyttelton, one of the ubiquitous Lyttelton clan. She was the daughter of General Sir Neville Gerald Lyttelton, one of Alfred Lyttelton's older brothers and a friend of Arthur Balfour's.

By the end of September, Conan Doyle had written the sabre-rattling *To Arms!* and Hodder & Stoughton had published it. It was a penny pamphlet with a foreword by F. E. Smith (later Lord Birkenhead). In a sense, Conan Doyle did not need to be recruited by Masterton, he was happy propagandising all on his own. Instead, it is possible that the government was seeking to gain some control over him.

Conan Doyle had decided to write a history of the war as it was being fought. As well as having contacts at the War Office and now the WPB, he established a wide network of sources among high-ranking officers directly engaged in the battles in France. He held out hopes of his account becoming the official version, but there were others vying

118 Andrew Lycett, *Conan Doyle: The Man Who Created Sherlock Holmes* (London: Weidenfield & Nicolson, 2007), p. 356.

for that honour – it would be written under the direction of Colonel (later Brigadier General) James Edmonds, former head of MI5 and a staff officer at the BEF's GHQ in France during the war, with Edmonds writing much of it himself.[119]

The Bureau would later earn infamy for its production of the *Report on Alleged German Outrages* in early 1915. The report exaggerated or invented reports of German atrocities for propaganda purposes and was widely criticised after the war, for example by Arthur Ponsonby in *Falsehood in Wartime* (1928). Rushed into print after the sinking of the *Lusitania*, the Bureau, seeking to capitalise on the tragedy, had 41,000 copies shipped to the USA and its findings were reported in *The New York Times*.

Richet: The Greatest Genius
and the Gravest Dangers

In 1914, the honour of being awarded the Nobel Prize for Medicine was still fresh for the French physiologist and psychical researcher, Charles Richet (1850–1935), Professor of Physiology at the Collège de France in Paris and former President of the Society for Psychical Research (1905). In September, Richet was in Italy, 'where,' he says, 'I felt the duty of carrying on an active propaganda for our holy national cause'. As if that were not enough, all five of his sons were then in the French army, fighting at the Front.[120]

Richet was staying at 'the Quirinal Hotel' – probably the Hotel Quirinale in Rome, although he does not specify the city – which was at that time 'almost deserted'. Sometime during the night of 22–23 September he was awoken from sleep by three knocks on his door,

119 Published as the *History of the Great War Based on Official Documents* in 28 volumes from 1922 to 1949.
120 Charles Richet, *Thirty Years of Psychical Research* (New York: Macmillan, 1923), pp. 280–1.

'very clear but not very loud'. He sat up in bed and switched on the light. Three knocks again sounded on the door.

'Come in,' called Richet, quite alert now.

'Doctor, doctor,' said a woman's voice from behind the door. Richet described it as 'speaking low and plaintively'.

'Very well, I am coming,' said Richet, swinging his legs out of bed. He expected someone needed medical assistance. He opened the door and was puzzled to find no one there. Returning to bed, he made note of the time, 1.20 a.m., wondering if he had had some sort of hallucination. He also wondered if it had been some sort of premonition: because he had heard a woman's voice, he supposed that it might refer to his daughter-in-law, then due to give birth; he did not think that it had anything to do with his five sons then at the Front and, in his words, 'exposed to the gravest dangers'.

A little while later he learnt that misfortune had befallen his son Jacques on 17 September. He had been severely wounded and captured by the Germans. Richet reported the incident, but remained sceptical. 'It is,' he wrote, 'absolutely impossible to prove that this was a monition of the wounding and capture of my son'; however, 'I am convinced [. . .] that the monition was real.'

Richet carried on his propaganda work. Later in the war, Richet was part of the French diplomatic mission to Romania, with the purpose of counter-acting German influence and bringing Romania into the war on the side of the Allies. They were in Moscow in the winter of 1915, apparently delayed *en route*, and the new British Consul-General Vice-Consul (acting Consul-General) there, R. H. Bruce Lockhart (later Sir), got to know France's 'eminent scientist'. 'In Richet,' he said, 'I met the greatest genius and most attractive personality I have ever known.' Lockhart also made the acquaintance of Aleister Crowley in Moscow, but did not record what he thought of him.[121]

---

121 R. H. Bruce Lockhart, *Memoirs of a British Agent* (New York and London: Putnam, 1932), p. 138.

'If Armageddon's On . . .'

On that fateful day in August, Rupert Brooke was staying with friends, the Cornfords, in Norfolk when he heard the news. In his veiled auto-biographical account 'An Unusual Young Man', Brooke puts into the heart and mouth of another, 'a friend', everything that he was thinking and feeling at the time war was declared. This friend was on a beach when a boy ran down with a telegram, exclaiming 'We're at war with Germany. We've joined with France and Russia.'[122]

During a visit to Germany before the war, Brooke had written to a friend, saying: 'I am wildly in favour of nineteen new Dreadnoughts. German culture must never, never prevail.' He thought them 'nice' but 'soft', although Munich café society gave him a poor base for general-isation. He reflected upon his time in Germany again as the news of war sank in and remembered instead friendship, drunken adventures and 'that air of comfortable kindness'; but now 'something in him kept urging, "You must hate these things, find evil in them" '.[123]

Rupert Brooke was in a music hall in London as the war deepened on 12 August. The show was interrupted by the projection of a hastily scribbled message: 'War declared with Austria'. Hands clapped, quick and low, 'a signal of recognition' rather than enthusiasm. The crowd discharged into Trafalgar Square to seek out 'midnight War editions' of the newspapers. 'In all these days,' wrote Brooke, 'I haven't been so near to tears; there was such tragedy and dignity in the people.'[124]

122 Marsh, 'Memoir', p. cxxiv; Rupert Brooke, 'An Unusual Young Man', in *Letters from America* (1916), pp. 173–80.
123 Marsh, 'Memoir', p. lxiii; Brooke, 'Unusual Young Man', pp. 174–5.
124 Marsh, 'Memoir', p. cxxv. Britain declared war on Austro-Hungary on 12 August, but this passage is also taken to refer to the declaration of war with Germany, see Alisa Miller, *Rupert Brooke in the First World War* (Liverpool: Clemson University Press/Liverpool University Press, 2017), p. 36. I am grate-ful to Dr Alisa Miller for checking Brooke's letters for me: Dr Alisa Miller, King's College London, personal communication, 5 April 2018.

The unusual young 'friend' was not moved to tears, but instead 'felt vaguely jealous of the young men in Germany and France'. 'Well, if Armageddon's *on*,' he surmised, 'I suppose one should be there.'[125]

After Brooke had dashed about London, considering enlistment in a London corps or returning to Cambridge for the Territorial Army, Winston Churchill offered him a commission in the newly formed Royal Naval Division. On 27 September, he and an old friend, Denis Browne, joined the Anson Battalion of the Royal Navy's new infantry formation. Another friend, Sir Edward Marsh, saw them off from Charing Cross as a train took them to Betteshanger Camp and military training. They were, he thought, 'excited and a little shy, like two new boys going to school'. Marsh had been Private Secretary to Alfred Lyttelton and then Churchill – it was Marsh's influence that led Churchill to offer help to Brooke over dinner at the Admiralty on 23 September. On 4 October, Brooke sailed for Dunkirk, from there by train to Antwerp and war.[126]

'They told us at Dunkirk,' he later wrote, 'that we were all going to be killed at Antwerp.'[127] The Germans were laying siege to the city; the 'Race to the Sea' had almost reached the sea. Armageddon, however, was not quite as Brooke had expected it:

> There's the empty blue sky and the peaceful village and country scenery, and nothing of war to see except occasional bursts of white smoke, very lazy and quiet, in the distance. But to hear – incessant thunder, shaking buildings and ground, and you and everything; and above, recurrent wailings, very thin and queer, like lost souls, crossing and recrossing in the emptiness – nothing to be seen [. . .] the whole thing is like a German woodcut, very quaint and peaceful and unreal.[128]

125 Brooke, 'Unusual Young Man', p. 180.
126 Marsh, 'Memoir', pp. cxxv-cxxvi; Miller, *Rupert Brooke*, p. 50.
127 Quoted in Marsh, 'Memoir', p. cxxxiv.
128 Marsh, 'Memoir', p. cxxx.

Soon they marched back again under cover of night, their way illumin-ated by burning houses. All in all, 'a queer picnic'. The war stirred up contradictory emotions: 'It's all a terrible tragedy. And yet, in its details, it's great fun.' He had already lost a friend at Cambrai and more would follow, but having seen the plight of the Belgian refugees, he felt that he was doing some good.[129]

Sir Oliver Lodge's Holy War

In November 1914, Lodge was at the Browning Hall in Walworth, London, talking ostensibly about 'Science and Religion'. His was the first in a series of lectures on the subject by seven distinguished men of science, but it degenerated into the sort of sermonising more appro-priate to religion than science.

Sir Oliver noted that 'the hall was crowded, people standing up and so on', estimating as many as twelve to fifteen hundred. The Mayor and Corporation of Southwark graced the platform, resplendent in their official robes: 'everything was done to lend some importance to the occasion'.[130] As the crowd fell silent, he began:

> We all know that there are powers of good and powers of evil. We all know, because we are fighting them at the present time. Why are we fighting this, the holiest war that we were ever engaged in? Because the powers of evil are loose, 'spiritual wickedness in high places', and in fighting them we are agents of God. It is a holy war. What is the doctrine opposed to us? That there is noth-ing higher than the State, that the State is the summit of every-thing, and that the State is entitled to do whatever it pleases, if it is conducive to its benefit. No moral law, no existence higher than a powerful State! Well, that is practical Atheism. That is

129 Marsh, 'Memoir', pp. cxxxii, cxxxiv.
130 Lodge, *Letters*, p. 41.

what we are at war with. If we had to live under the domination of a State like that, if the world ever came under such a domination, life would not be worth having. [. . .] We know that there is a moral government of the world. We know that there are high ideals: our enemy is taught otherwise. Our troops – how splendidly they are behaving – could not do the horrible, the treacherous the abominably cruel things that these people have done with this belief forced upon them, this kind of coercion and falsity of belief. [. . .] Right belief gives us strength, determination, and energy, and such vigour that we are irresistible and cannot be overcome. The other belief must succumb. The powers of good are stronger than the powers of evil.[131]

How they must have cheered in the Hall that night, but Lodge was lucky not to live, by his own admission, to see the inexorable rise of the state into the twenty-first century. Lodge's speech gives a good insight into his character and the humour of the times – it is certainly not an accurate analysis of the conflict. A. P. Sinnett would reproduce Lodge's speech in his 1915 book *The Spiritual Powers and the War*.

Sinnett's continually inaccurate predictions relating to the war did nothing to check his enthusiasm for developing wild occult theories of the hidden forces at play behind visible world events. Where Lodge at least still had his scientific credibility to temper his extremism, Sinnett was entirely abandoned to theosophical fantasising.

Sinnett's continual point of reference was the entirely fanciful history of Atlantis, spanning some four million years and all taking place 'more than nine thousand years before the Christian era'; his chronology seemed just as fantastic.[132] Here is the origin of Sinnett's White and Black Lodges as the people of Atlantis developed spiritual power and used it either for good or evil. Sinnett might give the impression of being deranged, but his theorising was only a reflection of what

131 Sinnett, *The Spiritual Powers and the War* (London: Theosophical Publishing House, 1915), pp. 11–12.
132 Sinnett, *Spiritual Powers*, p. 17.

was being pumped out by the Theosophical Society, founded by the failed fraudulent medium Madame Blavatsky. It is no surprise to learn that Sinnett was a member and that his books were published by the Theosophical Publishing House.

According to Sinnett, the Germans were now entirely under the control of 'dark influences'.[133] Sinnett's views were not unexpected. He was simply expressing the typical dehumanising and demonising of 'the enemy' that occurs whenever one group is at war with another. Sinnett had particular problems trying to reconcile the conflict with his ideas of karma and ideals of human brotherhood, but they need not detain us.

Sinnett was not content to leave his occult speculations there. He had an answer to the whole horrible business of industrialised slaughter, including the moment of death. In the words of Sinnett:

A man killed in the wild excitement of battle is wrapped in a confusion of thought which precludes him from realising that he has actually passed on to another condition of being. But that period of wild excitement need not be thought of as distressing, and in any case it is one from which multitudes of eager astral philanthropists are engaged in liberating those subject to it. And then they pass at once to the happier conditions of the higher astral region.[134]

Yeats had a counter to Sinnett's prophecy. He told the other Ghosts present that December night in 1914 – Sir William Crookes, Lt Col. Dudley Sampson, Alexander Ionides, Dr Abraham Wallace, Henry Withall (Hon. Treasurer of the London Spiritualist Alliance), Robert Gray, Lt Col. E. R. Johnson (late of the Indian Medical Services), and A. P. Sinnett, of course – of a prophecy he had heard in his youth, foretelling 'a period of brute force [that] would prevail beginning 1900 and lasting for 120 years.' The group fell to discussing another prophecy

133 Sinnett, *Spiritual Powers*, p. 27.
134 Sinnett, *Spiritual Powers*, p. 48.

doing the rounds at the time, the Johannes prophecy. But the time for prophecy was past.[135]

A Mid-Shipman on HMS *Hawke*

Abraham Wallace had recently been at a séance with the American medium Henrietta 'Etta' Wriedt – always called 'Mrs Wriedt'. This Mrs Wriedt used a technique called direct voice, meaning that the supposed spirits could talk in their own voices through her mediumship. For this she used a spirit trumpet, a cone of thin metal or stiff card, intended to amplify the weak voices trying to be heard across the divide between the living and the dead. Born in Detroit in 1859, she visited the UK several times during her career. She had a spinsterly air, hair centre-parted and brushed back, large almond-shaped eyes behind almond-shaped glasses, and a downward turn to a thin-lipped mouth. Prominent British Spiritualists, such as W. T. Stead and Vice-Admiral Usborne Moore, vouched for her abilities. Usborne Moore had even written a book about her mediumistic powers, *The Voices*, published in 1913. SPR members Baggally, Barrett, Lodge and Conan Doyle were all convinced.

Stead had had her over in 1911, before he was lost on the *Titanic* in 1912. Usborne Moore invited her to return in 1912 (she did not sail on the *Titanic*) and again in 1913. Now it was Wallace's turn.

Wriedt's so-called 'control', the principal spirit claimed to communicate through her, was a certain Dr John Sharp, deceased, a Glaswegian from the eighteenth century who had been taken to the USA by his parents and lived the rest of his life there as an 'apothecary farmer' in Evansville, Indiana. Other spirit controls appeared from time to time and sometimes all together, such as John King, Grayfeather, or Mimi and Blossom, as well as the alleged spirits of sitters' friends and family.[136]

---

135 Ghost Club Archive, British Library Add Ms 52264, p. 338 [182].
136 W. Usborne Moore, *The Voices* (London: Watts & Co., 1913), p. xix.

After Sinnett had finished talking about some prophecy given by a Portuguese priest in 1901, Wallace related the events of his séance with Mrs Wriedt, during which:

A boy's voice was heard and a statement made that he had come over three weeks ago. The speaker give a name like Hanan[?] and said he was getting on well and that his mother was anxious. Dr Sharp, the control, explained that the boy's father was Dr Harold; who was afterwards visited by Bro. Wallace, and he was shown a portrait of the boy, a mid-shipman [officer cadet], drowned when HMS *Hawke* was sunk some weeks ago.[137]

HMS *Hawke* was an Edgar-class protected cruiser launched in 1891 – a protected cruiser was a type of naval vessel with full armour plating limited to the deck to allow greater speed. Prior to the war, she had been assigned to the training squadron at Queenstown (Cobh) in Ireland, but in August 1914 was reassigned to the 10th Cruiser Squadron and sent out into the North Sea to form a blockade between the Shetlands and Norway. In October 1914, the Squadron was redeployed closer to Scotland to protect a troop convoy from Canada. She was patrolling off Aberdeen on 15 October when she stopped to pick up mail from the *Endymion*. The stop meant that she was no longer in formation with the rest of the Squadron, sailing abreast at ten-mile intervals, and had lost visual contact. Making steam at 13 knots in a straight line to regain her position, she was struck by a single torpedo. *Hawke* quickly began to take on water and capsized. The 7,890 tons of ship sank, taking Captain Hugh Williams and most of his crew of over five hundred men to the bottom with it.[138]

The rest of the Squadron only realised something had happened when the submarine responsible, SM U-9, unsuccessfully attacked

137 Ghost Club Archive, British Library Add Ms 52264, p. 338 [182].
138 Admiral Viscount Jellicoe, *The Grand Fleet, 1914–1916: Its Creation, Development and Work* (London: Cassell & Co., 1919), p. 141; Sir Julian Corbett, *History of the Great War: Naval Operations*, Vol. I (London: Longmans, Green & Co., 1920), pp. 207–8.

HMS *Theseus* and the order to retreat north-west at full speed got no response from the *Hawke*. A destroyer, HMS *Swift*, was sent out from Scapa Flow to search for the missing vessel. She found twenty-one men on a raft; another forty-nine were picked up by a Norwegian steamer. One of those rescued subsequently died of his wounds.

There was nobody with a first name of Hanan or a surname of Harold on board, or vice versa, and no midshipman with an approximate-sounding name.[139] Was it all bunk? Wallace claimed to have confirmed it.

On 22 September, U-9 had sunk three other British cruisers – HMS *Aboukir, Hogue* and *Cressy* – in a single engagement lasting just over an hour. Conan Doyle had seen red over it: 'A young German lieutenant with twenty men had caused us more loss than we suffered at Trafalgar'. He was right: U-9 had claimed 1,495 lives that day in September; only 458 of Nelson's men had lost their lives against the French at Trafalgar.

Conan Doyle wrote to the *Daily Mail* and *Daily Chronicle* demanding that all sailors be issued with inflatable rubber collars. The Admiralty took him up on the idea and expedited an order for 250,000 collars. The *Hampshire Telegraph* reported that 'the Navy has to thank Sir Conan Doyle for the new life-saving apparatus the Admiralty are supplying. There is little doubt that this swimming collar will result in the saving of many lives.'[140]

Johnson also had a story about a séance with Mrs Wriedt. A girl's brother had been gazetted as an officer and subsequently killed in action. She wanted to go to a séance, but feared the reaction of her relatives. A friend of her brother, a military chaplain, went instead and heard the girl's brother talking through the medium. There was an incident in their youth when he had broken a window, but for which she got the blame – she confirmed that this was so.[141]

---

139 http://www.naval-history.net/xDKCas1914-10Oct.htm, accessed 27 June 2016.
140 Quoted in Russell Miller, *The Adventures of Conan Doyle*, p. 323.
141 Ghost Club Archive, British Library, Add MS 52264, p. 340 [183].

Lucky Black Cats

Luck would be in high demand in the coming years, for it seemed only by luck that anyone could possibly survive the indiscriminate, industrialised slaughter of the Front. There would be many stories of lucky escapes, some, like Mons, verging on the miraculous. And, of course, the High God of Luck was the black cat.

Only weeks after the war had started, an unnamed writer spun the myth of the black cat in the pages of the *Evening News* to an audience eager for some evidence that luck could be courted, controlled and given to loved ones – husbands, fathers, brothers, sons – as they headed east, across the Channel to the charnel house of the Front. The story reached a large audience, being reprinted in the *Daily Telegraph* and *Daily Mail* on 4 and 5 September 1914.[142]

An unnamed regiment, 'sturdy fellows in khaki', are boarding the train at Waterloo Station with 'soldiers' wives, and soldiers' babes, and soldiers' sweethearts, all hugging and kissing and waving and sobbing "Good-bye"'.

A girl takes a black kitten out of a basket and holds it out to a 'stern-looking sergeant': 'Stroke it and love it for a moment, Daddy,' she says, 'it will bring you lots of luck – teacher told me so – and then you will be home again soon.'

The sergeant takes the kitten and strokes it. Other men reach out to stroke it as well and soon the animal is being passed up and down the carriage.

The writer describes a transport setting sail, full of soldiers, the familiar scenes of farewell. Many have 'packages of Black Cat cigarettes

142 'The Luck of the Black Cat: A Thrilling War Story from Last Night's "Evening Standard"', *Daily Telegraph* (4 September 1914), p.3; 'The Luck of the Black Cat: A Thrilling War Story from Last Thursday's "Evening Standard"', *Daily Mail* (5 September 1914), p.6.

or tobacco' tucked in their pockets. Nothing unusual about soldiers smoking, of course, but 'every package had the picture of a coal black cat on it – for luck'. And after the cigarettes and tobacco have been smoked, 'the torn cover with the black cat on it will be treasured in pocket or haversack – just for the luck of it'.

The superstition was not just for soldiers. The writer describes the man in the street on his way to work and the bobby on his beat, stopping to stroke a lucky black cat. Then he is in ancient times, describing how the great men of history did nothing without a black cat. Julius Caesar packs one in his galley as he crosses the sea to conquer Britain. Henry VIII has one with him when he meets Francis I at the Field of the Cloth of Gold. The Duke of Marlborough strokes a black kitten as he directs the Battle of Blenheim. Napoleon blames his failure in Russia on the accidental death of a black cat beneath his carriage wheels. All stories new to the historian.

And in each newspaper, an advert for Black Cat Cigarettes, Black Cat Mixture and Black Cat Double Broad Cut tobacco. Clever marketing? Perhaps, but not only that. The Imperial War Museum has examples of felt black cats used by soldiers as lucky charms.

Several ambulance units adopted the black cat as their symbol. A group of volunteers from the academically renowned Amherst College in Massachusetts, USA, formed Section Sanitaire Unit 539, taking the black cat as their mascot and themselves coming to be known as The Black Cats. They joined the US Army in 1917 and were assigned to the French, ferrying the wounded from the front lines in Ford Model Ts emblazoned with a black cat with arched back on a white square. A surviving example is SSU 627, now on display at the Air Force Museum in Dayton, Ohio.[143] Ernst Jünger described seeing British tanks painted with symbols of luck, the four-leafed clover and pig, as well as more menacing designs, such as death's heads and, in one case, a hangman's noose.[144]

143 William S. McFeely, 'The Black Cats of Amherst', *Amherst Magazine* (Spring, 2010), https://www.amherst.edu/amherst-story/magazine/issues/2010spring/blackcats, accessed 30 January 2018.
144 Ernst Jünger, *Storm of Steel*, trans. Michael Hofman (London: Penguin, 1961), p. 261.

A Maidservant at the Front

In November 1914, Francis Gilbert Scott, MRCS, of New Malden, Surrey, was having trouble with his new maid. She was a girl of sixteen years with 'no education except that of a village school'. It was not her age or lack of education that was the problem, instead 'she was rather untidy about her work'.[145]

Gilbert Scott as he was generally known, born 1869, had graduated from the London Hospital in 1892 and gone on to serve as District Surgeon in Selangor Government Straits Settlement in British Malaya, Southeast Asia. Home again, he would become Hon. Sec. of the Electro-Therapeutic Society in 1915 and President of the Section of Radiology at the British Medical Association's Annual Meeting in 1923. He was involved in Dr Edwin Ash's London Nerve Clinic and School of Psychotherapy from about 1913 onwards.[146]

He discussed this with a friend, a certain 'Dr S.', who advised trying suggestion on her when she was asleep. This he did. He does not give the particulars, but we must assume that he crept into her room (probably in the attic; probably sparsely furnished; and certainly at night) and said things over her sleeping form – I will be a better maid, I will not scatter the ashes when I sweep out the grate, I will not drop the

145 The sources for this story are to be found in the Notebook of Francis Gilbert Scott, MRCS, British Library, Ghost Club Archives Add MS 52269C; and the Ghost Club Archives, Vol. VII, Add MS 52264. The notebook is described as being that of Francis Gilbert Scott, but it is also possible that he is the 'Dr S.' referred to in the text and that it was, therefore, written by someone else. He is referred to as 'Dr Gilbert Scott' in the Ghost Club minutes and this is evidently how he styled himself.

146 Philip Kuhn, *Psychoanalysis in Britain, 1893–1913: Histories and Historiography* (Lanham, Maryland: Lexington Books, 2017), p. 94, note 67; Matthew Thomson, *Psychological Subjects: Identity, Culture and Health in Twentieth-Century Britain* (Oxford: Oxford University Press, 2006), p. 28, note 69.

peelings when I go out to the bin – 'I always told her she would remain soundly asleep, which she did.'

The next morning 'she carried out all my instructions well'. Dr S. must have been congratulated on his fine advice.

Having an experimental turn of mind, Scott started trying out how far he could push the power of suggestion. It was all well and good to get her to do things that she should be doing anyway, but what if he introduced suggestions that ran against what was expected or even desirable? One night he suggested that she should ask him if she should light a fire in the breakfast room, even though the days were still warm enough not to have one. Scott was pleased that this was her first question when she came down the stairs that morning. There were some frequently used cricket bats kept in a convenient place. Scott suggested to the maid that she would ask if she could move them. He noted her hesitancy the next morning when she asked exactly this, 'in all probability fearing the displeasure of the owners'. Scott could no doubt have gone on like this at some length, devising more and more difficult situations for the hapless and unwitting maid. Except that one morning she told him that she had had a most unusual dream.

Her boyfriend, Edgar, had joined up. He was with the Army Service Corps on the Western Front. Last night she had not just dreamt of him, but had dreamt that she was actually with him. She told Scott that she remembered going down some well-worn earthen steps into an underground bunker fitted out like a kitchen. A number of soldiers were there and shortly after her arrival Edgar came down the steps to join them. His arm was bandaged and he showed it to the others, but drew back as if it were painful. One soldier amongst them 'looked like a sneak' and the others 'did not chum with him'. Another man wanted a pencil and so they all turned out their pockets. Only the sneak had one. He handed it over and left 'at which they all seemed pleased'. It had all been so real, she said, that she would recognise everyone again if they should meet.

Scott was taken aback by the detail of her dream and asked the maid to send an account of it to Edgar, asking whether it were true or not. Edgar's reply took a fortnight to reach them. He was more taken aback than Scott. Everything she had described was correct. Yes, their kitchen was underground. Yes, his arm was bandaged: a horse had bitten it. Yes, there was a man who was a 'sneak', but he did not care to talk about him. And yes, they were often searching for pencils.

Scott excitedly told Dr S. about this latest development. Dr S. diagnosed her as having the gift of clairvoyance and suggested that they try a new experiment on her. Scott should try and consciously direct her clairvoyance in a situation that could afterwards be checked reliably for accuracy.

The next evening Scott directed the maid to sit in an armchair and 'put her to sleep', evidently meaning that he put her into a hypnotic trance. He told her to go over to Dr S.'s house and see what he was doing.

She discovered him in the hall, preparing to go out. He lit his pipe, got a bicycle out from behind a curtain, called his dog, and left the house. 'Is there anything else you can see?' asked Scott. There was a manservant upstairs, wearing black. He was pulling down the blinds; and there was a 'rather stout woman' with him. Scott recognised this as being the cook, the manservant's wife.

When Scott and Dr S. got together the next day, Scott related what the maid had seen. It was a 'By Jove!' moment. Dr S. confirmed that all these details were entirely correct. Scott realised that the maid was not just clairvoyant but had the power of what was then called 'travelling clairvoyance'; what the US military called 'remote viewing' when it undertook a multi-million-dollar research programme into the uses of psychic powers, codenamed Stargate Project, from 1978 to 1995.

Scott decided to try and send her back to France. Dr S. sat in on the next experiment. As before, Scott put the maid into a hypnotic sleep. He told her that as she had already visited Edgar in a dream she could easily do so again. They waited only a moment before she spoke excitedly, 'Oh, there he is!' Her voice became distressed, 'But he has been wounded. He has a wound under his right ear; no, the left. He is limping, too. I am sure he is hurt.'

She started to cry.

'Don't worry,' Scott told her, 'he is well enough to do his work. What is he doing?'

She replied that he was helping some others to store something in bags underground. They were brushing the dust of something – 'it looked like flour' – off their uniforms. Edgar's arm was still bandaged, but not as much as it had been before.

She started to laugh, saying, 'Oh, look at them, they are opening some tins of meat and they are doing it with nails and stones which they get out of the wall.'

Scott recorded in his notebook that 'she was much amused as they continued to do this'. He decided to end the experiment there and woke her up.

'Have I been crying?' she asked in surprise. 'My face is all wet.'

As before, Scott asked her to write to Edgar and describe the 'dream'.

When Edgar replied, his surprise was tainted with concern that she could apparently discover all this about him. He asked her if she were a thought reader, or was using one.

Again he confirmed the details. They had been storing flour underground. He had been wounded on both the left and right sides of his face – the one on the left being the more severe. He had been in hospital due to a leg injury and wondered if she knew that, too. His arm was on the mend, but not quite back to normal. He was most alarmed about her discovery of the way in which they opened tins after losing all their tin openers. He 'thought it hard they could not keep a secret a thousand miles away'.

The maid was also becoming interested in her travelling clairvoyance. Now that she had found Edgar, she wanted to see how her cousins (especially one called Bruce) were doing – they, too, were at the Front.

Scott put her to sleep once more. After only a minute or two, she found him: 'There is Bruce. He is polishing glasses. There are two others with him. One is cleaning boots and leggings.' After polishing the glasses, Bruce started laying a table: 'It is a small table – he has put the glass on it and something in a bottle – "Lemon",' she spelt out the next word 'S Q U A S H'. She thought that the place was nearer than

Edgar's underground kitchen, possibly headquarters. She described it as 'a kind of hut with wire and green bushes over the top held up by posts.'

She could see a general there and thought that he looked like pictures she had seen of General French.

The soldier who had been cleaning the boots looked up and asked, 'Where has the General gone?' Bruce said that he had gone to look after his horse.

'Oh,' said the maid, 'here comes a poor wounded horse. He is spitting and neighing. It is that gentleman's horse.' As she continued to watch, she described the men making it lie or go down and its being tethered to a tent pole. One man knelt beside it and put something down its throat. The general had gone inside and was lying on a 'couch' made of sacks and coats.

Scott instructed her to find out where she was, such as by finding a railway station. There was a short silence before she announced that she had found a crossroads with a signpost. She spelt out the names written on it: Nieuport, Lille and Dieppe. 'What direction is your cousin in?' asked Scott.

'Let me see,' said the maid, 'which way did I come? Oh, over those fields by the trenches.'

She announced that she was going to go back to Bruce and found him washing in hot water. He had hung up his watch.

'Look at the time,' instructed Scott.

'It is twenty minutes to eight. I thought it was later.'

Scott looked at the clock and saw that it was later: five minutes to eight.

From the description in Scott's notebook, it seems as if the next instruction and Bruce's reply occur during the clairvoyant session. 'Ask Bruce if that is the right time?'

Bruce replied that he did not know: 'His watch did not keep good time. He supposed it was because it had so much bumping about.'

Scott then enquired whether there were any Germans nearby.

She could not see any, but noticed that there was an observation post near and said that she would look through that. When she got there she found that 'someone else was looking now'. She waited and soon got her opportunity: 'Oh, yes, Germans. I can see them plainly now in the trenches firing – one behind the other.'

'Go over,' said Scott, 'and hear what they are saying.'

The maid went over and heard them, but could not understand their language.

They later learnt from a brother of Bruce that he was with a general – it was not General French – and that there was an observation post nearby. Scott simply records 'and other details' without indicating what they were: we might infer that the location was confirmed.

Scott next writes 'she visited the place again later', but it is not clear whether this was later in the same session or at another time. This time she sees one of Bruce's companions writing a letter and looks over his shoulder. She could read the address, a certain Mr or Mrs Crafter (the handwriting is difficult to read at this point) of Dulwich. 'What a funny address,' she remarked, 'I never heard of that place before.' Dr S. looked up a postal directory and found the name and address to be correct.

Finally, Scott writes, 'the closing pages of her career will be written later – at present the memory is sufficient'. There was no later. The rest of the notebook is blank.

Scott was a member of the SPR and friend of SPR Council member Dr Abraham Wallace (1851–1930). Wallace was also a member of the Ghost Club and Scott appeared as Wallace's guest at a Ghost Club dinner in Maison Jules on Wednesday, 3 March 1915, where he told his tale.[147]

The Captain's Curious Presentiment

The coughing of an engine made him look up. There it was, right on the dot. Fifth time that week. A black scratch on the morning clouds,

---

147 Conan Doyle mentions Wallace several times in his book *The Vital Message* (London: Hodder and Stoughton, 1919).

getting bigger, louder. Some of the men thought they knew what kind of plane it was, but it was hard to tell from the silhouette. An Albatross, perhaps. One thing was sure: it was German. And it would drop a bomb on them.[148]

He looked round at his men. Boots, hooves and wheels had run brown messy tracks through the November snow as they loaded up supplies of straw, coke and coal for the men in the front trenches.

Everyone had stopped to watch the plane. But no one ran for cover.

'Sergeant!'

'Yes, Sir!'

He smiled slightly at the crisp salute even under the wings of death. 'Tell the men to carry on.'

'Yes, Sir.' The sergeant turned on the men and got them back at it.

The plane spluttered and he looked up again. Nearly overhead. Will it get us this time?

'Take cover!' he yelled. Soldiers ducked under carts, darted back into doorways. But he could not take his eyes off it. Such a small thing way up there.

The bang was loud, sharp – just like the others. He hunched his shoulders involuntarily as earth and stones pattered towards him. A horse reared up, but a soldier was suddenly there, hand on the bridle.

Just like the others, the bomb had missed. It had fallen about fifty yards off – they all seemed to do that. Another pothole on the road to Ypres.

They talked about it that evening, the captain and the other officers. In five days they had only lost five horses and five men. How many bombs was it? A dozen, fifteen perhaps. Nothing so bad as they had to endure at the Front. But a funny thing all the same when you thought about it. Lucky. Not like those six Frenchmen at the hospital in the field just outside of town, wounded all over again by an unexpected bomb falling from the sky.

148 'Letters From The Front', *The Times* (2 December 1914), p. 6. The captain's letter is dated 19 November.

The Germans did not have 'bombers' in 1914. It did not stop them bombing. In a two-seater reconnaissance plane, the observer could still lob a bomb over the side. It was not very accurate, to be sure, but lob enough bombs – say twelve or fifteen – and you were bound to hit something sooner or later.

At 7 p.m. the captain had what he called 'a very curious presentiment'. He left the others and went round his men, ordering them to move location – and take the horses with them. They had settled in. There was grumbling. But orders were orders and with the sergeant at their heels they shifted their billets.

When he got back, the captain told his servant to make his bed up in the basement. He turned in at 9 p.m. with 'this strange feeling on me'. He mentioned it to the others.

The first shell landed at midnight. Either that or one shortly after blew the soldiers' former position all to smithereens. Shrapnel smashed through the window of the room the captain had always used before. A blast wave took out the windscreen of his car parked outside.

'We nipped out like greased lightning,' he later wrote, 'and mighty glad we were to leave the place.'

The captain in the Army Service Corps did not give his name when he wrote to *The Times* about his experiences, or if he did they did not print it. After Ypres he had a new billet in a village he did not name, staying in the house of a doctor who had been there during the German occupation. He listened to his stories of civilians being shot, houses looted. The Germans had put a machine gun up in the church tower, believing the British would not shoot at churches.

The captain continued to do his duty, striving to get the supplies through, but we cannot tell what became of him. His 'curious presentiment' had saved his life and that of his men that night; did it see him safely through all that was to come?

The Tale of the Noble Rose

Not long after the captain of the Army Service Corps left Ypres, the journalist George Herbert Perris (1886–1920) was there for a look around.[149]

'Ypres is, I believe, a mass of bricks now,' thought the captain. But Perris found that there was still a town, depopulated and crossed with 'dead streets'. The Allied positions were nearby and Perris could hear the 'boom and rattle of the guns, close, yet muffled like stage thunder'.

He came to 'the mud-bound causeway which is one of the main arteries of the war', but his escort, the inscrutable Commandant Count d'Harcourt allowed him to go no farther.

He had not seen any of the snow that the captain had talked of, but had also heard a story of luck. On All Saints' Day some Belgian officers were dining in an inn in Furnes called the Noble Rose. As they ate, 'a German shell went clean through the upper part of the building and fell into the narrow street'. It was the sort of story that would be repeated in many variations. War was half cruel misfortune and half unexpected good luck.

Perris ran into the Army Service Corps and talked to a sergeant. He was beginning to get a feel for the war. He had met bloodthirsty journalists, he said, but not one bloodthirsty soldier. The British were 'often shy, generally silent, hating heroics', though, 'if you want anything doing, here's your man'. He noted the French infantry marching without regimental band and standards, already covering up their resplendent uniforms and shining helmets and cuirasses.

'The solitude of the wide plateaux of Central France is broken day and night by a never-ceasing stream of traffic, all concentrated upon

149 G. H. Perris, 'A Tour of the Battle-Line', *Daily Telegraph* (2 December 1914), p.10.

one appalling task.' The war itself was 'a narrow red line, some ten miles wide and 350 miles long'.

He passed a British lady standing outside a little cottage. A Red Cross flag fluttered above it as she watched 'the mushroom smoke of bursting shells' and waited for the wounded.

'I Loathe Being a Medium'

Helen's friend Aelfrida Tillyard was not happy. Her elder brother Julius was interned in Germany at the Ruhleben Camp near Kiel for enemy civilians. Her younger brother Eustace had joined up and would soon leave for the Front and send home harrowing letters. Her husband was in Holland; for that, at least, she could be grateful as there was no longer any love between them. Her father had thought that she should 'marry a great man'; Lord Kitchener was his suggestion and she does seem to have been infatuated with him. Instead she had married a Greek: Constantine Cleanthes Michaelides, who changed his name to Graham, had a job in the Consular Service and betrayed her at the first opportunity. She herself had fallen under the spell of Aleister Crowley and was dabbling in Magick, much to her husband's displeasure, who ultimately forbade further contact, stifling her esoteric career.[150]

The 'other world' had been reaching out to her long before she turned to seek it. Frederic Myers had introduced her to the medium Eusapia Palladino at his home, Leckhampton House in Cambridge, in 1895, and the 'foreign-looking lady' had gazed intently at her before taking her hands and pronouncing 'You are a medium!' Twelve-year-old Tillyard had no idea what she was talking about, but Myers promised to 'initiate' her when she was older. Tillyard was even more perplexed by this; however, Myers was unable to keep his promise.[151]

150 Sheila Mann, *Aelfrida Tillyard: Hints of a Perfect Splendour* (Hitchin, Herts: Wayment, 2013), pp. 52–3, 75.
151 Mann, *Aelfrida Tillyard*, p. 30.

Helen had been the cause of the experimental turn in Tillyard's life. Her father was shocked that 'the Verralls were dabbling in Psychical Research', but Margaret Verrall assured him that such interests never entered her private schoolroom on the top floor of Selwyn Gardens where she taught Helen, Aelfrida and Sylvia Myers. She had had what she called 'visions' during her teenage years, but these were involuntary episodes; her conscious involvement began in 1902 when she was nineteen. Helen told her all about 'automatic writing and spirit rapping and wierd [sic] things'. She decided to give it a go: her hand wrote out 'briny' and 'briney' *ad infinitum*, much to Tillyard's bemusement. Helen and eventually Helen's mother told her more about their strange psychic world. Margaret Verrall pronounced her 'very psychic'.[152]

It may not have surprised Tillyard, then, when the deceased Myers showed up in July 1914 to ask if she knew Mrs Verrall and then again on 8 October 1914 to discharge a communication by automatic writing. She showed the results to Margaret Verrall a few days later. Myers had told her that the world beyond was a realm of pure idea, which she thought could only suit Bertrand Russell, and hated the feeling of being possessed when the communication took place. 'I loathe being a medium,' she confessed to her diary. Although she fought against it, whatever the 'spirit world' was, it was not finished with her.[153]

The Pulse of the Front

The experience of the Front was otherworldly in itself. The physical conditions of trench life are hard enough to imagine, never mind trench life under fire. For Ernst Jünger it was the sound that first orchestrated his experience. As he detrained in Bazancourt in the Champagne, fresh from training, one December day in 1914, he heard 'the slow, grinding pulse of the front' – the choice of the word 'pulse' of

---

152 Mann, *Aelfrida Tillyard*, pp. 30, 53.
153 Mann, *Aelfrida Tillyard*, p. 273.

course suggests that the Front was itself a living thing; it even exhaled a 'breath of battle'. This was no 'stage thunder'. His reaction was 'awe and incredulity'.[154]

In August 1916, on his way to join the Battle of the Somme, the artillery had found an even greater intensity. Here, 'a thousand quivering lightnings bathed the western horizon in a sea of flame'. This transformation of land, liquefied by shelling, was matched by the 'oceanic roar' of the guns and, as the bombardment increased, 'the sky seemed like a boiling cauldron'. Everything had been reduced to an elemental level of pure destruction.[155]

In such conditions people were also transformed; people lost their minds. An NCO 'went into a frenzy' to match the 'demented fury' of the bombardment. Jünger himself talks of an intensity of dread that was like entering 'a foreign country', a place in itself; a new dimension of reality, where he experienced 'an exalted, almost demoniacal lightness'. Inexplicable fits of uncontrollable laughter would shake him.[156]

The Front also had its own smell. The 'heavy smell of death' was there of course, but it mixed with the tang of 'piercing fogs of gunpowder' that was 'not only disgusting' but 'brought about an almost visionary excitement'. Jünger's choice of words increasingly verges upon the mystical. Even at the beginning, he was 'enraptured by war' – a feeling he extended to his fellow volunteers – but it was the intensity of the horrors inflicted upon him through every sense that produced the exalted state, truly a transcendental experience. For Jünger, perhaps for others, too, the Front was a spiritual experience, twisted and hellish, to be sure – a 'peak experience' in the lowest hell, a samadhi of slaughter.[157]

154 Ernst Jünger, *Storm of Steel*, trans. Michael Hofman (London: Penguin, 1961), p. 5.
155 Jünger, *Storm of Steel*, pp. 91, 95.
156 Jünger, *Storm of Steel*, pp. 93, 95.
157 Jünger, *Storm of Steel*, pp. 5, 93.

A Christmas Bombing

Helen spent Christmas 1914 at home with her mother in Cambridge. But even in the leafy serenity of Selwyn Gardens, the war caught up with them. Helen's cousin had been killed in action. Her mother mentioned this sad news in a letter, but only called him 'my nephew and godson', qualifying this with 'my husband's nephew really'.[158] This would have been Lt Christopher Francis Verrall, 2nd Battalion, Royal Sussex Regiment. He was mentioned in despatches for his part in the battle that led to his death, aged twenty-five, at L'Épinette between Béthune and La Bassée in northern France on 22 December. As the regiment's battle honours show, he was at the Battle of Mons and the long fighting-retreat after it.[159]

The Royal Sussex had been refitting at Hazebrouck when on 20 December they received orders to be ready to move at one hour's notice. They left camp on 21 December, being brought part of the way up to Epinette by 'motor buses'. The Germans had captured part of the British line and a desperate battle was about to ensue to recover it. On 22 December, the 2nd Battalion, Royal Sussex Regiment, moved forward to relieve the Seaforth Highlanders. Attacking and counter-attacking, the Germans got back into the British trenches. Hasty barricades were thrown up and both sides 'bombed each other vigorously'. During the fight, some of the Sussex were standing waist-deep in water. The 2nd Battalion was relieved at 6 p.m. on 23 December, although the process took until 6 a.m. the next day. The three-day battle cost the lives

158 Cambridge University Library, SPR.MS35/2704, Margaret Verrall to Sir Oliver Lodge, 1 January 1915.
159 L. A. Clutterbuck and W. T. Dooner (eds), *The Bond of Sacrifice: A Biographical Record of All British Officers Who Fell in the Great War*, vol. 1 (London: Anglo-African Pub. Contractors, 1917), p. 419; French, *The Despatches of Lord French* (London: Chapman & Hall, 1917), p. 173; Ray Westlake, *British Battalions in France & Belgium 1914* (London: Leo Cooper, 1997), p. 181.

of twenty-eight men and three officers, Lt Verrall amongst them.[160] On hearing the news, Helen's mother Margaret wrote 'it does bring home to one the waste from the human point of view'.[161]

Another of Helen's cousins was in the fighting; like his brother Christopher, Paul Jenner Verrall was a Trinity man. He won first-class honours in the Natural Sciences Tripos, part 1, in 1905 and went on to do clinical training at St Bartholomew's Hospital, becoming chief assistant to R. C. Elmslie from 1910 and a Fellow of the Royal College of Surgeons. During the war, he served in Egypt from 1915 to 1916, returning to Britain to join the staff of Sir Robert Jones as a surgeon at the Military Orthopaedic Hospital, Shepherd's Bush. He had joined the SPR in 1905, the same year as Helen, being proposed by Margaret Verrall and Eleanor Sidgwick.[162]

As the war ground on, Helen would recall the recently bereaved calling, almost daily, at the SPR offices – 'by no means all of them Members of the Society', she noted. It was Newton who dealt with them, especially those whose loss had come 'as a shattering blow', in Helen's words, and were 'finding it difficult to look forward into the future and face life'. Helen described Newton's 'skill and patience in setting them on the road again' as 'quite exceptional'. There were grim times ahead and the officers of the SPR unexpectedly found themselves in the role of bereavement counsellors.[163]

160 2nd Battalion, Royal Sussex Regiment, War Diary, National Archives, Kew, WO 95/1269/1.
161 Cambridge University Library, SPR.MS 35/2704, Verrall to Lodge, 1 January 1915.
162 'Obituary', The Lancet, Vol. 257, No. 6662 (5 May 1951), pp. 1021–2.
163 [Helen Salter], Proc. SPR, pt 178, p. 58.

1915

'The War Has Upset Everybody's Calculations'

For the SPR, 1915 began with the election of Professor Gilbert Murray as President of the Society. The Australian-born classicist was a top-tier academic and well-connected public figure. He was one of the so-called Cambridge Ritualists, who saw ritual origins in Ancient Greek myths and drama. He had been Professor of Greek at the University of Glasgow and was now Regius Professor of Greek at the University of Oxford. One of his students was E. R. Dodd, who himself also became a President of the SPR. He would have been another of the Society's 'sirs', if he had not turned down a knighthood in 1912.[1]

During the war Murray published pamphlets defending the justness of the British cause – 'we were right' to declare war on Germany he said, simply – despite declaring himself to be against war in general. It caused a rift in his old friendship with Bertrand Russell – Russell would be twice convicted for his principles under the Defence of the Realm Act 1914.[2]

The first council meeting was held on 29 January in the Society offices at 20 Hanover Street – actually, they held two Council meetings back-to-back that day, an AGM and an ordinary one. All the usual suspects were there: Schiller, Baggally, Barrett, Revd Bayfield, Crookes, Eleanor Sidgwick, Margaret Verrall, Alice Johnson, Isabel Newton and others. Afterwards they went over to the Robert Barnes Hall of the Royal Society of Medicine on Wimpole Street to listen to J. G. Piddington talk about 'Cross-Correspondences of a Gallic Type'.[3]

1 Nick Lowe, 'Gilbert Murray and Psychic Research', in *Gilbert Murray Reassessed: Hellenism, Theatre, and International Politics*, edited by Christopher Stray (Oxford: Oxford University Press, 2007), pp. 349–70.

2 Gilbert Murray, *How Can War Ever Be Right?* (Oxford: Oxford University Press, 1914), p. 4.

3 Published in *Proc. SPR* vol. 29 (November 1916).

During his Presidential Address on 9 July 1915, Professor Murray said that 'the war has upset everybody's calculations'. And so it had.

The SPR was running out of things to talk about. Towards the end of 1915 a notice was printed in the *Journal* giving further evidence of the effect of the war: 'Owing to the fact that public interest is now so largely centred upon the war, it has proved unusually difficult to obtain material for the *Journal*. Hence the delay in its appearance and the smallness of the present number.'[4]

The SPR was also running low on members. In total, seventy-five letters of resignation would be sent to the Society in 1915: thirty-eight gave no reason for the decision; of the rest, eight specifically mentioned the war and another ten gave reasons amounting to the same (reduced circumstances, the priority of other matters, etc.). Others mentioned ill health, inability to attend meetings, or going abroad (seven cases), some of which could also be connected with the war.

The blame lay not with the war alone. Three members expressed dissatisfaction with the direction of the SPR, one of them complaining that 'I cannot follow the present recondite investigations of the Society with much interest, as they are so very complicated, and the Council show such a very strange timidity in publishing any authoritative conclusions on any subject' (the correspondent was not named).[5]

He was, of course, talking about the cross-correspondences. The Society was later forced to address this issue. In the Council's report for 1915 we read 'some of our members are inclined to complain that so much attention is now devoted to the study of automatic writing', adding 'we may therefore observe that this circumstance is not wholly due to the perversity of investigators'. It was an interesting choice of words and shows that the Council was somewhat affronted by a challenge to its abiding concerns.[6]

There *was* something perverse about it. It enthralled and entertained the SPR elite; and failed to fully engage the broader membership or

4 *JSPR* (October–November 1915), p. 98.
5 'Report of the Council for the Year 1914', *JSPR* (February 1915), p. 21.
6 'Report of the Council for the Year 1915', *JSPR* (March 1916), p. 157.

interest the general public. At a time when the SPR complained of receiving few spontaneous cases, little effort was put into eliciting them. During the war years, only two requests for information on particular subjects were printed in the *Journal*.

In response to the criticisms, the Society launched a series of telepathy experiments in the Society's rooms. In February 1915, a notice was printed in the *Journal* asking for volunteers: ten came forward; seven were selected. Thirty sessions were held over the Spring months, but the results were not encouraging.[7]

Despite the problems, new members were still signing up. In 1915, one of these was the animal rights activist, the Duchess of Hamilton and Brandon – she was co-founder of the Animal Defence and Anti-Vivisection Society and founder of the Scottish Society for the Prevention of Vivisection. During the war, her husband, the 13th Duke, turned over the family seat, Hamilton Palace, to the Royal Navy to use as a hospital.

Several members at the Front had requested that the *Journal* be sent to them there. It was no doubt difficult collecting membership dues from members overseas and the drop in member numbers, generally, meant a drop in revenues. Income from the sale of publications also fell dramatically. Luckily, the Society was far from dependent on this income: it had a healthy Endowment Fund and other investments. Even so, rising costs, especially printing costs, would later compel it to solicit donations from members. Not only were membership numbers declining, but members themselves, who previously had put much energy into the Society, found other demands on their time and resources.[8]

7 James H. Hyslop, 'A Note on "Some Recent Experiments in Telepathy"', *JSPR* (March 1916), pp. 160ff. Only one individual, a Mrs Stuart Wilson, achieved scores above chance and even then not to any great degree.
8 Sales to the public through the SPR's London agent had dropped by almost two thirds (from £37 to £13) and sales to members had dropped by three quarters (from £16 to £4); however, 'no anxiety is felt as to its financial position', 'Report', *JSPR* (February 1915), p. 22.

The SPR Goes to War

SPR member Ernest Bennett was too old for frontline service, but he was no stranger to war. As a war correspondent he had covered the Cretan insurrection, Kitchener's expedition to Khartoum and the Italo-Turkish War, and had been in the Voluntary Ambulance Corps during the Boer War. In January 1915, Bennett set sail for Serbia with Sir Thomas Lipton in his yacht, *Erin*. Serbia was being ravaged by a typhus epidemic that eventually claimed the lives of some 150,000 people and brought military operations to a feverish collapse. Despite lacking any sort of medical qualification, Bennett took charge of a British Red Cross hospital. He was awarded the Serbian Order of the White Eagle (Third Class) in recognition of his services.[9]

With the epidemic under control, Bennett left Serbia in June 1915 and later joined the Staff of the 11th Infantry Brigade, BEF. Despite such a busy year, he was still able to attend a Meeting of the SPR Council in November 1915 and his name appears regularly throughout the war.[10]

Dr W. M'Dougall was reported as having 'gone to the front in charge of a motor-ambulance'. The Honourable Everard Feilding was 'appointed to the Naval Press Bureau' – there would be whispers that he was some sort of spy. Dr Woolley and M. R. Bullough had been to Elberfeld to study the so-called 'thinking horses', but the *Journal* noted that further investigation was no longer possible, with rumours suggesting that these miraculous animals had 'gone to the front'.[11]

---

9 *JSPR* (February 1915), p. 22; see E. N. Bennett, 'Some Recent Experiences in Serbia', *Nineteenth Century and After*, Vol. 78, (July–December 1915); James Berry, *The Story of a Red Cross Unit in Serbia* (London: J. & A. Churchill, 1916); and Richard P. Strong, et al., *Typhus Fever with Particular Reference to the Serbian Epidemic* (Cambridge, MA: Harvard University Press, 1920).
10 *JSPR* (December 1915), p. 106.
11 *JSPR* (February 1915), pp. 22, 24.

The war had also created opportunities for others. When Dr William Brown, the head of the Psychology Department at King's College, London, took a commission in the Royal Army Medical Corps, his absence created a hole in the curriculum that was filled by Helen Verrall's series of lectures on psychical research – the first time the subject had been taught in a British university, quite possibly in any university.

At least six SPR members – Drs Milne Bramwell, Constance Long, W. M'Dougall, T. W. Mitchell, Lloyd Tuckey and Maurice Wright – were involved in the formation of a Medico-Psychological Clinic in London to treat what was described as 'severe mental and nervous shock due to exposure, excessive strain, and tension'. Mitchell and M'Dougall took an active staff role, and another SPR member, Sir Lawrence Jones, was Chairman of the Board of Management. The SPR was also able to refer some patients. The clinic was a significant development in the recognition of 'shell shock' as a genuine condition and not the result of a lack of moral fibre.[12]

Enemies in the SPR

The war in Europe was not a war between strangers but a war between family and friends. Just as the conflict divided members of the same European royal households and divided members of the same ethnic groups – 'We Saxons, you Anglo-Saxons' the Germans were heard to shout over the trenches – so the conflict divided the SPR. Many important and influential members were now in what were designated enemy countries. Taking stock of the past year, the Council noted that eleven members were in Germany and another six in Austria-Hungary. [13]

12 *JSPR* (February 1915), p. 25.
13 'Report of the Council for the Year 1914', *JSPR* (February 1915), p. 12; Tony Ashworth, *Trench Warfare, 1914–1918: The Live and Let Live System* (Basingstoke: Macmillan, 1980), p. 34.

The biologist Professor Hans Driesch, known for his theories on vitalism and cloning the world's first animal (a sea urchin), was in Heidelberg, Germany. He would later be elected President of the SPR for 1926–1927. Then there was the German philosopher and psychologist, Dr Max Dessoir – he had coined the term parapsychology in 1889 – and Dr Freiherr von Schrenck-Notzing, who holds the Guinness World Record for being the first forensic psychologist (in 1896). The composer and philosopher Emil Mattiesen had studied in Cambridge and London before the war, and would produce major works on parapsychology after it.[14]

Dr Paul Pausnitz, one of the founders of the field of modern bacteriology, was assistant to Richard Pfeiffer in the German 14th Army Corps. When Lille fell to the Germans, Peiffer and Prausnitz went to the Institut Pasteur to restock their supplies of tetanus antiserum. Soldiers had found a dead pigeon on the premises and, thinking it was for carrying messages, laboratory staff were accused of being spies. Prausnitz's knowledge of French saved their lives, as he was able to translate documents showing that the pigeon had been used in medical experiments.[15]

Sigmund Freud, then still in Vienna, was a Corresponding Member. His close associate, the Hungarian psychoanalyst Sandor Ferenczi (Budapest), was also a member. Carl Jung, living in neutral Switzerland, would join the SPR in 1917, but had had visions of the European catastrophe in 1913. There were also two Austrian Princesses to add lustre to the list: Her Imperial and Royal Highness, the Hereditary Princess of Salm-Salm, Maria Christina; and Her Imperial Highness, the Princess Alexandra of Thurn und Taxis.[16]

14 Max Dessoir, 'Die Parapsychologie', *Sphinx*, 8 (June 1889), pp. 341–2. On Schrenck-Notzing, see http://www.guinnessworldrecords.com/world-records/first-forensic-psychologist, accessed 28 June 2018. Emil Mattiesen, *Der jenseitige Mensch* (1925) and *Das persönliche Überleben des Todes*, 3 vols (1936–1939).
15 A. W. Frankland, 'Carl Prausnitz: A Personal Memoir', *Journal of Allergy and Clinical Immunology*, vol. 114, issue 3 (September 2004), pp. 700–5.
16 On Jung's visions, see the editor's introduction in *The Portable Jung*, ed. by Joseph Campbell (Harmondsworth: Penguin, 1977), p.xxiv.

In the membership list for 1915, the name of Richard Knoller of Vienna appears. He was then Associate Professor of Aeronautics and Automobiles at Vienna's Technical University. During the war he redesigned the Albatross B.I biplane and developed his own models, the Knoller B.I and Knoller C.I and C.II, flown by the Austro-Hungarian air force, the *Kaiserliche und Königliche Luftfahrtruppen*.[17] Another member was the historian Carl Graf von Klinckowström of Munich. He was wounded in 1916 and spent the remainder of the war on the German General Staff in Berlin – he also wrote about magic and dowsing. The Council's report ended by saying 'It is hoped that communication will be resumed with those in Germany and Austria as soon as the war is over'.[18]

The Adventures of Captain Colley

The Ghost Club began 1915 with another cosy dinner at Maison Jules. Ten members were present: Percival, Sinnett, Ionides, Wallace, Fielding-Ould, Withall, Gray, with Johnson as Secretary and Crookes in the Chair, as well as someone we have not yet met, Captain E. R. Serocold Skeels of the Army Pay Department. There were also two guests present: Sinnett had invited Sir H. Griffin; and Withall, David Gow, the editor of *Light*. Gow was good company, giving an account of his life in a haunted house, but the real interest of the evening was a letter Skeels had received from Captain Clarence C. Colley, RA, son of the eccentric Archdeacon Colley of Stockton.[19]

Colley was a professional soldier, having joined the army before the war; and his father, Thomas, although a clergyman in the Church of

---

17 'Knoller, Richard', in *Österreichisches Biographisches Lexikon 1815–1950* (ÖBL), vol. 3 (Vienna: Verlag der Österreichischen Akademie der Wissenschaften, 1965), p. 448.

18 Hans Christoph Count of Seherr-Thoß, 'Klinckowström, Carl Graf', in *Neue Deutsche Biographie* (NDB), vol. 12, Berlin: Duncker & Humblot, 1980), p. 74.

19 British Library, Add. MS 52264, pp. 346–52.

England – he was rector of Stockton – was also a Spiritualist and an acquaintance of Conan Doyle's. 'Spiritualism,' he once said, 'comes as a godsend to millions who are incapable of believing the Christian faith without its aid. It teaches that death is the gate of life, hence that there is continuous and immediate and conscious being with no sleeping in the grave.' From the beyond, the Archdeacon was said to have projected letters written in his own handwriting onto photographic plates using the medium of a psychic photographer.[20]

The Archdeacon had died and now his son was facing death on the Western Front with the Royal Artillery. Colley wrote to Skeels on 2 December 1914, saying, 'Now that this hasn't to pass the censor I can tell you that on the great day when I got the guns away [. . .]'. He was evidently back in Britain and could write without having to go through the military censor. It was quite a ripping yarn.

The Captain was 'going through the wood to try and save them from behind and drag them out by hand', when he heard distinctly his father's voice, saying, 'Clarence, my boy, wait.' He found himself rooted to the spot: 'try as I would I could not move my right leg'. 'I was left balancing on my left foot,' he said, 'and was fixed there for all the world like the statue in Piccadilly Circus.' The effect lasted until 'as though by magic the firing ceased'. His gun teams 'got up with the limbers and then directly my right leg was unshackled and I actually fell forward with the release'. This moment of paralysis 'was just the time that gave us the chance to get the guns away although five minutes before the trees in that wood were being cut off short by the shell[ing] and fell like spears against our men and horses' – he had attached a small sketch to

---

20 For Clarence Colley's career: *The London Gazette*, (20 November 1908), p. 8545, referring to his promotion from Lieutenant to temporary Captain whilst seconded as Adjutant; *The London Gazette* (3 May 1912), p. 3178, recording his promotion to Captain in the Royal Regiment of Artillery. On Archdeacon Colley: Henry Thibault, *Letters from the Other Side* (NP: London, 1919); quoted in Grace Garrett Durand, *Sir Oliver Lodge is Right: Spirit Communication a Fact* (Lake Forest, Ill: Privately Printed, 1917), pp. 38–9. For some of the Archdeacon's work, see Thomas Colley, *Later Phases of Materialisation* (London: J. Burns, 1877).

illustrate the effect. 'More of the poor beasts,' he recalled of the horses, 'were impaled by falling timber than shell.'

At their next meeting, Skeel had a further letter to read from Captain Colley. A white dove had appeared 'at a critical moment in the fighting'. The Captain thought that this was 'a symbol relating', not to peace, but 'to White Dove the familiar control of Mrs Fairclough Smith'. The Ghosts debated the meaning of the story, with Sir Oliver suggesting 'a similarity with the Elberfeld horses and Baalam's Ass'.[21]

Sir Oliver had been invited to the Ghost Club's February dinner by Crookes and after they had talked about Colley gave the gathering an account of the SPR's work. In particular, he 'stated his conviction of the existence of SPR Committee "upstairs" which by every means in their power were endeavouring to establish communication with this plane'. This was primarily through 'the cross correspondence experiments made by the Verrall group at Cambridge'. He added that 'the exhibition of personality and manners was perfect and thus convincing'. He mentioned further that 'Mr Gerald Balfour in communicating with Gurney was similarly impressed.'

There were no more letters from Captain Colley. He was seconded to the Ministry of Munitions on 18 October 1915 and survived the war, reaching the rank of major, and joined the Ghost Club in 1926.[22]

The Battle of Dogger Bank

After the Battle of Heligoland, the Kaiser had effectively muzzled his navy out of fear of losing more ships, but the German captains were fighting men who would trade every moment in safe harbours to have the enemy in their gunsights. They also needed an opportunity to restore their honour after the Heligoland debacle. So it was that Admiral

21 British Library, Add. MS 52264, pp. 358–62.
22 https://livesofthefirstworldwar.org/lifestory/895766, accessed 2 April 2018.

Friedrich von Ingenohl, *Chef der Hochseeflotte der Kaiserlichen Marine* (Chief of the High Seas Fleet of the Imperial Navy), sent Admiral Franz von Hipper out with I Scouting Group (*I. Aufklärungsgruppe*) battle-cruiser squadron to raid the British coast like Vikings of old. On the morning of 16 December 1914, the battlecruisers' long-range guns bombarded the towns of Scarborough, Hartlepool and Whitby with apparent impunity. One of Lily's brothers, Captain Frederick Parland Loder-Symonds, commanding HMS *Forward*, was in Hartlepool at the time, but prevented from sailing by the German barrage. The Grand Fleet, apparently ruling the waves after Heligoland, had failed to prevent the attack and failed to intercept von Hipper's ships. 'Naturally,' wrote Churchill, 'there was much indignation at the failure of the Navy to prevent, or at least to avenge, such an attack upon our shores.'[23]

However, the British fleet had had a narrow escape. Von Ingenohl had brought out the High Seas Fleet behind von Hipper, looking to engage one of the British battlecruiser squadrons and, with the odds on his side, destroy it. Admiral von Tirpitz later wrote, 'Ingenohl had the fate of Germany in the palm of his hand.'[24] But as is so often the case in war, chance rather than strategy ruled the day; and the Germans had missed theirs.

As Thomas Frothingham recalled, 1915 began with bad weather, 'one storm following another', and the opposing fleets remained in harbour.[25] Instead, the Germans sent Zeppelins to bomb the Yorkshire coast. But the weather would change. On 23 January, Admiralty crypt-analysts in Room 40 decoded intercepted German communications showing that a large enemy force was operating in Dogger Bank in the North Sea. This was von Hipper's 1 Scouting Group and 2 Scouting Group sweeping the area for British spy ships posing as trawlers,

---

23 Churchill, *World Crisis*, p. 520.
24 Quoted in Churchill, *World Crisis*, p. 515.
25 Thomas G. Frothingham, *The Naval History of the World War: Offensive Operations, 1914–1915* (Cambridge, MA: Harvard University Press, 1925), p. 229.

although the British feared that more coastal raids were planned.[26] The Grand Fleet was launched to attack. Admiral Beatty led 1 BCS, comprising the *Lion*, *Tiger* and *Princess Royal*, Rear-Admiral Sir Archibald Moore led 2 BCS with *New Zealand* as his flagship and *Indomitable*, with Tyrwhitt bringing his Harwich Force of light cruisers and destroyers. Other ships – cruisers and pre-Dreadnoughts – were deployed in support and Jellicoe sent out the main force from Scapa Flow.

The lighter, faster vessels of the Harwich Force were scouting ahead of the main force. The light cruiser HMS *Aurora* was the first to make contact, sighting the German light cruiser SMS *Kolberg* (2 Scouting Group) as dawn broke on 24 January. Their guns barked into life and hits were scored on each side. The *Kolberg* and another light cruiser, SMS *Stralsund*, also sighted smoke on the horizon: the *Aurora* was not alone.

Von Hipper sought to break off the engagement, heading south-easterly away from the threat – perhaps with the intention, as Admiral Scheer said, of drawing his pursuers into the Heligoland Bight and the jaws of the High Seas Fleet.[27] But the British were faster. Putting on steam, Beatty had the scent and was closing the distance. Yet again, the older ships in 2 BCS fell behind: the crew of *New Zealand* looked on as the *Lion* and the other ships – the 'big cats' as they were known – pulled ahead. Soon they heard the big guns open up: first the *Lion's*, then the others as they came in range of the Germans.

The older armoured cruiser SMS *Blücher* (1 Scouting Group), with a top speed of just over 25 knots, was the first to come within range of the *Lion's* 13.5-inch guns at about 20,000 yards. As the rest of 1 BCS drew up, fire could also be directed at SMS *Moltke*. As he advanced, Beatty shifted fire to von Hipper's flagship SMS *Seydlitz*, letting the following ships engage *Blücher*.

26 Archibald Hurd and H. H. Bashford, *Sons of Admiralty: A Short History of the Naval War, 1914–1918* (London: Constable & Co., 1919), p. 87.
27 Reinhardt Scheer, *Germany's High Sea Fleet in the World War* (London: Cassell, 1920), p. 80.

German fire concentrated on the *Lion* and she began to suffer under repeated salvoes. Beatty watched as one of the guns of A Turret was put out of action and shells pierced *Lion*'s armoured hull allowing water to flood in. The flagship started noticeably to list to starboard. She was hit a total of fifteen times.

The *New Zealand* and *Indomitable* were now catching up. Captain Halsey 'got many messages from all over the ship hoping that the [*piupiu*] was again going to be worn'.[28] Whereas at Heligoland they had been 'startled', his men had now come to expect it.

Moore brought up 2 BCS to engage the already badly damaged *Blücher*, as Beatty veered off from the attack on *Seydlitz* to avoid what he believed was submarine action. The *Lion* was now listing 10 degrees to starboard and reduced to 15 knots. The rest of 1 BCS had turned with her, allowing the Germans to increase the gap between them. Beatty attempted to correct his mistake, but his signals caused confusion and the British ships concentrated on *Blücher*, letting the rest of the German fleet escape.

Sir Julian Corbett described the *New Zealand*, *Indomitable*, and other ships 'pouring in salvoes till she was a mere mass of smoke and flame'.[29] Gunnery records show that the *Indomitable* scored eight hits, the *New Zealand* zero.[30] The *Blücher* was still fighting back, putting one British destroyer out of action, but she was doomed. Rendered helpless at 11.45, Admiral Moore ordered ceasefire. The crew of the *New Zealand* watched as the *Blücher* capsized and sank just after 13.00. The captain had worn the Maori *piupiu*; they had survived the second battle.

28 Letter from Lionel Halsey, 17 February 1939, Royal New Zealand Navy Museum, Object information file for *piupiu* 2007.1.1.
29 Quoted in Frothingham, *Naval History*, p. 238.
30 Stephen W. Roskill, *Admiral of the Fleet Earl Beatty, the Last Naval Hero: An Intimate Biography* (London: Collins, 1980), pp. 118–19.

Wilson's New Wave Detector

David Wilson was a regular contributor to *Light*. Some say he was a chemist, a solicitor, even at one time Sir William Crookes's assistant. According to one who knew him, he was the son of David H. Wilson, MA, LLM, of Cambridge, 'a barrister and literary man', and studied law himself, becoming a solicitor but never practising, preferring instead to devote his time to 'mesmerism and electricity'.[31] The readers of *Light* knew him as the man who had given them the 'Message of Amen Rā-mes' – pseudo-Egyptian automatic writings that he had published throughout 1914 – and were probably largely non-plussed about it. In March 1915, he reminded readers that the Message had included the momentous information that:

> Any variation of kinetic state in any aggregation of the ethereal corpuscles will induce in some degree a variation in that particular form of ethereal corpuscular aggregation existing in the proximity of all grey matter.[32]

Whatever it meant, this – and one or two similar statements – gave Wilson the theoretical basis for a new communication device using 'ethereal vibration'. He already had a practical example to illustrate its possibility. A mysterious 'Continental experimenter' had told him two years earlier that when using a wireless radio receiver 'intelligible words' had been received even 'when the aerial receiving wire was entirely disconnected from the receiving circuit'. The words received

---

31 Anon., 'Mr David Wilson's "Radiograms", The Machine Described: Remarkable Messages', *Light* (24 April 1915), p. 194 – this was written by Wilson's 'very reliable witness' from his experiment of 10 January 1915.
32 David Wilson, 'The Ethereal Transmission of Thought', *Light* (13 March 1915), p. 123.

generally had some personal meaning for the experimenter, but he could never discover where they came from.

In January 1915, somewhere in Chelsea, Wilson duly built his device, consisting of a battery, 'a very sensitive galvanometer' and a detector. The detector was probably something along the lines of iron fillings in a glass tube designed to react to the existence of 'electric waves' and allow a current to pass through them (what he called 'oscillation detectors'). A visitor who saw the machine described it more thoroughly:

It is an easily portable machine contained in a wooden box lined inside with green baize. The parts consist of a copper cylinder, three inches in diameter, which [...] contains a substance discovered after careful experiment to emit an 'aura' or radiation essential to the results. This cylinder is fitted into the upper part of the box. Below it is a steel box containing two oscillation detectors of an original type, answering the purpose of the coherers used in some forms of wireless telegraphy. Besides the steel box stands a dry battery connected up with the detectors and with a small telephone which enables one to hear the sounds produced in the machine – the 'makes' and 'breaks' of the current as it passes.[33]

Wilson added that he was constantly modifying and improving this detector until one day 'for no assignable reason the needle of the galvanometer gave a pronounced jerk'. He observed that the needle moved in groups of four, three short 'deflections' then a longer one – three dots and a dash – repeating. He wondered if it might be Morse code, in fact, he called this the 'Morse call signal'. Then he received his first message in Morse code: 'Great difficulty, await message, five days, six evening.'

At the appointed time he waited, with 'a very reliable witness' on hand. At 18.04 the Morse signal came through. At 18.31, the next

33 Anon., 'Mr David Wilson's "Radiograms"', *Light*, p. 194.

message was delivered, both Wilson and the witness recording. The witness's transcription was a jumble of letters without any apparent meaning. Wilson's, however, seemed to say something and, with some filling in of the gaps, he made out of it 'Try eliminate vibrations. ARTK.' He did this by adding a telegraph key: 'I inserted into the circuit a Morse key which was to be operated by someone after the manner of automatic writing', but which would still occur in tandem with the electrical detector. This he christened the New Wave Detector.

Wilson was living the 'life of an owl', staying up night after night to catch the messages that seemed to prefer the hours between midnight and 4 a.m. He believed that he was back in touch with Ancient Egypt through 'those personalities who have elected to designate themselves Tehuti and Kha-em-Uast' and finally with Amen Rā-mes himself. The radiograms from ancient Egypt were often long and tedious, couched in archaic language and ultimately unrevealing. But there were many more besides and many of the so-called 'radiograms' received were unsigned, short, sometimes in foreign languages and strangely suggestive of communicators trying to get through:

> March 15th, 1915. 10.12 p.m. (Reference No. 7.)
> 'To all our friends and fellow workers, greeting.'
> March 17th. 10.56 p.m. (Reference No. 8.)
> 'Seien Sie vorsichtig Das Licht ist zu stark . . . Heinrich.'
> Translation: 'Be careful, the light is too strong . . . Henry.'
> March 19th. 11.[0]1 p.m. (Reference No. 10.)
> 'Nyet leezdyes Kogoneebond Kto govoreet pooossky.'
> Translation: 'Is there anyone who speaks Russian here?'[34]

A friend, 'J. F.', had set up another New Wave Detector in Paris and seemed to get the same message in Russian on the same date a little later in the evening at 11.07 p.m. One character, calling itself Jonquil and described as 'Puck-like', became something of a nuisance with

---

34 Anon., 'Mr David Wilson's "Radiograms"', p. 195.

'witty, flippant, and sometimes even ribald remarks'. Tehuti and Kha-em-Uast complained about him. Wilson found that turning up the lights sent him away, but one correspondent wrote in to *Light* asking for more from Jonquil and a little less from Amen Rā-mes.[35]

Messages were received in French, German, Russian, Greek, Portuguese, Norwegian, Japanese, Arabic and other languages that he could not identify. Many were intended for other individuals, some known, such as Miss H. A. Dallas, Miss Katherine Bates and Count Miyatovich, others not.[36] Reports of messages and experiments and debates about the machine were printed extensively throughout 1915. However, receiving messages in German was soon to get him in trouble.

'I Wonder If Bob Will Come'

Lily Loder-Symonds, who had already lost so much, was dealt a further blow when another brother, Captain Robert 'Bob' Francis Loder-Symonds, 1st Battalion, The Cheshire Regiment, was killed in what the authorities called an accident on 3 March 1915. An article even appeared in *The Times*: 'Four Brothers Killed and Wounded'. Bob left behind a widow, Muriel, and two-year-old son, Robert Guy, who would go on to become a distinguished soldier in the Second World War.[37]

Five days after his death, Sir Arthur and Lady Jean Conan Doyle attempted to contact his departed spirit in a séance.

'I wonder if Bob will come,' said Jean.

The words were barely out of her mouth when the table started moving. Jean's hand began to write, apparently controlled by Bob. He had been shot by a sniper, he wrote, but had already met brother John.

35 'Mr David Wilson's "Radiograms": Notes and Comments', *Light* (8 May 1915), p. 225.
36 'Mr David Wilson's "Radiograms": More Remarkable Messages', *Light* (1 May 1915), p. 214.
37 The Royal Artillery Commemoration Book 1939–45. Peter Wilkinson, MC, *The Gunners at Arnhem* (East Haddon: Spurwing, 1999).

Conan Doyle asked if he could try and find Malcolm Leckie – he did not know him, but said that he would try. Finally, he told them that the war would end in three months' time, with Britain triumphant. Of course, the war did not end in June 1915. Conan Doyle sent a sample of the handwriting to Lily and asked if it was like Bob's.

Conan Doyle also asked the spirits if his brother Innes would survive. Innes, when he found out, was not overly impressed.[38]

Raymond in the Trenches

With spring in the air, Raymond's company of the 3rd Battalion, South Lancashire Regiment, made its way back to Great Crosby and settled into tents and makeshift huts. The first batch of men was selected for the Front, but one of the new subalterns failed his medical due to 'some temporary indisposition', as Sir Oliver put it. A replacement was sought. When asked if he were fit, Raymond replied 'Perfectly'. He was to pack up and start for France that evening.[39]

He telegrammed home and arranged to meet his family *en route*, snatching some hours from the War Office to return home to Mariemont on the Westborne Road, Edgbaston. 'He seems quite well,' noted Sir Oliver afterwards, 'but naturally it has been rather a strain for the family.'

His brothers Alec, Lionel and Noel travelled with him on the midnight train to Euston. It was almost four in the morning when the train pulled in to the station. His brothers escorted him on to Waterloo where a Captain Taylor took charge of Second Lieutenant Lodge and got him on the train for Southampton.

Raymond made no (published) record of his Channel crossing; the first letter from France finds him in another train *en route* from Rouen to the Front. He was getting to know his servant – at that time all officers in the British Army had a soldier-servant to look after

38 Quoted in Lycett, *Conan Doyle*, p. 359.
39 Lodge, *Raymond*, pp. 15–30.

them. 'Altogether he is a very rough customer and wants a lot of watching,' he wrote, conceding that 'all the same he makes an excellent servant.' This servant – Bailey (forename unknown) – kept his officer supplied with hot tea during the long and much delayed train journey, with remarkable ingenuity. He improvised a brazier which he kept lit in his compartment to boil the water, darting out to gather supplies by the wayside whenever the train stopped or slowed down sufficiently.

The train took him to Flanders. Here he 'got a splendid reception from my friends' – these were the men he had trained with in Crosby and Edinburgh, subalterns like himself: Laws (probably William Laws), Eric Fletcher and Humphrey Thomas – and they got him into their company, 'C' Company, under the command of Captain Richard Taylor. Laws had been at the Front since 31 December and Fletcher since 4 January. Fletcher and Raymond had shared a room in Edinburgh; he now wrote of him, 'he has had some awful times'.[40]

Raymond was attached to the 2nd Battalion, and he found them resting up in the rear. 'This place is very muddy,' wrote Raymond. He spent the night in a tent before the Battalion found billets. The five officers from 'C' Company, their five servants and a cook squeezed into a farmhouse: 'the natives still live here,' he added.[41]

The next day the company were on a fatigue duty, but were sent the wrong way and wandered into view of the German artillery. They got out of the way just in time to avoid the shells that started falling. It was Raymond's first experience of the fighting – and he had not even reached the frontline trenches.

April Fool's Day found Raymond digging trenches under cover of darkness. The Germans were not more than 500 yards away and despite 'a very few stray bullets whistling over' he declared that he 'had a most peaceful time'.

40 Richard Arthur Ogden Taylor mentioned in the *London Gazette* (2 October 1914) and having a catalogue entry at the National Archives, Kew, WO 339/42968.
41 No. 11 Platoon, 'C' Company, 2nd Battalion, South Lancashire Regiment, 7th Infantry Brigade, 3rd Division.

On Saturday evening, 3 April, he was sitting in his dug-out, writing by candlelight. 'I am having quite a nice time in the trenches,' he wrote. He described his simple living arrangements: sleeping in his clothes on a straw bed covered with a tarpaulin, with 'my invaluable air pillow' and a big coat as a cover.

Everything was done under cover of darkness, not just digging trenches, but entering and exiting them. Fires were forbidden because of the smoke and could only be lit inside after dark, meaning that hot meals were restricted. Bailey's 'native cunning' (Raymond's words) turned their 'limited and simple rations' into 'excellent meals'.

As they manned the firing trench – the actual front line and only about 100 yards from the Germans – one of Raymond's men broke the rules and, letting curiosity get the better of him, peeked over the parapet. A bullet promptly put a hole in his cap. He smartly ducked down again and they all marvelled at how close to his head the shot had been.

For all that, he wrote 'things are awfully quiet here'. There was always the suspicion that it was the quiet before the storm, but on the whole Raymond found that 'if we don't stir them up with shots they leave us pretty well alone'.

His platoon were assigned six days' trench duty followed by six days' rest. It was a dangerous journey, trudging back down the line. Once night had fallen, they moved off in single file, negotiating rickety plank bridges and yawning shell holes. Every few minutes, the Germans would put up a star shell. The men froze in the sudden light, waiting the five seconds or so it took for the flare to burn itself out. Raymond found the details particularly interesting, describing the differences between the British 'Very' lights – pistol fired – and the German mortar-launched version. All the while, bullets would fly, like blind and angry wasps, through the flashing air.

Arriving back at their rest billets, they discovered that a shell had put a large hole through the roof of the farmhouse they had stayed in earlier. The remainder of the building was left in a dangerous condition: even the farmer and his family had left. They found another billet, but Raymond did not describe it.

Raymond had been looking forward to the rest break – 'ardently looking forward', he wrote – but now that he was back behind the lines he noted that the only real difference was that they had exchanged enemy rifle fire for enemy artillery fire. A shrapnel burst had caught 2nd Lieutenant Laws's servant and taken the fingers off his right hand, 'and I have been trying to forget the mess it made of his right leg'. Another shell fell amongst the men as they were playing football in a field. They threw themselves to the ground as the shrapnel whistled over their heads; luckily, no one was hurt. Raymond wrote home asking for morphia tablets: 'they might prove useful in the trenches, because if a man is hit in the morning he will usually have to wait till dark to be moved'. He was also pleased to announce that his revolver had arrived that morning – one presumes that he must have spent his first week in the trenches without one.

They got the daily newspapers only a day after publication, but no one much cared for them. Being in the thick of it, there was little desire to read about the war as well as live it. They preferred novels, anything in fact unconnected to the fighting. What had caught Raymond's eye in the *Daily News* was a chart showing 'The Night Sky in April'. He wrote home asking for a star chart. His father sent him a planisphere: 'an ingenious cardboard arrangement which can be turned so as to show, in a rough way, the stars visible in these latitudes at any time of day and any period of the year,' explained Sir Oliver. The family would send other things as well: dates and figs from his sisters; cigarettes and chocolate from his brothers – he liked to smoke Gourdoulis Egyptian Cigarettes; a periscope, ear defenders and sniper scopes from his father.

It was forbidden to reveal potentially sensitive information – information that could be useful to the enemy – but in his letters home, Raymond used a secret code to circumvent the censor and indicate his whereabouts. He was not just in Flanders, he was at Ypres, about 5 miles (8 km) south of the town at a place called Dickebusch.

Brooke's Corner of a Foreign Field

They all turned out, Rupert Brooke among them (now in the Hood Battalion), shoulders back, smartly to attention, as the King reviewed the Naval Division at Blandford on 25 February 1915. They were soon to be sailing to the Dardanelles. Brooke was jubilant: 'I'm filled with confident and glorious hopes' and imagined himself an Ancient Greek about to besiege Troy, 'I've never been quite so happy in my life.' As he sailed on the *Grantully Castle*, the war faded into the background. He fancied that they were all a 'lot of tourists', admittedly 'rather odd' ones. He wrote to Marsh that 'I can see that life might be great fun; and I can well see death might be an admirable solution'. Marsh thought this his normal state of mind rather than a premonition, but noted that Brooke 'certainly spoke to some people as though he were sure of not coming back'.[42]

Brooke never made it to Gallipoli. He was suddenly taken ill on 21 April whilst still in the Aegean, first complaining of back and head pains, with a swelling on his lip, then developing a dangerously high fever. He was diagnosed with acute blood poisoning (sepsis): 'and all hope was given up'. He was moved to a French hospital ship, the *Duguay-Trouin*, where his condition worsened. Now in a coma, his friend Denis Browne sat with him until the end came at 16.46 on 23 April, killed by an infected mosquito bite.

His corner of a foreign field is in an olive grove on Skyros, the Island of the Magnetes in Homer's *Iliad*, known in mythology as the place where the Greek hero Theseus was killed. It was, said Browne, 'one of the loveliest places on this earth, with grey-green olives round him, one weeping above his head'.[43]

The *Grantully Castle* sailed the next morning for Gallipoli. Within six weeks, Browne and most of his other friends from the Naval

---

42 Marsh, 'Memoir', pp. cxxxviii, cxl-cxli.
43 Quoted in Marsh, 'Memoir', p. clv.

Division were dead. Rupert's younger brother Alfred was also in the fighting: a 2nd lieutenant in the Post Office Rifles, he was killed in action near Vermelles on 14 June 1915.[44]

The Landing at ANZAC Cove

At 155 Sloane Street, London, Thomasine Grenfell White woke suddenly from a nightmare. She shook her husband awake:

'I *know* something has happened to George,' she said to him. 'I saw Vera crying dreadfully,' she explained, 'and I saw John very plainly, and he said to Vera, "I wish I could talk to you, but I can't."' Thomasine was Vera's sister and their brother John Chichester had been killed at Sumatra on 17 September 1914. She urged her husband to remember what she had told him that Sunday night on 25 April before any news had arrived.[45]

Earlier that Sunday, Captain L. C. Lampen of the Royal Marine Light Infantry had a letter to deliver. There was nothing especially remarkable about the letter, just a letter from a husband to his wife. The husband was Lieutenant Commander George Harley Pownall, Officer Commanding of the Submarine Flotilla at Malta, deployed to the Dardanelles, leaving his young wife, Vera, behind. No one had expected him to be deployed to Malta, except his Vera, who was garnering a reputation for having the second sight. When her husband had left for Gallipoli, she felt sure that she would never see him again: 'I had not a shadow of a doubt about it,' she said.[46]

Captain Lampen delivered his letter and asked if he might take a nap in the smoking room. Vera opened her husband's letter, dated 17

---

44 Marsh, 'Memoir', pp. xi, clvii. William Alfred Cotterill Brooke seems to have been generally known as Alfred.

45 Revd M. A. Bayfield, 'Recent Cases of Premonition and Telepathy', *JSPR* (January–February 1916), p. 134.

46 Bayfield, 'Recent Cases', p. 129. L. C. Lampen is given the pseudonym L. T. Esmond in Bayfield's account.

April. There was nothing much about naval matters except mention that he was 'going on to a transport' – the commander of a submarine flotilla lived aboard what was called a depot-ship rather than a submarine. She was about halfway through it when she was 'seized with an overpowering conviction' that a troop landing had taken place during which her husband had been killed.

She wanted to tell Lampen about it immediately, but as he was so very tired she thought it better to let him rest. It was about an hour later when Lampen returned to her in the drawing room. She told him of her impression.

'I was not aware that the landing had taken place,' said Lampen, 'and did not expect the attempt to be made for two or three days.' More especially, 'That Lieut. Comdr Pownall would land seemed to me improbable, as he was OC Submarines.' Lampen knew that ten 'beachmasters' had already been appointed for the landing: he had seen them passing through only a few days before. 'I did not think for a moment that a valuable submarine officer would be taken as a beachmaster.'[47]

Pownall had transferred from the collier *Hindukush* and was with the submarine depot-ship *Adamant* as part of the Second Squadron assisting the landings of the Australian and New Zealand Army Corps at 'ANZAC Cove'.[48] According to the Revd Bayfield, who presented this case to the SPR at a meeting of 22 November 1915:

> On Sunday, April 25, 1915, he was killed by a bursting shell while in charge of a boat taking part in the first landing on Gallipoli. He was wounded in the early morning and died at 10.30 a.m.[49]

47 Bayfield, 'Recent Cases', pp. 131–2.
48 *Supplement to the London Gazette* (16 August 1915), p. 8130; Don Kindell, *Royal Navy Roll of Honour: World War I, 1914–1918*, Pt 2 (Penarth: Naval-History.Net, 2009), p. 83.
49 Bayfield, 'Recent Cases', pp. 129–30.

The Sacred Heart of Gallipoli

The 1st Battalion, the Royal Munster Fusiliers, disembarked from the steamship SS *River Clyde* and waded towards V Beach on the Gallipoli Peninsula on 25 April 1915. Bullets were whistling in the air all around them. As they found their targets, the lapping waves turned red. Private Thomas Kelly felt a searing pain as a bullet passed through his hand to hit him in the chest. He fell into the water, salt water and other men's blood washing his wounds as the Turkish hail of bullets and shrapnel raked the landing zone.[50]

When he was pulled from the water two hours later, he was amazed to find that he was still alive. The bullet had passed clean through his left hand, which had been held over his chest – directly over his heart, according to the story. It had then struck a shield badge of the Sacred Heart sewn inside his tunic and been turned aside, cutting a gash across his chest and exiting on the right-hand side of his tunic through his paybook.

Back in Ireland and 'loudly proclaiming, to all whom he comes in contact with, his profound gratitude to the Sacred Heart', his wounds had healed and he was ready to go back to the Front with the firm conviction that the Sacred Heart would work miracles again for him, if need be, and see him safe home. At least, that is the story attributed to the Sisters of Mercy of Dungarvon, Waterford, as told by an Irish journalist in London in 1917.

It was not Michael MacDonagh's only story of a miraculous escape, although the others are undated and less specific. Private Edward Sheeran, Royal Irish Rifles, attributed his surviving a direct hit from the German artillery to his reciting 'O, Sacred Heart of Jesus, have

---

50 MacDonagh, *Irish on the Somme*, pp. 93–4. At least fifteen men called Thomas Kelly held the rank of private in the Royal Munster Fusiliers during the war, according to records in the National Archives, Kew.

mercy on us!' There was only enough mercy for Sheeran, though, as the shell burst destroyed one man's arms and blew another to pieces, 'parts of him over me' recalled Sheeran. Another soldier had a medal of Our Blessed Lady of Perpetual Succour that got him through twelve battles with only nine slight wounds. A certain Private Michael O'Reilly, of the Connaught Rangers, wrote to his mother from France, saying:[51]

> I have the Sacred Heart badge on my coat and three medals, a pair of rosary beads and father's Agnus Dei around my neck, so you see I am well guarded, and you have nothing at all to fear so far as I am concerned.

Mons Comes to *Light*

Towards the end of April 1915, a 'military officer' called at the offices of *Light* and asked to see a copy of the magazine. It was the issue containing an account of Machen's story about Mons. *Light* had reported on Machen's tale about the archers of Agincourt coming to the rescue of the BEF in October 1914.[52] Afterwards a 'well-known publisher' had asked Gow whether he could throw any light on statements being made that the story was actually true. Gow knew Machen and so wrote to him asking exactly that. Machen replied that it was 'merely a fanciful production of his own'. With that, Gow rather thought the case closed.

Now, this officer explained that:

> Whether Mr Machen's story was pure invention or not, it was certainly stated in some quarters that a curious phenomenon

51 MacDonagh, *Irish*, pp. 95–6. 'Medal Card of Sheeran, Edward J.', National Archives, Kew, WO 372/18/27601, shows that he was a private in the Royal Irish Rifles. There were four men called Michael O'Reilly in the Connaught Rangers.
52 'The Invisible Allies', *Light*, No. 1,761, Vol. XXXIV (10 October 1914), p. 490.

had been witnessed by several officers and men in connection with the retreat from Mons. It took the form of a strange cloud interposed between the Germans and the British. Other wonders were heard or seen in connection with this cloud which, it seems, had the effect of protecting the British against overwhelming hordes of the enemy.[53]

Gow observed that legends spring up quickly, but that there was always some element of truth to them, no matter how small. Whoever this 'military officer' really was, whether his report was true or not, his visit certainly had the effect of keeping the Mons legend alive. Gow ended his short note by saying, 'this legend of Mons is fascinating. We should like to hear more of it.' And so he would.

'A Little Holiday in Belgium'

Captain Bruce Bairnsfather, famous for his humorous 'Old Bill' sketches depicting life at the Front, was also heading for Ypres, marching up with the Royal Warwickshire Regiment. 'It was,' he said, 'a fine sight, looking back down the winding column of men. A long line of sturdy, bronzed men, in dust-covered khaki, tramping over the grey cobbled road, singing and whistling at intervals; the rattling and clicking of the various metallic parts of their equipment forming a kind of low accompaniment to their songs.'[54]

Even then Ypres was notorious. In the course of the war, five battles would be fought here. The first took place from 19 October to 22 November 1914, at the end of the desperate 'Race to the Sea' when the opposing armies attempted to envelop the western, seaward flank of

---

53 ' "The Invisible Allies": Strange Story from the Front', *Light*, No. 1,789, Vol. XXXV (24 April 1915), p. 201.
54 Bruce Bairnsfather, *Bullets and Billets* (London: Grant Richards, 1916), p. 255.

the other – neither did. The First Battle of Ypres resulted in over 100,000 casualties. But to Bairnsfather Ypres 'was what we had come here for'. As he sat at the side of the road watching men tramp past – 'battered, dishevelled looking men [. . .] dazed from shell-shock' – and heavy ordnance falling on the shattered city, he noted:[55]

> If one has ever participated in an affair of arms at Ypres, it gives one a sort of honourable trade-mark for the rest of the war as a member of the accepted successful Matadors of the Flanders Bull-ring.

The second battle began with a German attack near Langermarck, north of Ypres. In the faltering light of a late afternoon on 22 April, the Germans opened chlorine gas cylinders, letting the wind blow it across to the French lines.

To the south, Raymond was trying out his new periscope. It had arrived nicely packed in a canvas bag with spare mirrors and offered a less hazardous means of watching the German positions. In a letter home he used another one of his codes – an acrostic – to send a message to his family. It was not his location this time, but his heartfelt wish: 'peace'. Further up the line, six thousand French soldiers lay dead or dying from the gas attack.[56]

'We knew there was something wrong,' wrote twenty-year-old Private W. Hay of the Royal Scots. He was marching towards Ypres, but the road was choked with people fleeing the fighting. The Scots got off the road and used the railway line instead, still they saw people lying 'in a terrible state'. Hay heard them say it was gas: 'We didn't know what the hell gas was.' When they got to Ypres, they found the bodies of Canadians strewn across the battlefield: 'it was quite a horrible sight for us young men [. . .] I've never forgotten nor ever will forget it.'[57]

---

55 Bairnsfather, *Bullets & Billets*, p. 256.
56 Lodge, *Raymond*, p. 24.
57 Quoted at http://spartacus-educational.com/FWWypres2.htm, accessed 1 December 2017, original source not given.

Raymond was out digging communication trenches by night. For three nights in a row, he had been directing a working party, getting to bed just before dawn. 'What is wanted at the moment,' he observed, 'is not so much a soldier as a civil engineer.' He had also been damming a small stream to stop it flooding out the rear trenches and provide a water supply. He would wake up at midday and brew a cup of tea on his Primus stove, listening to a cuckoo singing in a nearby tree: 'It is amazing how tame the animals get. They have so much ground to themselves in the daytime [. . .].'

By Friday, 30 April, he was drawn back for another rest period. 'I wish you could see me now,' he wrote, 'I am having a little holiday in Belgium.' It was a bright, sunny day and he was sitting in the shade of a large tree, his back against its trunk. Across from him was a château, ruined by the war. He spent much of his letter describing it and sketched a front and aerial elevation. Some of the fruit trees in its orchard had been blown down by shellfire and lay in the moat, but even there bravely blossomed.

'C' Company were billeted in a former brewery. Raymond was stationed in a nearby house, sleeping in an outhouse with no door and straw on the floor for a bed. 'The place,' he wrote, 'is swarming with rats and mice.'

News of the gas attack had spread down the line. He reassured his parents that they had not used it on him; even so, 'on some days I have smelled distant traces coming down the wind from the north' – soldiers described chlorine gas as smelling like pepper and pineapple, with a metallic taste. German artillery had stepped up a gear and shells were raining down on the village they had earlier sheltered in: 'most of the companies have had to quit. We ('C' Company) are well back now . . .'

Before rest was over, he and his men were moved into woodland and designated as support, reserve troops to be used to bolster the line in case of a German attack in strength. Still the trench digging went on: Raymond and Thomas taking their platoons out into the uneasy night.

A Dream of Ypres

Back at Maricmont, Sir Oliver woke after a vivid, 'though not especially vivid', dream on 7 May. Sir Oliver was not much given to dreaming, especially vividly, or even not especially vividly, so he made note of it:[58]

> An attack was going on at the present moment, that my son was in it, but that 'they' were taking care of him. I had this clearly in mind before seeing the morning papers; and indeed I do not know that there is anything in the morning papers suggesting it, since of course their news is comparatively old. One might have surmised, however, that there would be a struggle for Hill 60, and I know that my son is not far off Ypres.

Hill 60 was an overgrown excavation heap at the side of a railway cutting about 3 miles (5 km) south-east of Ypres and bitterly contested. The British had taken it on 17 April, dislodging the Germans by exploding mines underneath it, but lost it again on 1 May when the Germans engulfed the area in greenish clouds of poison gas.

Some days later Raymond wrote again. 'We are within view of a well-known place' – Sir Oliver understood this as meaning Ypres – 'and the place has been on fire in three or four places for about two days, and is still going strong.' Bairnsfather had watched Ypres burning, too, and like Raymond found it most dramatic at night.

Bairnsfather and the rest of his battalion had been ordered to stop by the roadside and were waiting for the field kitchens to catch up with them. He spread his greatcoat out and sat on it to watch the show: 'we could hear and see the shells bursting in the city in darkness [. . .] Suddenly, a huge fire broke out in the centre of town. The sky was a whirling and twisting mass of red and yellow flames, and enormous

58 Lodge, *Raymond*, pp. 30–35.

volumes of black smoke [. . .] The tall ruins of the Cloth Hall and Cathedral were alternately silhouetted or brightly illuminated in the yellow glare of flames.' Bairnsfather asked some of the men in front of him to move out of the way to give him a better view.[59]

'I was awfully interested in father's dream,' Raymond told his mother. 'You say that the other night he dreamt I was in the thick of the fighting, but they were taking care of me from the other side.' He pooh-poohed the suggestion that he was in the thick of it, but conceded that 'I have been through what I can only describe as a hell of a shelling with shrapnel.'

On the morning of 7 May, 'C' Company were ordered forward. Marching in single file in four platoons, Captain Taylor led them closer to the fighting. Raymond was commanding No. 9 Platoon in the absence of Laws – Laws had been sent back 'on sick leave, as his nerves are all wrong,' explained Raymond – the Captain was leading Raymond's platoon, No. 11, and Fletcher and Thomas were bringing up theirs. They had not gone far when an aeroplane spotted them and started following their movements. Some message must have been sent to the German gunners because they started up, dropping some 'Johnsons' in their general vicinity – a reservoir embankment screened them from direct sight and the shells overshot their intended target. Their route took them through a ruined village – the German artillery already had its range, having been the ones to ruin it, and carpeted the streets with shrapnel. 'C' Company managed to pass through unaffected, but beyond the village was open ground: 'when we came out into the open on the far side, we caught it properly. Shell after shell came over and burst above us.'

Raymond and three other men turned a corner to hear a shell explode above them. Raymond looked up and 'saw the air full of flying pieces, some large and some small'. Shrapnel showered down over them. Miraculously, he was unharmed, but Bailey caught a piece on the knee. Although a slight wound, it rattled his nerves. Raymond helped him back round the corner and into a ditch. The rest of the platoon

---

59 Bairnsfather, *Bullets and Billets*, p. 265.

jumped in behind him. Looking round at them, Raymond decided that they should wait out the bombardment, but Fletcher shouted at them to move on. They left the wounded and went once more into the breach: 'we just walked along. It felt rather awful.' Their hearts must have been in their mouths, but Raymond wrote later 'I felt very much protected. It was really a miracle that we weren't nearly all "wiped out".' As it was, only one man had been killed and five or six slightly injured.

Eventually they made it to the support trenches. 'Things are very quiet,' he reported in a letter of 12 May, 'and I am enjoying myself very much. If it wasn't for the unpleasant sights one is liable to see, war would be a most interesting and pleasant affair.' Once again he was building things and 'did enjoy laying the sandbags and building a proper wall with "headers" and "stretchers"'. He made such a good job of it that a sergeant asked him in all seriousness if he had been a bricklayer before enlisting: 'I was awfully proud,' he confessed. His letter writing was interrupted by an order to provide rapid rifle fire during pauses in the British artillery bombardment. To the north, poison gas was giving the Germans the edge, pushing the allied lines back towards Ypres.

'With Wings to My Soul'

On 9 May, Aelfrida Tillyard wrote in her diary: 'Rupert Brooke came to talk to me a few nights after his death.' It was not the first ghost she had encountered: she first saw her deceased grandfather, Henry Joseph Wetenhall, in 1912. News of Brooke's death had already been reported in *The Times*: 'Rupert Brooke is dead' wrote Winston Churchill in the 26 April edition, adding, 'he was all that one would wish England's noblest sons to be in days when no sacrifice but the most precious is acceptable'.[60]

60 Tillyard quoted in Sheila Mann, 'Into the River of Death', *Paranormal Review*, 76 (Autumn 2015), p. 15; Churchill quoted in Marsh, 'Memoir', pp. clviii, clix.

Although Tillyard had never met Brooke, she had included four of his poems in her anthology of Cambridge poets published in late 1913. She was deeply affected by the news: 'of all the wanton destruction wrought by the war none seems more wanton than the death of a poet'. She had just had news from her brother Eustace – Eustace Mandeville Wetenhall Tillyard, OBE, who would become Master of Jesus College, Cambridge – from 'Somewhere in France' and must have been at once relieved to hear from him and doubly concerned about his future.[61]

'If I should die,' wrote Tillyard in her diary, quoting Brooke, 'think only this of me.' Tillyard expected that he had come back from the dead to apologise for missing their lunch appointment. Her biographer, Sheila Mann, thought this 'a typical Aelfrida touch'. She could not see him, only hear him, and asked whether he 'minded being dead'. Brooke did not mind, instead he felt liberated: 'it was glorious being free . . . and floating about looking at things'. She asked Brooke if there were 'any God "up there"'. 'No,' replied the atheist, 'not exactly God, but boundless light.'[62]

Brooke was a frequent visitor in June that year. Appearing in a dream – a 'true dream' according to Tillyard, using the phrasing of Margaret Verrall – the lonely ghost complained that everyone else was too busy and offered to be Tillyard's friend. She visited the Old Vicarage in Grantchester, Brooke's former and beloved home, and thought that 'there seemed a lot of him about'. On his next visit, she and Brooke collaborated on a poem, 'Settled Down', of which she remembered nothing and then another a week later: 'Light like the dreamy haze on distant hills / Of unimagined blue . . .' – she could not remember the rest. She found Brooke 'too funny, so eager and so excited about the spirit world and so keen to get a listener'. On his next visit he was again in 'tremendous high spirits' and 'awfully amusing'. 'Did you ever meet a ghost with a sense of humour?' she wrote in her diary.[63]

61 Aelfrida Tillyard (ed.), *Cambridge Poets, 1900–1913: An Anthology* (Cambridge: W. Heffer & Sons, 1913); Sheila Mann, *Aelfrida Tillyard*, p. 273.
62 Mann, *Aelfrida Tillyard*, p. 274.
63 Mann, *Aelfrida Tillyard*, p. 274.

Perhaps the spirits were aware that Tillyard was forgetting all the important stuff. When Rupert next appeared he said that Myers had told him to recommend automatic writing. Tillyard refused. She had been re-reading Myers's *Human Personality* and thought that she could not be sufficiently objective because of that. Brooke 'seemed rather hurt', but Tillyard went to bed and fell asleep. Later, she thought she woke up, hearing Myers say 'There! Now you've got it' to Brooke, who also had Edmund Gurney and Alfred Verrall with him. Brooke then 'seemed to take possession of my brain' and Tillyard dreamt about him in the spirit world. Again she thought that she woke up and started automatic writing. Finally, she did wake up and tried to record everything that she dreamt she had been writing: 'he plunged into the river of death [. . .]'. She was aware again of Brooke's presence and his triumph. Taking more paper, Brooke dictated to her and she wrote: '[. . .] both seekers of living harmonies'. The communication ended with Brooke telling her 'I don't feel like a discarnate spirit. I feel like me, Rupert, with wings to my soul instead of legs to my feet.'[64]

Brooke returned on 30 June to ask Tillyard to take a message to his mother. It was simple: 'Write to Mrs Brooke, 24 Bilton Road, Rugby thus: I know, I love, I understand.' She did as she was asked. Mrs Brooke wrote back, apparently confirming the message as genuine, but asking her not to write again because it would 'give her great pain to have her son send her messages through a total stranger'.[65]

She wrote no more to Mrs Brooke, but did send two letters to her old tutor Margaret Verrall. Verrall thought the messages were genuine, but did not take the matter further. Mann suggests, among several other reasons, that Tillyard's increasingly eccentric reputation may have warned Verrall off. There was no SPR investigation, nor publication of the events as described.[66]

64 Mann, *Aelfrida Tillyard*, p. 274.
65 Mann, *Aelfrida Tillyard*, pp. 274–5.
66 Mann, *Aelfrida Tillyard*, p. 275.

A Passage on the *Lusitania*

The American Society for Psychical Research (ASPR) was in turmoil. Founded in 1884, just two years after the SPR in London, the Society included first-rank American intellectuals, such as the mathematician and astronomer Professor Simon Newcomb (1835–1909), the pioneering psychologist Professor G. Stanley Hall (1846–1924), the psychologist and philosopher Professor George Stuart Fullerton (1859–1925), the Harvard Medical School anatomist Professor Charles Sedgwick Minot (1852–1914), the zoologist Professor Alphaeus Hyatt (1838–1902), the physicist and astronomer Professor Samuel Pierpont Langley (1834–1906), who was also the inventor of the thermal radiation detector known as a bolometer and founded the Smithsonian Astrophysical Observatory, the Edinburgh-born inventor Alexander Graham Bell, the physiologist Professor Henry Pickering Bowditch (1840–1911), then Dean of Harvard Medical School, and the psychologist Professor William James (1842–1910), often considered the 'Father of American Psychology'. The Society's first president was the astronomer Professor Edward Charles Pickering (1846–1919) of the Harvard College Observatory.[67]

Despite such promising beginnings, the ASPR soon ran into money troubles. In 1889, it was absorbed into the SPR and with the death of its dedicated secretary and tireless, if not obsessive, investigator Richard Hodgson in 1905, ceased to exist.

It was revived in 1907 by Professor James Hyslop (1854–1920). He had retired from his post as professor of logic and ethics at Columbia University on the grounds of ill health in 1902. His wife had died in 1900 and the indications are that he suffered a nervous breakdown. He

---

67 Seymour Mauskopf, 'Psychical Research in America', in Ivor Grattan-Guinness, *Psychical Research: A Guide to Its History, Principles and Practices* (Wellingborough: Aquarian Press, 1982); Announcement of Friend's death in *JSPR* (March 1916), p. 157.

originally intended that the ASPR would become Section B of his new American Institute for Scientific Research – Section A was to concentrate on psychopathology. But Section A never materialised and Hyslop's Institute officially reverted to the name of the ASPR in 1922.

During the war, Honorary Fellows included most of the SPR inner circle – Arthur and Gerald Balfour, Barrett, Crookes, Lodge – but also Freud, Jung, Max Dessoir, Schrenck-Notzing, Charles Richet and Pierre Janet. Everard Feilding and A. P. Sinnett were Honorary Members.[68]

Another high-level academic, he was nonetheless unpopular. Hyslop was said to have had a dictatorial style – Sir William Barrett thought him 'dogmatic and combative in the expression of his opinions'.[69] Hyslop had entered the field of psychical research as a sceptic – he thought Zöllner's famous experiments with the medium Henry Slade flawed (Slade was later unmasked as a charlatan) – but by the end of the war he was a firm believer.

In 1913 or 1914, he appointed twenty-six-year-old Edwin William Friend as Assistant Secretary (or Under-Secretary) and editor of the *Journal of the American Society for Psychical Research*. Friend had graduated from Harvard in classics and Indic philology, and was not long returned from Germany where he had been continuing his studies at the University of Berlin. Back in the USA, he had taught at Princeton before taking a higher degree at Harvard. His ASPR salary of $2,000 was made possible by a donation from the architect Theodate Pope. Pope even housed Friend and his new wife Marjorie on her estate of Hill-Stead in Farmington, Connecticut. It was she who pulled the strings to get him the editorship.

When war broke out, many of the original members had by now passed away – Newcomb, Hyatt, Bowditch, Langley, James – or were of advanced age. One languished in a German jail for the duration of hostilities.

68 *Journal for the American Society for Psychical Research*, vol. X, no. 3 (March, 1916), n.p.
69 Quoted in Arthur Berger, *Lives and Letters in American Parapsychology: A Biographical History, 1850–1987* (Jefferson, NC: McFarland, 1988), p. 62.

Professor Fullerton had been an exchange professor at the University of Vienna when the war broke out. He was arrested whilst lecturing in Munich and interned as an enemy national, presumably after the USA declared war on Germany on 2 April 1917. He remained in prison until the end of the war. The harsh conditions of his imprisonment left him with permanent health problems. In 1925, aged sixty-six, he committed suicide.[70]

At Hill-Stead, Marjorie started producing automatic writing and appeared to be in communication with those venerable members of the Society who had crossed over to the other side. Edwin neglected the articles that Hyslop was sending him for publication and started filling the journal with accounts of their Farmington séances.

Hyslop was incensed. He removed Friend from the editorship. Friend and Pope resigned in protest.

There must have been some communication with Sir Oliver Lodge, because Friend and Pope started packing their bags with the intention of staying with him in Britain whilst they sought the support of the SPR for their own American organisation.

Marjorie was already some months pregnant, so she would remain at Hill-Stead. Friend would travel with his patron Theodate Pope and Pope's maid, Emily Robinson. The next available sailing was on the RMS *Lusitania*.

It was a relatively new ship, the first of Cunard's new luxury ocean liners – its maiden voyage had been in September 1907 – and it was fitted with revolutionary turbine engines that enabled the quadruple-blade propellers to maintain a speed of 25 knots across the Atlantic, making it faster than the Royal Navy's pride of the fleet, the battleship HMS *Dreadnought*, even though it was longer and heavier. There were lifts inside, wireless telegraph and electric lighting, and the First-Class decks were divine. But because it was wartime, she had also been fitted with 6-inch gun mounts, although no guns had been installed.

On 4 February 1915, Germany had declared British waters to be a war zone, meaning that shipping would be sunk without warning.

70 'Dr. G. S. Fullerton Commits Suicide', *New York Times* (24 March 1925), p. 25.

Pope booked their passage, even though the German embassy in the USA had put an announcement in fifty American newspapers warning people not to sail on the RMS *Lusitania*.

Perhaps they felt safe that the international Cruiser Rules would protect the passenger ship, even though she was loaded with war munitions. The Royal Navy had further complicated the recognition of non-military shipping by using so-called Q-ships, merchant vessels with concealed gunnery designed to lure submarines to the surface. Cruiser Rules were effectively redundant.

Boston businessman Edward Bowen also had an important meeting in London and, like Friend, booked passage on the next available trans-Atlantic steamer from New York to Liverpool, also in spite of the German U-boat blockade. Nevertheless, 'A feeling grew upon me that something was going to happen,' said Bowen. He talked it over with his wife and cancelled his tickets. The meeting could wait.

The theatrical manager, Arthur 'Al' Woods, had taken a stateroom next to the famous playwright Charles Klein – in 1912 they had both cancelled their passages on the *Titanic*. On the morning of sailing, fear or foreboding again overcame Woods and he gave it up; but not Klein.

Alta Piper, the daughter of medium Leonora Piper, had been invited to the wedding of Sir Oliver Lodge's eldest daughter. Apparently the medium advised against sailing on the *Lusitania*, but Alta got as far as New York, still intending to sail. The night before the departure, a voice repeatedly called out to her 'If you get into your berth, you'll never get out'. She changed her mind. She tried various subterfuges to try and cancel her booking. She said her passport had not arrived: the Cunard agent said that they could send it on to her. She argued that she did not have enough time to pack all her luggage: she was told that the sailing had been delayed by two hours. She apparently spent the time packing and unpacking her suitcases, so as to be sure not to be ready before sailing, and so missed the ship's departure, at least according to the story.[71]

71 Michael Goss and George Behe, *Lost at Sea: Ghost Ships and Other Mysteries* (Edison, NJ: Galahad Books, 1994), pp. 260–2.

The ship was due to set sail on Saturday, 1 May, from Chelsea Piers' Pier 54, the same pier that RMS *Titanic* had sailed from in 1912. On the evening before sailing, the ship's mascot, a black cat called Dowie, made an escape down one of the large hawsers. The firemen and stokers saw in it a terrible omen.

'It's the best joke I've heard in many days, this talk of torpedoing,' said Captain William T. Turner as the ship prepared to cast off. The captain was confident that the *Lusitania*, with its superior turn of speed, could easily outrun any submarine. He had once made the Liverpool to New York crossing in a record twelve days. The crew were not so sure, especially as Boiler Room No. 4 had been shut down to save on fuel costs. Her 25 knots were now down to 22. Still, a German submarine could only make 15 knots on the surface and less than ten submerged. It was a different matter for torpedoes. Even an old-fashioned German Schwartzkopff torpedo could make 22 to 25 knots.[72]

'The Fortune of War'

Sir Oliver Lodge heard an account later from a lady whose name she desired to remain private. 'It would be absurd to say now,' she wrote, 'that from the beginning of the voyage I knew what would happen; it was not a very actual knowledge, but I was conscious of a distinct forewarning, and the very calmness and peace of the voyage seemed, in a way, a state of waiting for some great event.'[73]

Most of the 1,265 passengers were squeezed into Second Class: 601 people were booked into the 460 Second Class births. There was still room in First Class, with Klein, and plenty to spare in Third.

---

72 My account is based on Adolph A. Hoehling and Mary Hoehling, *The Last Voyage of the Lusitania* (New York: Holt, 1956), pp. 31–2; Frederick Ellis, *The Tragedy of the Lusitania* (Philadelphia: National Publishing Co., 1915), pp. 168, 172, 174–5; Senan Molony, *Lusitania: An Irish Tragedy* (Douglas Village, Cork: Mercier, 2002); and www.rmslusitania.info, accessed 12 May 2017.
73 Quoted in Lodge, *Raymond*, p. 300.

The cruise liners had renamed First as Saloon Class. Pope booked tickets in Saloon Class: she and her maid were in cabin D-54; Friend was in E-47. But as sailing got underway, she found her neighbours, the Cromptons, with their six children to be too 'noisy'. After one night she requested to be moved and took cabin A-10. Pope and Friend shared their dining table with Dr James Houghton and his travelling companion Marie Depage, wife of the Belgian royal surgeon. A fundraiser for the Red Cross, Depage had talked Houghton into giving his services as a doctor on the Western Front. Before sailing, Houghton had made his last will and testament.

In Room 40 of the Admiralty, British Naval Intelligence was attempting to track German submarine movements. They may or may not have known that a submarine had left the German port of Emden on 30 April, making the waters off Peterhead, Scotland, on 2 May, *en route* to the Irish Sea and rich pickings sailing in and out of Liverpool. On 5 May, a torpedo took the schooner, the *Earl of Lathom*, to the bottom of the sea, and another narrowly missed the *Cayo Romano*. That night, the Admiralty sent out the warning, 'Submarines active off the south coast of Ireland.' An update was released at midnight, 'submarine off Fastnet'.

On Friday, 7 May, heavy fog pressed at the windows and portholes, obliterating the surrounding waters. The ship was forced to reduce speed. Captain Turner doubled the lookout. They were nearly there, joy stifled by the grey wreath around them and the knowledge that they were only *nearly* there, still running the German naval blockade. The *Lusitania* was a few miles out from the Old Head of Kinsale Lighthouse on the south coast of Ireland. These were the most dangerous waters. Not far, now.

Somewhere out in the fog Kapitänleutnant Walther Schweiger ordered *Kaiserliche Marine* submarine SM U-20 to surface. They had been patrolling off the southern coast of Ireland as part of the German U-boat blockade of Britain since 30 April. The day before Schweiger had taken two cargo ships – the *Candidate* and *Centurion* – south of the Coningbeg Lightship, moored off the Saltee Islands, 9 miles (14 km) out from the Wexford coast. He was further south now and oil was running low. There were only two torpedoes left, and not their best ones.

The fog had cleared by the time Friend and Pope finished lunch, and they decided to take a stroll on deck. By now, the sea was a 'marvellous blue' and 'very dazzling in the sunlight'.

Standing in the conning tower, Schweiger swept his binoculars across the sea. At 14.20 (13.20 GMT) Schweiger spotted smoke stacks on the horizon. 'I saw it was a great steamer,' he said afterwards. It would make a great prize. He ordered diving stations to periscope depth and closed at high speed to around 2,300 feet (700 m). He launched a single torpedo.[74]

Captain Turner was pacing the *Lusitania*'s lower bridge, eyes on the sea. Suddenly, the second officer called out, 'There is a torpedo coming, sir.' The Captain turned and to starboard saw the tell-tale wake ploughing the sea towards them. It struck three metres below the waterline, punching through to the boiler room before exploding. Almost immediately there was another, much larger explosion.[75]

Friend and Pope had rounded the aft corner of the promenade ('B' Deck) when they heard the explosion. The noise had been tremendous. One passenger described it as sounding 'like a million-ton hammer hitting a steam boiler a hundred feet high'. A wall of angry water and debris was sent skywards.

'By Jove,' exclaimed Friend, punching his fist into his other hand, 'they've got us!'[76]

Schweiger's initial reaction must have been one of satisfaction: he had scored a bull's-eye. 'Torpedo hits starboard side right behind the bridge,' he wrote in his logbook. 'An unusually heavy detonation takes place with a very strong explosive cloud. The explosion of the torpedo must have been followed by a second one.' He could see the name *Lusitania* visible in big golden letters.

74 Lowell Thomas, *Raiders of the Deep* (New York: Doubleday, Doran & Co., 1928), pp. 94–5.
75 The 'Mersey Report': *Report on the Loss of the 'Lusitania'* (London: His Majesty's Stationery Office, 1915).
76 Hoehling and Hoehling, *Last Voyage*, p. 110.

As Schweiger watched the tragedy unfold before him, his mood changed. 'It looks as if the ship will stay afloat only for a very short time,' he continued in the log. 'I couldn't have fired another torpedo into this mass of humans desperately trying to save themselves.' He gave the order to dive to 82 feet (25 metres) and moved out into deeper sea. SM U-20 was on its way back to Wilhelmshaven.

Captain Taylor immediately ordered all lifeboats to be lowered, calling out 'Women and children first'. He gave the order to turn hard-a-starboard with the intention of getting as close to land as possible, but the engines were dead, drowned by the inrush of water. The radio operator sent out the SOS signal, followed by 'Come at once, big list, 10 miles south Head Old Kinsale.'[77]

Friend and Pope ran back inside, being hurled against the corridor wall as the *Lusitania* listed heavily to starboard. Making their way up to the Boat Deck ('A' Deck), they found it already crowded. An officer was shouting orders: stop lowering the boats; passengers to 'B' Deck on the starboard side where they should find the boats hanging down. The desperate crowd ignored him. A full lifeboat was lowered away. Momentum was still forcing the ship through the waves and, when the boat hit the water, it up-ended, throwing its occupants into the sea.

Friend and Pope made their way to the boats on the starboard side to see a lifeboat already getting away safely. By now the ship was listing so heavily that she threatened to roll over and crush anything beneath her.

'It's not a good place to jump from,' said Pope. Holding on to each other, they made their way back to where they had come from, passing Dr Houghton and Marie Depage.

Back on 'B' Deck, Friend urged Pope to board one of the lifeboats. Pope insisted that he join her, but Friend refused to take up a place whilst there were still women on the sinking ship. Together they headed to the back of the boat as the bow started to sink; as they did so they came upon Emily Robinson. Miraculously, Friend was able to find three lifebelts.

77 'Mersey Report'.

'You go first,' said Pope to Friend.

Friend jumped in. As he came back up after the dive, he gestured to the two women to follow him. Pope and Robinson jumped into the water.

Pope was 'washed and whirled' about in the water and hit her head on the bottom of a lifeboat as she came up. Momentarily knocked out, she opened her eyes to see that 'I was surrounded and jostled by hundreds of frantic, screaming, shouting humans in this grey and watery inferno'. But she could no longer see Friend and Robinson.[78]

A man 'insane with fright' jumped onto her and landed on her shoulders. He had no lifebelt on and his weight was pushing Pope under the waves. 'Oh, please don't,' she said before going under and losing consciousness again.

Captain Turner remained on the bridge as the ship went down. As water flooded in, he climbed a ladder to escape and grasped at a chair that floated by. The Captain clung on to the chair for nearly two hours before good fortune saved him. The chair turned over and the Captain flung up his arm. The gold braid on his uniform caught the light and was seen by a rescue boat. As he disembarked in Queenstown, cold to the bone and wet right through, he remarked, 'Well, it is the fortune of war.'[79]

Pope regained consciousness, floating on her back in 'brilliant sunshine and blue sea'. When she was finally pulled out of the sea, she was left for dead. Luckily, she was recognised and tended to, and, after some hours, regained consciousness. The bodies of Edwin Friend and Emily Robinson were never recovered.

78 Diana Preston, *Wilful Murder: The Sinking of the Lusitania* (London: Corgi, 2011), p. 277.
79 'Captain Turner Dead', *Montreal Gazette* (24 June 1933), p. 1.

'A Great Influence on the War'

Mrs Chenoweth went into a trance, with weary sighs interspersed with long pauses. Sounds of distress increased until:[80]

'Who drinks?'

'Can you tell me?' asked Professor Hyslop.

'Oh, my, I don't want to see that terrible thing.'

'What is it?'

'Oh, it's . . .' Chenoweth paused, 'perhaps it's, perhaps it's . . .' She seized Hyslop's hand, holding it tightly. 'It's the ocean . . . Oh, Oh, I'm dead.'

'Who is?' asked Hyslop, but he suspected he knew already.

Chenoweth relaxed her hold. 'Promised to report.'

'All right,' said Hyslop, 'I will be glad to hear from you and to have you tell me when you can who it is.'

Chenoweth sighed. The pressure of her grip increased. 'Went down . . . Down.'

'Why have you come here?' asked Hyslop.

'Yes, why?'

'What do you wish to say?' persisted Hyslop.

'It's all over. Perhaps I can help you more now.'

Edwin Friend was not allowed to rest in peace. On 10 May, Professor Hyslop attended a séance with Mrs Chenoweth and attempted to communicate with him. Mrs Chenoweth, also known as Minnie Meserve Soule, was the frequent subject of Hyslop's psychical researches. She was said to produce trance phenomena similar to Mrs Piper. Her spirit controls were Sunbeam, the spirit of a child, and the well-known Imperator.[81]

---

80 James H. Hyslop, 'Communications from Mr Friend, Who Was Lost on the *Lusitania*, Part I', *Journal of the American Society for Psychical Research*, vol. X, no. 3 (March 1916), pp. 148–87.

81 Nandor Fodor, *An Encyclopaedia of Psychic Science* (London: Arthur's Press, 1934); Hyslop, 'Communications', Part II, p. 179, n. 16.

The day after the sinking, the New York papers published lists of the passengers who had been onboard – Hyslop's stepmother pointed out to him that Friend and Pope were named – and possibly on the same day (Hyslop was not certain) a telegram arrived from Pope with the single word 'Safe'. The Sunday papers carried the news that Friend was listed as lost. On Monday, Hyslop was sitting with the medium. According to Hyslop, she had deliberately not read the news and knew nothing of Friend (he had sat with her previously under an assumed name), nor of Hyslop having had an assistant. Hyslop put much store in this, but it would have been quite easy to discover Friend's identity and role in the ASPR by reading the ASPR's *Journal*, and, most revealing, Hyslop lets slip in the footnotes to his séance that news of Pope and Friend's intended voyage had earlier been published in the newspaper.[82]

According to Aleister Crowley, writing in 1919, Chenoweth 'gives us a constant flow of the most terrible drivel which it is possible to conceive'. Crowley thought that 'it is plain to see that, by merely playing upon his vanity and flattering him to the skies, this "medium" has managed to ingratiate herself so thoroughly with the noted Professor, that he has become blind to evidence, to facts, and to common sense'. Being the pervert that he was, Crowley hinted that this was 'more than a mere scientific interest'.[83]

However, Friend was not only apparently communicating through Chenoweth, but also directly. Mrs Friend was an automatist herself and at 2.15 on the morning of Sunday, 9 May, she received a short communication: 'Take my message, darling. I am well. Boy.' Apparently, 'Boy'

82 'The American SPR at the Beginning of 1915', *JASPR*, vol. IX, no. 1 (January 1915), pp. 3–4. In a footnote, Hyslop also refers to the fact that news of Theodate Pope's intended voyage to the UK had been published 'in a New York paper' and that Friend's intention to visit Sir Oliver Lodge had also been published 'in the New York paper', Hyslop, 'Communications', p. 158, n. 11, and p. 159, n. 14.
83 Diana Preston, *Lusitania: An Epic Tragedy* (New York: Walker Publishing Company, 2002), p. 105; Aleister Crowley writing under the name of Hodgson Y. Knott, Review of "The Doris Case of Multiple Personality", *The Tank* (March 1919).

was his usual way of signing himself to his wife. At the time, she wrote that she was not sure 'whether I was receiving telepathically or whether the message came from across the border'. The wording would suggest that it was intended to convey that he was still alive; she would find out the truth later that day. Mrs Friend later joined Hyslop in séances with Mrs Chenoweth and an unidentified 'Miss D.'[84]

On 31 May, Hyslop received a letter from Friend's sister:

The other night I had a dream about Edwin in which he appeared to me very well and happy. I said to him: 'But Edwin, dear, I thought you were drowned when the *Lusitania* went down,' to which he replied: 'True enough, dear sister, I did drown, but I am not dead to those whom I love and know me. I live, but to all others I am dead.'[85]

After his own death in 1920 from a blood clot, Hyslop apparently returned from the grave to tell his research assistant and secretary, Gertrude O. Tubby, that 'I find it difficult to assume that I am dead'. The medium was Mrs Chenoweth.[86]

The tragedy of Edwin Friend did not end with his death. His wife, Marjorie Friend, was left destitute and survived on the mercy of friends. On 22 September 1915, she gave birth to their daughter. She called her Faith. According to the claim for damages, 'the record indicates that as a direct result of the great emotional shock sustained by the mother during her pregnancy following the announcement of her husband's death, and the grief and mental anguish suffered by her, the child was born and will always remain a defective'. Faith needed specialist care and Marjorie gave her over to the Massachusetts School for the Feeble Minded, paying out $364 a year. The Mixed Claims Commission formed to deal with reparations agreed under the Treaty of Berlin on 25

84 Hyslop, 'Communications', p. 153, n. 3.
85 Hyslop, 'Communications', p. 164, n. 22.
86 'Dr. James H. Hyslop Dies of Blood Clot', *New York Times* (18 June 1920); Gertrude O. Tubby, *James H. Hyslop – X His Book: A Cross Reference Record* (York, PA: The York Printing Co., 1929).

August 1921, decreed that she should receive $10,000 for her own suffering, a further $10,000 as the legal guardian of Faith, and the sum of $100 plus interest as repayment of the loss of her husband's personal property at the time of the sinking. She married a consulting engineer called Eastman A. Weaver in 1920 and one hopes she lived more happily after.[87]

Back at Windlesham Manor, the Conan Doyles and their friend Lily were conducting more psychical experiments. Lily's pencil moved unconsciously across the paper: 'It is terrible, terrible, and will have a great influence on the war.' Conan Doyle immediately thought that the message referred to the sinking of the *Lusitania* and later connected it to the entry of the USA into the war.[88]

Sang-Froid and Shrapnel

'No, I am not making things out better than they really are': Raymond's family were beginning to suspect that he was putting on a brave face. His letters portray a different sort of war than the one we are used to hearing about. 'I know that people think that everything in Belgium is chaos and slaughter, but it isn't so,' he wrote. 'Don't think I am having a rotten time – I am not.'[89]

He had spare time for writing when not in the front line, hence his letters tended to reflect what he was doing when he wrote them. There were the joys of a hot bath to report, the arrival of kippers, a gift of nectarines from the Belgian interpreter, fresh roses picked every day for the Officers' Mess, a private who played the Intermezzo from the *Cavalleria Rusticana* on his violin whilst they ate a candlelit dinner. There was time for horse riding across the fields and the officers' next

87 Mixed Claims Commission, 'Docket No. 422: Edwin Friend', signed by Edwin B. Parker and dated 23 September 1924.
88 Miller, *Adventures*, p. 364.
89 Lodge, *Raymond*, pp. 36–51.

rest billets were in a château, an undamaged one at that. It *was* bizarrely idyllic.

But it was still war. After Laws, Fletcher was next. 'His nerves are all wrong,' wrote Raymond on 18 May, using the same turn of phrase he had with Laws. Indeed, he explained Fletcher's condition further by saying 'he is going the same way as Laws did'. Laws and Fletcher had been at the Front the longest: the strain was getting to them, not the sudden derangement that we associate with the term shell shock, but a slow grinding away of normal functioning that was 'shell shock' nonetheless. Raymond began to worry for Thomas, as well: 'I am afraid of his going like Laws and Fletcher did,' he wrote.

As for Raymond himself: 'I do my best to keep cheerful and happy all the time – I don't believe in meeting trouble half-way.' Even then he conceded that 'If there was some indication of the termination of the war it would help matters – the unending vista is apt to be rather disheartening at times.'

As Sir Oliver had surmised, Raymond was sent up to Hill 60. Still keeping up his bravado, 'it was so interesting and exciting'. He and his men set about improving the trenches and digging a few new ones. Raymond's Battalion had achieved such a good reputation for this sort of thing that they were designated a 'Pioneer Battalion' and exclusively reserved for fortification work, going out at night and sleeping through the day.

A Brigadier-General inspecting the trenches had commended the Battalion on their work. Raymond's CO, Colonel Frederick Dudgeon was pleased as punch – 'he is an excellent man,' wrote Raymond – and told them that they would be relieved from other duties as a result. Captain Taylor was seized with enthusiasm and set about making 'C' Company the best in the Battalion: 'The result is that we have now nothing but parades,' groused Raymond.

Laws and Fletcher had been bombed out of their senses, but Raymond had made it through what would come to be known as the Second Battle of Ypres (22 April to 25 May 1915), a series of engagements – attacks and counter-attacks – that claimed over 59,000 British casualties, almost 22,000 French ones and more than 35,000 on the

German side. The Germans had beaten the allies back, the salient around Ypres was drawing tighter: the fighting continued.

At the beginning of June, he got a better look at Ypres. 'The town is almost unbelievable,' he wrote. It was still on fire, the occasional German shell exploding in the ruins. But to the ever cheerful Raymond this was 'very exciting'.

They passed a graveyard – ' "crumped" out of existence nearly!' It was the same one that Bairnsfather had walked past on his way to St Julien: 'A church and graveyard, both blown to a thousand pieces. Tombstones lying about and sticking up at odd angles all over the torn up ground.' 'It was,' wrote Raymond, 'an unpleasant place to pass.' Ypres must have been like a vision of hell: Bairnsfather talked of the 'charred skeleton wrecks of houses' and 'glimpses of yellow flames mounting to the sky'.

On 16 June, the 2nd Battalion were thrown into an attack. Raymond and 'C' Company were held in reserve at Ypres to receive prisoners. 'Poor devils, I do feel sorry for them,' he wrote, noting 'old men with grey beards' and 'many of the student type with spectacles' amongst the catch: 'not fit to have to fight'. Raymond excitedly reported that he had landed the machine-gun officer's position he was hoping for and had been given the dates for his course.

The night after the attack, the whole Battalion was ordered forward to consolidate the captured German trenches. 'C' Company headed out into the night, but got only halfway. The route was blocked by wounded men struggling back to safety. 'C' Company waited for an hour, watching the damaged soldiers go by. The Germans knew that under cover of night, the British would be on the move: 'though we could not be seen we had a good deal of shrapnel sent over us', and gas as well. They put their masks on, although Raymond reported that it was not very strong. Crouching in the darkness, gas swirling about them, shells exploding overhead, they waited. A piece of shrapnel hit Thomas on the head, knocking him out. He did not recover consciousness and died about an hour later.

When the Battalion finally got to the captured positions it was too late to do any work. They were ordered back, returning as dawn was breaking. Raymond felt the waste of Thomas's life acutely: they had gone out for nothing; his death had achieved nothing.

'He was a very fine friend to me,' he wrote in a letter to Thomas's mother. 'If he had to die, I am thankful he was spared pain beforehand. It made my heart ache this afternoon packing up his valise.' He spared her any mention of his thoughts on the matter.

By 22 June, Raymond had regained his *sang-froid*. Of the war he said, 'It is most like a long picnic in all sorts of places with a sort of constraint and uneasiness in the air.' Still, there was an undertone of strain in his letter: 'What a long war, isn't it?' he wondered, adding that 'I should think that never in this world before have there been so many men so "fed up" before'. The examples of Laws and Fletcher gave further resolve to his determination to remain cheerful at all costs: 'the less one worries about it the less it is'. For Raymond, it was off to Machine-Gun School at GHQ.

Cheiro recorded another instance of *sang-froid* at the front. He had seen an Exchange Telegraph Company message for 19 June: 'When Lord Kitchener came to the British Front, he met at Dunkirk Commandant de Balancourt, to whom he mentioned that a "Jack Johnson" had dropped not very far from him. "That did not alarm me," said the Field Marshal, "because I know I shall die at sea." '[90]

The 'Superstitious Exactitude' of the Beginning of the War

There was a widespread belief that things should happen on the same date as they did in the past. It seemed to give them added gravity.

The writer and politician Hilaire Belloc covered the war for the magazine *Land and Water*, and wrote several books about it.[91] In the first of these, published in 1915, he noted that the Germans – 'with

---

90 Cheiro, *Confessions*, p. 99.
91 Hilaire Belloc, *A General Sketch of the European War, The First Phase* (London: Nelson, 1915), and *A General Sketch of the European War, The Second Phase* (London: Nelson, 1916).

superstitious exactitude' – crossed the Belgian border on the same day and at the same hour as they had crossed the French border in 1870. There was a sense of history repeating itself, but here it was repeating itself exactly. Whether the Germans were supposed to have done this deliberately, or compelled by fate, is less important than the supernatural aura that began to develop around this occasion.[92]

Belloc made the point twice in his book and also in the pages of *Land and Water*. It must have made a considerable impression upon him – an impression that he wished to pass on to his readers. During the war, *Land and Water* had a circulation of over 100,000, so his readers were many.

Upon that same day, August 3rd, following with superstitious exactitude the very hour upon which, on the very same day, the French frontier had been crossed in 1870, the Germans entered Belgian territory.[93]

Unfortunately, Belloc did not seem to know what the right date was and gave different accounts each time he wrote about it. First he said that it was on 3 August, then he said it was on 4 August.

Its first bodies exchanged shots with the Belgian outposts early in the afternoon of Tuesday, August 4, 1914. The hour and date should always be remembered for the solemnity which attaches to the beginning of any great thing; and the full observer of European affairs, who understands what part religion or superstition plays in Europe, will note this enormously significant detail. The first Germans to cross the violated frontier accomplished that act upon the same day and at the same hour as that in which their forerunners had crossed the French frontier forty-four years before.[94]

92 'Mr. Belloc's War Book', *The Times* (1 June 1915), p. 6.
93 Belloc, *A General Sketch [. . .] First Phase*, p. 77.
94 Belloc, *A General Sketch [. . .] First Phase*, p. 211.

The Times' reviewer of Belloc's book spent most of it discussing this inconsistency. Sources tended to disagree, the reviewer confessed, but looking to 'authenticated dispatches' he found that the Germans invaded France at about 9 a.m. on 4 August in 1870. They were reported to have entered French territory on 2 August 1914; and on 3 August were reported in Belgium at Gemmerich near Verviers, which was only officially announced on 4 August.

However, *The Times*' reviewer concluded that Belloc was probably right in thinking that the Germans wanted to associate their latest invasion with that of 1870. In reality, it probably was just a coincidence. The timeline of events left little room for anything else. Archduke Franz Ferdinand was assassinated by Serbian terrorists on 28 June; the Austro-Hungarian Empire declared war on Serbia on 27 July; the German army mobilised on 1 August; and on 3 August the Belgian government refused the German ultimatum. The reviewer admitted that the matter was 'of no present military importance', but still thought it of 'the deepest historical interest'.

It was Belloc who famously wrote to his friend G. K. Chesterton in 1917, saying 'It is sometimes necessary to lie damnably in the interests of the nation'.[95] And sometimes it was necessary not to worry about the facts at all.

Back to Ypres

After Machine-Gun School in a commandeered convent, Raymond was home on leave (16 to 20 July). 'He had a great reception,' wrote Sir Oliver. 'I dropped into my old life just as if no change had occurred,' wrote Raymond. But all too soon it was over.[96]

Eighteen-year-old Alan Favell Ventris, the son of Major General Francis Ventris, and Holden (first name unknown) had been sent as

95 Letter to G. K. Chesterton (12 December 1917), quoted in Robert Speight, *The Life of Hilaire Belloc* (London: Hollis & Carter, 1957), p. 355.
96 Lodge, *Raymond*, pp. 51–71.

replacements for Raymond's old comrades, Laws, Fletcher and Thomas. First mentioned by Raymond on 29 July, he said little of them in his letters home and Holden, in particular, remains a mystery. Ventris had joined up on 10 November 1914 – at the outbreak of war, his father had been recalled from retirement, first to lead the 25th Division, part of Kitchener's Third New Army, then in 1915 to become the Commander of British Forces in China.[97]

Raymond's next letter home is dated 25 July. His new lodgings were 'quite a nice dug-out', it even had a table and chair in it, and a sandbag bed. 'Quite small and snug,' he wrote. Breakfast was bacon and eggs. 'It is a great thing to have a few comforts,' remarked Raymond's former platoon sergeant, 'it makes you forget there is a war.' Raymond agreed, that is 'until a whizz-bang comes over'. (Whizz-bangs were high-velocity, small-calibre shells that travelled so fast that there was little warning – the 'whizz' – before they exploded – the 'bang' when they did.)

There were mines, too. The rest of that week, the Germans were undermining the British line and detonating explosives. Raymond in his dug-out would be 'rocked for several seconds'. Then there were 'sausages': 'appalling things [. . .] great shell-shaped affairs, about 3 feet along and 9 inches in diameter'. Raymond could see the Germans firing these trench mortar bombs 100 yards up into the air and watch them drop onto the British positions. They would fall side on and explode a few seconds after landing. According to Raymond, 'there is the most appalling explosion I have ever heard', and he was getting to hear rather a lot of them. Once during a bombardment, a soldier froze, standing open-mouthed pointing to one as it landed. A corporal had the presence of mind to give him a mighty shove, sending him ten yards and out of danger. Raymond reported that they had had only one casualty so far 'and that a scratch'. In *Lingo of No Man's Land*, Lorenzo Smith wrote of them 'even though no fragments touch him the concussion is so great that a man's insides burst like a kernel of popcorn and

97 Holden, possibly Frederick Albert Holden, later a Captain in the 2nd Battalion, South Lancashire regiment, mentioned in *Bond of Sacrifice*; for Ventris, see *London Gazette* (10 November 1914), p. 9142.

death is usually instantaneous'. They were also known as flying pigs, rum jars and minnies; Raymond guessed that they were intended to destroy British mine galleries.

After the mines and sausages, the Germans were also using armour-piercing shells to penetrate the mud and destroy entrenchments. On 2 August, the Germans were traversing the South Lancashire's section of the line with these shells. Raymond was in his dug-out, trying to make a cup of tea: 'every shell blew out the Primus, and covered us in dust'. But the shells were getting nearer: one blew in the parados, the raised earthwork behind the trench, the next blew up his neighbour's dug-out – the man inside made a miraculous escape. Raymond judged that it was time to leave. A second bombardment that evening blew his dug-out to pieces. It took two men the best part of an hour to dig Raymond's belongings out.

Later that day, a piece of shrapnel hit Raymond's servant Bailey in the leg. The wound was not serious, but Bailey was out of the action. He was replaced by a man called Gray, 'who shapes very well. He is young and willing, and quite intelligent'.

They were sent up the line 'north of Ypres, to St Julien or there-abouts', he wrote with little thought for the censor. By the next rest period on 16 August, he had spent nineteen continuous days in the trenches, in the same clothes. Still the shells kept falling. As the Battalion's officers stood with the Colonel, holding what they called 'Orderly-Room', a shell could be heard overhead: 'Well, that's nothing unusual, but this one got crescendo, and we all looked up in alarm. Then it got very crescendo, and finally cleared us and landed with a loud explosion about 50 yards beyond us.'

On 29 August he reported home that he was at Hooge – again he did not trouble to encode it in an acrostic – due east of Ypres and north of Hill 60. The lack of subalterns meant that he was taken off machine-gun duties and back with 'C' Company still doing trench work by night. On one evening, they worked in the open under a full moon and Very lights, only 30 yards out from the Germans, who were liberally using hand grenades and sniper fire to try and kill them. Despite that, casual-ties were light.

Other than prisoners, Raymond had not actually seen any German soldiers up until this point. He was engaged on construction work when a German star shell lit up the ravaged landscape. Caught in the open, he stood stock still, hoping to blend into the general devastation around him. He was turned towards the German position along a line of woodland and saw one of them 'quite distinctly walking into the wood'. This, more than any other single feature of Raymond's experiences, exemplifies the industrialised nature of the war: his brother officers Laws, Fletcher and Thomas had already become casualties, but this was the first time that Raymond had seen the enemy face to face.

On their forays, the soldiers were apt to collect souvenirs. Raymond was delighted to find a half-buried German machine gun; but the souvenir he took with him was 'a Hun rifle', which he found whilst they were digging a trench, lying with its previous owner: 'we were obliged to move him elsewhere'. The Captain got hold of a Pickelhaube, the distinctive spike-topped helmet that the Germans had worn during the early stages of the war. The only problem was that 'he had to have it cleaned out, because part of the owner was still inside it!' Raymond hung the rifle over the door of his dug-out.

Raymond had been in the Army less than a year and at the Front for a little over five months. By now he could recognise every sort of munition by its sound and tell the difference between a dead man and a dead horse by smell alone. Construction work on the trenches invariably meant digging through corpses. Men worked with their gas masks on, but despite that they were often physically sick.

As early as June, one of his brothers, Alec, had applied to have Raymond recalled from active service to work in munitions. Then, Raymond had had mixed feelings, 'I should love to come home again,' he had written, 'although I don't feel as if I had done my bit yet – really. I haven't been in any big scrap, and I haven't killed my man even . . .' At the end of August, he was enquiring whether anything had come of this. He was still prevaricating – 'I don't know what you think about it, and whether you think I ought to carry on out here' – but the protest was wearing thin. 'I am sure,' he wrote, 'that after six months I shall be just about fed-up with this business.'

But the Army was not fed up. Planning was already underway for the next big push: the Autumn Offensive.

Superstitious in Paris

In Summer 1915, the American short-story writer Emma M. Wise was in Paris. She had had her work published in the *New York Times Magazine Supplement* many years ago and in the *Black Cat* magazine many more years before that. And now, although no one knew how old she was, she might be considered to be enjoying something like a retirement, or at least an extended holiday.[98]

After those first worrying months of the war, the front line had been pushed well away from the French capital and the panic of 1914 had given way to more frivolous pursuits. The war was a distant thunder cloud, menacing the horizon, while the summer sun was bright and warm overhead for those with the leisure to enjoy it.

'Superstitions,' said Emma, 'hover, like birds, in the Paris air. By patient endeavour they may be snared.' And so saying, she had caught a few.

We might picture her sitting in La Rotonde. Although Hemingway was yet to make it famous, thirty-four-year-old Pablo Picasso was a frequent patron, having his studio nearby – possibly still working on

---

98 Emma M. Wise's writing career seems to have begun in the 1890s. The earliest pieces I could find were in *The People's Advocate* (1895), *The Hartford Republican* (1896), 'The Worth of the Warning' in *The Puritan* (July 1897), and 'My Detective Instinct' in the Bostonian short-story magazine *The Black Cat* (February 1898). The highpoint of her career must have been 'The Girl Who Suited' in *The New York Times Magazine Supplement* for 27 September 1903, p. SM11. There is a considerable gap before we find her again writing, this time for the British press. A short story appeared in the *Evening News* in 1914, http://eveningnews.atwebpages.com/history1.htm, accessed 10 April 2017; and the article referred to, 'Latest Superstitions from Paris', *Daily Mail* (8 June 1915), p. 4. I found nothing after this, but a more thorough search may reveal more.

his *Nature morte au compotier* ('Still Life with Compote and Glass'). Here she might meet friends and swap gossip, or sometimes sit alone, an ear open for the conversation at other tables.

Her favourite was a story about a woman who went every day to the Church of Saint-Sulpice. Dipping her fingers in one of the two enormous shells within the entrance – gifts to Francis I from the Venetian Republic and now serving as fonts – she would progress to the Baroque Lady Chapel. Daylight from hidden windows fell across Francois Lemoyne's fresco of the Assumption of Mary and Jean-Baptiste Pigalle's white marble statue of the Virgin with Child as she made her prayers.

She prayed because of the war. She prayed for all her loved ones caught up in it. She even prayed for herself. The list grew shorter as the war grew older until she prayed only for one, a soldier at the Front:

'If he have anything to suffer, let me suffer it for him.'

There was nothing surprising in this; the whole of France, the whole of Europe, was praying for loved ones. Unlike many, if not all, of the others, she was an atheist.

'And I say with the faith of a good sceptic, "If he have anything to suffer, let me suffer it for him."'

She chose Saint-Sulpice because of Balzac – and her story must have especially appealed to Emma because of Balzac. In his short story 'The Atheist's Mass', Desplein, the atheist of the story, goes to the Lady Chapel of Saint-Sulpice to hear mass said for his old friend and guardian, Bourgeat the water-carrier.

The woman's prayer was from Balzac's tale. Her sentiments, too. She prayed, like Desplein, not because she believed, but because the one for whom she prayed believed. Emma added that on account of this tale, the woman also believed that a prayer said here must be more effective than a prayer said anywhere else.

Then there was the Moroccan. He talked English, only English. She found him in a café surrounded by a great crowd. Even the policeman who had come to clear the pavement ended up joining them. They were all listening to him recount his adventures in English. None of them understood English. The Moroccan gestured now and then to his bandaged left arm, so everyone surmised that the tale must involve it.

Another soldier in the French army sitting with him at the table could understand a little English. The Moroccan constantly addressed him with 'You see?' and 'You understand?' as he tried to translate for the rest of the audience.

When the Moroccan realised that Emma spoke English, he spoke even faster in his excitement. Finally, the overworked translator gave up: 'Tell it in French! You speak French as well as me.'

'Well, yes,' the Moroccan was forced to confess, 'I do.'

But he still would not speak it.

'I was brought up on French,' he said, 'but I learned English in Alexandria years ago, and I like it better. I speak it now on principle. I am superstitious about speaking English. I believe that it would be black ingratitude to speak anything else. It was due to an Englishman that I got off with only this.' He gestured to his bandaged arm. 'Only for him and a command given in English, or I'd be back in the Argonne to stay.'

A surprise attack had thrown them into confusion, he explained. Men were losing their heads, the Moroccan amongst them. He could no longer understand the orders in French being shouted all about him, fear had knocked it out of him, and so, try as he might, he could not obey them.

A sharp command in English cut through the din: 'Duck, I say, duck!'

The Moroccan ducked. Shrapnel from an exploding shell nearby whizzed by him. A piece hit him in the arm. If he had not ducked, it would have taken his head off.

'Only for that "duck" I should have been gone, and since I am still here to tell it I should expect to be struck by something more deadly than shrapnel if I ever told it in anything but English.'

English became, for him, 'lucky'. For others, it was Scottish.

On another occasion, perhaps in another café, this time in the Quartier Latin, Emma was amused by the strange commotion attending on the entrance of two soldiers from a Highland regiment.

From every table came the shout of 'Sit here, Monsieur!' Every hand reached out to them.

They sat down next to Emma, perhaps because she was the only one in the whole café not shouting at them. 'What do you think the row is all about?' asked one of the Highlanders. Emma shook her head. 'Luck,' answered the other, 'that is what they want us for, good luck. Every man, woman and child in Paris has the idea that to drink with a man in a kilt will bring good luck. They nearly had a free-for-all fight to get us. For a chap who was always considered an unlucky penny at home that is a cheering experience. Maybe they'll think more of me when I get back and tell them about it.'

Then there was the Canadian soldier with a thing about the number 888. When he enlisted he became No. 888 in his regiment. When he was bayoneted in Flanders, his attacker was also No. 888.

'And a jolly good thing for both of us that it was,' he explained to Emma, 'for I am sure that we let each other off easier than we would have done if we had had different numbers.'

The run of coincidences did not end there. Motor ambulance No. 888 took him to the base hospital. As he lay in bed recovering, he talked so much about 888 that they gave one of the nurses the number. It 'eased his mind', wrote Emma, and gave the nurse 'a chance to pull him through'.

Still the coincidences did not end. His wife wrote to him and by-the-by mentioned how business in their little general shop had been. A rich townsman owed them $8.80 and had no intention of repaying it.

'Send another eight cents' worth of something around to his house,' he wrote back to his wife, 'then make out a bill for eight dollars and eighty-eight cents. He will be sure to pay up.'

'And did he?' asked Emma.

The Canadian chuckled and took a cheque from his pocket: 'Here you are, $8.88.'

Emma took the cheque. Right enough: $8.88.

'She was so proud of me that she sent the cheque all the way over here just for me to look at.'

In desperation, people turned to strange measures: an atheist prayed in church; a soldier spoke a language his listeners could not understand, not to annoy them, but so as not to break the luck; people jostled for the presence of men in kilts because it was lucky, although no one could tell them why; no. 888 became 'the Canadian's creed'. People turned to the irrational because the rational could no longer help them. Luck stuck to odd coincidences because it was hoped that the luck would work again.

'A Few Earthly and Sympathetic Believers'

Emma had no doubt heard of other new fancies of the Parisians, fortune-tellers and séances, perhaps she had even been to something of the sort herself. She would certainly have read about them in the newspapers.

The Times correspondent in Paris wrote back to London that 'the Paris police have been very active recently in their efforts to spare ingenuous persons the expense occasioned by visits to "mediums" and other charlatans'. In late July or early August two cases were heard before the magistrates: Mme Amouroux and George Debord.[99]

Mme received visits from ladies anxious about their husbands serving in the forces, or people simply wanting to find out what fate had in store for them. *The Times* correspondent must have been in the gallery as he was able to say that many witnesses came forward to testify to the absolute accuracy of Mme Amouroux's predictions. The magistrate surely rolled his eyes at this. A cobbler came forward with a complaint: Mme Amouroux's powers had not been evident on his account. She had told him that in 1915 he would kill his wife and children and then die himself. The lawyer for the defendant politely reminded him that 1915 was not yet over. At any rate, the cobbler must surely have been glad that her prediction had not come true, at least for the first half of the year – who knows what was to follow.

George Debord had been a singer until 'he suddenly became aware that he was the possessor of extraordinary powers of divination'. He

99 'Ex-Singer And Credulous Paris Ladies', *The Times* (6 August 1915), p. 5.

gathered 'several old ladies, experts in the doctrine of Spiritualism' and arranged a séance. Debord was a natural, it seemed. At once the most prestigious spirits made themselves known, conveniently speaking through the medium.

'We have formed a committee of patronage,' they told the 'old ladies'. 'King David has been nominated president.'

Lamartine was an assessor and Tolstoy, Musset and Gambetta were members. It was a curious mix. Alphonse de Lamartine (1790–1869) was a politician and writer, noted for his romantic tragedy *Graziella* (1852). Leo Tolstoy (1828–1910), of course, is still widely remembered, especially for his epic *War and Peace* (1869). Alfred de Musset (1810–1857) was a Parisian Romantic poet and dramatist. Léon Gambetta (1838–1882) had been a prominent French statesman, notably organising French resistance during the Franco-Prussian War. One wonders how they would have got on with the Old Testament's King David, who reigned over Israel from around 1002 to 970 BCE.

They wanted, said *The Times* correspondent, to 'form a society in order that their astral entities might be able from time to time to come and hold converse with a few earthly and sympathetic believers, and thus break the monotony of their ethereal solitude'.

'Scratch His Way to the Devil'

They had other notions at the Front. That summer the *Daily Chronicle*'s special correspondent, Philip Gibbs, was at British Headquarters in France. He was struck by the gallows humour of the troops – 'not exactly suitable for drawing rooms, but it is marvellously effective in an atmosphere of high explosives'. He thought it quite 'healthy and true' to laugh at the destruction of the enemy, whatever it was, it was probably inevitable.[100]

100 'Jests of Battle in the British Lines', *Daily Telegraph* (31 July 1915), p. 9.

There were other 'customs', too, among some of the soldiers 'from the rural districts'. In one case a sergeant major came upon his men engaged in burying a German who had been dead for three weeks – one can imagine the state the corpse must have been in. They were burying him face downwards.

'What on earth are you doing?' roared the sergeant major, annoyed by the unregimental activity.

'Well, it's like this, Sarg,' began one of them, perhaps leaning on his spade as he might once have done in 'the rural districts'. 'If the beggar begins to scratch, he will scratch his way to the Devil. It's an old belief in our parts and it took our fancy.'

He had heard another story, although not rooted in ancient rustic custom, that managed to combine the sentimental and macabre – at once horrible and touching. A company of British soldiers was filing down a trench; a dead German lay on the parapet, his hand hanging over.

'Poor old buffer,' said one and shook the hand. The others following did the same. It was a curious tribute, recognition that little separated the living and the dead.[101]

The Ghost of Skobelev

A telegram from Petrograd to the offices of the French newspaper *La France de Demain* in Paris stated that Russian sentries on the Eastern Front had seen General Skobelev in a white uniform riding a white charger. Mikhail Skobelev (or Skobeleff) had earned the nickname of 'the White General' for this habit and had gained his fame in the Russo-Turkish War of 1877–1878. The only problem was that he had died in 1882. According to tradition, his apparition appears at moments of crisis to sow panic in the ranks of the enemy.[102]

---

101 Robert Graves had a similar story, see his *Good-Bye To All That* (1929), pp. 153–4.

102 'The Ghost of Skobelev', *The Cambria Daily Leader* (4 August 1915), p. 1.

And a crisis there had been. The front-page news on 4 August 1915 was all about the German offensive along the river Narev (or Narew). The Russians reported heavy losses, but had checked the German advance. That telegram from Petrograd travelled as far as the *Cambria Daily Leader* in Wales and the *Ghoulburn Evening Penny Post* in New South Wales.

Using this to support the Angels of Mons story, Ralph Shirley, Editor of the *Occult Review*, wrote that 'Stories have been widely current in the Russian army that many Russian sentinels have seen the famous ghost of General Skobeleff in white uniform and riding his white charger'. But there were no more details forthcoming.[103]

Touch Wood

The men of the 6th Battalion, City of London Rifles, were lined up in Regent's Park. One by one they filed up to a large open-topped car where West End star, the French actress and singer Alice Delysia, handed them a lucky charm, a Touchwood or Touchwud. To 'touch wood' is a popular superstition to avert bad luck. She handed out 1,200 that day, 14 August 1915, even tying one to the collar of the regimental mascot, an Irish Wolfhound. 'Never,' wrote Irish journalist Michael MacDonagh, 'has there been such a public exhibition – uncontrolled and unashamed – of the belief in charms.' A Pathé news team was there to film the event.[104]

As this instance shows, lucky charms were officially condoned, publicly promoted and mass-produced, even if they are almost entirely

103 Ralph Shirley, *The Angel Warriors at Mons* (London: Newspaper Publicity Co., 1915), p. 10.
104 MacDonagh, *Irish on the Somme*, p. 88; Owen Davies, 'The Supernatural and the First World War', https://everydaylivesinwar.herts.ac.uk/2015/01/supernatural-beliefs/, accessed 22 June 2018; Sandy White, 'Fumsup and Touch Wood Charms', https://www.sandysvintagecharms.com/pages/fumsup-and-touch-wood-charms, accessed 22 June 2018; 'Luck Charms Presented', film ID 1848.11 (British Pathé, 1915).

absent from the historical record. MacDonagh was one of the few contemporary writers to mention the Touchwood:

> 'Touchwood' is a tiny imp, mainly head, made of oak, surmounted by a khaki service cap, and with odd, sparkling eyes, as if always on the alert to see and avert danger. The legs, either in silver or gold, are crossed, and the arms, of the same metal, are lifted to touch the head.

They came in several varieties. In my collection, I have a 'John Bull' type with the Union Flag painted on his wooden belly.

One manufacturer, Mr H. Brandon, reported sales of 1,250,000 Touchwoods since the beginning of the war. He received many letters from frontline soldiers attributing their survival to his charm. MacDonagh had seen one such letter with five signatures:

> We have been out here for five months fighting in the trenches, and have not had a scratch. We put our great good fortune down to your lucky charm, which we treasure highly.[105]

In a ruined farmhouse near Kemmel Hill (Kemmelberg, Flanders), the official war correspondent Philip Gibbs came upon a group of artillery officers who had no need for small anthropomorphic representations to touch wood for them. 'Have the Huns found you out yet?' asked Gibbs. 'Not yet,' replied one of them at which they all got up from the table where they were lunching and 'making a rush for some oak beams, embraced them ardently. They were touching wood.'[106]

The poet Robert Graves was an officer in the Royal Welch Fusiliers during the war. One evening in the trenches in 1916, near the spot they called Trafalgar Square, he was standing with some other officers discussing the military situation. Pritchard, the battalion trench-mortar officer,

---

105 MacDonagh, *Irish on the Somme*, p. 89.
106 Philip Gibbs, *Now It Can Be Told* (New York: Harper & Brothers, 1920), p. 143 – the British title was *The Realities of War*.

was explaining his role with the new Stokes mortar. The adjutant commented that 'we've had about five hundred casualties in the ranks since Loos and not a single officer.' According to Graves, 'he suddenly realised that he had said something unlucky.' One of the other officers, David Thomas, said 'Touch wood.' Everyone immediately tried to find a piece of wood. Graves noted that it was a French trench without wooden rivets holding it together. Graves pulled a pencil out of his pocket: 'that was wood enough for me'. Richardson said, 'I'm not superstitious, anyway.'[107]

The next day, Thomas was shot through the neck and died at the dressing station. Richardson was blown up by a shell, but seemed all right; he, too, died at the dressing station. The adjutant brought Graves the news: 'You know, somehow I feel, I – I feel responsible in a way for this.' As they were talking, whizz-bangs landed about twenty yards off. Pritchard took a direct hit. Casualties that night: three officers and one corporal.

How could one resist superstition in such conditions? Even Arthur Balfour as the First Lord of the Admiralty (1915–1916) had been seen touching wood in parliament.[108]

Fumsup

Another mass-produced charm combined the lucky qualities of wood with the 'thumbs up' sign. Called 'Fums Up' or 'Fumsup', it was a small mannikin with a wooden head and metal body, the hands fixed in the 'thumbs up' position. Adverts for the Fumsup were often accompanied by a rhyme extolling their lucky properties, such as this one from an advert by jeweller J. C. Vickery in 1916:[109]

107 Robert Graves, *Good-Bye To All That* (London: Jonathan Cape, 1929), pp. 247–8.
108 *T. P.'s Weekly* (4 December 1915).
109 I have two examples in my collection, one is identified with the Reg. No. 831991, the other is unmarked. 'Fumsup! – A First World War Lucky Mascot', http://blog.maryevans.com/2014/02/fumsup-a-first-world-war-lucky-mascot.html, accessed 26 June 2018.

Behold in me
The birth of luck,
Two charms combined –
Touchwood – Fumsup

The picture shows a baby, with winged feet and a four-leafed clover on its forehead, holding both thumbs up. The Vickery model came in four versions: silver 'with natural eyes'; 9ct gold; 15ct gold; and 15ct gold 'with real gem eyes'. A simple version could come in brass with a painted wooden head, sometimes also wearing a 'tin hat', or Brodie helmet, after their introduction in September 1915. Vickery also offered lucky white heather and lucky number charms. One could also buy gold-plated Fumsups in Harrod's for 3/6.[110] Demand continued after the war. A jeweller, W. H. Wilkerson, in Victoria, British Columbia, imported Fums Ups from the UK, selling silver gilt models for $1.90 and solid gold for $5. 'Always we have sold them at an astonishing rate,' was the claim.[111]

The psychoanalyst Ernest Jones was aware of the practice, writing in 1916 about 'anxious relatives who press a horseshoe or a "fums up" on their man when he leaves for the front'. He explained the symbolism behind the Fumsup as being due to 'the exaggerated association in the primitive mind between the genital organs and the idea of power or potency'. Luckily, those anxious relatives 'have not the faintest idea of the meaning of their superstitious act'.[112]

110 John Lewis-Stempel, *Six Weeks: The Short and Gallant Life of the British Officer in the First World War* (London: Orion, 2010), unpaginated digital edition.
111 *The Daily Colonist*, No. 245 (30 September 1919), p. 8.
112 Ernest Jones, 'The Theory of Symbolism', in Ernest Jones, *Papers on Psycho-Analysis*, revised and enlarged edition (Toronto: Macmillan, 1918), p. 171.

'If Your Name is Not on a Bullet'

Everyone is familiar with the superstitious concept of a bullet having one's name on it. Journalist Michael MacDonagh attributed the saying to Irishman Sergeant Dwyer, VC, during a recruiting meeting in Trafalgar Square:

> I don't know what the young men are afraid of,' said he. 'If your name is not on a bullet or a bit of shrapnel it won't reach you, any more than a letter that isn't addressed to you.[113]

A bullet with his name on it found the Sergeant at the Somme, said MacDonagh; however, the only Sergeant Dwyer with the Victoria Cross was John James Dwyer of the Australian Machine-Gun Corps, who survived the war.

Trooper Rupert Henderson of the 6th Australian Light Horse heard the same thing at Gallipoli: 'I remember one of the men in my squadron saying, "If your name's on a bullet you're going to stop it."' He recalled that 'soon afterwards a four-point-seven got him'.[114]

Charles Edmund Carrington, an officer in the Royal Warwickshire Regiment, knew the superstition, too. His servant 'Stanley' had often told him, 'Why, the shell ain't made yet with my name on it, sir.' The German munitions factories were extremely productive, however. He was killed by small-arms fire during the Third Battle of Ypres in 1917.[115]

---

113 Macdonagh, *Irish on the Somme*, p. 103.
114 Walter Wood (ed.), *In the Line of Battle: Soldiers' Stories of the War* (London: Chapman & Hall, 1916), p. 72.
115 Carrington wrote under the pseudonym Charles Edmonds, *A Subaltern's War* (London: Peter Davies, 1929), pp. 141, 181.

'I Saw a Ghost at Béthune'

At the Front in 1915, Lieutenant Robert Graves, 3rd Battalion, Royal Welch Fusiliers, was counting his lucky escapes. On 28 May in the chaotic trenches among the brick stacks at Cuinchy in the sector between Ypres and the Somme, he had met a rifle-grenade at close range. Landing about six feet away, it should have exploded and done him some damage, but against the odds it had landed the wrong way round and stuck in the wet clay 'looking at me'. Later in June, he was walking along a trench at Cambrin (near Cuinchy) when he suddenly threw himself flat on his face. 'Two seconds later,' he recalled, 'a whizz-bang struck the back of the trench exactly where I had been.' A sergeant who had been walking a few yards ahead came rushing back to ask, 'Are you killed, sir?' Graves reasoned that as the shell was fired from a German battery only a thousand yards off it must have landed before the sound of it being fired could be heard. 'How did I know that I should throw myself on my face?' he wondered.[116]

Not everyone was so lucky. Jenkins was introduced to Graves when he joined 'A' Company at the Front as 'one of those patriotic chaps who chucked up his job to come here'. Billeted in Vermelles in between trench duty, there was time for cricket and eating the ripe currants in abandoned gardens. Graves and Jenkins went to explore the ruins of the village's old Norman church. The remains of the bell tower were being used for artillery observation and it had eight unexploded shells lodged in it. The two men went inside where everything was either broken, smashed or ripped. Graves climbed on the altar to pull a large piece of broken stained glass from the east window.[117]

'Souvenir,' he said, handing it to Jenkins.

116 Robert Graves, *Good-Bye To All That* (London: Jonathan Cape, 1929), pp. 160–1.
117 Graves, *Good-Bye*, pp. 137, 158–9,

Jenkins held it up to the light and they could see that it was St Peter's hand clutching the keys to heaven. Graves thought it must be medieval. 'I'm sending this home,' Jenkins said.

On their way out they met two soldiers from the Royal Munster Fusiliers, Irish Catholics. One of them spoke to Jenkins: 'Shouldn't take that, sir, it will bring you no luck.' Graves recorded that 'Jenkins was killed not long after'.

Summer 1915 saw Graves in and out of the Cambrin and Cuinchy trenches, with rest periods billeted in Béthune or one of the surrounding villages, such as Vermelles. Although this sector of the line does not have the infamy of Ypres or the Somme, despite the fact that the Royal Munster Fusiliers had lost 11,000 men the month before, Graves reported that casualties were high. Pessimism crept into the men's bones along with the chill of the long night watches. Graves noted that 'pessimism made everyone superstitious'. Graves became pessimistic and superstitious, too: 'I found myself believing in signs of the most trivial nature.'

He came across instances of apparent presentiment as well. Sergeant Smith told Graves a story about his predecessor as platoon commander:

He was a nice gentleman, sir, but very wild. Just before the Rue du Bois show he says to me: 'By the way, sergeant, I'm going to get killed to-morrow. I know that. And I know that you're going to be all right. So see that my kit goes back to my people. You'll find their address in my pocket-book. You'll find five hundred francs there too. Now remember this, Sergeant Smith, you keep a hundred francs yourself and divide up the rest among the chaps left.' He says: 'Send my pocket-book back with my other stuff, Sergeant Smith, but for God's sake burn my diary. They mustn't see that. I'm going to get it *here*!' He points to his forehead. And that's how it was. He got it through the forehead all right. I sent the stuff back to his parents. I divided up the money and I burnt the diary.[118]

118 Graves, *Good-Bye*, p. 160.

One evening in late June, Graves and the other officers were having a special dinner in the 'C' Company billet to celebrate having made it though another tour of duty at Cuinchy. Graves recounted their menu with relish, including the 'three bottles of Pommard'. He looked up and saw Private Challoner, 1st Battalion, Royal Welch Fusiliers, at the window. Challoner saluted and walked on. 'There was no mistaking him,' said Graves, 'or the cap-badge he was wearing.' Graves knew that there was no Royal Welch Battalion within miles of Béthune. He jumped up and looked out of the window. There was no one there 'except a fag-end smoking on the pavement'. Graves also knew that Challoner had been killed at Festubert in May. Graves had known him from the regimental depot at Wrexham where they were in 'F' Company together and the Lancaster internment camp where both were sent on detachment duty. When he went out with a draft to join the 1st Battalion, he shook Graves's hand and said 'I'll meet you again in France, sir.' That was the last time he saw him alive. 'Ghosts,' he wrote, 'were numerous in France at the time.'[119]

The Man Who Could Stop the War

Alphonso Watters of Woolton Grove, Woolton, Lancashire, was a man with strong ideas about the war. He wrote article after article propounding his views on bringing an end to it. No one would publish them.[120]

No one that is, except Arthur Samuel Freeman. This Mr Freeman managed to arrange things, or appear to arrange things, that Watters's views found their public platform in the shape of Watters's *Woolton Magazine*.

---

119 Graves, *Good-Bye*, p. 161.
120 'Occult Indian "Prince"', *Daily Mail* (13 August 1915), p. 3; 'Prince with Occult Powers', *Cambria Daily Leader* (19 August 1915), p. 5.

The War Office objected to what was said in the *Woolton Magazine* and prosecuted the printers. The War Office won their case and the printers lost £150 in fines.

Freeman continued to call on Watters at his Woolton Grove mansion. They shared a common interest, for Freeman also knew someone who wanted to end the war and, what is more, claimed the power to be able to do so. There was an Indian prince living in Mayfair, London, who had influence in high places. But more than that he had 'pronounced spiritual power'. Watters should write to the prince, Freeman suggested; and so he did.

On 10 July, Watters received a telegram announcing that the prince was on his way to see him. A taxicab brought them up from a hotel in town and deposited the prince and his 'secretary' Daniel Bray on Watters's doorstep. Bray presented 'His Highness'. One can only hope that the prince was swathed in exotic fabrics. His accent, at least, must have sounded strange in the Lancashire air.

Watters discovered that the prince shared his interests in Spiritualism and fruitarianism. It was decided that they should establish a fruitarian restaurant in London. The prince would give lectures and lead a health campaign to promote the astounding benefits of eating a fruit-only diet.

Fruitarianism, some would argue, was the original diet of the human race because Adam and Eve only ate fruit. To return to paradise, we should give up meat, bread and dairy produce. Even vegetarianism is too barbaric because the plant must die, but the fruit (and nut) have evolved to be eaten as a means of seed dispersal. (Fruitarians are also allowed to eat nuts and seeds, so could also be called Nutters.) So Watters and the prince had their scheme of a fruitarian revolution to bring peace to humankind, overlooking the fact that, according to Christian tradition, a certain apple had caused all the trouble in the first place.

The prince was fortunately well connected. He had known King Edward. He knew King George and Kaiser Wilhelm. He would ask them to stop all the fighting.

The prince 'possessed extraordinary occult powers'. He was a psychologist and thought-reader, known amongst all intelligent people as Professor Akldar. Perhaps he gave Watters some demonstration.

But even with such connections, such powers, there was always the question of money. The fruitarian restaurant needed funding. Lord Rothschild, said the prince, had already agreed to give £1,000. All the prince wanted from Watters was a mere £500. He left with a cheque for £250.

Mr Watters may have wondered why the prince should seek him out when he was a regular chum of Kings and Lords. Perhaps he felt flattered. Perhaps he smelt a rat.

Old Mr Watters had a gardener, no doubt one particularly skilled in the cultivation of fruit. This Thomas Hayes was his only help about the place, since no one else lived with him and he kept no other servants. Hayes was going about his business when he saw the prince and his secretary leaving the house. 'They were rubbing their hands, M'Lord,' he later said, 'and seemed very satisfied.'

Doubts certainly entered Watters's mind. 'I understand that he wanted my money,' he said of the prince, 'and I did not believe the stories he was telling me.' And that was what he told the police.

Liverpool Police Court: Arthur Sam Freeman, Daniel Bray, Samuel Bray, and a certain Ludwig Kahn alias Professor Akldar, posing as an Indian prince, were in the dock charged with conspiracy. Now the sordid truth came out. The Indian prince was in reality a thirty-two-year-old German Jew, who specialised in predicting horse-racing winners and reading words on folded pieces of paper (so-called billet reading). He had learnt his art in America under the tutelage of the fraudulent medium Bert Reese around 1888. At some point he had joined the 'Independent Order Free Sons of Israel', a curious Jewish fraternal organisation in America, founded in New York in 1849. Based on Freemasonry, with rituals, regalia and secret passwords, it raised money for the Red Cross and the Jewish Welfare Board during the war.[121]

Kahn and his co-conspirators were found guilty of attempting to obtain money by false pretences. They were sentenced to two years'

---

121 Independent Order Free Sons of Israel, *World War Activities of the Independent Order Free Sons of Israel* (New York, 1919).

imprisonment, except Samuel Bray, who was sentenced to six months.[122]

Kahn continued to profess psychic powers after the war, although he tried to get rid of his other personas. Harry Price knew him for a 'billet reader', but others were calling him 'one of the most remarkable clairvoyant mediums at the present time'.[123] This undeserved reputation was based largely on experiments conducted by Eugene Osty and Charles Richet in Paris.[124]

He would usually gather some four to six people. He would give them sheets of paper and ask them to write something on it, then fold it in eight so that all should look the same, but only when he was out of the room. He would leave. The sitters would write and fold. He would return and ask one of the sitters to gather all of the folded papers, mix them up and redistribute them. Now, Kahn would go round the group, stating what was written on each piece of paper. The sitter would unfold it and, surprise, read out what Kahn had just said.

The German Dr Moll was not impressed by Osty and Richet. Examining their evidence he concluded that all of Kahn's effects could be produced through trickery. Moll also remembered him as the Professor Akyldar or Akldar whose adverts were carried around Regent Street, London, by sandwich-board-men in 1920.[125] Even today some people still entertain the possibility that Kahn may have had genuine powers as well as being an out-and-out charlatan.[126]

122 'A Bogus Indian Prince with Occult Powers', *The Times* (23 November 1915), p. 19.
123 Campbell Holms, *Fundamental Facts of Spiritualism*.
124 See Max Schottelius, 'Ein Hellseher', *Journal für Psychologie und Neurologie*, xx (1913), pp. 236–62; and for Osty and Richet, see Eugène Osty, 'Un homme doué de connaissance paranormale', *Revue Métapsychique* (1925), pp. 65–79, 132–43.
125 Moll, *Zeitschrift für Kritischen Okkultismus*, vol. 1, No. 3, reported in 'Notes on Periodicals', *JSPR* (June 1926), pp. 93–4.
126 Mary Rose Barrington, Ian Stevenson, Zofia Weaver, *A World in a Grain of Sand: The Clairvoyance of Stefan Ossowiecki* (Jefferson, NC: McFarland & Co., 2005) p. 154.

Return of the Living Dead Man

In 1913, Ella Wheeler Wilcox was living in London. She already knew Elsa Barker from Paris and was a great admirer of her work, in particular her poem 'When I Am Dead and Sister to the Dust'. Now, 'she spoke to me of a strange experience through which she was passing, and vaguely hinted that it was of a psychic nature'. Before Wilcox left Europe, Barker had confided that 'she was receiving messages from some disembodied intelligence'. Wilcox noted that 'she seemed profoundly impressed by her experience'. Before the war broke out, she would discover the truth of the mystery.[127]

It had started in 1912 when Barker was still living in Paris. 'I was strongly impelled to take up a pencil and write,' she later explained. She had no idea what she should write about, but picked up a pencil anyway: 'my hand was seized as if from the outside' and proceeded to write 'a remarkable message of a personal nature'. It was signed 'X'. The next day she showed the message to a friend and asked if she knew who 'X' was.

'Why,' she replied, 'don't you know that that is what we always call Mr—?'

She did not know. Furthermore the person identified was, as far as she knew, alive and well some six thousand miles away back in western USA. Some one or two days later, a letter arrived informing her that Mr— had died a few days before communicating with her.

The identity of her communicant was later revealed: in an interview for the *New York Sunday World* in 1914, Bruce Hatch said he was convinced that 'X' was his late father Judge David P. Hatch (1846–1912), formerly of Los Angeles. As well as having served on the Los Angeles Supreme Court, Hatch had also written *Scientific Occultism*.

127 Wilcox, *The Worlds and I*, p. 169.

Barker continued to call him 'X', but she printed the identification in the second volume of her received communications.[128]

Now Barker was back in New York. On 4 February 1915, she felt the presence of 'X' and her pencil began to move:

> When I come back and tell you the story of this war, as seen from the other side, you will know more than all the Chancelleries of the nations.[129]

The first of his war messages was delivered on 5 March 1915. 'X' conveyed the, by now, usual occult interpretation of the war: that it was some sort of battle for spiritual evolution – 'a new race has to be born' were his words; that it was a war between good and evil. The letters are all in much the same vein: a great deal of pontificating and nothing in the way of fact. Some of the statements were morally repellent. For example, 'X' blamed the fate of the Belgians (the imagined 'Rape of Belgium' that the propagandists had cooked up) on their behaviour in the Congo: 'race karma', 'X' called it. 'X' not only demonised the Germans, but demonised their victims to make it all seem acceptable in some greater scheme of things.

Barker would argue otherwise and drew attention to what she called 'The *Lusitania* letter'. Barker claimed to have received it one hour after the ship was sunk and fully nine hours before she knew of it. There was no mention of the *Lusitania*, or even of a ship being sunk, however. The closest 'X' got was 'They seek now to embroil the United States'; and perhaps 'the trial by water, the trial by air, the trial by fire', if one ignores the other trials and draws undue attention to the mention of water. The letters ended on 28 July 1915.[130]

The great French psychical researcher, Charles Richet, was not impressed. Of her books he said, 'These show the same vague and

---

128 Elsa Barker, *War Letters from the Living Dead Man* (New York: Mitchell Kennerley, 1915), pp. 1–2; David P. Hatch, *Scientific Occultism: A Hypothetical Basis of Life* (Los Angeles: Baumgardt, 1905).
129 Barker, *War Letters*, p. 2.
130 Barker, *War Letters*, pp. 283, 284.

well-meaning idealism as most other writings of the kind', concluding that 'There is nothing, absolutely nothing, to show the presence of any intelligence other than that of the automatist', and, hence, were of 'but slight scientific interest'.[131]

German Black Magic

The Germans are proving their weakness by reviving in modern Hamburg and in over-civilised Berlin an ancient rite of savagery. Firm in the faith that they are owing (or will owe) their victory to the twin deities – the Submarine and von Hindenburg – they have set up vast images of wood of 'the conqueror of the *Lusitania*' and the hero of Russia, into which all who are willing to pay for the privilege are invited to drive nails. It is a barbarous and ill-omened rite, and it is difficult to see how an act of violent worship is likely to benefit either the wooden deities or the German Empire.[132]

Not only, then, was it barbarous, but also ineffective. The writer really was having his cake and eating it; yet still he wanted more:

Many precedents may be found for this last act of German ferocity, and not one of them is designed to bring solace to the Kaiser's arrogant subjects. The savage tribes which are accustomed to drive tenpenny nails into their idols do it in no spirit of reverence. It is the anger of disappointment, not the spirit of worship, which strengthens their arms. It is when their prayers are unanswered, when their ardent desires are unfulfilled, that they attack their Joss with hammer and nails. Is this, then, the interpretation that we must put upon the ecstatic action of the Germans?

131 Richet, *Thirty Years of Psychical Research*, pp. 80, 286.
132 'Tenpenny Nails', *Daily Mail* (11 September 1915), p. 4.

So, not only was it barbarous and ineffective, but also a sign of disappointment. The only reasonable response to this is to ask whether it was written by the War Propaganda Bureau or MI7. It is possible that such was taking place: rituals of this sort still take place today. On a visit to the Christian pilgrimage site of Conques in France in 2016, I came across a block of wood into which pilgrims or anyone else could hammer tacks for the price of a small donation. The children found it to be immense fun. The religious institution that runs Conques would be alarmed to hear the practice described as black magic.

Interestingly, in 1917 a certain Mr Rose wrote to *The Times* complaining that 'the Church is apparently doing nothing to help in getting good crops by means of prayer.'[133] Priests up and down the land were praying for victory, of course, and there seems little distinction between that, good crops and tenpenny nails.

The Faunus Message

Miss Robbins had gone to see a medium. She was now sitting in her parlour in Greenfield, New Hampshire. Mrs Leonora Piper had already built up a considerable reputation for spirit communication – William James had studied her and could not rule out that her messages were genuine. However, since her return to America in October 1911, her powers of trance mediumship had faded; indeed, one of her spirits, 'Imperator', informed her that her mediumship had been suspended. There were still some communications received through automatic writing – often intended for Sir Oliver Lodge – but otherwise Mrs Piper seemed to all the world to be in retirement.[134]

A recent automatic writing message (of 5 August 1915) had been addressed to Lodge:

133 John Watson, 'Prayers for the Crops', *Daily Mail* (13 March 1917), p. 4.
134 Lodge, *Raymond*, pp. 91–5; Alta L. Piper, *The Life and Work of Mrs Piper* (London: Kegan Paul, Trench, Trubner & Co., 1929).

For the moment, Lodge, have faith and wisdom [and confidence?] in all that is highest and best. Have you all not been profoundly guided and cared for? Can you answer 'no'? It is by your faith that all is well and has been.

At the time it seemed cryptic. At the time it seemed innocent.

Miss Robbins knew Mrs Piper – she had been one of her earliest sitters – and was, therefore, somewhat surprised to be sitting before the medium. Mrs Piper had received an automatic writing message from the 'Rector' instructing her daughter Alta to invite Miss Robbins to the house for 'a meeting "as of old"' on Sunday, 8 August 1915. Were her powers about to return? Expectations were running high.

The renowned Mrs Piper went once more into a deep sleep-like trance and an old member of the SPR, Richard Hodgson, whom she had known in life and who had so often talked through her in death, returned to speak once again.

Hodgson greeted Miss Robbins and gave her some advice on her forthcoming trip to California.

'Now Lodge,' Hodgson abruptly changed the subject, 'while we are not here as of old, i.e., not quite, we are here enough to give and take messages. Myers says you take the part of the poet, and he will act as Faunus'; Then once more with emphasis, 'FAUNUS'.

Miss Robbins was puzzled, 'Faunus?'

'Yes,' said Hodgson, 'Myers. *Protect*. He will understand.'

Alta made a note that Hodgson was evidently referring to Sir Oliver Lodge.

Hodgson continued, 'What have you to say, Lodge? Good work. Ask Verrall, she will also understand. Arthur says so.'

Poor Miss Robbins was still rather puzzled, 'Do you mean Arthur Tennyson?'

'No,' replied Hodgson, 'Myers knows. So does [name withheld]. You got mixed [addressing Miss Robbins], but Myers is straight about Poet and Faunus.'

Alta sent the cryptic automatic writing message and séance transcript on to Sir Oliver, but it took almost a month to reach him. Sir

Oliver was holidaying with his wife in Scotland at the time, getting some golf practice at Gullane, a popular seaside town on the east coast.

Sir Oliver knew, of course, that the 'Arthur' referred to was former SPR member Arthur Verrall, now deceased. He wrote to his widow Margaret Verrall in Cambridge. 'Does The Poet and Faunus mean anything to you?' he asked. 'Did one "protect" the other?'

'The reference,' replied Verrall, 'is to Horace's account of his narrow escape from death, from a falling tree, which he ascribed to the intervention of Faunus.' She quoted one of Horace's Odes:

Me the curst trunk, that smote my skull,
Had slain; but Faunus, strong to shield
The friends of Mercury, check'd the blow
In mid descent [. . .][135]

The friends of Mercury (*Mercurialium*), were generally interpreted as being poets. Sir Oliver took it to mean that some blow would fall, but that Myers would be able to protect him from it. His first thoughts were that some financial catastrophe was in the offing.

Sir Oliver wrote to Alta to thank her. 'The reference to the Poet and Faunus,' he began, 'in your mother's last script is quite intelligible, and a good classical allusion. You might tell the "communicator" some time if there is opportunity.

'I feel sure,' he continued, 'that it must convey nothing to you and yours. That is quite as it should be, as you know, for evidential reasons.'

From this we can infer that Sir Oliver thought that it *was* evidential. It had been a coded message that, among the SPR inner circle, the classical scholar Mrs Verrall could best decode. His letter to her on 'The Linga Private Hotel' headed notepaper was dated 12 September. As he

135 Horace, Ode II, Poem 17, here quoted from *The Odes and Carmen Saeculare of Horace*, trans. John Conington (London: George Bell and Sons, 1882). This was one of the translations used by Sir Oliver at the time.

waited for the blow to fall, the letter returned to him on 14 November, sent back by the Dead Letter Office.

Preparation for the Attack

'Great happenings are expected here shortly,' wrote Raymond in early September, 'and we are going to have our share.' The Autumn Offensive was about to begin.[136]

The Autumn Offensive was a full-out attempt to break the German lines using Allied numerical superiority. The French would attack in the Artois region towards Givenchy and Vimy (the Third Battle of Artois) and in the Champagne east of Rheims (the Second Battle of Champagne). The British would attack at Loos (Loos-en-Gohelle), immediately north of the French push in the Artois, with diversionary attacks at Ypres. Raymond would be the diversion.

September started wet and muddy: 'the rain was incessant, and presently I found the floor of my dug-out was swimming'. Raymond slept in wet clothes and worked in wet clothes, sometimes in water a foot deep.

Out of the trenches again, Raymond and Captain Taylor rode into Poperinghe (due west of Ypres) for a meal: 'I had a really good dinner there – great fun.' A cake had arrived from home and more cigarettes – Virginias this time. He wrote back asking if they could send *The Motor* or *The Autocar* magazines.

Raymond was still with 'C' Company. Captain Taylor fell off his horse one night and sprained his ankle. He was sent to the rear to rest, likely to be gone a month. Raymond was now commanding 'C' Company.

The Army V Corps Commander, Lieutenant General Sir Herbert Plumer, called by to inspect the troops. The fifty-eight-year-old was a

136 Lodge, *Raymond*, pp. 35–6, 71–80. Second Battalion, South Lancashire Regiment, war diary, National Archives, WO 95/1414/1.

veteran of the Mahdist, Matabele and Boer Wars – he had been at the Siege of Mafeking. It had been Eton, Sandhurst and straight into the infantry. He was Army through and through. Raymond called his company to attention and went round with Plummer.

'How long have you had the Company?' he asked.

'Three days, sir.' The answer must have raised an eyebrow.

'And how long have you been out?'

'Since March, sir.'

'Have you been sick or wounded?'

'No, sir.'

Raymond imagined that he might reply, 'Good lad for sticking it!' But he did not. Raymond did not record his actual words.

On 12 September, Raymond wrote a hurried note to say that he was taking 'C' Company back to the front line. Motorbuses would collect them at 5 p.m. – he was thrilled at the thought. They were going back to Hooge in the Ypres salient.

'During September,' wrote 2nd Lt William Roscoe, Raymond's friend from the Machine-Gun School, 'times grew worse and worse up in the Ypres salient, culminating in the attack we made on the 25th, auxiliary to the Loos battle. The trenches were ruins, there was endless work building them up at night, generally to be wrecked again the next day. The place was the target for every gun for miles on either side of the salient.

'Every day our guns gave the enemy a severe bombardment, in preparation for the attack, and every third or fourth day we took it back from them with interest: the place was at all times a shell trap.'

Roscoe remembered Raymond's cheerfulness one particular night as he took 'C' Company forward for 'a particularly unpleasant bit of trench digging in front of our lines' out by the old château stables, 'a mass of ruins and broken trenches where no one could tell you where you might run across the enemy'.

Tuesday 14 September was a dull, warm day. The Germans had been shelling the front line throughout the night, and although disrupting supplies had only succeeded in wounding two men. 'During the morning,' reads the 2nd Battalion war diary, 'information was received that our guns were to shell the enemy's trenches immediately in front of those held by "C" Company.' The distance between the opposing lines was not great and the order was given to pull 'C' Company back to a safer distance. Ventris and Raymond got the men out of the front firing trenches and down a communication trench, staying behind to make sure that everyone was safely out of the forward positions. 'But their movement must have been seen by the enemy,' continued the diary, 'as hostile shrapnel fire was at once directed on to the trench.'

Lord Kitchener Expresses His Sympathy

In Scotland, Sir Oliver was having a poor day on the Gullane Links. A special game had been arranged for the morning of 15 September by Roland Waterhouse and Sir Oliver had been looking forward to it. 'I was in an exceptional state of depression,' he wrote. 'I could not play a bit. Not ordinary bad play, but total incompetence, so much so that after seven holes we gave up the game, and returned to the hotel.' He made special note of it; afterwards it would seem more meaningful.

With enemy shrapnel exploding all around them, Raymond's servant, Private Gray, was hit and went down. A piece of shrapnel had struck him on the head. Raymond bent over him and could see that he was still alive, but in a bad way. He went farther down the trench to instruct the sergeant major to arrange assistance. German artillery continued to pound their position. Ventris was hit and killed outright. A piece of shrapnel caught Raymond on the left side of his back.

Lieutenant Case from 'A' Company, 2nd Battalion, rushed over to Raymond when he heard the news. He found him, still conscious, lying in a dug-out. Raymond recognised him and asked some questions. Case went to get a doctor, but the telephone wires had been cut by the bombardment. The stretcher-bearers did all they could, but that was not much. When Roscoe got to him, Raymond's eyes were closed and his breathing difficult.

In the early morning of 17 September, Raymond's brother Alec – staying in a hotel near Swansea – woke from what was described as 'an extraordinarily painful and vivid dream', apparently 'quite an exceptional occurrence for him', according to Sir Oliver. It was the worst dream Alec had had in his whole life. It had not been about anyone in particular and seemed to have no significance. He wrote it down, nonetheless.[137]

Still at Gullane, Sir Oliver received a telegram from the War Office, dated 17 September. Was this the blow? He hastily scanned the lines:

Deeply regret to inform you that Second Lieut. R. Lodge, Second South Lancs, was wounded 14 Sept. and has since died. Lord Kitchener expresses his sympathy.

'Death is Not the End'

Raymond was buried next to Ventris in the garden of a ruined farmhouse. A simple wooden cross in the shade of some tall trees marked his final resting place. The garden was full of simple wooden crosses. Nothing grew here any more, the farmer had long gone; only Death remained to plant the South Lancashires in neat rows.

Of the others who remained, not all survived. Gray also died of wounds that fateful day. Case was killed shortly after on 25 September. Fletcher recovered his nerves sufficiently to return to active duty and was killed on 3 July 1916.

They had taken unnecessary risks, there was no doubt about it. Reckless behaviour demonstrated their insouciance. It was part of being an officer in the British Army. Raymond had even written about it to Thomas's mother after her son had been killed:

137 Unfortunately, Alec's dream has not been published and the whereabouts of his record are unknown.

Humphrey was splendid always when shells were bursting near. He hated them as much as any of us, but he just made himself appear unconcerned in order to put heart into the troops.[138]

On one particular occasion the Germans had been bombarding them for the best part of an hour, putting 'every sort of shell over us and some came very close'. Raymond looked up to see Thomas, 'a lone figure walking calmly about as if nothing was going on at all. It may have been foolish but it was grand.'

Fletcher said much the same about Raymond when writing to his mother: 'heaps of times I've had to tell him to keep down when he was watching the men working'. Roscoe remembered his 'cheerfulness' when sent out on dangerous work.

Captain A. B. Chieves of the Royal Army Medical Corps wrote to the Lodges to tell them where their son was buried and give what other information he could. 'There was no chance of saving his life,' he wrote, 'and this was recognised by all, including your son himself.' Afterwards, when his body was brought down, Chieves had noted that 'the expression on his face was absolutely peaceful', adding, 'I should think that he probably did not suffer a great deal of pain.'

Raymond is now interred at Birr Cross Roads Cemetery, Zillebeke, near Ypres in Belgium. His grave lies on the right-hand side, still next to his friend and comrade Alan Ventris. The inscription reads 'Raymond who has helped many to know that death is not the end'.[139]

For Sir Oliver various pieces of a still incomplete jigsaw puzzle fell into place: Alec's dream, Hodgson's message, his own uncharacteristic attack of depression. He also consulted Revd Bayfield about the meaning of Faunus. Bayfield was of the opinion that Horace had not been spared being struck by the tree, but that the blow had been lightened. Sir Oliver was keen to accept this interpretation as more nearly fitting

138 Lodge, *Raymond*, p. 50.
139 Plot reference II.D.5.

the facts of the case: he had not been spared Raymond's death, but Myers would make it easier for him. But was it enough to be any sort of consolation?

Raymond Returns

Katherine Kennedy was sitting in her garden on 21 September, writing about something quite ordinary and uninteresting. Suddenly it seemed as if someone else were controlling her hand and words that were not her own were written across the page:[140]

'I am here . . . I have seen that boy, Sir Oliver's son; he's better, and has had a splendid rest, tell his people.'

Kennedy was not surprised. After learning of Raymond's death, she had asked her son Paul about it. Paul was also dead.

Paul had died before the war. He had been injured in an accident and died eight weeks later on 23 June 1914. On 25 June he started to communicate:

'(Without my asking for it or having thought of it) I felt obliged to hold a pencil,' explained Mrs Kennedy, 'and I received in automatic writing his name and "yes" and "no" in answer to questions.' She wrote to Sir Oliver about it because of his widely known interest in psychical research and Sir Oliver took her to see the medium Mrs Wriedt: 'and there she received strong and unmistakable proofs', or so he claimed. Kennedy went on to see other mediums, including Vout Peters and Gladys Osborne Leonard.

It was through Kennedy that Lady Lodge arranged to see Mrs Leonard. She wanted to take a French woman, Madame Le Breton, a widow who had lost both of her sons in the war – Madame Le Breton had 'been kind to our daughters during winters in Paris', explained Sir Oliver, and was at that moment staying with Lady Lodge at Edgbaston. Using Kennedy as an intermediary meant that she could withhold their

140 Lodge, *Raymond*, pp. 49–50, 75, 96–125.

names from the medium to hinder any less than paranormal detective work.

Even as Lady Lodge was visiting Kennedy to make these arrangements, Kennedy's hand started writing a message:

'I am here, mother . . . I have been to Alec already, but he can't hear me. I do wish he would believe that we are here safe; it isn't a dismal hole like people think, it is a place where there is life.'

The next day, 24 September, Lady Lodge, Madame Le Breton and Mrs Kennedy were sitting before Gladys Leonard. At thirty-three, Leonard was already an established medium, but now she was about to become famous. Leonard had only met Kennedy before and, as far as they were aware, did not know the identities of the other sitters. Lady Lodge made notes: 'Mrs Leonard went into a sort of trance, I suppose,' she observed, 'and came back as a little Indian girl called "Freda", or "Feda", rubbing her hands, and talking in the silly way they do.' 'Feda' was Leonard's 'spirit control', although even Leonard herself wondered if it might not be some other part of her personality.

Leonard or 'Feda' had messages for Kennedy and the Madame, but, as Feda explained, there were many others standing beside the three women:

Then Feda described some one brought in lying down – about twenty-four or twenty-five, not yet able to sit up; the features she described might quite well have belonged to Raymond. [. . .] Feda soon said she saw a large R beside this young man, then an A, then she got a long letter with a tail, which she could not make out, then she drew an M in the air, but forgot to mention it, and she said an O came next, and she said there was another O with a long stroke to it, and finally, she said she heard 'Yaymond' (which is only her way of pronouncing it). Then she said that he just seemed to open his eyes and smile; and then he had a choking feeling, which distressed me very much; but he said he hadn't suffered much – not nearly as much as I should think; whether he said this, or Paul, I forget; but Paul asked me not to tell him to-morrow night that I was not with him, as he had so much the feeling that I was with him when he died, that he (Paul) wouldn't like to undeceive him.

I then asked that some one in that other world might kiss him for me, and a lady, whom they described in a way which was just like my mother, came and kissed him, and said she was taking care of him. And there was also an old gentleman, full white beard, etc. (evidently my stepfather, but Feda said with a moustache, which was a mistake), with W. up beside him, also taking care; said he had met Raymond, and he was looking after him, and lots of others too; but said he [W.] belonged to me and to 'O.' I asked how and what it was he had done for me, and Feda made a movement with her fingers, as though disentangling something, and then putting it into straight lines. He then said he had made things easier for me. So I said that was right, and thanked him gratefully. I said also that if Raymond was in his and Mamma's hands, I was satisfied.[141]

The three ladies returned the next day, with Dr Kennedy in tow to take notes. This time it would be a table sitting, as Sir Oliver explained: 'The three ladies and the medium sat round a small table, with their hands lightly on it, and it tilted in the usual way.' Each letter of the alphabet would be called out and the table would tip until it came to the one intended. By this means simple messages could be laboriously spelt out. Although the sitting was mainly for Madame Le Breton's benefit, they managed to make contact with 'Raymond' again.

'Are you lonely?' (Sir Oliver's transcript does not indicate who asked the questions, but from the following 'conversation' we may conclude that it was Lady Lodge, as one might expect.)

'No,' said Raymond.

'Who is with you?'

'Grandfather W.'

'Have you anything to say to me?'

'You know,' answered Raymond, 'I can't help missing you, but I am learning to be happy.'

141 Lodge, *Raymond*, p. 121.

'Have you any messages for any of them?'

'Tell them I have many good friends.'

'Can you tell me the name of anyone at home?'

'Honor.' This was the name of one of Raymond's sisters.

'Is there anything you want to send?'

'Tell father I have met some friends of his.'

'Any name?'

'Yes, Myers.'

Myers was there, like a prophecy fulfilled. Lady Lodge would have known of the Faunus message. It was surely this that compelled Sir Oliver to visit Leonard for himself. But during the sitting Madame Le Breton had mentioned Lady Lodge by name; uncertainty would now seep through that crack in her anonymity.

Sir Oliver's Séance

Just before noon on 27 September 1915, Sir Oliver rang Mrs Leonard's doorbell. He was alone. He gave no name. But Lodge was a public figure; most especially, Lodge was well known in Spiritualist circles. He had been a president of the Society for Psychical Research from 1901 to 1903 (and would be again in 1932), and had published *The Proofs of Life After Death* in 1902 and *The Survival of Man* in 1909, ending the book with 'In Memory of Myers', so his regard for Myers was also public property. Raymond's death had also been reported in the newspapers.[142]

In the parlour, Mrs Leonard went into a trance. Soon, a little girl's voice was heard. It was 'Feda':

---

142 Lodge, *Raymond*, pp. 125–8. Some conversation reconstructed. Raymond Lodge's death was announced in several newspapers, e.g., the first was 'Sir Oliver Lodge's Son Killed', *Birmingham Mail* (18 September 1915), and the most visible was the *Daily Mirror* (21 September 1915); and his photograph was printed in the *Sheffield Daily Telegraph* (21 September 1915).

There is some one here with a little difficulty, not fully built up; youngish looking; form more like an outline; he has not completely learnt how to build up as yet. Is a young man, rather above the medium height; rather well-built, not thick-set or heavy, but well-built. He holds himself up well. He has not been over long. His hair is between colours. He is not easy to describe, because he is not building himself up so solid as some do. He has greyish eyes; hair brown, short at the sides; a fine-shaped head; eyebrows also brown, not much arched; nice-shaped nose, fairly straight, broader at the nostrils a little; a nice-shaped mouth, a good-sized mouth it is, but it does not look large because he holds the lips nicely together; chin not heavy, face oval. He is not built up quite clearly, but it feels as if Feda knew him. He must have been here waiting for you. Now he looks at Feda and smiles; now he laughs, he is having a joke with Feda, and Paulie laughs too. Paul says he has been here before, and that Paul brought him. But Feda sees many hundreds of people, but they tell me this one has been brought quite lately. Yes, I have seen him before. Feda remembers a letter with him too. R, that is to do with him.[143]

Feda muttered, as if to herself, 'Try and give me another letter.' There was a pause before she continued. 'It is a funny name, not Robert or Richard. He is not giving the rest of it, but says R again; it is from him. He wants to know where his mother is; he is looking for her; he does not understand why she is not here.'

'Tell him he will see her this afternoon,' said Sir Oliver, 'and that she is not here this morning, because she wants to meet him this afternoon at three o'clock.' Lady Lodge had an appointment to see another medium that afternoon, but Sir Oliver gave no more details away.

'He has been to see you before,' continued Feda, 'and he says that once he thought you knew he was there, and that two or three times he was not quite sure. Feda gets it mostly by impression; it is not always

143 Lodge, *Raymond*, p. 126.

what he says, but what she gets; but Feda says "he says", because she gets it from him somehow. He finds it difficult, he says, but he has got so many kind friends helping him. He didn't think when he waked up first that he was going to be happy, but now he is, and he says he is going to be happier. He knows that as soon as he is a little more ready, he has got a great deal of work to do. "I almost wonder," he says, "shall I be fit and able to do it. They tell me I shall."'

Feda was not finished: 'He seems to know what the work is. The first work he will have to do, will be helping at the Front; not the wounded so much, but helping those who are passing over in the war. He knows that when they pass on and wake up, they still feel a certain fear.' Feda's link with 'R' seemed to waver. She missed a word and went on in a more general vein.

Even in the afterlife, the war went on, as Feda explained: 'Some even go on fighting; at least they want to; they don't believe they have passed on. So that many are wanted where he is now, to explain to them and help them, and soothe them. They do not know where they are, nor why they are there.'

Sir Oliver was beginning to get impatient. He thought that this was just the usual 'Feda talk' and much the same as that which could be heard from other mediums at that moment in time. 'Though the statements are likely enough,' he wrote, 'there is nothing new in them.' He decided to interrupt the garrulous spirit with a question:

'Does he want to send a message to anyone at home? Or will he give the name of one of his instructors?' He immediately regretted asking two questions at once.

'He shows me a capital H,' said Feda, 'and says that is not an instructor, it is some one he knows on the earth side. He wants them to be sure that he is all right and happy. He says, "People think I say I am happy in order to make them happier, but I don't."'

What must Sir Oliver have thought about this vague and ultimately useless answer?

Feda continued: 'Now the first gentleman with the letter W is going over to him and putting his arm round his shoulder, and he is putting his arm round the gentleman's back. Feda feels like a string round her head; a tight feeling in the head, and also an empty sort of feeling in the chest, empty, as if sort of something gone. A feeling like a sort of vacant feeling there; also a bursting sensation in the head. But he does not know he is giving this. He has not done it on purpose, they have tried to make him forget all that, but Feda gets it from him. There is a noise with it too, an awful noise and a rushing noise.

'He has lost all that now, but he does not seem to know why Feda feels it now. "I feel splendid," he says, "I feel splendid! But I was worried at first. I was worried, for I was wanting to make it clear to those left behind that I was all right, and that they were not to worry about me."

'You may think it strange, but he felt that you would not worry so much as some one else; two others, two ladies, Feda thinks. You would know, he says, but two ladies would worry and be uncertain; but now he believes they know more.'

The medium came out of her trance. Feda had returned to wherever she came from and it was Mrs Leonard once again who sat in her chair.

'Mrs Leonard,' began Sir Oliver, 'do you know who I am?'

'Are you by chance connected with those two ladies who came on Saturday night?'

'Yes,' Sir Oliver nodded.

'Oh! Then I know, because the French lady gave the name away, she said "Lady Lodge" in the middle of a French sentence.'

Sir Oliver's attempt at anonymity had been blown. It threw everything the medium had said into doubt. But Sir Oliver was more concerned that Mrs Leonard might be overstraining herself by holding too many séances a day.

'I prefer not to have more than two or three a day,' said Mrs Leonard, 'though sometimes I cannot avoid it; and some days I have to take a complete rest.'

'Three per day is rather much,' said Sir Oliver.

'There are so many people who want help now,' she explained, 'I feel bound to help those who are distressed by the war.'

Sir Oliver was keen to report all of this, because he felt that the sheer volume of people she saw added weight to the information given to a member of his family who was new and unknown to her, that is, his wife during the first sitting before Madame Le Breton had given the game away and, as he himself admitted, a lot of what Feda had said was just 'ordinary "Feda talk"', such as she might say to all and sundry.

Moonstone

Sir Oliver's sitting with Mrs Leonard had finished at one o'clock. At three o'clock Lady Lodge was waiting to begin another séance – not with the overworked Mrs Leonard, but with Alfred Vout Peters. She was in the home of Mrs Kennedy when the doorbell rang. The forty-eight-year-old medium entered.[144] Arnold Bennett thought him 'short [. . .] quick and nervous' – although bald on top he still had dark hair at the sides and Bennett conceded that he had a good forehead; small round glasses made him look bookish, but his pointed beard added an aristocratic touch, even if Bennett elitistly added that he was the 'son of a barge-owner' (Bennett was the son of a solicitor).[145]

Peters lived in Westgate-on-Sea, but kept a room at 15 Devereux Court, Fleet Street, in London, for seeing clients. Sir Oliver thought him to be 'a man who takes his mediumship seriously', leading a 'simple life altogether', which was apparently arranged around his spiritual practice, at least Sir Oliver interpreted the fact that he went 'into the country at intervals, and stops all work for a time' as measures intended to allow him to gather his powers.

At 3.30 p.m., Mrs Kennedy began taking notes. As Peters fell under the control of his spirit 'Moonstone', he remarked 'I feel a lot of force here, Mrs Kennedy.' The spirit greeted Mrs Kennedy and reminded her of his Dvinsk prophecy – apparently some great battle of the war would be fought there. Dvinsk was then a city in Russia; now it is known as

144 Lodge, *Raymond*, pp. 129–32, 136, 162–3, 174–5, with additional details from A. F. Pollard, *A Short History of the Great War* (London: Methuen & Co., 1920), ch. X.
145 Bennett's description dates from 1917, quoted in Newman Flower (ed.), *Journals of Arnold Bennett* (London: Cassell and Co.,1932), p. 185.

Daugavpils in Latvia. After Russia's great retreat in 1915, it became part of the Eastern Front and notably withheld massed German assaults on 25 September and 2 October. It was said at the time that the failure to take Dvinsk had cost the Germans 'more than all the greater fortresses they had captured'. Moonstone was evidently pointing out a successful 'hit'.

Now Peters/Moonstone turned to Lady Lodge:

'What a useful life you have led, and will lead. You have always been the prop of things. You have always been associated with men a lot. You are the mother and house prop. You are not unacquainted with Spiritualism. You have been associated with it more or less for some time.'

So far Moonstone's remarks had seemed more like fishing for responses than making factual statements. Now, he started tentatively to explore a more specific path.

'I sense you as living away from London – in the North or North-West. You are much associated with men, and you are the house prop – the mother. You have no word in the language that quite gives it – there are always four walls, but something more is needed – you are the house prop. You have had a tremendous lot of sadness recently, from a death that has come suddenly. You never thought it was to be like this.'

Even Mrs Kennedy seemed to be bored by this and added in parentheses: 'Peters went on talking glibly, and there was no need for the sitter to say anything.' But the tone was to pick up.

'There is a gentleman here who is on the other side – he went very suddenly. Fairly tall, rather broad, upright' (here the medium sat up very straight and squared his shoulders) – 'rather long face, fairly long nose, lips full, moustache, nice teeth, quick and active, strong sense of humour – he could always laugh, keen sense of affection.'

Raymond had a longish face and nose, but no moustache.

'He went over into the spirit world very quickly,' continued Moonstone. 'There is no idea of death because it was so sudden, with no illness. Do you know anything connected with the letter L?'

The ladies gave no answer.

'What I am going to say now is from Paul – he says: "Tell mother it is not one L, it is double L." He says: "Tell mother she always loved a riddle" – he laughs.'

Both Lady Lodge and Mrs Kennedy said that they did not understand the reference, although secretly they both took 'L.L.' to mean Lady Lodge.

'Moonstone' continued: 'They don't want to make it too easy for you, and funnily enough, the easier it seems to you sometimes the more difficult it seems to them. This man is a soldier – an officer. He went over where it is warm.'

It *was* warmer in Flanders, but would anyone describe it like that? Several newspaper reports of Raymond's death had mistakenly located it in the Dardanelles.

'You are his mother, aren't you – and he does not call you ma, or mamma, or mater – just mother, mother.'

Lady Lodge knew this to be true, but whether she said or not is not recorded.

'He knew of Spiritualism before he passed over, but he was a little bit sceptical – he had an attitude of carefulness about it. He tells me to tell you this: the attitude of Mr Stead and some of those people turned him aside; on one side there was too much credulity – on the other side too much piffling at trifles.

'He holds up in his hand a little heap of olives, as a symbol for you – then he laughs. Now he says – for a test – associated with the olives is the word Rowland. All of this is to give you proof that he is here.

'Before you came you were very down in the dumps. Was he ill three weeks after he was hurt?'

'More like three hours,' added Sir Oliver later, 'probably less.'

Moonstone made repeated guesses as to what the number three could mean, before asking Lady Lodge directly:

'I see the figure 3 so plainly – can't you find a meaning for it?'

'The 3rd Battalion?' suggested Lady Lodge – Raymond had technically been in the 3rd Battalion whilst training and attached to the 2nd Battalion at the Front.

'He says "Yes,"' continued Moonstone, 'and wasn't he officially put down on another one?

'He says: "Don't forget to tell father all this."'

Moonstone made several comments in relation to photographs of 'this boy'. At the time, they seemed off the mark, but the Lodges later discovered several photographs that they believed fitted Moonstone's descriptions and took these comments as evidential.

'When he was younger, he was very strongly associated with football and outdoor sports. You have in your house prizes that he won, I can't tell you what.'

Sir Oliver noted later that this was a miss. He thought that there was 'possibly some confusion in record here; or else wrong'.

'Why should I get two words – "Small" and "Heath"?'

Sir Oliver later remembered that Raymond had had some, but not very close, association with a place called Small Heath near Birmingham.

'Also I see, but very dimly as in a mist, the letters B I R.'

Lady Lodge may have thought of Birmingham.

'You heard of either his death or of his being hurt by telegram. He didn't die at once. He had three wounds. I don't think you have got details yet.

'Was he not associated with chemistry? If not, some one associated with him was, because I see all the things in a chemical laboratory. That chemistry thing takes me away from him to a man in the flesh.

'And connected with him a man, a writer of poetry, on our side, closely connected with Spiritualism. He was very clever – he too passed away out of England. He has communicated several times. This gentleman who wrote poetry – I see the letter M – he is helping your son to communicate.'

M for Myers: Lady Lodge's recognition must have flashed upon her face, even if only momentarily.

'At the back of the gentleman beginning with M and who wrote poetry is a whole group of people. They are very interested. And don't be surprised if you get messages from them, even if you don't know them.'

Lady Lodge would have thought of the SPR's Upstairs Committee, all those deceased grandees eager to communicate now that all doubt had passed.

'This is so important that is going to be said now, that I want to go slowly, for you to write clearly every word.' Moonstone started to dictate carefully:

'Not only is the partition so thin that you can hear the operators on the other side, but a big hole has been made.

'This message is for the gentleman associated with the chemical laboratory.

'The boy – I call them all boys, because I was over a hundred when I lived here and they are all boys to me – he says, he is here, but he says: "Hitherto it has been a thing of the head, now I am come over it is a thing of the heart. What is more ..." Peters/Moonstone suddenly jumped up in his chair, snapped his fingers in excitement, and went on speaking more loudly:

'Good God! How father will be able to speak out! Much firmer than he has ever done, because it will touch our hearts.'

Lady Lodge also became excited: 'Does he want his father to speak out?'

'Yes, but not yet – wait, the evidence will be given in such a way that it cannot be contradicted, and his name is big enough to sweep all stupid opposition on one side.

'I was not conscious of much suffering, and I am glad that I settled my affairs before I went.'

Lady Lodge knew that Raymond had done so. Before leaving for the Front, he had made a will and put his affairs in order.

'Have you a sister of his with you, and one on our side? A little child almost, so little that you never associated her with him. There are two sisters, one on each side of him, one in the dark and one in the light.'

With a pang in her heart, Lady Lodge thought of her last child, Laura: she had died only a few minutes after being born. That had made Raymond their youngest surviving child: his sister Violet had been born before him. 'Raymond,' as Sir Oliver later explained, 'was the only boy sandwiched in between two sisters.' They would have understood 'one in the light' to mean one who had died, and 'one in the dark' to mean one still living.

'Your girl is standing on one side, Paul on the other, and your boy in the centre.' Peters/Moonstone put his arm round Mrs Kennedy's shoulder – in ordinary circumstances this would have been unheard of. 'Now he stoops over you and kisses you there,' said Moonstone indicating the forehead.

'Before he went away he came home for a little while. Didn't he come for three days?'

Mrs Kennedy noted that 'there is a little unimportant confusion' about the matter of 'days'. There followed more confusion about an attempt to describe the interiors of three of the Lodges' previous homes. Sir Oliver later edited this part out as being 'hardly worthwhile' – already he was selecting the evidence, treating mistakes as 'some confusion in the record' and brushing them aside.

Moonstone continued: 'And he wanted me to tell you of a kiss on the forehead.'

'He did not kiss me on the forehead when he said good-bye,' said Lady Lodge.

'Well, he is taller than you, isn't he?'

'Yes,' said Lady Lodge.

'Not very demonstrative before strangers. But when alone with you, like a little boy again.'

'I don't think he was undemonstrative before strangers,' said Lady Lodge.

'Oh yes,' replied Moonstone, 'all you English are like that. You lock up your affection, and you sometimes lose the key.'

Moonstone decided to change the subject. 'He laughs. He says you didn't understand about Rowland. He can get it through now, it's a Rowland for your Oliver.'

Sir Oliver later thought that this was 'excellent'. As he explained, 'By recent marriages the family has gained a Rowland (son-in-law) and lost (so to speak) an Oliver (son).'

'He is going,' said Moonstone. 'He gives his love to all.

'It has been easy for him to come for two reasons: first, because you came to get help for Madame; secondly, because he had the knowledge in this life.'

'I hope it has been a pleasure to him to come,' said Lady Lodge: she must have been wondering if she had mentioned Madame Le Breton to

Peters; she was sure she had not. Sir Oliver explained it later: 'it is a simple cross-correspondence,' meaning that it was an evidential comment because it was shared between two unconnected sittings.

'Not a pleasure, a joy,' said Moonstone.

'I hope he will come to me again,' said Lady Lodge.

'As much as he can. Paul now wants to speak to his mother.'

'A Lovely Night for Zeppelins!'

'I feel that there will be a Zep. raid to-night or to-morrow at 9.45 p.m. V. Pownall. Oct. 12.' Vera Pownall had written the note on the back of a bill from Selfridge's whilst in her flat in London at about 7.15 p.m. on the evening of 12 October. She then rather forgot about it.[146]

The next evening Miss Cyrille Bayfield – the daughter of SPR stalwart, Revd Bayfield, then staying with her – and Mr J. Knox were dining with her at her flat. Vera felt distracted.

Cyrille noticed her uncharacteristic behaviour. 'What is the matter with you? I never knew you so vague!'

'I feel something is going to happen,' said Vera.

'What?' asked Cyrille.

'I do not know,' said Vera. 'I did not think of Zeppelins,' she wrote afterwards.

'To whom?' asked Cyrille.

'To all of us.'

'When?'

'Oh, soon.' Vera apologised for being so vague and they all laughed about it.

146 Revd M. A. Bayfield, 'Recent Cases of Premonition and Telepathy', *JSPR* (January–February 1916), pp. 137–8. Original papers, including the Selfridge's bill, are in the SPR Archive, Cambridge University Library, SPR.MS/Journal Vol. XVII 1915–1916.

Getting ready to go out to the theatre after dinner, Cyrille was still probing for answers. 'Is it going to happen to you or me?' she asked.

'Oh no; we are all in it,' replied Vera.

'Is it something awful?' asked Cyrille.

'No,' said Vera.

It was a clear, still night as they made their way to the theatre.

'What a lovely night for Zeppelins!' exclaimed Cyrille.

They were sitting in the theatre when they heard the first bomb explode.

Suddenly Vera remembered. 'I wrote that down yesterday and put it in my dressing-table drawer.'

She looked at her watch. It read 9.40. However, she noted that her watch loses five minutes every day – she would set it each morning at 9.30 using the clock of the Great Central Hotel, which she could see from her flat window.

When they got back to her flat, Vera showed Cyrille the note.

Family Gatherings

Despite, or possible because of, Sir Oliver's interest in mediumship, the rest of the family were rather sceptical: 'It may be thought,' he wrote, 'that my own known interest in the subject was naturally shared by the family, but that is not so. So far as I can judge, it had rather the opposite effect; and not until they had received unmistakable proof, devised largely by themselves, was this healthy scepticism ultimately broken down.'[147]

Sir Oliver already believed in life after death when he started looking for Raymond after Ypres; even then, the communications had seemed to seek out the Lodges rather than the other way round. For the rest of the family, their experiences, indeed their conversion, is particularly interesting.

147 Lodge, *Raymond*, pp. 164–70, 180–7.

Lady Lodge had had her first sitting in 1889 with the celebrated Mrs Piper, yet it would not be until '1906 or thereabouts', according to Sir Oliver, that she changed her mind, having had 'some extraordinarily good evidence'. The rest of the family 'neither read my nor anyone else's books on the subject'.

Raymond, when still alive, had written to one of his sisters (just called 'Mrs Rowland Waterhouse' by Sir Oliver) during the winter of 1905–1906. Raymond was still at Bedales School; his sister was in Paris, no doubt making the acquaintance of Madame Le Breton. 'I should like to hear more about table turning,' he had written, adding, 'I don't believe in it.' He knew some girls who had told him that they had tried it at Steephurst (presumably another school) and 'attribute it to some sense of which we know nothing'. Raymond thought that, if real, this power could be put to good use 'driving a dynamo or something'.

Despite their natural scepticism, the family would, in due course, be won round to the side of Spiritualism. They cannot all have been as disinterested as Sir Oliver makes out, since there had already been some private sittings at the family home at Mariemont that have gone unpublished. Sir Oliver perhaps plays up, even if unintentionally, their scepticism in order to make their conversion all the more convincing.

Raymond's brother Alec was the first to visit one of the professional mediums. On 23 October 1915, he went with his mother, Lady Lodge, to Mrs Kennedy's and there met Vout Peters.

It was a Saturday and they arrived at Mrs Kennedy's at five minutes to eleven in the morning. Little time was spent on pleasantries: five minutes later the séance began. They shook hands with Vout Peters and sat down in Mrs Kennedy's private room – the one generally reserved for séances. The blinds had been pulled down, but the midmorning daylight fought its way in. Street noises from below broke the silence. The medium took up the ladies' hands, holding first Mrs Kennedy's, then Lady Lodge's. He shifted in his seat, rubbed his face, rubbed his eyes. Suddenly, he sat upright as though having received a shock and began speaking quickly in broken English. Moonstone had arrived.

'Good morning! I generally say, "Good evening," don't I? Don't be afraid for Medie; he has been prepared since six o'clock this morning. Magnetism has to be stored up, and therefore it is best to use the same room and the same furniture every time.'

The first 'spirit' to arrive was that of Lady Lodge's mother.

'She has been with you and comforted you through this trial,' said Moonstone. 'She has been, and will go on, looking after the boy.'

Moonstone turned to Alec and pointed at him: 'She is related to *him*. She puts her hand on his shoulder. She is very proud of what he is doing at the present time. He has been a great help to you. Since the passing away of him who is loved by you both, he has looked on Spiritualism with much more respect, because previously it has not touched his heart. It is not only a thing of the head, it is now a thing of the heart.

'She put her finger on her lips and says: "I am so proud of O.!"' Moonstone also put his finger to his lips.

Moonstone's next pronouncement was oddly prophetic.

'It has always been what I thought: the triumph (?) has been a long time coming, but it will come greater than had been anticipated. There have been difficulties. I am glad of success. It will come greater than before. The book that is to be will be written from the heart, and not the head. But the book will not be written now.' Moonstone repeated loudly, 'Not now! Not now! Not now!' before returning to a normal tone of voice. 'Written later on. The Book which is going to help many and convert many. The work done already is big. But what is coming is bigger.'

We know that 'O.' – presumably Sir Oliver – would write a book – *Raymond* – and that it would be influential. At this early stage, with little in the way of mediumistic 'evidence', it is unlikely that Sir Oliver had yet conceived of writing a book about Raymond.

Alec was taking notes during the sitting, but at one point the medium reached across and grabbed his hand so that he could not continue writing. A new spirit control – 'Redfeather' – had taken over the trance. Peters was stretched out across the small table they were sitting round, both of his arms reaching across to grasp Alec. He spoke as though choked with emotion, sobbing and shaking, face flushed. Alec thought that the medium's voice was 'extraordinarily like Raymond's' and that even Peters' grasp on his hand was 'a grasp just like Raymond's'.

After a time, Peters released his grip, the high emotional intensity relaxed. Alec began making notes again, but for him this had been the 'central part of the sitting'.

Another control – an old washerwoman called 'Biddy' – took over Peters. He again seized Alec, taking hold of both of his hands, speaking all the while. When the sitting ended, Peters came out of the trance, seemingly struggling to breathe. He said that he had been very deeply under and returning to normal consciousness was like 'coming to after an anaesthetic'. It must have been an intense experience for the sitters. Sir Oliver made a brief note, saying 'It was evidently difficult to get over for the rest of the day.'

Lionel was the next of Raymond's brothers to try and communicate with him, sitting with Mrs Leonard on 17 November 2015. Alec also sat with Mrs Leonard in December.

Lionel went alone and unintroduced. Even the letter he had sent to arrange the sitting had been delivered to Leonard's old address in Warwick Avenue and had not been redirected. Lionel also sent himself to the wrong address, but at least *he* was redirected. When he turned up at her new address, she did not know who he was and had not been expecting him.

Luckily, Leonard was free. Inside she drew down the blind and lit a red lamp. She explained the process, that she was controlled by an entity called Feda, and in about two minutes had gone into trance.

'Good morning!' said Feda in her chirpy, childish way. 'Why, you are psychic yourself!'

'I didn't know I was,' said Lionel, unimpressed.

'It will come out later,' decided Feda. 'There are two spirits standing by you; the elder is fully built up, but the younger is not clear yet. The elder is on the tall side, and well built; he has a beard round his chin, but no moustache.' Feda repeated this several times as if puzzled by it. 'A beard round chin, and hair at the sides, but upper lip shaved. A good forehead, eyebrows heavy and rather straight – not arched – eyes grey-ish; hair thin on top, and grey at the sides. [. . .] Letter W is held up.'

It was Grandfather W. whom Lady Lodge had already met at her first séance with Mrs Leonard; and whom Lady Lodge and Sir Oliver had subsequently encountered during a table sitting with Leonard on 28 September. Sir Oliver reproduced a photograph of him: we see a typical Victorian, black suit, froth of grey-white hair orbiting his face – and no moustache.

'There is another spirit,' continued Feda. 'Somebody is laughing.' Feda's voice dropped to a whisper and she seemed to talk to someone else, 'Don't joke – it is serious.'

'It's a young man, about twenty-three, or might be twenty-five, judg-ing by appearance. Tall, well built; not stout, well built; brown hair, short at the sides and back; clean shaven; face more oval than round; nose not quite straight, rather rounded, and broader at the nostrils.'

Lionel must have brought a picture of Raymond to his mind: tallish, he supposed; thin rather than well built; long face, not really oval; clean shaven, yes; long nose, a bit squint, a bit broader at the nostrils perhaps; she had not mentioned the ears, everyone noticed the ears. Was it Raymond?

Feda's voice dropped to a whisper again: 'Feda can't see his face.'

She spoke loudly, 'He won't let Feda see his face; he is laughing.

'L, L, L,' she whispered, before saying loudly, 'L. This is not his name; he puts it by you.'

Lionel could only draw one conclusion, but why only the initial and not the whole name?

'Feda knows him,' she whispered to herself again, 'Raymond.' Then loudly, 'Oh, it's Raymond!' Feda hopped up and down in her chair, hands in a delighted fidget.

'That is why he would not show his face, because Feda would know him,' she continued. 'He is patting you on the shoulder hard. You can't feel it, but he thinks he is hitting you hard.'

Lionel remembered the way Raymond would pat his brothers on the shoulder, gently at first, then getting harder until the other had to beat him off.

'He has been trying to come to you at home,' said Feda, 'but there has been some horrible mix-ups; not really horrible, but a muddle.'

There *had* been an attempt to contact Raymond at home and when Lionel told him later, Sir Oliver thought that this reference 'shows specific knowledge' and was another 'cross-correspondence'.

'Do you remember a sitting at home when you told me you had a lot to tell me?' asked Lionel.

'Yes,' said Feda, 'What he principally wanted to say was about the place he is in. He could not *spell* it all out – too laborious. He felt rather upset at first. You do not feel so real as people do where he is, and walls appear transparent to him now. The great thing that made him reconciled to his new surroundings was – that things appear so solid and substantial. The first idea upon waking up was, I suppose, of what they call "passing over". It was only for a second or two, as you count time, [that it seemed to be a] shadowy vague place, everything vapoury and vague. He had that feeling about it.'

Feda spoke more carefully, as though it were more difficult to get the facts right: 'The first person to meet him was Grandfather. And others then, some of whom he had only heard about. They all appeared to be so solid, that he could scarcely believe that he had passed over.'

'He lives in a house – a house built of bricks – and there are trees and flowers, and the ground is solid. And if you kneel down in the mud, apparently you get your clothes soiled.' Then Feda appeared to speak directly as Raymond: 'The thing I don't understand yet is that the night doesn't follow the day here, as it did on the earth plane.' Feda explained that 'it seems to get dark sometimes, when he would like it to be dark, but the time in between light and dark is not always the same. I don't know if you think all this is a bore.'

Lionel had been busy writing everything down. He had just used up the first of his pencils and had started on the other, and was distracted by wondering if it would be enough to last the sitting.

'What I am worrying round about,' Feda/Raymond continued, 'is how it's made, of what it is composed. I have not found out yet, but I've got a theory. It is not an original idea of my own; I was helped to it by words let drop here and there. People who think everything is created by thought are wrong. I thought that for a little time, that one's thoughts formed the buildings and the flowers and trees and solid ground; but there is more than that.'

The communication switched back to Feda: 'He says something of this sort: there is something always rising from the earth plane – something chemical in form. As it rises to ours, it goes through various changes and solidifies on our plane,' but appeared to become Raymond again, 'Of course I am only speaking of where I am now.'

To Lionel it must have seemed in character: the practical-minded Raymond, who would have turned table-turning into electricity, was now trying to work out how his new world was made. In later séances he would make a more thorough description of the 'after life'.

At 1.30 p.m. the sitting was over. Lionel tumbled back out into London's streets. Had he been convinced? From her responses, Lady Lodge really did seem to think that she had been able to talk to her son through Moonstone. The séances continued until 26 May 1916, with a total of twenty-four sittings of the Lodge family with various mediums (mostly Leonard) published by Sir Oliver in his 1916 book *Raymond, or Life and Death*.

The Authenticity of Angels

Despite the death of cousin Christopher at L'Épinette in 1914, the war had its advantages for Helen. She had been assisting Dr William Brown, head of the Department of Psychology at King's College, London. When he received a commission in the Royal Army Medical Corps, the resulting hole in the syllabus gave Helen the opportunity to teach. During the Lent Term, 1915, she gave a course of lectures on psychical research to third-year students. It was noted in the *Journal* that this was quite probably the first time that such a course had been taught in a university. Her mother privately remarked 'these young psychologists are just the people we want to catch'.[148] Now, she was about to undertake the biggest case of her career.

It was not just her biggest case, it would be the SPR's biggest wartime case, too. Although events reputedly occurred at or following the Battle of Mons on 23 August 1914, speculation about the Angels reached its height in 1915. An appeal for information was posted in the July 1915 edition of the *Journal* and 'the correspondence which resulted [. . .] was voluminous'. The Secretary, Isabel Newton, did most of the work, answering letters and following up leads; Assistant Research Officer Helen Verrall sifted through what was left over.

Despite the popularity of the angels, perhaps even because of it, there was a certain tone to the request for further evidence of the 'Alleged Visions on the Battlefield' that appeared in the July edition of the *Journal*. It was unsigned, so we may attribute it to Alice Johnson, then Honorary Editor as well as Research Officer. She argued that 'practically all these accounts are identical' and that 'it thus appears that the account was repeated and circulated on purely hearsay evidence'. This was hardly the basis for an objective enquiry and may, indeed, have prejudiced it.

To make matters worse, before Helen's investigations were completed, it was reported that a dim, if not derogatory, view was taken of the subject by certain members of the SPR. Several were said to have 'laughed jeeringly' at Professor Gilbert Murray's humorous mention of angels during his presidential address on 9 July 1915.[149]

On 28 September 1915, Helen married William Henry Salter (1880–1969); her strange friend, Aelfrida Tillyard, was a bridesmaid. Salter was, in the words of Helen's mother, 'an old friend whom we have known since he was a Classical scholar at Trinity'; he had been a pupil

148 'Report', *JSPR*, 17 (February 1915), p. 25; Cambridge University Library, SPR.MS35/2703, Verrall to Lodge, 24 December 1914.
149 Cambridge University Library, SPR.MS/Journal Vol. XVII 1915–1916, Clement Ord to Isabel Newton, 13 August 1915.

of Helen's father.[150] After their marriage, he would heed Lord Kitchener's cry of 'Your Country Needs You!', but was deemed unfit for active service: he would spend the war doing legal work in the Ministry of Munitions.[151]

Helen's mother was by then battling the illness that eventually claimed her in 1916. Helen had already lost her father in 1912. She and her husband had rooms in London, but towards the end of 1915 spent increasing amounts of time visiting her mother in Cambridge.

Whilst this was going on, a public battle over the Angels was carried out between the writer Arthur Machen, who claimed to have invented them in the pages of the London *Evening News*, and Harold Begbie – a member of the SPR, incidentally – who claimed to have more than enough evidence to prove otherwise in *On the Side of the Angels*. Ralph Shirley, the editor of *The Occult Review*, weighed in with a pamphlet of his own, *The Angel Warriors at Mons*, showing the proof for angelic interference. Helen disagreed with all of them. She concluded that it was possible that some men had seen something, but as the result of fatigue rather than divine intervention.

Mrs Salter Investigates

Helen analysed eleven accounts of the 'angels' from ten separate sources, most of them already published elsewhere.[152] One of them came from Private Robert Cleaver, subsequently proven, as Helen was aware, not to have been at Mons nor on the retreat; another, from Phyllis Campbell, was merely glossed, no names, no pack drill; and one attributed to 'Miss R.' was merely inserted as an example of third-hand hearsay with precious little in the way of detail. Of the rest, three

150 Cambridge University Library, SPR.MS 35/2710, Verrall to Lodge, 25 August 1915.
151 C. D. Broad, 'Obituary: Mr W. H. Salter', *JSPR*, 45 (March 1970), p. 204.
152 In contrast, Harold Begbie mustered thirty accounts for *On the Side of the Angels* (London: Hodder and Stoughton, 1915).

specified the Battle of Mons itself, five the retreat afterwards. Four named 'angels', in the plural, another mentioned angel-like figures with 'outspread wings' and 'loose-hanging garment of golden tint'; two mentioned riders; and one simply 'some bright pulsating light'. So we see some variation in the accounts and none of them mentioned St George or ghostly bowmen as in Machen's story; the majority pointed to the arduous retreat from Mons rather than the battle itself, again in contrast to Machen. She followed up on several of these cases, writing to Phyllis Campbell for example, but most often received no reply, or, at the least, a not very helpful one.

As already argued in the July notice, Helen had found that many of the stories could be traced back to one source, not Arthur Machen as he claimed, but an article, 'The Angelic Guard at Mons', that had appeared in *The All Saints' Clifton Parish Magazine* for May 1915 (and reprinted in July). It concerned a 'Miss M.', daughter of the well-known 'Canon M.', who had heard the story from two unnamed officers she knew: 'Both of whom had themselves seen the angels who saved our left wing from the Germans, when they came right upon them during the retreat from Mons.'[153]

In the SPR Archives there is a small sheet of paper folded once in two and written on three sides marked 'Copy' and 'Angels Seen'. This appears to be a copy of the original subsequently published in *The All Saints'*, the points of difference between it and the 'Angelic Guard' story merely showing the work of the editor.[154]

The story begins as if the officers had shared the same experience of the Germans being 'dazed' and unable to attack, allowing the British to escape, but as the narrative develops it seems that each officer had a different version to relate. The first officer – 'one of Miss M.'s friends' – 'saw a troop of Angels between us and the enemy and has been a changed man ever since'. He seems to be the one connected to the 'dazed'

153 Mrs W. H. Salter (H. de G. Verrall), 'An Enquiry Concerning "The Angels at Mons"', *JSPR* (December 1915), p. 107. The SPR Archives contain a hand-written copy of this story, entitled 'Angels Seen'.
154 There is another in the same hand, but more hurried, with the title 'A Vision of St George'.

Germans. The other officer – whom 'she met in London last week' – 'saw between them and the enemy a whole troop of Angels' and gave a much more detailed account of pursuing cavalry being routed by the angels, allowing the British to, again, escape to a nearby 'fort, or whatever it was'. A final note in square brackets states 'During the retreat to the Marne'.[155]

Helen did not print Miss M.'s full name, but letters in the SPR Archives show that she was a certain Miss Marrable; with less compunction, Ralph Shirley, editor of the *Occult Review*, published her full name of Sarah Marrable in the July 1915 issue. When Helen wrote to her, she stated that she did not know the officers involved, nor did she know their names.[156] Helen concluded that Marrable's accounts were 'no more than rumours'.[157]

What Helen considered to be her strongest piece of evidence was a letter that Arthur Machen had received from an unnamed 'lieutenant-colonel at the Front':

> As I rode along I became conscious of the fact that, in the fields on both sides of the road along which we were marching, I could see a very large body of horsemen. These horsemen had the appearance of squadrons of cavalry, and they seemed to be riding across fields and going in the same direction as we were going, and keeping level with us.[158]

The lieutenant colonel claimed that 'many men in our column' also saw them, but that when they investigated 'found no one there'. Events were dated to 27 August 1914 during the night-march after the battle of Le Cateau, which was fought by the BEF during the 'great retirement' from Mons.

155 Quotations from 'Angels Seen'.
156 Marrable to Salter, 28 May 1915, as referred to in the published article; however, no copy was found in the files in the SPR Archives.
157 Salter, 'An Enquiry', p. 108.
158 Machen published this in the *Evening News* (14 September 1914).

Helen compared this with a letter from Lance Corporal A. Johnstone,[159] also published in the *Evening News*. Again the sighting was of 'large bodies of cavalry, all formed up into squadrons'; again, several people apparently saw it. As the soldiers approached 'the horsemen vanished and gave place to banks of white mist'. The location was again on the retreat, this time at Langy, outside Paris.[160]

These appeared to be honestly reported experiences. Both were quite different from Machen's story: both involved horsemen; both took place during the retreat; both occurred at night. Crucially, neither appearance of the horsemen was as a saving intercession during battle. Both accounts noted the general exhaustion of the witnesses.

Helen had her explanation – hallucination caused by fatigue – but was there more to her 'enquiry' than that? From the many letters referred to in the article, the article itself seemed like only the tip of the iceberg of a much more detailed investigation. The game was afoot.

Secrets in the Archive

There is no collection of Helen's papers in the SPR's Archives at Cambridge University Library. Here and there, her name appears in the collections of other people, but upon inspection none of them bears upon the case of the Angels of Mons. There is nothing to be found in the most likely subject collections, either. After some days of fruitless searching, it looked like there was nothing to be found at all. It was only the knowledge and insight of the late archivist Peter Meadows (d. 2015) that led me to an uncatalogued box marked SPR.MS/Journal Vol. XVII 1915–1916.

159 The only match I could find was Andrew Johnstone described as a 'Driver Royal Engineers Special Cable Sect. Date of Death 16/12/1916 Service No 17459', no rank recorded ('Machy Churchyard Somme France)', http://www. inmemories.com/Cemeteries/machy.htm, accessed 7 October 2015), but in Helen's 1915 article he is already called 'late' by which one supposes deceased.
160 *Evening News* (11 August 1915).

At the bottom of the box was an old brown envelope marked 'Letters and papers relating to "An Enquiry Concerning 'The Angel at Mons'" '. Inside were letters, press cuttings and some printed matter. The precise outlines of rust stains from paper clips on some of the letters told me that no one had gone through all of these pages since they were bundled up a hundred years ago. In seeing the marks of real people – their handwriting, their signatures, even some grubby fingerprints on the back of one letter – the immediacy of the investigation was brought to me with a jolt.[161]

The contents of the envelope were not ordered by date or by correspondent, but in a rather more haphazard way. In the order retrieved: (A) loose correspondence from Clement Ord; (B) a bundle of letters fastened with a stud at the corner from Clement Ord with enclosures from other correspondents; (C) a newspaper clipping, 'Strange Battlefield Visions', from the *Weekly Dispatch* (no date); (D) a copy of *The All Saints' Clifton Parish Magazine*, vol. XXVII, no. 4 (July 1915); and (E) another bundle fastened with a paperclip from various correspondents with further press cuttings.

The extant correspondence on the enquiry runs from May 1915 to February 1916. Several of the letters referred to in the article have not been preserved, nor have the many enquiries also referred to. One thing the files revealed immediately was the larger role that the then secretary Isabel Newton had played in conducting the actual investigation, writing to people for more information and so on. Alice Johnson, Research Officer, was also involved, as was Shirley Thatcher, Hon. Secretary, although their roles appear to have been minimal.

In addition, Helen had disguised her sources. Pseudonyms were used, or names omitted altogether, sometimes at the correspondent's request, sometimes because permission had not been sought. This was no secret, but, until now, no one has uncovered their identities.

One such previously unnamed correspondent was Clement Ord (1858–1939), the editor of the *All Saints' Clifton Parish Magazine*. He

161 The SPR Archives, Cambridge University Library, SPR.MS/Journal Vol. XVII 1915–1916.

was to prove particularly helpful. Ord was a Cambridge man, taking a BA (1884) and MA (1888) at King's College, and went on to become a lecturer in German at University College, Bristol. At the time that he wrote to Newton, he was head of the department there. His son Rudolf was already in the thick of the fighting; he would suffer twenty-six separate injuries at the Third Battle of Ypres in 1917 and spend the remainder of the war (and some time after it) in hospital.[162] Another son, Bernhard (inexplicably known as 'Boris'), would join the Artists Rifles in 1916 before taking to the skies with the Royal Flying Corps – he, too, would survive the war and go on to become the organist of King's College; the fame of the choir today owes much to his efforts.[163]

As well as twice publishing the story itself – in the May and July issues of 1915 – Ord also printed a notice that further information should be sent to the SPR. One of those who responded to Ord's call was Charles H. Malcomb of Leamington. Writing to the Society in a neat copperplate on 2 July 1915, he said:

> Members of my family have a great friend in Mr Wells, Vicar of Sefton near Liverpool, he preached a sermon which was heard by my brother in law Captain Murray who tells me that Mr Wells stated that he had seen letters from two different officers for whose bona fides he would pledge himself, describing the appearance of the Angel Guard in very much the same terms as it was described in the All Saints Magazine.[164]

Surely, here was something worth following up. A reply was sent asking for first-hand testimony – Malcomb referred to it in his next letter – but

162 *Despatch* [The Western Front Association, Lancashire North Branch], Issue 8 (November 2011), pp. 11–14.
163 National Archives, http://discovery.nationalarchives.gov.uk/details/ rd/80b86b7a-1f8c-4732-bae7-bdee56595ceb, accessed 8 October 2015; 'The Papers of Bernhard ('Boris') Ord', http://janus.lib.cam.ac.uk/db/node.xsp?id= EAD%2FGBR%2F0272%2FPP%2FBO, accessed 8 October 2015.
164 Cambridge University Library, SPR.MS/Journal Vol. XVII 1915–1916, Malcomb, 2 July 1915.

instead of pursuing this line Malcomb recommended that the Society follow-up the story of 'Miss M.' instead. He must have done something, however, as there is also a brief note from Mr Wells on 'Sefton Rectory' headed paper, saying that 'if I can send you any useful information I will do so'. It is the only letter from Mr Wells. Helen chose not to publish the account in her report.

Ord himself received correspondence on the subject that he was happy to forward. On 13 July 1915, he wrote to Newton, saying that he was enclosing a letter that he claimed contained 'direct testimony'. This was what Helen had been waiting for, or at least that is what one would assume.

Unfortunately, the Ord correspondence is somewhat disorganised. In a group of letters fastened together (group B), Ord referred to a total of four enclosed items: two letters, a 'note' and the 'direct testimony'. On 6 July 1915 he referred to two enclosed letters 'which are also not positive in any way'. On 9 July he referred to an enclosed note. On 13 July he referred to an enclosed letter containing the 'direct testimony'. What we find in the bundle approximating to these references is a letter from Mrs Casman to Ord, dated 11 June 1915; a letter from Harold Gibson to Ord, 22 June 1915; and a letter from L. [?]aroche to Ord , 7 July 1915.[165]

Only three items are preserved. It is not clear which letter he meant and the order in which the letters are arranged does not illuminate this, either. Indeed, the letter itself may not be among those preserved; certainly, none of them appears to contain 'direct testimony', if by that we are to understand 'first-hand'.

The earliest of these is a letter from Mrs Casman of Brenchley, Kent. Dated 11 June 1915, the essential part reads:

A diary of a young man who has been killed, has been sent to his mother, a lady at Tunbridge Wells, and it contains several

---

165 The name of [?]aroche seems to be quite clearly written as 'J Saroche', but this makes no sense. The letter is in a very untidy hand, but not otherwise difficult to decipher. There is no mention of the name in Ord's correspondence.

references to similar experiences, as those referred to in your magazine.[166]

Mrs Casman does not say where she got this information or whether she personally knew any of the people involved. There is no indication in the files as to whether this was followed up or not. A note in red ink in the top left corner reads '2 copies', possibly referring to the two copies of the parish magazine referred to elsewhere in the letter. In any event, Helen did not refer to it in her report.

The letter from Gibson possibly refers to some query made by Ord: 'I heard of the case you mention of the "Angel Guard" but the man is not here now. He was not a parishioner he was only stationed here for a time.' And that is all there is to it.

The final extant letter is from L. [?]aroche of Tunbridge Wells. Again it seems to be a reply to an enquiry by Ord and the writer states 'With regard to the name of the man who told his Sister about the Angelic Guard at Mons, my friend would not give up his name, she heard it from his Sister, that is all I know.' Given the nearness of the dates, this is probably the 'note' referred to by Ord on 9 July.

When Ord wrote again on 13 July, his excitement was palpable: 'I am enclosing a letter I have just received which may open up some new clue. This is the first direct testimony I have had of the apparition [. . .] Can all this be explained in Mr Machen's offhand way?' Ord had high hopes for this document. It is simply a mystery that it is not there when much else has been so carefully gathered together and preserved.

Luckily, however, correspondence on the subject did not end there. The SPR received another letter, bringing the possibility of first-hand testimony again within their reach.

166 Cambridge University Library, SPR.MS/Journal Vol. XVII 1915–1916, Casman to Ord, 11 June 1915.

What the General Saw

In July 1915 the Society for Psychical Research put out an appeal for further information concerning 'Alleged Visions on the Battlefield'. The Society received few replies, but among them was an important statement that had, until I found it in the SPR Archives in Cambridge, remained unpublished and unknown for a hundred years.[167]

Writing to the Society's Research Officer and Hon. Editor, Alice Johnson, a certain L. E. Cotesworth told the following story:

> I saw the article about the 'Phantom Army' in the Magazine and as I am an associate I thought I would write and tell you that a cousin of mine who is [three words, illeg.] has a cousin, Brig. Gen. Prowse who is said to have seen these much talked of figures. She was told by a mutual cousin who had it from Gen. Prowse's wife. Of course this is indirect, but supposing you cared to write to Mrs Prowse, I can get her address though I don't know if that [illeg.] was in the '[illeg.]' then very near the German lines and it seems he said he saw a host of figures between his line and the Germans. – I felt angry with Dean Hensley Henson who in a sermon in [two words, illeg.] on Sunday denounced the stories as absurd superstition and the result of a [illeg.] which but [crossed out] no doubt many of them do come to that. But he should not pronounce judgement before the matter has been thoroughly investigated.[168]

The letter was forwarded to Johnson, care of a Miss or Mrs Berry. Strangely, Johnson wrote to Shirley Thatcher, the Society's Honorary

---

167 Leo Ruickbie, 'An Unpublished Account', *Paranormal Review*, 76 (Autumn 2015).
168 Cambridge University Library, SPR.MS/Journal Vol. XVII 1915–1916, Cotesworth to Johnson, 27 July 1915.

Secretary, and asked her to reply on her behalf, saying all of the things that she could have said herself:

> I think Miss Newton will not be at the Rooms tomorrow, so will you write to this person (I don't know if it is Mr, Mrs or Miss) saying that you are writing for me, as I am away – I think the best thing would be to ask her to write to Mrs Prowse, asking if it would be possible to get a first-hand account from General Prowse of what he saw for the SPR explaining that no names would be mentioned without permission. Of course thank her for the letter, and indicate that only first-hand accounts are of value to us.[169]

And there the trail runs cold. The SPR Archives contain no further letters on the subject. If Johnson had cared to check the Society's membership records, she would have seen that Cotesworth was a 'Miss', full name: Lilias E. Cotesworth of 45 Westminster Mansions, Great Smith Street, London.[170]

On the face of it, the story is of the typical friend-of-a-friend type, only this time it is the wife of a cousin of a cousin. Even worse, the story is introduced with hesitation: 'it seems he said'. But we have a name: we have so few names in connection with these stories and here we have, not just a name, but an identifiable person: Brigadier General Prowse.

Charles Bertram 'Bertie' Prowse was born in West Monkton, Taunton, Somerset, in June of 1869. He was schooled at Cornish's School, Clevedon, and Marlborough. He joined the Militia and from there went into regular service with the Somerset Light Infantry. He went with his regiment to South Africa and fought in the Second Boer War (1899–1902), being appointed adjutant.[171]

169 Cambridge University Library, SPR.MS/Journal Vol. XVII 1915–1916, Johnson to Thatcher, 30 July 1915.
170 'Members and Associates', *Proc. SPR*, vol. XXVI (1914–1915), p. 517
171 Frank Davies and Graham Maddocks, *Bloody Red Tabs: General Officer Casualties of the Great War 1914–1918* (Barnsley: Pen & Sword, 2014), unpaginated digital edition.

On the outbreak of the First World War, he was a major in the 1st Battalion, the Somerset Light Infantry. His regiment formed part of the 11th Brigade of the 4th Division of the British Expeditionary Force and was in the thick of it almost from the beginning.

The 4th Division detrained at Le Cateau on 25 August, about 33 miles (53 km) south of Mons, and took part in the fierce fighting there on 26 August. As at Mons, the odds were too great and the BEF was forced to retreat further. They had at least won some time, pulling out whilst they observed the enemy artillery continuing its bombardment of their abandoned positions.

Prowse would now lead his men on a gruelling, desperate march as the BEF tried to escape. First they crossed the Somme, then the Aisne, then the Marne before halting and turning to face the Germans once more for the First Battle of the Marne on 5 September 1914. Since the Battle of Mons on 23 August, the soldiers had marched nearly 200 miles (320 km); Prowse and the 4th Division a little less.

We next catch sight of Prowse in the military record when he was awarded the Distinguished Service Medal at the First Battle of Ypres. The 4th Division were spread along an eight-mile front between the Douve stream and Armentières. The Germans had been concentrating their offensive against the Ypres salient, but on 30 October 1914 also moved against Ploegsteert Wood. Part of the line was overrun, but Major Prowse led his company of the 1st Battalion, the Somerset Light Infantry, in a counter-attack and retook the position. 'God bless them,' said General Hunter-Weston, 'They have restored the situation.' The spot was named Prowse Point.[172]

On 1 July 1916, his unit was in the fray at the Somme. Before the battle, Prowse put on his best uniform complete with white dress gloves.[173] Captain G. A. Prideaux, writing in the regimental history, states 'At about 9.45 a.m. the General decided to move his H.Q. into

172 Andrew Rawson, *British Expeditionary Force: The 1914 Campaign* (Barnsley: Pen and Sword, 2014), p. 196.
173 Anthony Seldon and David Walsh, *Public Schools and the Great War: The Generation Lost* (Barnsley: Pen and Sword, 2013), p. 57.

the German front line, thinking that it was cleared of all the Germans. Just as he was getting out of our front line trench, near "Brett Street", he was shot in the back by a machine gun in the "Ridge Redoubt".' Lt G. A. Robinson, MC, also recorded 'Brigadier-General Prowse gave me orders to open the brigade ammunition dug-out that had been blown in. Immediately afterwards he was mortally wounded while assembling men of the Seaforth Highlanders in our front-line trench. Brigadier-General Prowse showed great gallantry in his efforts, ignoring the great breaches in our parapet exposing himself to great danger.'[174]

Forty-seven-year-old Prowse was taken to the casualty clearing station at Doullens, but died there of his wounds.[175] Prowse was the most senior officer to be killed during the Battle of the Somme. One soldier who served under him remembered him 'as good a soldier that ever went across the Channel'.[176]

And there the story almost ends. In 2012, Prowse's battalion diary came up for auction: 184 slightly browned, carbon-copied pages with bumped corners and rubbed edges, covering the critical period from 4 August to 16 December 1914. It was sold by Antiquarian Books in Bloomsbury, London, to an unknown bidder for £900. Having briefly surfaced, it has once more disappeared, its secrets, if there are any, still awaiting discovery.[177]

Helen Salter decided not to publish Cotesworth's letter in her report on the Angels of Mons. Was it suppressed evidence? Or did she think

174 Davies and Maddocks, *Bloody Red Tabs*, unpaginated.
175 Martin Gilbert, *The Somme: Heroism and Horror in the First World War* (New York: Henry Holt and Company, 2006), p. 59.
176 Tim Machen (ed.), *Coward's War: An 'Old Contemptible's' View of the Great War* (Leicester: Matador, 2006), p. 84.
177 'Full list of lots – Dreweatts 1759: The Fine Art Auction Group', http://webcache.googleusercontent.com/search?q=cache:gQcqHUUOQpAJ:bcva.dnfa.com/search.asp%3Fview%3Dkeyword%26auction%3D36007%26keyword%3D%257C%257C%26lotno%3D%26noperpage%3D20%26cat%3D%26pg%3D40%26orderby%3D%26noofresults%3D419%26catname%3DFull%2520list%2520of%2520lots+&cd=3&hl=de&ct=clnk&gl=de, accessed 4 October 2015.

that it was just more hearsay that could not be verified? There is at least one element to the story that might be considered valuable. The description of 'a host of figures' is too vague to be of any real use, but our reconstruction of Prowse's war record shows that he could only have seen what he allegedly saw during the retreat from Mons. This accords with what Salter considered to be her strongest evidence: two letters published in the London *Evening News* by ostensible eyewitnesses describing the event as having occurred during the retreat. They were not the Angels of Mons at all.[178]

Matron Baldwin's Letter

On 17 September 1915, the SPR received a letter from Mrs A. P. Pynnington, residing in Gstaad, Switzerland, now in the last bundle (E). Pynnington wrote that she was enclosing part of a letter she had received from a certain Miss Baldwin, with her permission, 'containing the account of the Angels appearance at Mons which I think would interest the society'. Baldwin had written to Pynnington with the news of her appointment as matron at Crother's Hospital in Tunbridge Wells. Crother's was a so-called Voluntary Aid Detachment (Kent 94),[179] an *ad hoc* hospital set up to deal with the huge influx of casualties from the Front. Including Baldwin, there was a staff of four, with a doctor making daily rounds, to care for the wounded: 'We take twenty and the beds are full all the time.'

The letter begins with an unexceptional preamble about the weather; however, it is worth quoting the passage mentioning the Angels in full:

[. . .] One of my men who was at Mons tells me he saw the Angels in a long line. It is most interesting to listen to him. He says they

178 Salter, 'An Enquiry', pp. 106–18.
179 See 'The First World War – Tunbridge Wells Hospital', www.mtw.nhs.uk/ userfiles/The First World War.pdf, accessed 20 October 2015.

came down in a fine sort of mist between the English and German lines and for seconds he and two other men saw them quite distinctly – one man said there is my mother 'Who had been dead many years' then he says they disappeared for a time and came as before a second time. They have wonderful stories to tell of the battlefield – they all say the same thing – that the Germans will not fight the English if they can help it also the Belgians. It's quite true that the Saxons and our men used to talk together from trench to trench for a whole month and never fired a shot at each other. The Germans say to our men – we are Saxon, you are Anglo Saxon and we don't want to fight you or you us. When I read that the enemy and our men talked and 'chummed up' I said I don't believe it – but it's quite true [. . .][180]

What is interesting stylistically is how Baldwin positions one unbelievable account with another subsequently shown to be true: the Angels *vis-a-vis* fraternisation. The rhetorical implication is that if one could happen, then so could the other.

Both Baldwin's account and that attributed to Prowse share the element of there having been a multitude of angels, but otherwise there is not much else to go on. Assuming that Prowse did see *something*, then it could only have been after Le Cateau. Baldwin's soldier 'was at Mons'. Baldwin's account also mentions several witnesses and one of them identifies his mother among the angelic host. Baldwin's account also shares with several other reports the theme of there having been a mist.

Baldwin wrote this a little more than a year after the supposed event and there is no indication when she herself heard the story from the soldier. Her familiarity with the theme – 'saw *the* Angels', not 'saw Angels' – shows that she must have read of it elsewhere, so there is room for influence from these other sources.

180 Cambridge University Library, SPR.MS/Journal Vol. XVII 1915–1916, Baldwin to A. P. Pynnington, Crother's Hospital, Southborough, Tunbridge Wells, Kent, 12 September 1915.

There is a note in red ink in the top left corner of Pynnington's letter. Dated 4 October 1915, it records that Baldwin has been written to with a request either to put the soldier in direct contact with the SPR or to furnish a written statement from him. There is also a reminder not to publish any names without permission. If Baldwin or the soldier replied, there is no record of it here. Another trail runs cold.

This letter fits in with the pattern of nurses relating soldiers' stories of the Angels: we can identify the nurses, but never the soldiers. Furthermore, the nurses' re-tellings seem quite genuine. Here Miss Baldwin is simply writing to her friend Mrs Pynnington, and after the usual pre-amble about the weather, some concern as to when she last wrote and the conveyance of the good news that she had been appointed matron, comes the story of the Angels. She is not writing to a national newspaper or even a parish magazine, so the motives of fame or religious propaganda would seem to be ruled out.

Mere Rumour

The investigation had failed to elicit any strong evidence; the best Helen had was a letter that Arthur Machen had received. Helen concluded that many of the reports were 'founded on mere rumour', but she conceded that some statements demonstrated that 'a certain number of men who took part in the retreat from Mons honestly believe themselves to have had at that time supernormal experiences'. However, given the condition of the soldiers, 'sensory illusion due to extreme fatigue', rather than veridical apparitions, was the more likely explanation. Of the authenticity of angels, 'the result of our enquiry is negative'. There were no angels, only tired, desperate men.

The wording of Alice Johnson's July request, Professor Murray's facetiousness, even Helen's opening remarks in her December report, suggest that a core group of Society members had come to some sort of understanding about the case. And had already dismissed it. By treating it as 'folklore' from the beginning, the investigation had only compounded that conclusion.

We can also see that Helen chose as her best evidence accounts that were more obviously amenable to a psychological explanation. In the case of both Machen's 'lieutenant-colonel at the Front' and Lance Corporal Johnstone, an unusual phenomenon is witnessed by several people, but when investigated by them is found to be non-existent. Then there is the number of accounts analysed: only eleven in contrast to Harold Begbie's thirty. There is no record of any correspondence with Begbie in the Angels' envelope. It seems that Helen simply chose to ignore her fellow SPR member.[181]

There was nothing in the archives to challenge Helen's report; however, some of the correspondence was missing, such as the reply from Sarah Marrable, the letter from 'Miss R.' and, perhaps crucially, the 'direct testimony' referred to by Clement Ord. Other correspondence was ignored in the printed report. Perhaps more effort could have been made in following up leads, although the often one-sided nature of the files may give a false impression – if only copies had been made, or at least a record of letters sent. Strangely, Helen was not involved in much of the correspondence herself, leaving most of it to Isabel Newton. Part of the reason for Helen's absence during the crucial investigative research could have been her mother's increasing ill health, but there is no mention of this in the correspondence.

The disappearance of Ord's 'direct testimony' is a real mystery. If the SPR did not receive it, then there appears to have been no documented attempt to recover it. Given the fact that we have Ord's enclosing letter, we can only assume that the SPR did receive it. The obvious question is what happened to it? Perhaps it was not as convincing as Ord claimed, as in January 1916 he wrote to Newton to say that he agreed with the conclusions of the SPR report and made no mention of the fact that all of the material he had sent them had been left out.

181 However, elsewhere in the SPR Archives there is correspondence between Sir Oliver Lodge, sometime President, and Begbie: SPR MS 35 Sir Oliver Lodge.

I would not argue with her conclusions either, but with the manner in which she has reached them. The handling of the evidence, the conduct of the enquiry in general, and the missing 'direct testimony' in particular, all raise significant doubts as to the credibility of the investigation.

Despite the conclusions reached, for Helen, the enquiry still had value: 'the whole history of the case throws an interesting light on the value of human testimony and the growth of rumour'. This was particularly important because for those engaged in psychical research 'it is upon human testimony that their conclusions must to a great extent be founded'. What she had discovered, but restrained herself from saying, was that human testimony was deeply flawed and driven by motives more complex than the truth; we may say the same for investigations into it.

Helen's report certainly did not settle the matter. Its reach was circumscribed by the number of members the SPR had, the *Journal* being sent out to them as part of their membership. Going into 1915, the SPR had 1,212 members.[182] This would have been supplemented by the readers of *The All Saints' Clifton Parish Magazine*, but that could not amount to many more. Instead it was still Machen's claim that was being debated as the war years dragged on. 'I was in France,' said Forbes Phillips in 1916, 'hearing stories of angelic intervention long before Mr. Machen wrote his delightful yarn.'[183] It seems unlikely, but the feeling that something ought to be true often overrides consideration of whether it is true; and Phillips was so very sure of himself. The SPR made no attempt to contact him to prove the veracity of his statement. The power of the story of the Angels of Mons quite exceeded the ability to resist it.

182 'Report of the Council for the Year 1914', *JSPR* (February 1915), p. 21.
183 Forbes Phillips and R. Thurston Hopkins, *War and the Weird* (London: Simpkin, Marshall, Hamilton, Kent & Co., 1916), unpaginated digital edition.

A Strange Presentiment at Gallipoli

They were going over the top tomorrow. Private Tom Arnold was a long way from his home in Briton Ferry, West Wales, a long way from his job in the office of the Steel Smelters' Association in Neath, a long way from everything he knew. He thought of his parents there and got out pen and paper.[184]

> I have a strange presentiment that something is going to happen, and if I lose my life in tomorrow's battle I want you to banish all grief or sorrow for me and keep up your heads as true British parents. Show those around you that you can share the sacrifice and show courage and honour for your country.
>
> Your boy cannot die a more glorious death than to fall with his face toward the enemy and die with the secure consciousness that you, the parents I love, will be proud of me even in death. My only desire is that you will just smile upon me, say 'Well done,' and be pleased and proud that your own loving boy died as a hero.

The next day, Tom Arnold was reported wounded, missing in action. Sergeant Orr said, 'We found him this morning in a small gully shaded by trees. We dug a grave and laid him to rest, marking the place carefully so that we could identify it again.'

At least, that is the account that appeared in the newspapers for 21 September 1915. A presentiment is one thing, but it seems like a strange sort of letter to write. The style does not sound like a Welsh private on the eve of battle. It sounds like British Intelligence waging information warfare on the home front.

184 'Soldier's Presentiment: Farewell Letter on Eve of Death in Battle', *Daily Mail* (21 September 1915).

Was there a Private Tom Arnold? There was a Thomas Richard Arnold (S 693) in the Royal Marine Light Infantry (Plymouth Battalion, Royal Navy Division), who died in the Gallipoli Campaign on Sunday, 9 May 1915. According to his Royal Navy record, he was born in Briton Ferry in 1895. He joined up in November 1914, just after his nineteenth birthday and never got to see his twentieth.[185]

The First Battle of Krithia had failed. What was left of the 29th Division after 28 April were holding out against repeated Turkish counter-attacks. The Australian and New Zealand Army Corps (ANZAC) had landed at ANZAC Cove and the Officer Commanding, General William Birdwood, felt his position secure enough to send two brigades amounting to around five thousand men to reinforce the 29th. The British also sent in reinforcements, including brigades from the Royal Naval Division. The Second Battle of Krithia was as disastrous as the First. Over the course of the battle from 6 to 8 May, around a third of all the British and ANZAC troops involved became casualties.[186]

Saved by a Ghost at Ypres

December 1915, in a frontline trench somewhere in the Ypres salient, Belgium, Second Lieutenant William M. Speight of the 3rd Battalion, West Yorkshire Regiment (Prince of Wales's Own), sat in his dug-out. The First and Second Battles of Ypres had already been fought and around 200,000 men had already died in them – there were three more Battles of Ypres yet to come. But men did not only die in the great battles of the war, they died all the time. Speight's

185 Don Kindell, *Royal Navy Roll of Honour: World War 1 by Date and Ship/ Unit*, Part 2 (Penarth: Naval-History.Net, 2009), p. 91; National Archives, Kew, ADM 159/176/693.

186 Charles Bean, *The Story of ANZAC from 4 May 1915, to the Evacuation of the Gallipoli Peninsula, Official History of Australia in the War of 1914–1918*, vol. II (11th ed.) (Australia: Angus & Robertson, 1926).

friend, another officer whose name has not been recorded, had died that day.[187]

December in Ypres is generally remembered for the Germans' first use of poison gas against the British, although the French had had an earlier whiff of it in April that year. On 19 December ahead of raiding parties at Wieltje to the north east of Ypres, gas was discharged along the front. Further gas attacks were made on 20 December, turning into high-explosive shelling that continued into the evening of 21 December. It may have been during these attacks, or to a sniper's bullet, or a shell blast, or fragment of shrapnel that Speight's friend lost his life. Speight sat in his dug-out in the dim glow of a candle-stub, a melancholy watch in a godforsaken hole, when who should walk in, but his friend. Speight did not record his reaction, nor what the ghost did, but he invited another officer to come to his dug-out the following evening in case the ghost should return:

'The dead officer came once more and, after pointing to a spot on the floor of the dug-out, vanished.'

Speight had a hole dug at the spot indicated. About three feet down spades broke through to a narrow tunnel running beneath them. It was packed with fused explosives. The Germans had undermined them. The timers still had thirteen hours on the clock, time enough for the British to defuse the danger.

187 *Pearson's Magazine* (August 1919), quoted by Conan Doyle, *History of Spiritualism*, vol. II, p. 234 – neither source gives Speight's exact rank or regiment. There was a William M. Speight; according to the Census Records for 1901 and 1911, he was born in 1895 and came from Bingley, Keighley, in Yorkshire. This was probably also the same William M. Speight who was commissioned into the West Yorkshire Regiment as identified in 'Medal Card of Speight, William M.', National Archives, Kew, WO 372/18/211994, and WO 339/35587 where his middle initial is given as Moorhouse; *Supplement to the London Gazette* (14 April 1915), p. 3689.

1916

'A Day to be Denied'

Always in frail health, Lily Loder-Symonds's spirit had been battered by the war. The repeated shocks as the battles unfolded of losing brother after brother must have been as unbearable as they are unimaginable. Finally, on 28 January, influenza snuffed out what life remained. Conan Doyle called her a 'high soul upon the earth' and in his diary for that day he wrote '*dies neganda*', a 'day to be denied'.[1]

She had been a decisive factor in convincing him of the reality of spirit communication and hence of an afterlife. In May 1915 he had written to her, saying: 'You know what I think of death. It is a most glorious improvement on life, a shedding of all that is troublous and painful and a gaining of grand new powers which are a supreme happiness to the individual.'[2]

In early 1916, it was not just Lily who was fighting for her life, the Conan Doyles' son Adrian, then only five, had pneumonia. Jean was by his bedside day and night. On one occasion, she had to leave him to get something from the nursery. As she hurried through, she startled Denis, who jumped up from a chair and accidentally squashed a platoon of lead soldiers underfoot. When she got back to Adrian, he opened his eyes and said, 'Naughty Denis, breaking my soldiers!' Jean could not imagine how he knew and of course told her husband all about it.

He wrote into *Light* about it and his account was published in the March 1916 issue:

I can only explain it by the supposition, which can be supported by a volume of evidence, that the soul can be, and probably always is, out of the body at such times, and that occasionally under rare

1 Lycett, *Conan Doyle*, p. 362.
2 Miller, *Adventures*, p. 366.

conditions which we have not yet been able to define, it can convey to the body the observations which it has made during its independent flight.

Helen's mother, Margaret Verrall, a stalwart of the Society, had been in ailing health for some time before finally passing away on 2 July 1916. She left a generous bequest of £500 to the Society. Eleanor Sidgwick was moved to complain about the obituary notice that appeared in *The Times*, 'which I think hardly does justice to her many-sided activities', in particular:

> It is quite true that in connexion with the Society for Psychical Research (which is not rightly described as a small band of Cambridge Spiritualists, nor indeed as Spiritualists at all) her work both as an investigator and as herself an automatist is scientifically important and of lasting value.[3]

Winifred Coombe Tennant heard the news of Verrall's death from Helen some days later, but her sympathy was only for herself, writing in her diary 'How anxious and solitary seems my state, left in this battle and turmoil of life [etc.]'. She would later record dreaming vividly of her.[4]

Ill health also forced Alice Johnson to resign as Editor and Research Officer, with an SPR pension of £120 and status as Honorary Member. Helen Salter was appointed in her place.

Humbug and Rum

In early March 1916, someone calling themselves 'Anti-Humbug' wrote in to *The Sunday Times* decrying the fact that 'to the thinking public

---

3 Eleanor Mildred Sidgwick, 'The Late Mrs Verrall', *The Times* (6 July 1916), p. 9.
4 Tennant, *Between Two Worlds*, p. 192, dream of Margaret Verrall on 4 February 1917, p. 208.

there must appear an undulating wave of superstition among our military' due to the fact that 'We read that a regiment has gone to the front with its "mascot"'. According to Anti-Humbug, 'The word "mascot" is a French barbarism of the Portuguese word "Mascotto", which means Witchcraft.'[5]

Anti-Humbug dismissed the whole idea – 'there is no such thing as luck or chance' – quoting the Austrian statesman and diplomatist Klemens von Metternich as his authority: 'They say I am lucky. It is not so, but I am more competent than my adversaries.' Consequently, British soldiers have no need of 'an incongruous incentive to make them fight like British soldiers'. But it is admissable for Johnny Foreigner: 'Let the Russian have his "Icon", the Turk his "fetisch", the Frenchman his "portebonheur", the Italian his "amuleto" and his "talismano", and the German his "Glücksgöttin", but let the British soldier rely on his innate courage.'

The choice of the Austrian Metternich rather deflated Anti-Humbug's castigation of foreign and especially enemy superstitiousness. In his enumeration of the range of lucky charms being used among the warring nations, we get an accidental insight into the pervasiveness of the idea.

Anti-Humbug's stern denunciation of, well, humbug, was soon forgotten. The 'undulating wave of superstition among our military' proved to have come in with the tide. An anonymous story appeared in the *Daily Mail* for 8 November 1916 taking a certain delight in detailing the power of humbug.[6] The piece began by discussing the Angels of Mons.

What the author thought was the chief point of interest in the Angels story was 'the fact that hundreds of practical, unpoetical, and stolid English soldiers came forward and testified to having seen the vision' – soldiers, certainly, but that does not logically imply that they were an

5 Anti-Humbug, 'Mascotto', *Sunday Times* (5 March 1916), p. 2.
6 'The Rum Jar', *Daily Mail* (8 November 1916), p. 4; later published in Vernon Bartlett, *Mud and Khaki: Sketches from Flanders and France* (London: Simpkin, Marshall, Hamilton, Kent & Co., 1917).

unimaginative and unexcitable lot, as the many poets, writers and artists enlisted in the ranks amply testify. Still, the author was building a case.

'Before the war,' he argued, 'the unromantic Englishman who thought he saw a vision would have blamed, in turn, his digestion, his eyesight, his sobriety, and his sanity before he allowed that he had anything to do with the supernatural.' But now how the times have changed, and the same type admits without embarrassment 'that he has put his faith in superstitions and charms and mascots, and that his lucky sign has saved his life on half a dozen occasions'.

The superstition that the author calls 'the most popular' in the British Army is that of the rum jar.[7] The story goes that 'once, long ago', perhaps as far back as 1915 or 1914, a supply party was bringing up rations to the front line. Those rations included their allotment of spirits, the rum jar, and the supply party succumbed to the temptation to check to see if this rum was properly regimental. The jar passed round and they conceded that it was regulation British Army rum, but to be on the safe side they decided to check again. A merry little party was had in the communication trench until with horror they realised that the jar was empty. An explanation would be needed. One quick thinker suggested breaking the jar and saying that it had been smashed by a bullet. So they staggered on to the front firing trench and handed over the jar's handle wrapped up in a fine story of how a German bullet had almost taken the soul of Private Hawkes, but had robbed the jar of its spirit instead. It may be that the unsteadiness of the supply party was put down to the terrible shock they had received, particularly Private Hawkes in his brush with Death. From this incident arose the belief that rum jars had a magnetic attraction for German bullets. The author notes that 'a few stray shots have helped to strengthen the superstition', so that it is almost ubiquitous in the British line that he who carries the rum jar is at a doubled risk of being shot.

The rum 'jar' was made of stoneware and stamped SRD, meaning Supply Reserve Depot, but usually interpreted as 'Seldom Reaches

7 Tim Cook, 'Rum in the Trenches', *Legion* (1 September 2002).

Destination'.[8] When it did reach its destination, soldiers were given a tot of ½ gill (⅛ pint), initially only in exceptional circumstances, but quickly becoming a daily ration as the war ground on; and it might be mixed with hot tea or coffee.[9] Rum was dear to the soldier's heart. Robert Graves observed that his comrades 'look forward to their tot of rum at dawn stand-to as the brightest moment of their twenty-four hours'.[10] As the Canadian officer Captain Ralph Bell wrote:

> When the days shorten, and the rain never ceases; when the sky is ever grey, the nights chill, and the trenches thigh deep in mud and water; when the front is altogether a beastly place, in fact, we have one consolation. It comes in gallon jars, marked simply SRD.[11]

The opinion was widespread. M. A. Searle, 18th Canadian Battalion, said 'most of us carried on [. . .] because of not limitless but more than ordinary issues of rum'; whilst Private G. Boyd, 8th Canadian Battalion, added, 'If we had not had the rum we would have died.'[12]

For the officers it was a powerful tool for discipline (when distributed for good behaviour) and Dutch courage (when going over the top). Extra rum rations were given as a reward for dangerous volunteer

---

8 The exact meaning of SRD is still the subject of debate with some suggesting that it stood for Services Rum Diluter or Special Red Demerara, see Jason Wilson, *Soldiers of Song: The Dumbells and Other Canadian Concert Parties of the First World War*, (Waterloo: Wilfrid Laurier University Press, 2012); but an example in the collection of the Imperial War Museum (FEQ 802) clearly shows 'Supply Reserve Depot' stamped on the wax seal stopper. For obvious reasons the stoppers themselves were rarely preserved, leading to the confusion around the term today.

9 Fiona Reid, *Medicine in First World War Europe* (London: Bloomsbury, 2017), p. 120.

10 Graves, *Good-Bye*, p. 211.

11 Ralph Bell, *Canada in War-Paint* (London and Toronto: J. M. Dent & Sons, 1917), p. 122.

12 Quoted in Tim Cook, ' "More a Medicine than a Beverage": "Demon Rum" and the Canadian Trench Soldier of the First World War', *Canadian Military History*, 9.1 (2000), pp. 10–11.

duties, such as raiding parties. Graves reported the custom of a double tot before going over the top. Some old hands still remember getting a British Army rum ration in the 1980s, although no longer, it would seem.[13]

'The Strange Tricks that Fate Will Play'

If men avoided carrying the rum jar, there were other things that they preferred to have with them. The author of the rum jar piece also told of a soldier he knew who always used to carry a rosary that he had found in the ruined streets of Ypres. When shrapnel from a trench-mortar bomb broke his leg in two places, he refused to be taken off to the dressing station until a search had been made to confirm that he still had the rosary with him. The author writes as if he were there at the time and even recalled the wounded man's words on the occasion: 'If I don't take it with me, I shall get hit again on the way down.'

His was not an isolated case:

Nearly every man at the front has a mascot of some sort – a rosary, a black cat, a German button, a lucky elephant, or a weird sign – which is supposed to keep him safe.[14]

Vogue reported in 1916 that jewellers were doing a roaring trade in gold and diamond lucky elephants. Their trunks were upward-pointing to keep the luck 'in', just as beliefs surrounding the horseshoe stipulated that the points should be upmost.[15]

As we saw at Mons, lucky coins were especially popular. Nineteen-year-old Private Shore joined the Machine Gun Corps when it formed

13 Graves, *Good-Bye*, p. 197; 'Army Rum Ration', https://www.arrse.co.uk/community/threads/army-rum-ration.18855/, accessed 8 July 2017.
14 Vernon Bartlett, *Mud and Khaki: Sketches from Flanders and France* (London: Simpkin, Marshall, Hamilton, Kent & Co., 1917), p. 124.
15 Pearl Binder, *Muffs and Morals* (London: G. G. Harrap, 1953), p. 134.

in 1915. He carried with him a lucky silver shilling from 1906 with the picture of King Edward VII on one side, and a brooch pin soldered on to the back. He was wounded by shrapnel in the leg and hospitalised, but returned to the Army, serving until 1920.[16]

Lucky coins came in all shapes and currencies. I have a 1916 farthing with the middle delicately cut out to highlight the King's head and pierced with a chain link so that it could be worn. Another is a Belgian five-centime piece from 1914 mounted with a red stone, either a ruby or cut glass. I also have an example of a penny from 1904 shot through with a bullet. This combined the belief in lucky coins with that of there being a particular bullet destined to hit the soldier.

'Luck' could inhabit any sort of object, either through the imagined indwelling properties of the item (such as silver), or through association with some incident. The author mentioned that he had a servant, letting slip that he was of the officer class. One such always used to wear an old shoe-button on a piece of string around his neck. It had been given to him by 'a tiny girl' when he had been billeted at some village in France and was forever treasured by him 'as carefully as a diamond merchant would treasure the great Koh-I-noor stone'. British soldiers also carried lucky swastikas, long before the Nazi party adopted it as its symbol.[17]

Bullet-stopping Bibles have become legendary, but there are some authenticated instances. Lieutenant General Sir Arthur Smith survived the war thanks to his Bible. He won the Sword of Honour at Sandhurst and was commissioned into his father's regiment, the Coldstream Guards, in 1910. On the outbreak of war, his father gave him a pocket Bible, with a verse from the 91st Psalm on the flyleaf: 'Because thou hast made the Lord thy refuge. There shall no evil befall thee. For he

---

16 Dave Shore, personal communications, 22 July 2014. Twenty-two men with the surname Shore served in the Machine Gun Corps during the First World War; unfortunately Mr Shore did not supply the first name.

17 '51. Collection of amulets and charms worn by the troops', *Medicine and Surgery in the Great War, 1914–1918: An Exhibition* (London: Wellcome Institute, 1968), p. 16. See also the discussion in Vanessa Chambers, 'A Shell With My Name On It: The Reliance on the Supernatural During the First World War', *Journal for the Academic Study of Magic*, 2 (2004), pp. 79–102.

shall give his angels charge over thee to keep thee in all thine ways.'
His father had carried it through the Boer War and now he trusted that
it would keep his son safe.[18]

It was tested early in the war. In November 1914, Smith was on
night reconnaissance when German shells started falling. Something
hit him with force and he was thrown some distance. At the dressing
station he discovered that the Bible had taken the brunt of the damage
from a piece of shrapnel. It had cut through the book before stopping
at the 91st Psalm. He described it as 'a very significant thing and
encouraged my faith'.[19]

Private Leonard Knight was also given a pocket Bible, this time from
his Aunt Minnie in July 1915. His edition stopped a German bullet. It
has been passed down through his family and still exists today, the
bullet still embedded. The Imperial War Museum has a Bible said to
have belonged to Gunner John Dickinson, Royal Artillery, that took a
German bullet in 1915.[20]

Lieutenant Colonel T. E. Lawrence, 'Lawrence of Arabia', came
across something similar during his military operations in the Middle
East. One of his allies, Auda abu Tayi, carried an 'amulet Koran' and, he
claimed, in the thirteen years he had carried it had not once been
wounded. He showed it to Lawrence after a volley of rifle fire had shot
his camel from under him and torn his equipment to shreds, but otherwise left him unhurt. Auda had paid £120 for it, but Lawrence noted
that it was a cheap edition printed in Glasgow: truly, magic is in the
mind of the believer.[21]

Pilots accumulated their share of lucky things, too. Russian flying
ace Alexander Alexandrovich Kazakov carried an icon of St Nicholas.

18 Brigadier Ian Dobbie, OBE, 'Lieutenant General Sir Arthur Smith (1890–
1977)', in *The Fight of Faith: Lives and Testimonies from the Battlefield*, edited by
Michael Claydon and Philip Bray (London: Panoplia, 2013).
19 Quoted in Lewis-Stempel, *Six Weeks*, unpaginated.
20 'Pocket Bible Saved WWI Soldier's Life', *Daily Mail* (16 January 2017);
Imperial War Museum, 'Bible, Bullet Damaged', EPH 2024.
21 T. E. Lawrence, *The Seven Pillars of Wisdom* (London: Jonathan Cape, 1935
[1926]), p. 307.

Captain E. F. 'Tab' Pflaum of the Australian Flying Corps had a stuffed baby kangaroo named 'Joey'. Britain's highest-scoring fighter ace at the time of his death in 1917, Captain Albert Ball, VC, DSO and Two Bars, MC, carried a slice of his mother's plum pudding. French flying ace, 'The Sentinel of Verdun', Jean Navarre, carried a lady's silk stocking. American Aviator John McGavock Grider, who flew with the RFC/RAF rather than wait for the US to organise its own air force, was reported to have a considerable collection of lucky items: a piece of wreckage from his first crash; a doll given to him by the British actress Billie Carlton; a Columbian half-dollar; a sixpence; and a stocking.[22]

Superstitions surrounding luck were not solely concentrated in physical objects. The 'Rum Jar' author had come across a wide variety of superstitions: one man believed that he would be killed on a Friday; another would never light a third cigarette with the same match; one man thought that seeing a cow on the way to the firing line was a lucky omen. There was still another type who would volunteer for patrols, go over the top without a second thought, indeed face any and every danger because he has 'got a feelin'' that he will survive, and, noted the author, 'he generally does'.

Robert Graves would recite a line of poetry by Nietzsche – in French – as a charm. Charles Edmund Carrington, an officer in the Royal Warwickshire Regiment, wrote of his own superstitious practices under the pseudonym Charles Edmonds: 'You think of absurd omens and fetishes to ward off the shell you hear coming' that included touching some especial object, sitting a particular way, or finishing whistling a tune in time. It gave them the illusion of control in uncontrollable situations; something to do when nothing could be done.[23]

Unlike 'Anti-Humbug', the anonymous author of the 'Rum Jar' article (since identified as Vernon Bartlett) was speaking from

22 Eric and Jane Lawson, *The First Air Campaign: August 1914–November 1918* (Cambridge, MA: Da Capo Press, 2002), pp. 147–8; Mike Polston, 'John McGavock Grider (1892–1918)', The Encyclopedia of Arkansas History and Culture, http://www.encyclopediaofarkansas.net/encyclopedia/entry-detail.apx?entryID=5277, accessed 1 June 2018.
23 Graves, *Good-Bye*, p. 272–3; Edmonds, *Subaltern's War*, p. 163.

first-hand experience. And it was the soldiers' experience of the vagaries of war that led them down the path of superstition. The author had heard of men who had had premonitions of their death, which turned out to come true, or others who had survived hard fighting only to be killed on the same day they lost their lucky charm. As he explained:

> To you in England it seems ridiculous that a man should hope to save his life by wearing a shoe-button on a piece of string. But, then, you have not seen the strange tricks that Fate will play with lives. You have not watched how often a shell will burst in a group of men, kill two outright, and leave the rest untouched; you have not joked with a friend one moment and knelt by him to catch his dying words the next; you have not stood at night by a hastily dug grave and wondered why the comrade who is lying there on the waterproof sheet should have been killed while you are still unhurt.[24]

The author recognised the helplessness of the individual soldier, the fact that it was not skill at arms that brought him through, but simply Death's lottery, unpredictable and unsympathetic. The lucky charm, and here he puts them all together as is right – 'the Bible, the Crucifix, a cheap little charm' – was an attempt to enlist some help on his behalf. He also saw another, psychological factor in the power of amulets: 'a man who has confidence that he will come through a battle unhurt generally does so'. On the other hand, the soldier 'who has no belief in some shielding power', even if it is only a shoe-button on a string, 'is taken by death very soon'. The author was a champion of the charm. Not just because they were unavoidable, but also because they were psychologically valid, and he called on the reader to sympathise:

> The penny lucky charm that can bring comfort to a man in danger is not a thing to be ridiculed. It may be a proof of

24 Bartlett, *Mud and Khaki*, p. 124.

ignorance, but to the man it is symbolical of his God, and therefore worthy of all respect and reverence from others.

The Battle of Jutland

The SPR's experiments in 'thought-transference' continued into 1916 with Professor Murray as the receiver. But the really interesting information came from the rank-and-file membership. In early summer 1916, the most impressive was what the Society termed a 'Coincidental Hallucination', concerning a dream or vision of Mrs Florence Baxter about her brother, George William Malpress. The son of George and Hannah Malpress had set off from their family home at 56 New Road, Peterborough, to become Able Seaman SS 3854 Malpress and sail the Seven Seas on board HMS *Queen Mary*.[25]

HMS *Queen Mary* was a sight to behold, over 700 feet long, bristling with sixteen 4-inch guns and eight 13.5-inch guns (later, two anti-aircraft guns were added), with armour up to 10 inches thick and a top speed of 28 knots. Malpress joined a crew of 1,275 sailors and officers to sail a ship that had cost over £2 million to build. The battlecruisers balanced armour and armament against speed, making them faster but less deadly than the Royal Navy's battleships, and better fitting the battlecruisers for reconnaissance roles.

She was assigned to the 1st Battlecruiser Squadron (1 BCS) under the command of Rear-Admiral David Beatty. We do not know exactly when Malpress enlisted, but he may already have seen action at the Battle of Heligoland Bight (28 August 1914) and the Raid on Scarborough in December 1914. Due to re-fitting the ship had missed the Battle of Dogger Bank in 1915.

In 1916, the Germans were suffering under the naval blockade that the superior British fleet had managed to enforce in international waters. The blockade is seen as one of the key factors that led to the

25 'Case L. 1204', *JSPR*, No. CCCXXXI, Vol. XVII, (July 1916), pp. 204–7.

defeat of Germany. As well as depriving the German munitions indus-
try of supplies, the blockade caused severe food shortages. Estimates
suggest that almost half a million German civilians – ordinary men,
women and children – starved to death.[26] The Battle of Jutland was all
about breaking the blockade and to do that the German *Kaiserliche
Marine* had to break the British fleet.

Germany had challenged the might of the Royal Navy during the
pre-war naval arms race, when from 1898 onwards, Wilhelm II had
ordered a massive building and modernisation plan. Britain reacted in
kind, taking the lead with the revolutionary new Dreadnought design,
concentrating fire-power in heavy main batteries rather than in second-
ary armaments and using steampower to increase speed. By the start of
the First World War, Britain could put twenty-nine large warships to
sea, compared to Germany's seventeen.[27] At the Battle of Jutland,
Admiral Sir John Jellicoe commanded the Royal Navy's Grand Fleet of
151 fighting vessels, comprising twenty-eight battleships, nine battlecruisers, eight armoured cruisers, twenty-six light cruisers, seventy-
eight destroyers, a minelayer and a seaplane carrier. It was said that the
Grand Fleet when cruising all together covered an area larger than the
County of London.[28] Against him, Vice-Admiral Reinhard Scheer
commanded the ninety-nine-ship strong High Seas Fleet of sixteen
battleships, five cruisers, six pre-Dreadnought class ships, eleven light
cruisers and sixty-one torpedo boats.

Scheer knew that he could never defeat the Royal Navy in a head-on
confrontation. His strategy was to lure out part of the Grand Fleet and
bring the full force of his naval might down upon it. But the British

26 Leo Grebler, *The Cost of the World War to Germany and Austria-Hungary*
(Yale University Press, 1940), p. 78. The German authorities estimated that as
many as 763,000 had perished due to the blockade, see C. Paul Vincent, *The
Politics of Hunger: The Allied Blockade of Germany, 1915–1919* (Athens, Ohio:
Ohio University Press, 1985), p. 141.
27 Niall Ferguson, *The Pity of War: Explaining World War I* (London: Basic
Books, 1999), p. 85.
28 Archibald Hurd and H. H. Bashford, *Sons of Admiralty: A Short History of
the Naval War, 1914–1918* (New York: Doubleday, 1919), p. 165.

blockade was keeping German warships in their harbours, too. Patrolling the cold northern waters, Jellicoe's ships denied the enemy the open seas, although under the sea German submarines had evaded detection to pursue a counter-blockade of Great Britain. British belligerence could still be relied upon.

Scheer sent out Vice-Admiral Franz Hipper's fast reconnaissance formation of battlecruisers – I Scouting Group – five modern ships with the turn of speed to out-distance pursuers, intended to lure out Vice-Admiral Sir David Beatty's battlecruiser squadrons. The Germans also positioned submarines along likely British patrol routes and waited.

A flurry of signal intercepts told the British that something big was on. The Battle Cruiser Fleet put on steam and headed out from Rosyth on the Firth of Forth to intercept – just as the Germans had intended. However, the signals intelligence had allowed the British to put to sea before the Germans, gaining a significant advantage. Jellicoe, too, realised that this was no ordinary manoeuvre and gave the order to send out the rest of the Grand Fleet, sailing from Scapa Flow and the Moray Firth to rendezvous with Beatty.

The German High Seas Fleet put out from Wilhelmshaven, sailing north in open seas off the coast of Denmark, Hipper and I Scouting Group ahead of the main formation under Scheer. The Royal Navy had already crossed most of the North Sea and were *en route* to intercept the Germans in the waters of Skagerrak, the straits running between Denmark and the southerly coasts of Norway and Sweden.

The German submarines were ineffective, only radioing back the crucial information that the British had taken the bait, but misreporting of their directions – due to submarine-evading zig-zagging – gave the impression that the British forces were moving apart rather than heading for a rendezvous. On 31 May 1916, Seaman Malpress was sailing to his fate.

The *New Zealand* was still the flagship of 2nd Battlecruiser Squadron, leading HMS *Indefatigable*, but the *New Zealand*'s former captain, Lionel Halsey, was now Captain of the Fleet, sailing on HMS *Iron Duke*, the flagship of Admiral Sir John Jellicoe. When he handed over command to his successor in June 1915, he also handed over the *piupiu* and *tiki* to the new Captain, John Frederick Ernest Green, obtaining his agreement to wear the ceremonial items whenever the *New Zealand* went into action.[29]

Green was an unexceptional, if not incompetent, sailor. He had come twenty-ninth out of thirty-seven successful candidates for naval cadetship in 1879. Low points of his career include running the cruiser HMS *Forte* aground in 1910 and smashing the armoured cruiser HMS *Natal* into a fishing boat in 1913. Despite that he was constantly promoted beyond his abilities, reaching the rank of Admiral in his retirement. If his reputation had preceded him, then the crew of the *New Zealand* could not have greeted his arrival with much enthusiasm: the Maori chief's prophecy had not covered accidents due to ineptitude.[30]

The 2nd Battle Cruiser Squadron was a ship down before the biggest sea battle of the First World War: HMS *Australia* was in dock for repairs after HMS *New Zealand* had collided with her, twice, on 22 April. Although the official investigation cited procedural errors, Green had prior form. HMS *Lion* had hoisted the signal to zig-zag as the ships entered a bank of fog a few miles off Heligoland. The *Australia* zig-zagged. The *New Zealand* crashed into her and knocked her again with her port outer propeller as she turned away. 'Apparently,' wrote Captain Trevor Wilson Ross, then a junior officer on HMS *Australia*, '*New Zealand* were unaware that they had lost the propulsion of the port outer propeller.' So *New Zealand* suddenly appeared again, cutting across *Australia*'s bows. The *Australia* could not avoid the second collision. Green was a liability.[31]

More than one sailor must have drawn comparison between Drake famously finishing his game of bowls before attending to the Spanish Armada and the events before the Battle of Jutland. On the eve of the

29 *The Navy List* (December 1916), p. 396f.
30 Green Service Record, The National Archives, ADM 196/42/335, f. 260.
31 Trevor Wilson Ross, 'Battle Cruisers in Collision', *Naval Historical Review* (December 1975).

battle – a battle of which all were as yet unaware – the Grand Fleet 'was in an unusual state of excitement': it was the finals of the Grand Boxing Competition.[32]

A general order had been issued for Tuesday, 30 May: 'make and mend clothes'; this was Saturday routine, thus allowing as many men as possible to ferry themselves over to the *Borodino* for the finals. The *Borodino* had been a Hull liner before the war, and then she had been requisitioned for the Royal Fleet Auxiliary, serving first as a prison ship for German civilians, now as the Fleet's 'sports-ship'.

But before the winning punch was thrown, the rumour was going round: 'The German Fleet is out at last.' The British warships were already underway, the *Borodino* steaming alongside the super-Dreadnoughts as drifters and picket-boats took the men back to their ships. The main fleet sailed from Scapa Flow; the 2nd Battle Squadron put out from Cromarty; Beatty took out his battlecruisers from Rosyth, the *New Zealand* (2 BCS) and *Queen Mary* (1 BCS) among them. The hunt was on.

According to Admiral Scheer, Vice-Admiral von Hipper had left the mouth of the Jade River at 4 a.m. on the morning of 31 May, with I Scouting Group: *Seydlitz, Moltke, Derfflinger, Lützow* and *Von der Tann*. A screen of U-Boats was already stationed off the British northern naval bases and their radio reports alerted von Hipper to the British movements, but as Scheer explained, these movements did not reveal any strategy and the Germans felt reassured in their plan to draw out a smaller force with the Scouting Group and crush it with the hammer of the High Seas Fleet.[33]

Lighter, faster vessels – British destroyers and the German equivalent, torpedo boats – had already made contact: gunfire and smoke coloured the early afternoon. Von Hipper's I Scouting Group had been caught out in the open. The Battle Cruiser Fleet put on steam to intercept.

32 W. L. Wyllie, C. Owen and W. D. Kirkpatrick, *More Sea Fights of the Great War* (London: Cassell, 1919), p. 112.
33 Scheer, *Germany's High Sea Fleet*, p. 140.

That Wednesday, back in Peterborough, Florence Baxter was lying ill in bed. 'I was taken worse,' she said, 'and thought I was going to die.' Sometime in the afternoon she had what she called 'a vision', rather than dream: 'I was with my brother on his ship and he was so happy and singing, and then it changed and he was at home on leave.' She tried speaking to Able Seaman Malpress, but he did not reply. She was much upset by that, thinking 'he would not speak because I was disfigured'. Later, she asked her mother whether he had gone back – the vision had been so real that she really thought that he had been there – but she replied that he had not been home.[34]

'Enemy in Sight'

Captain Green reported that the day of the battle was hazy and becalmed, with visibility between 7 and 10 miles (11 to 16 km). By early afternoon, the Battle Cruiser Fleet was already far out into the North Sea. The *New Zealand* was ahead of the pack, steaming north-north-east, the *Indefatigable* close behind, to rendezvous with the Grand Fleet further north. Off to the port side, some two or three miles back, the newer ships of 1 BCS were coming up – Beatty leading in the *Lion*, with *Princess Royal*, *Queen Mary* and *Tiger* following in that order. To starboard, the light cruisers *Nottingham* and *Dublin* protected 2 BCS's flank, with the rest of the 2nd Light Cruiser Squadron, HMS *Southampton* and *Birmingham*, bringing up the rear. A good 5 or 6 miles (8 to 10 km) further to port, the 5th Battle Squadron – four Queen Elizabeth-class battleships: HMS *Barham*, *Valiant*, *Warspite* and *Malaya* – was steaming towards them.[35]

Scouting ahead of the big warships were the light cruisers of Commodore E. S. Alexander Sinclair's 1st Light Cruiser Squadron:

34 'Case L 1204', *JSPR* (July 1916), p. 204.
35 'The Battle of Jutland: The Battle Cruiser Action, from 3.15 to 3.30 p.m.', Ordnance Survey, 1923. W. L. Wyllie, C. Owen and W. D. Kirkpatrick, *More Sea Fights of the Great War* (London: Cassell, 1919), p. 113, gave a somewhat different disposition of the fleet.

HMS *Galatea, Inconstant, Cordelia* and *Phaeton*. At 14.20 Sinclair spotted two ships in the far distance. He signalled back to Beatty: 'enemy in sight'.

Across the Battle Cruiser Fleet, bugles sounded action stations as Beatty adjusted course to meet the Germans. At 15.30, he made out five enemy battlecruisers with destroyers and light ships: von Hipper's I Scouting Group. Sinclair had already turned his ships to screen the battlecruisers as Beatty ordered his ships to increase speed to 25 knots. According to Scheer, though, the British cruisers turned north when spotted and it was the Germans who gave chase. At 15.48, with 18,500 yards between them, firing commenced.

At 15.51 the *New Zealand* began ranging on what she identified as the fourth ship from the right – this was SMS *Moltke*, a battlecruiser armed with 11-inch guns, and a veteran of Heligoland and Dogger Bank. Six minutes later, the *New Zealand* opened fire at a range of 18,100 yards. Lieutenant Commander Arthur Douglas Wales Smith was the ship's gunnery officer. He had been sailing with the *New Zealand* for almost a year: this would be his first big battle.[36]

The gunners of the *New Zealand* found range-taking and spotting difficult. 'It was,' said Green, 'very difficult to distinguish hits, but occasional bursts of smoke with a salvo seemed to denote a hit.' In contrast, 'the firing of the enemy was extremely good'.[37] Admiral Scheer was of the same opinion: 'superiority in firing and tactical advantages of position were decidedly on our side' – at least until the 5th Battle Squadron got within range.[38]

The *New Zealand* was closing fast on the enemy. At just after 4 p.m., range was down to under 11,000 yards. The guns of the *Lützow* were already firing on Beatty's flagship, the *Lion*: Q Turret amidships was destroyed and only emergency flooding of the magazine prevented it from going up – Major Harvey, Royal Marines, was awarded a

36 Smith Service Record, The National Archives, ADM 196/51. f. 103.
37 'Captain's Report on Action of 31st May 1916. H.M.S *New Zealand*' in Admiralty, *Battle of Jutland 30th May to 1st June 1916: Official Despatches with Appendices* (London: His Majesty's Stationery Office, 1920), pp. 393–5.
38 Scheer, *Germany's High Sea Fleet*, p. 142.

posthumous Victoria Cross for his forethought in saving the ship and her crew from annihilation. Malpress watched as the *Queen Mary's* sister ships, the *Tiger* and *Princess Royal*, were also hit. A few minutes later, a tight cluster of German shells from the battlecruiser *Von der Tann* struck the *Indefatigable*, landing on the upper deck and smashing through the lighter armour there into the bowels of the ship. There was a terrific explosion in the magazine. *Indefatigable* pulled out of the battle line, but a second salvo caught her. She keeled over and sank, 'leaving only a great towering cloud of brown-grey smoke and steam'.[39] There were only two survivors out of a crew of 1,019.

Admiral Evan-Thomas's battleships were now closing, with a range of between 19,000 and 20,000 yards, the big 15-inch guns opened up. The 'tawny cordite' from firing guns and black smoke from hits drifted across the sea, obscuring an already hazy day – the German destroyers also deployed smokescreens to their advantage. The battlecruisers churned the waves with their zig-zagging evasive manoeuvring.[40]

At the same time, destroyers on both sides were heavily engaged. Admiral Scheer reported that V 27 and V 29 were sunk early in the battle, with the British also losing two or three destroyers – other stricken ships were later picked off by the High Seas Fleet at its leisure.[41] As well as salvoes gouging chunks out of sea and ship, torpedoes from the destroyers streaked the waves.

An anonymous midshipman working in one of the gun turrets captured the strain and intensity of the action:

> A constant flow of ammunition is coming up the hoists, and this is your job, your life and death, success or failure – you must give your mind to nothing else [. . .] The noise is incessant, for besides the salvoes of the heavy guns the 6-inch battery is bursting out at intervals with rapid fire [. . .] If you stop for a moment and look through one of the sights of the control

39 Wyllie, et al., *More Sea Fights*, p. 115.
40 Wyllie, et al., *More Sea Fights*, p. 118.
41 Scheer, *Germany's High Sea Fleet*, p. 144–5.

cabinet you catch a glimpse of the ship ahead, all but hidden by the mighty jets of spray which tower far above the mastheads, the intervening water torn and tormented by the shells which have gone wide.[42]

It might have been the view of Malpress, a battle more heard than seen by most of the sailors involved. Only a few officers in their armoured conning towers could grasp the dreadful enormity of the sea battle raging round them.

Suddenly, there was 'another tremendous explosion' and 'again a dreadful towering cloud of brown-grey smoke mounted thousands of feet into the air'. The *Queen Mary* had been hit. Her stern stood upright upon the sea, propellers whirling in the air. Another explosion ripped through her. A midshipman onboard watched as one of her 50-ton guns seemed to stand on end before crashing, breech first, down into the ship. A shower of debris was blasted over her neighbours, falling upon the *Tiger* and *New Zealand*. In its collection, the National Museum of the Royal New Zealand Navy has a piece of ring bolt from the *Queen Mary* that landed on the quarterdeck of the *New Zealand*. Not much more than that was left.[43]

'When the smoke from the explosion cleared away,' said Scheer, 'the cruiser had disappeared.' A destroyer picked up eighteen survivors: Malpress was not among them.

The *New Zealand*'s guns were still firing. At just after 16.00, she had shifted fire to the fifth (last) ship in von Hipper's line. At 16.22, smoke obscured that ship and she shifted fire back to SMS *Moltke*. Twenty minutes later, the enemy was out of range at 18,850 yards. The *New Zealand* attempted to close the distance, ranging again at 18,000 yards, but before she could fire the enemy was again too far off. It took the best part of an hour for the *New Zealand* to get the enemy within her sights again, firing on a German battlecruiser for about ten minutes before smoke made spotting impossible.

42 Wyllie, et al., *More Sea Fights*, p. 124.
43 Wyllie, et al., *More Sea Fights*, p. 120.

At the beginning of the battlecruiser action, the British had outnumbered the Germans six to five and out-gunned them with 13.5-inch and 12-inch guns to the Germans 12- and 11-inches. But better armour and subdivision of the internal compartments – a lesson learned at Dogger bank – had swung the odds in the Germans' favour. The big battleships kept their distance in order to take advantage of their better gunnery range, but poor visibility – the fog of war, quite literally – hampered their efforts; their lesser speed also kept them at the tail end of the engagement.

During this time, Jellicoe was still bringing the main part of the Grand Fleet from the north-west, whilst Scheer was steaming with the High Seas Fleet from the south-east. The Germans still had the impression of chasing the British: reconnaissance squadrons were constantly scouting ahead and turning back again when they encountered superior opposition, while the main forces manoeuvred and counter-manoeuvred across the miles of open sea between them. Charts of the battle are a mess of dotted lines showing ship movements, full of arrows and arcs, and about-turns. The second phase of the battle was about to unfold, the Battle Fleet Action.

Geoffrey and the *Black Prince*

Geoffrey Harry Verrall Bayfield was born in 1893, the youngest son of the Revd M. A. Bayfield, man of the Church and member of the SPR, and his wife Helen Campbell. He was already serving in the Royal Navy when war was declared. Initially, he sailed with the Dover Patrol on the ships *Nubian* and *Mohawk*, and in 1916, aged twenty-three, he was a Lieutenant on board HMS *Black Prince*.[44] The *Black Prince* was a Duke of Edinburgh-class armoured cruiser assigned to the 1st Cruiser Squadron under Rear-Admiral Sir Robert Keith Arbuthnot.

44 National Archives, ADM 196/55/79.

In addition to the *Black Prince*, Arbuthnot's squadron of armoured cruisers consisted of his flagship HMS *Defence*, HMS *Warrior* and HMS *Duke of Edinburgh*. The point of the armoured cruisers, being faster than the battlecruisers and battleships, was to provide a forward screen for the Grand Fleet as it steamed for the rendezvous with Beatty's force. So it was that Lieutenant Bayfield found himself on the *Black Prince* with the rest of the 1st Cruiser Squadron, the 2nd Cruiser Squadron, a squadron of light cruisers and Rear-Admiral Hood's 3rd Battle Cruiser Squadron scouting ahead of Jellicoe's Battle Squadrons of Dreadnoughts and Super-Dreadnoughts, and their destroyer escorts.

When wireless operators aboard the *Iron Duke* intercepted Commodore Sinclair's message to Beatty saying that he had sighted the enemy, Jellicoe ordered full steam ahead. Belching black smoke from their funnels, the battleships threw the coal into their furnaces until they were making 20 knots. Just after 17.00, the *Black Prince* received the order 'Take station for the approach'. A moment later, the whole of the Grand Fleet was signalled 'Prepare for action in every respect'. Bayfield's heart must have been in his mouth as he steamed southwards into the greatest naval battle in history.[45]

The *Black Prince* cleared for action. Sailors raced to and fro making ready: all woodwork on the quarter-deck was removed, buckets and barrels were filled with water, hoses rigged and extra ammunition stacked in place. All hands stood by their posts, life-jackets and respirators on. They cheered as they heard the news: 'enemy sighted'.[46]

Arbuthnot's squadron was 10 miles (16 km) in advance of the main battle fleet. By 17.40, Lt Bayfield would have seen gun flashes ahead and heard their distant rumble. Arbuthnot's battle line had the *Defence*, *Duke of Edinburgh* and *Black Prince* steaming abreast with 8 miles (13 km) between each ship and the *Warrior* following on in column behind the *Defence*. As the minutes ticked on, enemy ships were sighted at 17.47. They adjusted course to meet them. The *Defence* signalled 'Open

45 Wyllie, et al., *More Sea Fights*, pp. 138–9.
46 Wyllie, et al., *More Sea Fights*, pp. 140, 143.

fire, ship interval 12 seconds' and salvoes roared from the big guns, falling short at the extreme range.[47]

Shortly after 18.00, officers on watch aboard the battleships observed the battle already raging ahead as the Fleet's forward ships met the enemy. Rear-Admiral Hood had engaged his three Invincible-class battlecruisers against the German vanguard. The *Defence* and *Warrior* could be seen in hot pursuit of the stricken *Wiesbaden*.[48]

An officer on HMS *Yarmouth* observed that 'Admiral Arbuthnot was anxious to engage any enemy that might turn up and pressed forward with great impatience.' That impatience brought his ships directly in the path of Beatty's battlecruisers. From HMS *Badger* they saw that 'the *Defence, Warrior, Black Prince* and one other cruiser [*Duke of Edinburgh*] also appeared suddenly out of the mist, and cut across the *Lion*'s bow'.[49]

From the *Yarmouth*, Arbuthnot's squadron 'looked a very fine sight, turning and firing in succession'. However, Arbuthnot's charge had brought his ships within close range of the German big guns and the squadron received 'overwhelming gunfire from the enemy ships'.[50]

Three salvoes were seen to strike the *Defence* across the quarter-deck and bridge, causing 'a huge column of flame and smoke' to tower into the air and 'the ship was gone'. Rear-Admiral Arbuthnot and all hands were lost, some nine hundred men.[51] HMS *Warrior* was in flames; heavily damaged, she was engulfed in the smoke of her destroyed flagship as she raced forward. The *Duke of Edinburgh* managed to haul northwards and escape. From the *Yarmouth* it looked as though the *Black Prince* had met the same fate as the *Defence*.[52]

47 H. W. Fawcett and G. W. W. Hooper (eds), *The Fighting at Jutland: The Personal Experiences of Forty-Five Officers and Men of the British Fleet* (London: Macmillan, 1921), p. 84.
48 Wyllie, et al., *More Sea Fights*, p. 140.
49 Fawcett and Hooper, *The Fighting at Jutland*, pp. 82, 135.
50 Fawcett and Hooper, *The Fighting at Jutland*, p. 82.
51 Wyllie, et al., *More Sea Fights*, p. 140. The third salvo reported may have been an explosion of one of the ship's magazines.
52 Fawcett and Hooper, *The Fighting at Jutland*, pp. 82–3.

The North Sea by Starshell

The *New Zealand* checked fire just before 18.30 and it would be two hours before she had the enemy again visible and within range. At 20.24 she picked up the '3rd ship from the right' and with the distance falling to under 10,000 yards opened fire. In the *New Zealand*'s 'Record of Ranges' there is a note at 20.30: 'enemy on fire forward and hauling out of line, listing heavily'. But darkness brought the engagement to a close and at 20.39 the *New Zealand* again checked fire.[53]

As night fell, searchlights snapped on and starshells burst in the darkness above. Muzzle flashes from the great guns added their brief illumination and fire flickered upon the floating wreckage. The smell of coal and cordite hung in the air. Dim outlines of ships drifted through the smog and explosions reverberated through the black sea. In the darkness, the British destroyers came upon the German battleships and felt their wrath. From the upper deck of the *Agincourt* the men crowded to watch the unequal battle: 'volumes of tawny smoke intermixed with red flashes, and above, brilliant starshells lit up the clouds,' recalled one eyewitness.[54]

The *Black Prince* had not been sunk, but she had lost contact with the rest of the British Grand Fleet. Between about 18.30 and 23.30 there was no news of her. Drifting in the middle of the biggest sea battle in history for five hours, it is impossible to say whether Lt Bayfield was still alive. A ship was spotted by the crew of the destroyer HMS *Spitfire* some time just after 23.30, after they had narrowly avoided being rammed by a German ship. A few hundred yards off their starboard side a burning cruiser emerged from the smoke and darkness on a direct course for the *Spitfire*:

---

53 'Record of Ranges', in Admiralty, *Battle of Jutland*, pp. 393–5.
54 Wyllie, et al., *More Sea Fights*, pp. 151, 154. The eyewitness is not named.

To our intense relief she missed our stern by a few feet, but so close was she to us that it seemed that we were actually under her guns, which were trained out on her starboard beam. She tore past us with a roar, rather like a motor roaring up hill on low gear, and the very crackling and heat of the flames could be heard and felt. She was a mass of fire from fore-mast to main-mast, on deck and between decks [. . .] flames were issuing out of her from every corner.[55]

Onboard the *Spitfire* they came to the conclusion that the ship could have been the *Black Prince*. At about midnight they heard an explosion coming from the direction in which she had gone. Officers of the watch onboard the light cruiser HMS *Active* saw a ship caught in the search-lights of several vessels off her starboard side. Salvoes rained down, sinking her. They recorded the time as 23.00 and thought that this may have been the *Black Prince*. In the darkness and confusion, the exact fate of the *Black Prince* was unknown, but come the dawn she was seen no more. Lieutenant Bayfield's body was never recovered. His name is inscribed upon the Portsmouth Naval Memorial.[56]

The *Piupiu*

On paper, the British had all the numbers in their favour: more ships, especially more battleships, more battlecruisers, more light cruisers, more ships of every description; more ships meant more guns and more battleships meant more bigger guns. Providence, they say, is always on the side of the big guns. At sea, the Germans had inflicted the greater losses upon their enemy: more ships sunk; more men killed; more men wounded.

55 Fawcett and Hooper, *The Fighting at Jutland*, p. 169
56 Wyllie, et al., *More Sea Fights*, p. 160; Sir Henry Newbolt, *A Naval History of the War, 1914–1918* (London: Hodder and Stoughton, 1921), p. 112.

The *New Zealand* fired 420 12-inch shells during the battle, more than any other Dreadnought there. She scored only four hits. She herself took only one hit, an 11-inch shell to X Turret, but without sustaining serious damage or casualties.[57] As Captain Green put it in his report:

> We were fortunately only hit once by a heavy projectile, about 1 foot above the deck on the port side of 'X' Turret (the after turret) which punched a hole about 2 feet in diameter. It also went through the tongue of the towing slip which was secured round the turret. The shell must have burst on deck as there were sputterings round about there. It also damaged the deck, cutting through it and through the deck below into the Engineer's Workshop.[58]

As the anonymous midshipman observed, 'some of the escapes seemed miraculous'. A shell splinter had reached the main steam-pipe, but had come to rest against it rather than catastrophically puncturing it. Another shell blasting through the ship *en route* to the magazines had been stopped by the flour store.[59] Then there were the other strange relics of blind destruction shaped by strange forces: a wooden model of HMS *Barham* carried onboard the battleship was hit by shrapnel and 'scarred as though to scale in exactly the same places as the ship was damaged'. Onboard HMS *Warspite* a heavy shell exploded outside the ship's chapel: 'Everything inside was wrecked, chairs broken, splinters everywhere. In spite of all the ruin the crucifix was quite unhurt and still stood upon the broken altar.'[60]

There was a reason why people thought sailors superstitious: when their lives hung by a thread, only blind luck seemed to play a role. And

57 *Conway's All the World's Fighting Ships 1906–21* (London: Conway Maritime Press, 1985).
58 'Captain's Report on Action of 31st May 1916, HMS *New Zealand*,' in Admiralty, *Battle of Jutland*.
59 Wyllie, et al., *More Sea Fights*, p. 126.
60 Wyllie, et al., *More Sea Fights*, p. 136.

then there was the *New Zealand*: in the thick of the fighting and only one hit to show for it, while around her two ships had exploded with almost total loss of life. The belief persisted that the *New Zealand* had escaped entirely unscathed: 'untouched though right in the thick of all the fighting', wrote Wyllie, et al., adding 'the prophecy seems to have been fulfilled'. Even Green had managed not to crash into anything. Did he wear the *piupiu*? The National Museum of the Royal New Zealand Navy thinks he did.

The *piupiu* was loaned to the National Museum of the Royal Navy in Portsmouth and went on display in a major exhibition, 'Jutland 100', in 2016. The First Sea Lord, Admiral Sir Philip Jones, and the High Commissioner for New Zealand, Sir Lockwood Smith, attended the opening ceremony of the exhibition to watch a *haka* dance and traditional songs performed by the Cultural Group of the Royal New Zealand Navy.[61] Lieutenant Commander Ian Andrew, a logistics adviser for the New Zealand Defence Force, told *Portsmouth News*:

> Throughout history sailors have generally been quite superstitious and anything that brings good luck is welcome on board a ship. A ship is more than just the nuts and bolts, the engines; it's the people on board, it's the crew. They are the life and soul, they are the actual spirit of the ship. Having something like the *piupiu* presented from the people of New Zealand to the ship HMS *New Zealand*, would naturally give the crew something to bond to or identify themselves with and pull them all together, which is hugely important on any ship.[62]

---

61 'First Sea Lord Receives Maori Welcome at Jutland Exhibition', Royal Navy Website (5 June 2016), https://www.royalnavy.mod.uk/news-and-latest-activity/news/2016/june/05/160605-first-sea-lord-receives-moari-welcome-at-jutland-exhibition, accessed 14 February 2018.
62 'Skirt Worn by Naval Captain During Battle of Jutland Goes on Show in Major Exhibition', *Portsmouth News* (19 May 2016), https://www.portsmouth.co.uk/news/defence/skirt-worn-by-naval-captain-during-battle-of-jutland-goes-on-show-in-major-exhibition-1-7390241, accessed 14 February 2018.

To all onboard, it seemed as though the *piupiu* had again saved the *New Zealand*. Mrs Baxter's vision must have perplexed her until news of the battle was published on 2 or 3 June 1916, but her heart would have been in her mouth until the casualty list was published on 8 June.[63] Revd Bayfield would have read that casualty list, too, and seen his youngest son's name.

The press initially reported the battle as a German victory, but despite their heavier losses, the British had repulsed the German attempt to break the blockade and still held the numerical advantage in the North Sea. The Germans never again risked a confrontation on the same scale.

The Grand Fleet's losses forced the Royal Navy to re-organise her squadrons. Amongst the many changes, the *New Zealand* was posted to the 1st Battle Cruiser Squadron to take the place of the *Queen Mary*, although she would later be shifted back again. The *piupiu* remained onboard throughout the rest of the war.

After the war, the *piupiu* was returned to Halsey and after his death in 1949 it passed to his youngest daughter Ruth Halsey, despite the fact that 'Lord Mountbatten tried hard to get hold of the Maori skirt when my father died'.[64] After Ruth died in turn in 2002, her nephew (and Halsey's grandson), John Wood, offered it to the Royal New Zealand Navy Museum – Ruth had always wanted it to return to New Zealand – and there it lies to this day.

63 'Case L. 1204' *JSPR*, No. CCCXXXI, Vol. XVII (July 1916), pp. 204–7. A later note says first news was in the evening papers of 2 June (JSPR, October 1916, p. 211). The existence of Malpress is confirmed by Don Kindell, *Royal Navy Roll of Honour: World War 1 1914–1918, Pt 2: By Date and Ship/Unit*, ed. Gordon Smith (Penarth: Naval-History.net, 2009), p. 206; and National Archives, ADM 188/1097/3854.
64 Letter from Mrs J. Wood to Lt.-Commander P Dennerley, 24 March 1994 (Object information file for *piupiu* 2007.1.1).

Mrs Baxter's Vision

In 1916, the SPR still had a mystery to solve: what had Mrs Baxter's vision meant? The SPR's Secretary, Isabel Newton, went to Peterborough to interview Mrs Baxter on 29 June 1916. Baxter was suffering from erysipelas (St Anthony's Fire), a bacterial infection of the skin that can be fatal in severe cases, and experienced the vision whilst in a delirious state.[65]

Her mother, Mrs Hanna Malpress, told Newton how her daughter had been 'lightheaded on and off' during the course of her illness, but on the afternoon of 31 May was 'listless and blank'. Mrs Malpress rushed out to find someone who could fetch the doctor: 'I thought she was dying,' she stated.

Florence Baxter also thought that she was dying. She 'felt something snap inside her, and part of herself seemed to have gone out of her'. Newton made notes on how the vision unfolded:

> Then she seemed to be on a ship, or very near it; she could see sailors moving about, and heard them singing; they were very happy. She spoke to her brother on the ship; he wouldn't answer. She called for a scarf he had given her, so that she could hide her face, as she was disfigured.

The vision changed and she found herself back at home:

> Her brother was at home, she spoke to him, but he wouldn't answer. She cried, thinking it was because she was disfigured.

The vision faded. When Mrs Malpress went back upstairs, she found her daughter in tears and greatly upset. She asked her what the matter

65 'Case L. 1204', *JSPR* 17 (1915–16), pp. 204–7.

was. Florence asked if her brother had returned; 'She said Will had been to see her, and he wouldn't speak to her.'

'How did Will look?' asked Mrs Malpress.

'Just as usual,' said Florence, 'I thought he was here on leave. He was in his uniform, and very bright and happy.'

Miss Newton also contacted Mrs Baxter's doctor. Dr H. Latham was able to provide a few more details of Baxter's condition: her delirium had lasted from the night of Monday, 29 May, to 'the end of the week'. During this time she 'appeared to ramble' and, in her mother's words, say 'queer things', but only at night. When Dr Latham had visited her – he could not remember on what day – both Mrs Baxter and her mother told her about the 'vision'. Naturally, he asked Baxter about it: 'She told me quite simply that she had seen her brother on the deck of his ship, that he looked quite as usual, but never spoke a word.' The doctor gave strict orders that Mrs Baxter should not be told about the battle – he evidently feared that the shock would be too much for her – and it was not until 'a full week' afterwards that she read of it. He stated that this was the only such hallucination described to him: 'I am quite sure that neither Mrs Malpress nor Mrs Baxter have ever had any other previous experience of the kind.'[66]

Reconstructing events, the *Journal* Editor had a copy of Admiral Sir John Jellicoe's despatch on the battle as published in the newspapers for 7 July. According to the Admiral, the battle began at 15.48 GMT. From the *Daily Telegraph* for 6 June, she had an account saying that the *Queen Mary* sank 'quite early in the action'. She compared this to Mrs Baxter's statements, she 'saw' her brother in 'the afternoon', according to the account published in the newspaper, or at 'about 5 o'clock', according to Miss Newton's interview. As it was British Summer Time, Jellicoe's 15.48 is 16.48; add some minutes to bring it up to 'quite early in the action' and the Editor thought it close enough in time to represent something significant.

66 Letters of H. Latham, MB, 3 July and 15 July 1916, in 'Case L. 1204', *JSPR* 17 (1915–16), pp. 206–7.

'Contrary to our practice of excluding hallucinations occurring during illness where delirium is present,' the Editor decided to publish. G. W. Malpress is commemorated on Panel 13 of the Portsmouth Naval Memorial, just one of the 24,023 names inscribed upon it.

Kitchener's Sixty-Sixth Year

In June, in his sixty-sixth year, Lord Kitchener embarked on a dangerous mission. A special sleeping carriage had been hitched to the regular eight o'clock Sunday train from King's Cross, London, but only two or three senior officials knew that Kitchener was on board.

Kitchener had boarded quickly to avoid being seen any more than was necessary. Uncharacteristically, he reappeared on the platform. 'Look after my things while I am away,' he is reported to have said, 'very quietly – and a little sadly' to a friend who had accompanied him to the station. According to one of his biographers, 'as if unable to explain to himself the impulse which had prompted him to have a last word, he quickly regained his seat and looked away out of the window until the train started'.[67]

The train paused briefly on the cold and largely deserted platform of Edinburgh's Waverley Station at 4 a.m. Monday, 5 June. His final destination was not printed, but one would guess it was Thurso, like the later special wartime service dubbed 'the Jellicoe Express' designed to move naval personnel fast across the length of the land. Thurso lies 717 miles (1,150 km) from London on the far northern coast of Scotland with sea links to the Orkney Islands where the Grand Fleet was based.[68]

The light cruiser HMS *Hampshire* had only just returned to port at Scapa Flow after the Battle of Jutland. In the words of Petty Officer Wilfred Wesson, 'the din of battle still rang in their ears' and the 'strain

---

67 Sir George Arthur, *The Life of Kitchener*, vol. III (London: Macmillan & Co., 1920), p. 353.
68 'Lord Kitchener Lost at Sea', *The Guardian* (7 June 1916).

of high-pressure warfare showed in their eyes'. Now she was on stand-by for a special mission. The crew speculated that a further battle was in the offing, but as a pinnace from Sir John Jellicoe's flagship, HMS *Iron Duke*, drew near, they saw that their special mission was Kitchener.[69]

It may have been summer, but one of the worst storms in years was blowing in and the pinnace struggled through the heavy swell. At lunch aboard the *Iron Duke*, Jellicoe had tried to persuade Kitchener to delay his voyage. He would not. His mission was vital to the war effort. As a compromise, Jellicoe suggested taking a different route, more protected from the storm winds, away from Scapa Flow. With the wild wind whipping his greatcoat, Captain Herbert T. Savill welcomed him on board the *Hampshire* and soon the whole crew knew their top secret destination: Archangel, Russia.

With an escort provided by the destroyers *Unity* and *Victor*, the *Hampshire* put out into what Wesson called 'the very teeth of the most terrific gale in my experience'. The wind had veered north-west: it 'whipped the sea to a fury'; 'it moaned and shrieked in her rigging'; and 'mountainous seas swept her decks in great frothing sheets'. The hatches, all but one, were battened down against the onslaught. The storm beat back the destroyers; soon they were 'mere specks on the livid horizon'. Wesson could make out the 'iron coast' of the Orkneys off to starboard: 'great towers of jagged black rocks rose sheerly against the skyline'. The air was full of the sound of 'rushing water and scream-ing wind'.

The supper bugle had called Wesson down to the messroom and over bread and cheese he debated the threats of submarines and mines with his comrades. The weather was too rough for submarines, they argued, and the waters had been swept for mines, or so they thought. That was when the explosion rocked the ship. Wesson felt the *Hampshire* lurch. From somewhere deep within the ship came 'a dreadful grating sound'. Escaping steam hissed like a nest of vipers. Feet could be heard pounding like a drunken drum roll and shouts filled the air. The lights flickered and went out.

69 Wilfred Wesson, 'How Kitchener Died', *Sunday Express* (8 July 1923).

Wesson and the others made for the open hatch, wading through the water that was already pouring into the corridors. Up on deck, people were talking of having hit a mine. Officers were shouting orders, but they could barely be heard above the storm. Waves crashed over the decks as the men struggled to lower the lifeboats – they were electrically controlled and the power was out. In the wild confusion Wesson saw Kitchener come out on deck: 'he looked grave and calm'. As the *Hampshire* listed to starboard, Kitchener made his way to the bridge to join the captain.

The *Hampshire* was doomed. Men surged into the boats. Men jumped overboard. The wounded screamed again as the brine bit into their wounds. Wesson was in charge of the Carley raft stations to starboard and got his raft safely away, even as the waves swept men overboard – the Carley rafts resembled giant lifebelts with rope handles round the sides to enable fifty or so men to cling on. They paddled with all their strength to get clear of the stricken ship. Behind them, the *Hampshire* rolled over and, as she went down, the vortex sucked in men and boats. They were only 2 miles (3 km) off the Orkney coast, but they were still in the teeth of the gale and soaked to the skin by the ice-cold water. Gunner Tom Jennings roared out a desperate rendition of *Tipperary* at the top of his lungs. Many would die of exposure, Jennings among them. Nearly eight hundred men lost their lives. Wesson was one of the lucky twelve who survived.[70]

That Monday evening, Cheiro was sitting in the music room of a country house. A world away from the knife-edged wind and raging sea of the north, he and some friends were chatting about the war. A crash startled them. The sound had come from the north end of the room. They went to investigate. A large heraldic shield carved out of oak and painted with the royal coat of arms had fallen to the floor and broken in two. Cheiro picked it up and seeing that the wood had split through the arms of England and Ireland, pronounced that 'this is evidently an omen that some terrible blow has at this moment been dealt to England.

70 Estimates of crew numbers vary from 655 (*Sunday Times*, 28 August 1988) to 800 (Wesson).

I feel that some naval disaster has taken place in Ireland or at least the name of Ireland is in some way concerned.' As he finished speaking, the clock struck the hour: 8 p.m.[71]

The next day in London, the Admiralty received a telegram from Admiral Jellicoe:

> I have to report with deep regret that His Majesty's ship *Hampshire*, Captain Herbert J. Savill, R. N., with Lord Kitchener and his staff on board, was sunk last night at about 8 p. m., to the west of the Orkneys, either by a mine or a torpedo.[72]

Kitchener had, of course, been born in Ballylongford, County Kerry, in Ireland.

Lord Kitchener Lives

The rumour mills started to grind immediately after Kitchener's death. 'The public mind,' reported the *Daily Mail*, 'has been quick to associate his death with the work of spies.' The *Morning Post* declared that 'circumstances point at espionage or treachery'. Crowds gathered in London – at the Stock Exchange, in Whitehall and outside the news-paper offices – demanding news. Across the country, official flags were lowered to half-mast and the Army was ordered into mourning by the King himself. A memorial service was held in St Paul's Cathedral. For a week, all officers wore a black band around their left arms.[73]

The conspiracy theories were not restricted to spies and treachery: there was also a Spiritualist conspiracy. In 1922, a strange book appeared

71 Cheiro, *Confessions*, pp. 99–100.
72 Quoted in Capt. Logan Howard-Smith, Thomas F. Trusler and Viscount James Bryce, *Earl Kitchener and the Great War* (Philadelphia: International Press, 1916), p. 12.
73 Quoted in Howard-Smith, et al., *Earl Kitchener*, p. 14; other details, pp. 15–16.

– *The Message: Lord Kitchener Lives* – written by one Ala Mana (apparently the only book written by 'Ala Mana'), claiming to be the direct communication of Kitchener from beyond the grave. According to this 'Kitchener', as the HMS *Hampshire* got underway, 'I had a depressed feeling, a strange inward foreboding'. After dinner he took a turn on deck, settling into a chair to gaze into the darkness of the night. He fell asleep, but was awoken by the sound of someone calling his name. He could see no one. This happened a second time, then 'slowly in the darkness, I saw a light'. The light began to take form and soon he recognised his mother.[74]

'My boy,' said the apparition, 'danger awaits you on every hand and if you are not careful you will come to the spirit. Watch – watch, my beloved son.'

Kitchener was rooted to the spot. It was fifteen minutes before he could raise himself from his chair. Then he heard someone cry out, 'Submarine!'

Leaning out over the railings he peered into the blackness of the night. Suddenly, in the flash of the ship's searchlight, a torpedo could be seen streaking towards them. Then he saw the submarine, as the searchlight swept on, diving back below the waves. The torpedo missed, but the HMS *Hampshire* fired back, launching its own torpedo and finding its target. Nevertheless the *Hampshire* had sustained some damage astern. It was not severe, but back in his cabin, it put Kitchener in the mood to commit a statement to paper:

> I hear the cries for peace ring on the tongues of the beaten and I hear it ring on the tongues of the victors, the people. The people must choose lest destruction sweep the world and trample down both good and bad. For peace must come soon or men will die; rivers will run blood-red.[75]

The message was not just about the present war. He saw 'a might army' rise up – 'the army of the world sent by the Devil from Hell' – which

74 Mana, *The Message*, pp. 17–18.
75 Mana, *The Message*, p. 19.

would 'crumble civilization'. The time was not far off when 'this terrible war, one more spectacular than the one now raging' would be 'caused and made by the mighty army of disembodied spirits'. The ranks of this spirit army would be drawn from 'the present fields of battle', all those killed 'in horrified moments of bloody fight' who 'seek to go on with the fight' because 'they feel only a fight can relieve them'. For his own part, he wrote 'I will watch the world when I am gone [. . .] I hope I may help to stay this mighty army.'[76]

After a great many more words in similar vein, the prophetic moment finally passed. 'What a strange thing for me to write,' remarked 'Kitchener'. Ala Mana then proceeds to give an account, as if related by Kitchener, of the Field Marshal's death: he finds himself locked in his cabin, there is an explosion, he smashes the door open, water floods the ship, he drowns, but his consciousness lives on. His mother appears again to lead him through the separation of body and spirit, and he learns the fundamental truth from her: 'there is no death'. The book goes on for another four hundred pages as 'Kitchener' settles into his new world, undergoes a sort of training programme (including a bizarre astral operation) and other tedious adventures before meeting Queen Victoria, Admiral Nelson and Abraham Lincoln, amongst others, to learn all sorts of nonsense from them.[77]

Kitchener's martial character is immediately changed by his passing over, so that when he overhears another spirit 'say something about hanging being too good for the murderer' finds that 'this rather upset me'. His guide tells him that this spirit is 'in darkness' and that 'an entity' caused the murderer to commit the crime. This blanket pardon for criminals – a version of 'the Devil made me do it' – is symptomatic of Mana's sickly sweet Spiritualist afterlife. Like many other Spiritualist accounts, the afterlife is structured as a vast schoolroom where the deceased study outlandish subjects, such as 'penmanship of the language of the astral', so that they may teach others, and everyone conveniently speaks English (everyone, conveniently, seems to be

76 Mana, *The Message*, p. 20.
77 Mana, *The Message*, pp. 24–8.

English, with a smattering of foreign worthies, such as Moses and Tolstoy, and the odd American).[78]

In Ala Mana's Other World the spirits are divided into a White Circle and a Black Circle. The Black Circle is ruled by 'the Devil' – no surprises there – and comprises demons from the 'lower planes' and 'earthbounds'. Kitchener undergoes a sort of 'harrowing of Hell', has an interview with the Devil where they argue over his soul and gets through it all to find out that he is one of the White Circle. And there are circles within circles: a Circle of Constructors, a Circle of Free Spirits, a Circle of Intelligence, and so on, within the White Circle itself. Kitchener joins a 'convention to help bring about the end of the war', with the special task of harassing military planners so that 'they will know and do the right thing'. Unfortunately, the Black Circle has 'made its impression and the conflict has been most terrible and unnecessary'; apparently, the White Circle did not intend for the war to run so long. Ala Mana creates an earthly world without Free Will: every evil deed is the result of the Black Circle's influence; every good one, that of the White. Even the influenza epidemic was 'caused by atmospheric thought waves'. As for Kitchener, his mother explains that 'Your death was accomplished by the Black Circle who had a legion there'. Jesus comes in at the end of the book, apparently arriving by cloud, and, with the tolling of a great bell and a fanfare of trumpets, announces the end of the war. Fortunately, volume two seems never to have been written.[79]

As we know, there was no submarine prowling the raging seas around Orkney. There had been: U-75 had laid thirteen mines just before the Battle of Jutland; twelve of them had been found by minesweepers. That and the dead Kitchener's uncharacteristic squeamishness put sizeable holes in Ala Mana's narrative before its other claims had been questioned.

Ala Mana is identified in the catalogue of the British Library as Margaret Malel O'Brien, but this must be Margaret Mabel O'Brien. She

78 Mana, *The Message*, pp. 38, 49.
79 Mana, *The Message*, pp. 191, 204, and *passim*; 271, 294, 375.

may have been Margaret Mabel O'Brien of Carbonear on the Avlon Peninsula, Newfoundland, who lost a brother, James O'Brien, during the war. He had served with the Newfoundland Mercantile Marine (Canadian Merchant Navy) and lost his life aboard the schooner *Jorgina* on 24 March 1918. Again, it may have been the Margaret Mabel O'Brien who danced barefoot as one of the 'harem girls' at the Little Theatre, Los Angeles, in 1916. The book was published in both Vancouver and Los Angeles, so both are possible; and the two names could refer to one and the same person.[80]

Conan Doyle Goes to the Front

Sir Arthur Conan Doyle's son, Kingsley, spent a year in Malta before changing his mind. He took a commission in the Hampshire Regiment and in April 1916 found himself on his way to France. Conan Doyle was delighted. He also got his chance when he was invited to survey the Italian front as a British observer, although his mission was one of war propaganda. The Italian Army had been castigated in the press for its poor performance against the Austro-Hungarians: Conan Doyle would write a pro-Italian piece to counterbalance the criticism.[81]

He managed to tour some of the British lines *en route*. He was arrested by the strange beauty of shrapnel shells bursting round a lone aeroplane; dead landscapes of rusty barbed wire under wheeling crows disturbed by the occasional sniper's bullet.

80 *Merchant Navy Book of Remembrance*, p. 54, http://www.veterans.gc.ca/ eng/remembrance/memorials/books/page?page=54&book=6&sort=pageAs c, accessed 7 March 2018; 'Harem Girls Will Dance in Bare Feet in Revue of Plays', *Los Angeles Herald* (28 April 1916), p. 1; the copy in the British Library was published by the Sun Publishing Co. of Vancouver, also in 1922. The name turns up again in the Louisville, Kentucky, *Courier-Journal* for 29 July 1928.
81 Sir Arthur Conan Doyle, *A Visit to Three Fronts* (London: Hodder & Stoughton, 1916); Conan Doyle, *Memories*, unpaginated; Miller, *Adventures*, pp. 329–30.

At Bailleul he met his brother Innes, now a Colonel and Assistant Adjutant-General of the 24th Division. He dined with him in the officers' mess and lodged in the town. After dark, he went out on a drive to see the lights of the Ypres salient at night. The next day, Innes drove him into Ypres, utterly ruined by war. Conan Doyle 'marvelled at the beauty of the smashed cathedral and the tottering Cloth Hall beside it'. Later in the afternoon they reached Sharpenburg and Conan Doyle reflected on the battles already fought, 'the spots which our dear lads, three of them my own kith, had sanctified with their blood'.[82]

Some days later he met Kingsley. Field Marshal Douglas Haig had arranged it all and now father and son had an hour to talk. Kingsley talked of a coming 'big push' – the Battle of the Somme. As Conan Doyle left, he must have wondered if he would ever see him again.

Later that day he had lunch with his friend and former secretary Alfred Herbert Wood, now a major in the 5th Royal Sussex Territorials and acting as Mayor of Beauquesne. At fifty, he had already seen fighting at the Battle of Festubert and elsewhere during his two years in uniform.

They travelled on to Amiens together where Conan Doyle got the train to Paris: 'a very dead and alive Paris'. An uneventful two-day journey from Paris brought Conan Doyle to Padua. When he reached the Italian front he found it much like Flanders, although blessed with better weather. Conan Doyle's official guides kept him away from the frontline trenches, but even so, he had a narrow escape. On the road to the recently liberated port of Monfalcone, the Austrian artillery had him in their sights as his speeding car tried to outrun the bursting shells. He never got to Monfalcone, but he did make it back to Paris.

Conan Doyle spent little time in Paris; after all, the Front was only a short car drive away. He motored out to Soissons. Soissons 'proved to be a considerable wreck'. Inside the cathedral they crunched across broken stained glass lying across the aisles and were greeted by a stray dog climbing over the roof, now lying untidily in the central aisle. Conan Doyle stooped to gather up some brightly coloured shards as

82 Conan Doyle, *A Visit*, pp. 24, 26.

souvenirs for his wife. The abbé came out to greet them and give them a tour of the desecrated ruin.[83]

He had a store of stories about the war, but one struck Conan Doyle particularly. It was one of those amazing coincidences, so rare during peacetime, so common in total war. A woman serving in the local ambulance said she would kiss the first French soldier to enter the town as the Germans were forced to retreat. The first Frenchman turned out to be her husband. Conan Doyle noted that although the abbé was 'a good, kind, truthful man', he had 'a humorous face'.[84]

He left the abbé not quite sure if he had been the butt of a joke. His tour of the French positions taught him that 'trenches are trenches' and only the colourful French characters and ever present danger kept him from becoming bored or jaded. One of those characters was General Georges Louis Humbert (1862–1921), commander of the French Third Army. 'Why is Sherlock Holmes not a soldier in the British Army?' demanded the general. 'He is too old for service,' replied Doyle.[85]

Conan Doyle's adventure at the Front was soon over and he made his way home again. Before he reached Windlesham, Kingsley was appointed Temporary Lieutenant (15 June 1916). The 'big push' was coming.

'Worse Than France'

'I remember screaming,' wrote Captain Robert Graves, now in the 2nd Battalion, the Royal Welch Fusiliers, as he recalled being moved from the field hospital. They had taken him there after the attack on High Wood during the Battle of the Somme on 20 July. Graves had joined the army a day or two after war was declared. Expecting garrison duty on the home front and a short war, before the end of 1915 he was a

83 Conan Doyle, *A Visit*, pp. 54–5.
84 Conan Doyle, *A Visit*, p. 55.
85 Conan Doyle, *A Visit*, p. 72.

Captain. Now, he was officially reported as dead. He was not dead and, when he was able to, posted a notice in the newspaper:

> Captain Robert Graves, Royal Welch Fusiliers, officially reported died of wounds, wishes to inform his friends that he is recovering from his wounds at Queen Alexandra's Hospital, Highgate.[86]

He did not spend long at Highgate. By September he was well enough to go on leave and arranged to spend it with Siegfried Sassoon in Harlech. At Harlech they worked on poetry together. After he had gone, Graves visited a friend from the 1st Battalion. Recently wounded, he had been sent home to Kent. His elder brother had been killed at Gallipoli and when Graves arrived he found that the mother had preserved his bedroom exactly as he had left it. Not exactly: the mother aired his sheets, laundered his linen, kept the flowers fresh and put cigarettes by his bedside. 'She was religious,' Graves explained, 'and went about with a bright look on her face.'

The two friends sat till after midnight talking about the war. Graves noted that he fell asleep around one o'clock, but was soon awakened by 'sudden rapping noises'. He tried to ignore them, but they were getting louder and, mysteriously, seemed to come from everywhere. It was unnerving. 'I lay in a cold sweat,' he wrote.[87]

At about three o'clock, he heard 'a diabolic yell and a succession of laughing, sobbing shrieks'. He jumped up and tore open the door. In the passage outside he ran into his friend's mother, still fully dressed.

'It's nothing,' she said, 'One of the maids has hysterics. I am so sorry you have been disturbed.'

Graves went back to bed, but lay awake until daybreak. 'I'm leaving this place,' he said to his friend in the morning, 'it's worse than France.' Graves said no more about the event. In November, he was back with the Battalion; and back at the Front the following January.

86 Graves, *Good-Bye*, p. 283.
87 Graves, *Good-Bye*, pp. 289–90.

The Spectre of the Somme

September 1916, Captain W. E. Newcome relates that he was moving down the line with the 2nd Battalion, Suffolk Regiment, from Loos to the northern sector of Albert in the Somme. Here he would witness something that would stay with him for the rest of the war, even for the rest of his life:[88]

> Whilst in the front line trenches of that sector I, with others, witnessed one of the most remarkable occurrences of the war.

The great Battle of the Somme was underway, the biggest battle in military history: four and a half million men fought each other; over one million lay dead or wounded afterwards. Since 1 July 1916, the British and French had been attempting to dislodge the Germans from their entrenched positions in the Somme Valley and would continue until 18 November.

Captain Newcome reported that 'we were actually holding that part of the line with very few troops'. On 1 November, the Germans attacked Captain Newcome's position. 'The assault was sharp and short,' wrote Newcome, 'a very determined attack,' but the enemy 'never gained a footing in our trenches' and was repulsed.

'We had settled down to watch and wait again for his next attack.' They did not have to wait long before they could make out German troops advancing across No Man's Land in 'massed waves'. Could they hold the line again? They sent what Newcome called an 'SOS signal', when he was surprised to see someone stand up in front of the advance:

88 First published in *Pearson's Magazine* (August 1919), pp. 190–1, and retold by Conan Doyle, *History of Spiritualism*, vol. II, pp. 234–5.

Before they reached our wire, a white, spiritual figure of a soldier rose from a shell-hole, or out of the ground about one hundred yards on our left, just in front of our wire and between the first line of Germans and ourselves.

Newcome watched the 'spectral figure' walk slowly along the Suffolk's front for about a thousand yards. It made him think 'of an old pre-war officer' in a 'shell coat, with field-service cap on its head'. The figure regarded the oncoming Germans before continuing its slow walk, passing along the Captain's sector.

Their SOS had now been answered by artillery and 'shells and bullets were whistling across No Man's Land'. The spectre continued unaffected. 'It steadily marched from the left of us till it got to the extreme right of the sector,' he wrote later, 'then it turned its face right full on us. It seemed to look up and down our trench, and as each Verey light rose it stood out more prominently.'

After this survey, the figure turned abruptly and headed directly towards the Germans. Newcome was astonished to see that before this solitary figure 'the Germans scattered back and no more was seen of them that night'.

'Angel of Mons, that was,' said one man.

'Just like before, sending the Germans packing!'

'Call that an angel? Didn't have no wings!'

'Looked more like Kitchener!'

Field Marshal Horatio Herbert Kitchener, 1st Earl Kitchener – Kitchener of Khartoum; the famous face of British Army recruitment – had died on 5 June 1916 when the ship he was sailing in struck a German mine and went down.

'I saw his face: spitting image of Lord Roberts, if you ask me.'

Frederick Sleigh Roberts, 1st Earl Roberts, with more honours and titles than we have room to mention, had died of pneumonia on 14 November 1914, aged eighty-two. Kitchener and Roberts had extremely dissimilar faces: Kitchener was bold, all moustache and hair parted with parade-ground discipline; Roberts was floating whiskers and big forehead, made bigger by male-pattern balding.

'I know that it gave me personally a great shock,' wrote Newcome. The others, too: 'for some time it was the talk of the company'. What is more, 'its appearance can be vouched for by sergeants and men of my section'.

Most of the original 2nd Battalion had been killed or captured at Le Cateau during their astonishing rearguard action to allow the BEF to continue its retirement. Out of a thousand men, 720 were listed killed, wounded or taken prisoner. What was left was transferred to GHQ Troops and from October 1915 to the 76th Brigade, 3rd Division.

It was strange of Newcome to say that they were coming from Loos, about 56 miles (90 km) north of Albert. The 2nd Suffolk had been involved in the Battle of the Somme from 8 July, first at Carnoy to the east of Albert, moving north to Montauban and Longueval as the battle progressed. In early October they were re-deployed north of Albert at Courcelles-au-Bois and the frontline trenches facing the German-held village of Serre, about 9 miles (15 km) north of Albert, taking part in the attack on Serre on 13 November.[89] Of Captain W. E. Newcome himself, assuming the spelling of his name is correct, I could find no trace.

Cruff, The Wise One's Half-Brother

Winifred Coombe Tennant's role as one of the SPR Automatists influenced her son Cruff, who tried his hand (or someone else's, as it may be) at automatic writing for the first time on 21 August 1915. 'He soon succeeded,' she wrote, getting 'a confused lot of stuff about a fire caused by a fuse'. Strangely, she did not want him to continue his experiments in this direction.[90]

As the war continued into 1916, with conscription being introduced, Winifred became 'very agitated over Cruff's fate'. He was still at

89 http://somme-roll-of-honour.com/Units/british/2nd_Suffolk.htm, accessed 19 April 2017.
90 Tennant, *Between Two Worlds*, p. 173.

Winchester, having tried and failed to get into Trinity College, Cambridge, in December 1915 – during his entrance exam, Winifred's mind had been awhirl with thoughts of the SPR's Trinity men, Sidgwick, Gurney and Myers, and no doubt thought of her boy following in the footsteps of her heroes. Fearing that he might end up as cannon-fodder in the Army, she wrote to Gerald about getting him into the Admiralty or the Flying Corps. A medical examination found him unfit for flying due to a weak heart, but not weak enough for the other Services.[91]

Discussions with Gerald Balfour concerning an Admiralty position led to nought and Winifred wrote to Cruff suggesting that he enter Sandhurst, i.e., join as an officer. 'Anything,' she wrote in her diary, 'to save him from the hell of the life of the ordinary Tommy!' She might have thought the ranker's life to be hell, but junior officers suffered higher casualty rates. Nevertheless, she busied herself writing letters 'to powers that be' to try and get him into the new Welsh Guards or Glamorgan Yeomanry. Meanwhile, Cruff joined the Officer Training Corps (OTC) at Winchester.[92]

With the OTC, Cruff was drilled by Sergeant Bawket, who had been at Mons and the retreat after it and, all told, spent nine months in the trenches. He must have been greatly impressive to the young cadets, with his tales of marching eighteen miles a day during the Great Retirement and showing them real trenches. Cruff acquitted himself on the firing range, with his sergeant remarking that 'there was nothing in [his] shooting to worry about'.[93]

Winifred's letter-writing paid off. The Welsh Guard's Colonel-in-Chief, Lord Harlech, summoned Cruff for an interview. As long as he had £500 a year or more, a place was his, whether he got into Sandhurst or not. She confessed to having 'mingled feelings'. On the positive side, she had saved him from being a Tommy and got him into the finest Welsh regiment. On the negative, she had gone against her principles,

---

91 Tennant, *Between Two Worlds*, p. 187.
92 Tennant, pp. 187, 188. The Welsh Guards had been created in 1915 after a letter to *The Times* pointed out that unlike the other countries in the United Kingdom, Wales did not have its own regiment of foot guards.
93 Tennant, *Between Two Worlds*, p. 190.

describing herself as a conscientious objector (although one who regarded Kitchener as one of her heroes), and was appalled at the thought of Army life in general and, in particular, 'of his being thrown among dissolute rich men' and 'the standard of extravagance implied by the need of a subaltern of £500 a year'.[94]

By August 1916, they had news of Cruff's try for Sandhurst: he had come fifteenth out of 302 in the entrance exams, winning a prize cadetship. Winifred's feelings were again mixed, 'rejoicing' at his success, yet deploring what it meant.[95]

At Sandhurst, Cruff felt like a new boy at school all over again, lost in the unfamiliar maze of buildings. It was like being in barracks, he thought, but he had a room to himself, looking onto a square. The door had no key to the lock and the sink was without a plug, but he had a rifle of his own. Before mess, 'juniors' were only allowed the lower end of an ante-room he described as being like a 'large smoking lounge' and the invisible line between the seniors at the upper end was guarded by the rumoured threat of transgressors being thrown into an ink bath. 'Very barbarous,' wrote Cruff in a letter to his mother.[96]

In another letter, he described training: 'we spent all morning digging trenches, in canvas trousers'. Each cadet had a 6x3 plot in which to dig a 3-foot-deep hole, throwing up the excavated earth in front. At the Front they dug deeper and put the earth behind. He found it 'very hard work'.[97]

Winifred visited Cruff at Sandhurst in September, describing him as 'looking very tall and boyish' but in 'hideous vile Khaki livery'. They had lunch together and went for a walk in the surrounding woods. Later she was treated to what she called 'a disgusting spectacle of a parade' and complained about the 'futility and silliness' of the punishments meted out for untied bootlaces and imperfect trouser creases (seven days confinement), unaware that such practices instilled the

94 Tennant, *Between Two Worlds*, p. 189; views on Kitchener, p. 191.
95 Tennant, *Between Two Worlds*, p. 196.
96 Tennant, *Between Two Worlds*, pp. 196–7.
97 Tennant, *Between Two Worlds*, pp. 197–8

sort of discipline they would need when facing an enemy intent on killing them. Instead, Winifred wrote in her diary 'it is an outrage to every fibre of my soul'.[98]

As Cruff continued his training, he heard news of the Hon. Edward Wyndham Tennant, known as 'Bim', a friend who had preceded him to France. He was the son of Lord and Lady Glenconner and they had been at West Downs and Winchester together, and now he had been killed in action at the battle of the Somme, aged nineteen. His last letter to his mother was printed in *The Times* and Cruff wrote to his own mother remarking that 'I felt it was just the sort of letter I might have written to you'. As his time went on at Sandhurst it brought him nearer to his inevitable deployment, Winifred thought she saw the anxiety of it beneath his everyday manner; she certainly felt it.[99]

America's Premier Psychic

Describing herself as 'America's Premier Psychic', the fifty-nine-year-old Madame Almira Brockway had arrived in Britain to give a lecture series in London, beginning on 5 November 1916. The *Daily Mail* reported that she had taken 'a richly furnished house in Bayswater – No. 8 Linden-gardens' where she entertained a 'very large and a very lucrative clientèle, and her rich drawing-room is daily the scene of miracles'.[100]

The *Daily Mail*'s unnamed Special Correspondent – research reveals this to have been Harold Ashton – visited her in December to test her psychic powers. He found her 'a quick, nimble, little woman with smooth grey hair and sharp grey eyes, and extremely businesslike and

---

98 Tennant, *Between Two Worlds*, pp. 198–9.
99 Tennant, *Between Two Worlds*, pp. 199, 203.
100 Our Special Correspondent, 'Mme. Brockway', *Daily Mail* (15 December 1916), p. 3; 'Psychist Again in Court', *Sunday Times* (31 December 1916), p. 10.

brisk in her methods'. They sat together in the drawing room on oppo-site sides of an elegant card-table. A pencil and writing pad lay between them.

'Take the pencil,' she said, 'and write down the names of, say, a couple of spirits you knew before they was spirits. Write the name distinct, and underneath it two or three questions, and if the spirits are anywhere about I guess we'll get through to 'em all right. If not, don't blame me, but them!'

The Correspondent thought she treated 'these astral voyages in the Beyond' as if 'she were dealing in dry-goods'. But he picked up the pencil and pad, and wrote down two names – Richard Hoskins, his grandfather, and Fred Davis, a childhood friend – and three questions apiece on separate sheets of paper; and folded the two sheets in four.

Madame Brockway warned that current conditions made communi-cation with the afterworld especially fraught: 'The spirit world is exceed-ingly powerless just now. All the spirits are at sixes and sevens, and it may be difficult to get through to them.'

With that she fixed a pair of pince-nez on her nose and picked up one of the pieces of paper. She pressed it to her forehead and began talking. They were sitting under a bright overhead electric light and the Correspondent said that he was shading his eyes but still 'watching carefully'. As she 'chattered on', he watched her shift the paper from her forehead to her lap where it was obscured from his view by the edge of the table. The movement was quick and the paper – 'apparently the same slip of folded paper' – was soon back on her forehead. He noted that while it was in her lap 'the rustle of her silk dress did not hide the rustle of paper'. Even with the folded sheet back on her forehead, the rustling of paper continued. She then put the piece of paper to her ear 'and "rang up" the Beyond'.

'Say! You there,' she called out. 'Yes, I guess it is . . . Will you ask the spirit of the person this gentleman is asking for to come through? He's there, is he? What? Guess I can't quite catch his name.'

Doing a very good impersonation of one end of a telephone call, she shifted her position to get a better view of whatever it was that she had in her lap. The Correspondent caught her glancing down for the briefest of moments. Suddenly the line to the spirit world seemed to improve.

'Speak up, please,' she continued, 'Who is it speaking? Oh – Ned – Ned . . . Davis!'

She addressed the Correspondent: 'Is that the name you want?'

'Not quite,' he said. In parentheses he informed the reader that his 'Fr's and 'N's are difficult to tell apart.

Brockway shot another look down at her lap. 'If it isn't Ned, it's Ted,' she said, the Correspondent noting her cross tone of voice.

'It's Fred,' he said, finally putting her out of her misery.

'Oh, I see.' Her eyes flashed downwards again. 'I guess he's a bit shy. He's one of them lonely spirits. He's never been called up before, and he's so excited over it that he don't quite know what he's saying.'

The real Fred Davis had died of measles in childhood and now went on to answer all the questions put to him 'with a knowledge beyond his years'. The Correspondent called her account a 'long rigmarole'.

One of his questions to Fred was 'Shall I be better in health in this year?'

'The spirit says,' said Brockway, 'you will have rather a bad time, but you will be all right if you take great care.'

His other two questions were: 'What is the immediate future in store?' and 'Will the East Pioneer be profitable?' – and Brockway answered them together.

'You are going to the East,' she said, 'you are going on a very dangerous mission; you must take great care, very great care, but at the end of it you will come out all right through the danger.'

'Thanks, madame,' said Ashton, 'I am very much relieved.' The East Pioneer was a Stock Exchange listing he was considering speculating in.

The next spirit 'promptly answered the telephone call', but gave his name as Hopkins instead of Hoskins. One of the questions the Correspondent had written down was, 'Is she all right?'

Brockway immediately got to work on this one, 'She is, in a way,' she said, adding, 'and she isn't. Beware of those dark eyes. She'll lead you on . . . and then you'll regret it! You'd better go slow – better still, cut her out of your scheme of things!'

The Correspondent was quite alarmed to hear of his missing black kitten being talked of in such a way. Altogether fed up with the performance, the Correspondent cut it short and asked her to name her fee.

'A guinea, please,' she said, and as he handed it over, he 'congratulated her on the money-making success of just a little sleight-of-hand – substituting one piece of a paper for another, reading the first in her lap while the dummy document is still held to the forehead'. Finally, however, he 'told Mrs Brockway flatly what I thought of her'.

Her reaction was dramatic: 'first she stormed and turned pale and trembled', then she asked him why, if he had seen through the trick, he had let her go through with it.

'I wanted to see the end of the experiment,' he replied.

'You are cruel – unkind, wasting my time and upsetting me like this!'

'Anyway, madame,' said the Correspondent, 'you have got your guinea.'

To this she became indignant. 'The money doesn't go to me. It all goes – every penny – to the Psychic Research Society!'

Later that day the Correspondent was able to ask the secretary of the Society for Psychical Research if this were true. 'We have never had anything to do with the woman,' came the reply.

Experiments with Table Turning

In the archives of the Society for Psychical Research in Cambridge University Library there is a bound notebook with blue marbled covers. A small, gold-edged sticker on the front reads 'Experiments with Table', giving the initials 'F. U.' and date 'Dec 1916 to Jul 2 1917'. The price of 7/ is still pencilled on the inside and on the inside back a sticker reads 'A & N. C . S. Ld Stationery Dept 105 Victoria St SW'. Inside are ninety-seven hand-numbered pages, with a few loose, handwritten sheets towards the back. There are no names, only the initials of those taking part: E. L., M. L., M. B. and F. U. The description in the catalogue provides no clues.[101]

After painstakingly decoding it, I discovered that it was, in fact, the record of Edith Lyttelton's table-turning experiments with the writer Florence Upton and others. An American, Florence Upton had been living in Britain since about 1893 and working as an illustrator. In 1895, she published the first book in her hugely successful Golliwog series of children's stories – Edith's children all loved them. M. L. was probably Edith's daughter Mary Frances Lyttelton; M. B. was probably Gerald Balfour's daughter, Mary (1894–1980), who also dabbled with the crystal ball.

Edith was born a British subject in St Petersburg, Russia, in 1865, the first child of the merchant Archibald Balfour. He moved his family back to the UK and Edith grew up in aristocratic circles, becoming one of 'The Souls', along with Arthur Balfour, Margot Tennant (who married Asquith) and Alfred Lyttelton. Her interest in the paranormal is well known. After the death of her husband, Alfred Lyttelton, in 1913, she turned to Spiritualism in her grief, although she had been a member of the SPR since 1885. She became one of the SPR Automatists operating under the *nom de guerre* of Mrs King – her true identity was only revealed in 1923. In later years, she wrote several books on the subject and served as President of the SPR (1933–1934).[102]

During the First World War she was busy with the War Refugees Committee (she founded it), the British Club for Belgian Soldiers

101 Cambridge University Library, SPR MS 57/ Table Turning Experiments, 1916–17. I first examined this in 2015 and, after I decoded it, have since provided an explanation to the Archivist.

102 Identity revealed in J. G. Piddington, 'Forecasts in Scripts Concerning the War', *Proceedings SPR*, vol. 33 (1923), p. 441. For her books, see *The Faculty of Communion* (London: Longmans & Co., 1925), *Our Superconscious Mind* (London: Philip Allan, 1931), and *Some Cases of Prediction* (London: G. Bell, 1937). See also Churchill Archives Centre, Cambridge, The Papers of Alfred Lyttelton and Dame Edith Lyttelton, and their son Oliver Lyttelton (1st Viscount Chandos), GBR/0014/CHAN, especially 'Psychic Experiences', CHAN I/6/11, covering 1913 to 1943.

(President, 1916) and the Women's Branch of the Ministry of Agriculture (Deputy Director, 1917), as well as sitting on the Central Committee of Women's Employment (1916–1925). In 1917, she was made a Dame of the British Empire in recognition of her war work and in 1929 was made a Dame Grand Cross (GBE) for her work with the League of Nations.

The experiments took place in the library 'with its book-lined walls' at Wittersham House in Kent. It is difficult to reconstruct their exact method, but to begin with they mainly used a simple yes/no system, with some spelling out of words, sometimes involving 'rapping out', before developing something capable of receiving more complex messages, with 'letters arranged in a semicircle on Table. A small silver box for pointer which sometimes moved with great speed' – a Ouija board to all intents and purposes. But they also called out the alphabet – a process they found tiring.[103]

Edith's son Oliver was at the Front and one can imagine that they were all anxious for news of the war. The first meaningful message came through on 5 December 1915 from 'J. R. Woosnam', apparently killed in the fighting at a place called Morveaux on 1 September 1916. He wanted to give a message to his mother: 'hope'. Woosnam returned the next evening to say 'Shake a little malt over the dog.'

Edith and the two Marys were back in the library again on 9 December. A new name was spelt out: 'Charles Fisher' and then 'Black Sweater', apparently a nickname Charles had for Edith. Amongst other messages, Charles had information for those at the Front: 'Haig [. . .] try again can advance west of [. . .] Ginchy'. On 11 December, Charles told them 'Jolly host of angels helped me'.

They received the first mention of Oliver on 19 December. A communicator giving its name as George Davies told them 'You tell Crystal Wood stop with Lyttelton willing to wed Oliver'. They did not record what they thought this might mean.

At first M. B. and F. U. sat at the table on 27 December. No messages came through, but they heard a 'continuous tapping'. M. L.

103 Description of the library from Edith Lyttelton, *Alfred Lyttelton: An Account of His Life* (London: Longmans, Green and Co., 1917), p. 339.

then took over and George immediately came through: 'Mistyrious little note note to Oliver from (Loos) Milne written Loos please'. 'We don't understand, quite (read it aloud),' wrote Edith. 'Stop reading please,' said George, 'Loos is right – September Nineteen Fifteen – Milne (Mom Moms) Mons Monste Mons'; then, 'Milne was not at Loos'. It still made no sense. Another communicator interrupted to say 'God is love' and 'Gilbert Talbot is very happy', ending by asking them to 'Send Hermione his love'. They sat up late into the night, getting further messages.

They sat round the table almost every night that December, receiving these strange, nearly meaningful messages. Then on 31 December, they asked one of the communicators directly: 'George, could you get hold of Bobby Palmer, Lord Selborne's son, killed in Mesopotamia?'

'I will try to find him,' said George.

Madame Brockway on Trial

Before the end of December, Almira Brockway had been arrested and was standing in the dock of West London Police Court on a charge of professing to tell fortunes under Clause 4 of the Vagrancy Act of 1824. Presiding was the then well-known metropolitan magistrate Mr Charles King Francis (d. 1925), known for a good game of amateur cricket in his youth.[104]

'I do not tell fortunes,' she protested, 'but simply get into communication with the spirits – that is, if I can get in touch with them. In some cases I do not succeed. Spiritualism will be the universal religion. If you prosecute all those who come to us you will have to prosecute more than half the people of London.'

104 'Psychist Again in Court', *Sunday Times* (31 December 1916), p. 10; additional details from 'Fortune-Telling Case', *Daily Telegraph* (1 January 1917), p. 5; and 'Spirit Messages', *The Times* (1 January 1917), p. 5; Obituary [of Charles King Francis], *Gloucester Citizen* (28 October 1925).

But Mr Barker for the prosecution was not out to prosecute Brockwell's clients; and for their part, Ernest Wild, KC, and Walter Frampton, for the defence, sought to preserve her from the charges.

The court heard how a Mrs Annie Betts and a Mrs White had discovered Brockwell – now 'the prisoner' in the official language of court proceedings – at a Spiritualist meeting at Bechstein Hall on 20 December and had arranged to call upon her at her 'rich lodgings' in Notting Hill Gate the next day.

The now familiar procedure was enacted. Each lady was to write down the names of three departed souls along with two or three questions for them.

Brockway picked up one of Betts's folded papers. Putting it to her ear, she said, 'Yes, who is it?' and then 'What, dear?' Addressing Betts she asked if the name was Nancy Bruce. Betts said that it was. 'Do you know anyone by the name of Edward William Lang?' Betts again said yes. Brockway continued:

'Yes, yes; he is pleased to see you, to meet you, and tell you that Chris is quite safe at present, but he has been in the thick of it, and he says Will— Wal— William – he is out there too. I think he will return, but there are many dangers out there, but we in the spirit will do all we can to guide and guard him.'

Next, Mrs White's father came through from the Beyond and had told her that 'she was not to worry as he was going to be with her and do all he could for her'. He added that 'perhaps next year she would be happily married'. Mrs White was astonished: she already had a husband, currently at the Front.

Wild laid out his case for the defence: it would hinge upon the fact that the prisoner was indeed a psychic and had the power of communicating with the dead.

The magistrate Mr Francis was also astonished: 'Are they going to ask me to believe that?'

Barker assured him that his beliefs on the matter were beside the point: 'this was not a prosecution as to whether it was allowable to get into communication with the spirits, for it was not for any magistrate to say whether it was possible'.

The court heard from Detective Inspector Sanders that an inspection of the prisoner's accounts showed that she had received £115 in the last thirty-four days. She did not, however, pocket the whole sum. There was a letter from 'J. Hewat McKenzie' detailing her 'half-month's salary' of £25, minus deductions for a certain Mrs Willoughby. Various books and pamphlets written by McKenzie were also found in her possessions: 'Spiritual Intercourse' and 'If a Soldier Dies, Shall He Live Again?'

Wild, KC, turned out to be a representative of the 'British College of Psychic Science' and tried to impress the court by announcing 'Would it surprise you to learn that the President of the college is Sir William Crookes, and amongst the members are Sir A. Conan Doyle and Mr Hewitt, KC?' But it was not reported whether he mentioned that McKenzie was the founder of this organisation.

Sanders then said that 'he thought that the receipts showed that the money received from visits was handed over to the college.' Wild was trying to make it all seem above board and quite noble in character, but this in no way could explain the fact that the prisoner had pretended to be in communication with the dead to extort money.

Harold Ashton, star of the *Daily Mail*'s sting operation, was then called. He detailed his séance to loud laughter. He added some new information that he had withheld from his newspaper article. When paying for the sitting and being told that she did not keep it for herself, he had asked 'Who did it go to – your friend Mackenzie, or that other man, von Bourg?'

Her fuller reply had been, 'It does not go to either of them. Every penny I make out of this business goes to the National Psychic people, or society.'

Ashton had qualified this by asking if she meant the 'Psychical Research Society'.

She had replied, 'Yes, I do.' Despite the connection with McKenzie she was strangely sketchy about where the money was going.

Wild cross-examined the witness: 'You asked her whether you would be successful in a certain venture. Had you one in view?'

'I had several,' replied Ashton to laughter.

'Are you a believer in psychic science?' persevered Wild.

'That is rather a wide question,' countered Ashton.

Wild tried to be more specific: 'Do you believe in communion with the dead?'

Ashton refused to be precise: 'I have an open mind on that point.' And so their banter continued.

Ashton admitted that he did have orders to go abroad – the location was not specified – but the East was 'improbable'. These were later cancelled. And he further admitted that his question 'Is she all right?' was a trick question.

Almira Brockway, as it turned out, was an ordained minister in the USA. She was a widow – her husband was described as an 'X-ray professor' – and her son was currently someone important in the Red Cross in France. Brockway had apparently 'practised occult science' in the USA for the past thirty years and had been invited to Britain by McKenzie to help promote his College of Psychic Science.

McKenzie was described as 'a hard-headed Scotchman and an engineer', as if these things should make him immune to fraud, who 'did not make a penny out of his connection with the science'. Clearly, he did make money out of Brockway on the evidence of the receipts produced; but even that is incidental to the question of whether Brockway was a charlatan.

Wild argued that the prosecution must prove that Brockway had intended to deceive her clients. He noted in her defence that there was 'the absence of the usual paraphernalia', whatever that might be, 'or any evidence that she was practising charlatanism with intent to deceive'.

Wild was getting on his high horse again: 'He hoped the magistrate would treat with respect the fact that eminent men did not think that Spiritualism or psychic research was so much rubbish. It was not a subject to be laughed at. The point was as to whether the woman was an imposter.'

The magistrate replied, 'That is not the question. I am not going to discuss psychic questions.'

Wild called his witnesses. William S. Hendry, a self-described 'healer', had also been at Brockway's demonstrations at Bechstein Hall and had had a private sitting. He told the court that he was convinced that she was 'a genuine person' and had told him 'nothing about the future'. John H. Miller, a former actor now working for the Navy League, told the court that he had had two sittings with the prisoner and 'the answers he received were satisfactory'.

The case was adjourned and Brockway released on bail.

1917

'Stop Playing with Powder and Shot'

....

The adventures of SPR members Sir Oliver Lodge and Sir Arthur Conan Doyle tended to overshadow the rest of the Society, even more so now in retrospect, but other prominent people were taking a major role in the Society. The President for 1917 was the educator, philosopher and Unitarian minister Lawrence Pearsall Jacks (1860–1955), usually known as L. P. Jacks. Little remembered now, he rose to prominence in this period up until the Second World War.

Jacks fell in love with Olive Brooke (a daughter of Queen Victoria's chaplain Stopford Brooke) on a transatlantic crossing and married her in 1889. Of their six children, the three sons were in the war. Jacks knew Oscar Wilde, George Bernard Shaw, and Sidney and Beatrice Webb. He also personally knew Edward Stanley Russell, the subject of the SPR's case L. 1217. He accepted a Professorship at Manchester College, Oxford, in 1903, teaching philosophy and theology, with a focus on Henri Bergson and Spinoza. He was also editor of the *Hibbert Journal* and published *The Alchemy of Thought* in 1910. He served as Principal of the College from 1915 until his retirement in 1931. So despite the name not ringing many bells today, Jacks was an influential and well-connected person, although the President of the American SPR, James Hyslop, was somewhat hostile. Jacks was elected President of the SPR on 31 January 1917.

The SPR had reduced the *Journal* from monthly to every two months, due to lack of material and the cost of paper. Jacks's presidential address was delayed until 28 June owing to pressure of work. Meanwhile, there were others in the Society with plenty of material.

On 1 January, M. L., E. L. and F. U. were in the 'studio', presumably in Wittersham House. It was their twenty-fifth table-turning experiment. M. L. was at the table: 'George' came through. 'I think sitting is very good,' he said. The table 'skipped badly' and they had to put it on a rug.[1]

1 Cambridge University Library, SPR MS 57/ Table Turning Experiments, 1916–17.

'Wish the war would end – So many people here too young,' said George.

'I say, George,' said M. L., 'have you found Bobby Palmer yet?'

'Not yet.'

George left and F. U. tried her hand at the table, but the spirits wanted her to stop.

They were back in the studio at 6.30 the following evening. George came through, saying 'Speak to Lord Selborne – Tell him his son wants to find the way to speak to him.'

One of the ladies asked, 'Are we to bring him here?'

'Please do not yet – He is not ready – I think he finds it hard as yet – He is happy – George – trust me – I will look after him – It is all right.'

On 4 January, George communicated: 'Please tell Lord Selborne – Bobby is ready – I will be there.'

Bobby was the Honourable Robert Palmer, second son of William Waldegrave Palmer, 2nd Earl of Selborne, KG, GCMG, PC, Under-Secretary of State for the Colonies (1895–1900), First Lord of the Admiralty (1900–1905), High Commissioner to South Africa (1905–1910) and an elected member of the SPR since 25 October 1916. When war broke out, Bobby was already an officer in the 6th Battalion, the Hampshire Regiment. Stationed in India, he transferred to the 4th Battalion in the Near East and was killed on 21 June 1916 at the Battle of Um El Hannah against the Turks.[2]

Edith, her daughter Mary and Lord Selborne gathered at the appointed hour, Wednesday, 10 January. Mary operated the table with Edith recording.

'Palmer – Are you there?'

'Who do you want to speak to?'

'My father – Tell him I think the time has come for Luly to stop playing with powder and shot – Do not stop him writing to Nellie Balfour.' (Luly was Bobby's younger brother – Lord Selborne's youngest son

---

2 See Lady Laura Riding, *The Life of Robert Palmer, 1888–1916* (London: Hodder and Stoughton, 1921); and Robert Palmer, *Letters from Mesopotamia* (Privately printed, no date).

– the Hon. William Jocelyn Lewis Palmer (b. 1894), also in the Hampshire Regiment; Nellie Balfour was Gerald Balfour's daughter Eleanor.)

'I never thought of stopping him writing to Nellie,' said Lord Selborne. 'Dear Bobby, explain yourself more carefully.'

The table moved away from Mary towards Selborne, spelling out 'AOP'.

'Dear Bobby,' continued Selborne, 'I'm so glad you're thinking of Luly, but I don't know what you mean. He is on Carmichael's staff and is going back to Lord Ronaldshay. Should he go back to his regiment?'

'I think he ought not to leave Carmichael.'

'Yes, but Carmichael is leaving him in April. Why should he not go with Ronaldshay if R. asks him?'

'He had better go on staff.'

'Bobby, dear, what do you mean by "playing with powder and shot"? – I thought you meant he ought to go back to his regiment – now you say "stay on staff".'

'He should not be afraid of staying on staff – It is better for him than regiment.'

'You mean, Luly should stay on staff, and not go back to regiment?'

'Yes.'

Perhaps somewhat exasperated, 'Bobby' changed the subject, asking about Selborne's work. Selborne for his part tried to get 'Bobby' to give some evidence that it was truly he. 'Bobby' gave no answer to any of these questions. Selborne left after 11 o'clock, but the ladies continued with another sitting at midnight.

Sir Oliver Lodge joined them on 12 January. M. L. was at the table, E. L. recording, F. U. observing and Sir Oliver asking most of the questions. Soon after they began, 'Raymond' came through, but he said little worth reporting.

There were also communications from 'Hawarden'. This must have been William 'Will' Glynne Charles Gladstone (b. 1885), Lord of the Manor of the family estate of Hawarden Castle in Flintshire, Wales, at the time of his death. He was commissioned into the 3rd

Battalion, the Royal Welch Fusiliers, in August 1914, going over to France in March 1915. He was killed in action near Laventie on 13 April 1915. Later Raymond Asquith also apparently communicated. He was the eldest son of the Prime Minister H. H. Asquith. He was a Lieutenant with the 3rd Battalion, the Grenadier Guards, at the Battle of the Somme and was killed during an assault near Ginchy on 15 September 1916.[3]

Their experiments continued until 2 July 1917, moving around mid-June to the Balfours' residence at Fisher's Hill and involving Gerald in the sittings. Edith must have been relieved never to get a message from her son Oliver: he survived the war. Through 'Hawarden' she communicated the progress of his military career to her deceased husband Alfred.

'I Know I Have the Power': The Trial Continues

Almira Brockway returned to the West London Police Court on Saturday, 6 January. More evidence was to be heard in the case.[4]

A newspaper owner, Justice of the Peace and town councillor of Enniskillen, Ireland, William Copeland Trimble (1851–1941), was called. No Irish rebel this, but a staunch Unionist: the report noted that Trimble had raised a troop of horse for the Ulster Volunteer Force – his newspaper, *The Impartial Reporter*, was decidedly partial in favour of the Union. However, 'until recently he was not a believer in psychic matters'.

He had three sons fighting in the war. Lieutenant R. S. Trimble of the 6th Battalion Royal Irish Fusiliers had been wounded in the

3 Viscount Gladstone, *William G. C. Gladstone: A Memoir* (London: Nisbet, 1918). Raymond Asquith first appears in their record on 21 March 1917.
4 'Psychic's Own Story', *Sunday Times* (7 January 1917), p. 10; 'Fortune-Telling Swindle', *Daily Telegraph* (8 January 1917), p. 12; *Daily Telegraph* (19 January 1917), p. 4.

Dardanelles campaign in August 1915. His father had sent bundles of fly-paper out to the battalion (and others there) to combat the plagues of flies that spoiled food, disturbed sleep and tormented the wounded. Second Lieutenant A. E. C. Trimble of the 7th Battalion Royal Inniskilling Fusiliers, had twice received the 'Parchment of the Irish Division' and was mentioned in despatches by Major General W. B. Hickie, Commanding Officer 16th (Irish) Division. His youngest son, Noel Desmond Trimble, had obtained a commission in the 12th (Reserve) Battalion Royal Inniskilling Fusiliers on 23 June 1915. On arriving in France he had been posted to the 8th Royal Inniskilling Fusiliers. He had been a brilliant scholar at Enniskillen Royal School and Trinity College, Dublin, and a promising university career lay ahead of him. He lasted less than a year at the Front, being killed in action on 9 June 1916.[5]

Grief had brought Trimble to London to search for news of his dead son in the capital's séance rooms. He found himself in the company of Brockway in November 1916:

She was tired; the evening was gloomy, and the gas was not lit. She told him to write down on slips of paper the names of those with whom he wished to communicate. On one of the papers he wrote the name, 'Noel Desmond Trimble'.[6]

Brockway told him that Noel had been trying to 'impress himself upon Rex'. From the context, Rex must have been the unusual name of Trimble's daughter. Brockway added that 'his daughter had a faculty for communicating if she chose to develop it'.

Trimble later talked to Rex about Brockway's revelations. She said,

5 W. C. Trimble, editorial, *The Impartial Reporter* (5 August 1915); G. A. Cooper Walker, *The Book of the Seventh Service Battalion The Royal Inniskilling Fusiliers, from Tipperary to Ypres* (Dublin: Brindley & Son, 1920), pp. 32, 50, 84, on p. 128 Noel Desmond is listed as having 'died of wounds'; 'Second Lieutenant Noel Desmond Trimble', http://ourheroes.southdublinlibraries.ie/node/16747, accessed 11 July 2017.
6 'Psychic's Own Story', *Sunday Times* (7 January 1917), p. 10.

'Noel has been with me frequently.' In connection with having 'a faculty', she replied, 'Yes, I know I have the power, because I have both seen and heard.'

Trimble was still sceptical, but went back to see Brockway again. He had composed 'a set of test questions' in his hotel room before-hand. He thought one to be particularly good concerning whether Noel had suffered pain at the end. Noel's elder brother had been with him at the end and wrote home to say that Noel died without pain.

In Linden Gardens, Trimble put his questions to the spirit world. Brockway 'went through all the contortions of suffocation, so much so that it was painful for him to look upon her'. He asked her to stop. She told him that 'Noel's body turned black and that he had been gassed.'

At the time this probably hardened Trimble's scepticism. Some time later he learnt that Noel had been gassed and that his body was discol-oured. When cross-examined about this in court, Trimble said he now thought that his other son had written about a painless death to spare any further anguish on his mother's part.

The next witness called was Revd Carew Hervey Mary St John-Mildmay (1863–1937), a scion of a noble house, distantly related to the medieval King of England, Edward III. He was a younger son of Sir Henry St John-Mildmay, 5th Baronet. The Revd's elder brother, also called Sir Henry, had inherited the title in 1902 and had been a major in the Grenadier Guards, serving in the Egyptian War of 1882 and the Suakin Expedition in 1885; he died of old age in 1916. The court noted Carew's distinguishing achievement as being a member of the Athenaeum Club; however, there was more to him than that. He had graduated from Trinity College, Cambridge, with an MA and went on to become Rector of Aldham in Essex. He was not the stay-at-home sort and became Chaplain to the Forces, which took him off to the Boer War from 1901 to 1902. Some time after returning he became Rector of St Mary's in Stamford, Lincolnshire. Now he was in the West London Police Court explaining why he had gone to see a medium. Apparently, he was trying to find the whereabouts of an old friend's tombstone. He told the court that he believed Brockway to be 'perfectly genuine'.[7]

The next witness was Miss Ethel Webling (1859–1929), an artist trained at the Slade School of Art who had exhibited at the Royal Academy. Her nephew was with the Royal Flying Corps and had been reported missing. Worry brought her to Brockway's door. She asked the boy's deceased grandfather if he were still alive and he replied in the affirmative. Three weeks after, news came from Berlin that the nephew was a prisoner in Germany.

The American prisoner, Almira Brockway, was now invited to make a personal statement. She had been born in Wisconsin in 1858, married in 1877 and widowed in 1913. The exact details were confused: her husband had been an 'X-ray doctor' and an 'inventor of electrical appliances', but also owned 'a large department store'. She had worked there as a dressmaker and also 'had charge of dressmaking'. She lost what she described as 'her fortune' in a fire.

Soon after their marriage they began investigating Spiritualism together. Almira discovered a talent for it herself and began 'working as a medium by means of slate writing' – so-called 'slate writing' was another sleight-of-hand trick – and claimed that she offered her services free of charge.

Good intentions do not fill hungry mouths. Luckily, her guides in the spirit world pointed out that Jesus had said 'a labourer was worthy of his hire'. After that, her palms were crossed with silver. As to her mediumship:

> She only told people what the spirits told her. She was possessed by a spirit and very frequently did not know what her mouth might be saying. She only passed on communications which the spirits gave to her.[8]

7 'Obituary – Sir Henry St John-Mildmay', The Times (18 July 1902), p. 8; 'Carew Hervey Mary St John-Mildmay', Burke's Peerage, vol. 3 (2003), p. 3493; 'Major Sir Henry Paulet St John-Mildmay', http://www.holmesacourt.org/hac/3/8613.htm, accessed 11 July 2017.
8 'Psychic's Own Story', Sunday Times (7 January 1917), p. 10.

She had been a pastor at more churches than you could shake a crucifix at: Boston, Chicago and elsewhere. She repeated that she had been invited to Britain to open the British College of Psychic Science and made a point of saying that 'she left a church where she was making more money than she was making in London today'.

Her real motive for coming to London was to be nearer her son, who was 'holding a responsible Red Cross position' in France. 'He had,' she said, 'received several medals for heroic conduct.'

Mr Wild, KC, for the defence, asked her 'how it came about that sometimes apparently untrue answers were given'. She had an answer ready for this: 'the law of spirituality was that like attracted like, and that if anyone brought three questions they brought with them also some lying spirits'.

Mrs Cecil Porch, wife of Lieutenant Colonel Cecil Porch, was brought out. Lt Col. Porch, attached 23rd (Service) Battalion, Northumberland Fusiliers, would be awarded the DSO for gallantry in leading his battalion only a few months later. As he was in the thick of the fighting, his wife may well have been visiting Brockway to find out how he fared. Mrs Porch told the court that Brockway 'had no opportunity of knowing who she was and yet gave her full name'. She believed that the papers on which she had written her questions were 'so twisted' that Brockway 'could not have undone them to read them'. As to the answers she gave, they were 'true'.

Mr Barker, for the prosecution, was not to be sidetracked. 'I suggest to you,' he said, 'though it may be very painful, that your son was wanted by the police in America in 1911 and that he has not been there since?'

'I never knew that he was wanted there,' she replied, disingenuously.

Barker continued, 'As a fortune-teller and a much-wanted criminal?'

'That is news to me.'

'It is curious that he has not been back to America since 1911?'

'He had business in France.'

'Does he not run a cinematograph show in Paris?'

'Yes, for the last six weeks. He works for the Red Cross.'

'He has been running it for big prices, say $10,000?'

'I do not know.'

When asked about the alleged offence, she stated that at the time 'she was in a semi-conscious condition, and did not know what she was saying'.

The magistrate observed that a new defence was being offered with this.

Wild piped up, 'This fact of unconsciousness is one of the first elements of psychic work. I am afraid, sir, that you do not know the first elements; therefore, you should not try this case.'

One can imagine how delighted the magistrate must have been by this remark. He addressed the prisoner: 'Are you only unconscious when they come with lies?'

'I am unconscious at all times,' she replied.

'You are conscious when you ask for the guinea fee,' retorted Francis.

Wild brought up Sir Oliver Lodge and talked about his book *Raymond*. Francis said that 'he had heard Sir Oliver Lodge's name introduced in the case', but added that he had not read the book and 'was very sorry'.

Wild gave him another blast along the lines of not being capable of hearing the case. Having made sure of thoroughly annoying the magistrate, Wild continued:

'Have you,' he said to Brockway, 'ever played any conjuring tricks by opening papers and reading names on them?'

'Never, sir,' Brockway replied, 'with emphasis' as the court report recorded, 'I swear by God. The moment I touch the paper the spirit will be by my side, and he or she will read out the name on the paper.'

'Do you ever see the spirit form?'

'Sometimes I see it as clear as I see you. At other times I do not.'

James Hewat McKenzie was then called as a witness. He was an engineer by occupation, he told the court. For a number of years he had been 'interested in psychic science' and had spent 'thousands of pounds on it'. Indeed, he was paying for Brockway's defence – and Mr Wild, KC, would not have been cheap; he would pick up a knighthood during his career and become Recorder of London (1922–1934) and High Steward of Southwark. Speaking in 1926, Sir Arthur Conan Doyle said he 'had been a great criminal lawyer'.[9]

McKenzie 'considered Spiritualism to be a most important science'. He managed to mention Sir William Crookes's name again as the president of the 'College of Psychic Science which was being formed'.

Wild must have asked him something about the séance itself, for the report records that he gave the opinion that someone attending a sitting 'with the intention of deceit would upset the psychic balances' and 'would create such a disturbance in the psychic atmosphere that the medium would say almost anything she heard'.

'Are these lying spirits?' asked Wild.

Barker interjected: 'What is the use of asking Mr McKenzie or anyone else such a question?'

'I ask,' asked Wild, 'for the magistrate's ruling on the question.'

'I call it a ridiculous question,' said the magistrate.

'I feel it is impossible to have the case tried in anything like the atmosphere in which it ought to be tried, and I cannot carry it any farther.' With that, Wild gathered up his papers and left the court room.

Mr Francis, the magistrate, said that he was sorry to see Wild take the course of action that he had. Brockway herself must have been more than sorry to see her defence storm out of the room, especially as the other barrister, Frampton, appeared to have done almost nothing (he may have been an assistant, in which case he would also have flounced out of court).

'I have no hesitation,' said Francis, 'in ruling that there ought to be a conviction. I would be the last in the world to say anything that would be the propaganda of psychical science.'

Brockway was fined £50 and ordered to pay 30 guineas costs. Notice of appeal was given. Mr Barker recommended deportation. The magistrate concurred, but the deportation order would not be put into effect

9 'Death of Sir Ernest Wild', *The Argus* [Melbourne] (15 September 1934), p. 23; 'Crowborough's Hospital Bazaar', *Kent and Sussex Courier* (8 October 1926).

until after the appeal. The news made *The Sunday Times* and Monday's *Daily Telegraph*. The *Telegraph* called it a 'fortune-telling swindle'.

Interestingly, at the same time as it could condemn Brockway for her Spiritualist swindle, the *Telegraph* could recommend Elliot O'Donnell's latest book on the supernatural, *Twenty Years' Experience as a Ghost-Hunter*. Although a 'strange book', O'Donnell was 'obviously a genuine and honest believer' and so 'for those who like to feel their flesh creep and enjoy good ghost stories, we can confidently recommend *Twenty Years' Experience as a Ghost-Hunter*'. The deciding factor may have been O'Donnell's attitude towards mediums: 'he has in this volume shown how strongly opposed he is to Spiritualism, automatic writing, table-turning, and any commerce with paid mediums'.

Because of Ashton's mention of the SPR, Eleanor Sidgwick later wrote to the *Daily Mail* to point out that the SPR had nothing to do with the British College of Psychic Science or with Almira Brockway.[10]

The Danger of Spiritualism

The trial of Almira Brockway inspired the journalist Edward Bolland Osborn (1867–1938) – he always signed himself E. B. Osborn – to take up the pen against Spiritualism in general: a 'Spiritualist craze' he called it, and 'a growing danger'. War, he argued, reveals a nation's weaknesses as well as strengths. The stress of interminable warfare had produced 'symptoms of "nerviness"', such as Spiritualism.[11]

Writing in *The Sunday Times* – the same issue that carried the conclusion of the Brockway case – Osborn developed his theme by stating that there was nothing new in it. He looked back to Mlle Lenormand in the Napoleonic period, who was much consulted by the Empress Josephine – 'as curious and credulous as a Creole', he wrote. In the

---

10 *Daily Mail* (20 January 1917), p. 4.
11 E. B. Osborn, 'The Spiritualist Craze: A Growing Danger', *Sunday Times* (7 January 1917), p. 7.

countryside, there was a 'recrudescence of witch-hunting'. Perhaps the imputation was that war here had also led to an outburst of the 'irrational'.

More pertinently he noted the 'futility of exposure': 'it was, and is, a curious fact that such exposures never cause the convinced Spiritualist to suffer the slightest loss of conviction'. Brockway had clearly been caught cheating by Ashton, but Wild, 'the convinced Spiritualist' in this case, still agreed to defend her and threw in the towel in protest when his occult defence of 'lying spirits' was not admitted. Osborn talked about other tricks involving such things as 'the luminous inflated India-rubber hand' and noted that 'the medium's faithful clients, so far from taking such an exposure seriously, would blame the detective for risking a fatal shock to the poor woman's nervous system' – it is an argument still used today.

In peacetime, Spiritualism was, according to Osborn, 'a matter of small account', but in wartime was 'a real danger'. He imagined that 'crystal-gazers and clairvoyants, etc.' were raking in 'several thousands a month' – money that could be put to better purposes – and should be shut down. He bizarrely thought that 'a fine is always an advertisement' and so argued for imprisonment. These were not even the most dangerous of their species, for that was the 'private medium'.

Perhaps as a nod to Brockway's American origins, Osborn argued as 'a fact' that 'nearly all these mediums come from Boston', which he called 'the world's capital of psychical crankdom'. More particularly they were 'born in what are known as the "burnt-over areas" of New England', scene of 'raging revivals' and 'bogus religions' (and here he was thinking of Mormonism). He was right to see this area as a focal point: modern Spiritualism had originated here with the Fox sisters in 1848. However, it was disingenuous to paint 'nearly all' mediums in these 'burnt-over' colours.

There did seem to be something of a trade route for mediums. Osborn had it on 'good authority', whatever that might be, that these Yankee necromancers came to London via Paris. Paris had been in the grip of its own Spiritualist craze until the police deported as many mediums as they could catch. We might remember that Brockway's son was also accused of fortune-telling and had fled the States to set up in Paris.

He noted that the demand for mediums had greatly risen, 'thanks to the pathetic folly of bereaved persons, mostly women, who, crediting the incredible, hope to get with a medium's help some tidings of a son or lover or husband who has fallen in action'. The danger here lay, not only in fiscal harm, but also in the fact that, 'as many doctors know, the attendance at "sittings" often leads to a mental breakdown'.

Osborn castigated Lodge's *Raymond* as propaganda for the charlatans: the 'regrettable circulation' of the book had 'helped to increase the Spiritualist craze not a little'. He doffed his cap to the 'son who died a noble death in the field' and admitted that Lodge's accounts of the supposed conversations he had with him are 'set forth in good faith'. Notwithstanding that, Osborn sought to diminish the evidence by pointing out that 'much stress is laid on two curious small coincidences between facts and the matter of the conversations in question'. Rather than attack the minimal coincidences, Osborn used a comparison with Jules Michelet's account of a seventeenth-century possession case from France. The case revolved around several allegedly possessed nuns who implicated Father Louis Gaufridi (or Gauffridi) as a Satanist and chief cause of their possession. Michelet was an excitable writer whose vivid reinterpretation of witchcraft in *La Sorciére*, while entertaining to read, is limited in its historical accuracy. Having introduced the taint of witchcraft, Osborn connects the possessed nun with the entranced medium and brings them both to the door of hysteria as understood by Freud. The medium is a 'professional hysteric'. However, this is not the conclusion of his denunciation. Ultimately, Osborn falls back upon fear and hatred of the 'foreigner':

Fortunately, people of sound common sense are not in need of such confutation. They wisely prefer the Christian ideals of life after death. So that the vast majority of Britons will, no doubt, agree with me that these mediums are undesirable aliens, and ought to be quietly sent back to their own countries.

As might be expected after such a broadside, the letters pages of the following Sunday's edition carried readers' reactions. Private E. K. Collett of the 224 Canadian Forestry Corps, Virginia Water, Surrey, suggested that Osborn should read Camille Flammarion's *The Unknown* (published 1900), then 'he would get food for thought':[12]

> That mediums do have communication with the spirit world has been proved so often that it is useless adding any more evidence on the subject.

Dudley Wright, the former editor of *The Annals of Psychical Science* – Sir William Crookes, Charles Richet and Camille Flammarion had been on the editorial board – also wrote in to the newspaper. In large part he actually agreed with Osborn's criticisms, although a confessed Spiritualist himself – he called Osborn's piece 'fair though trenchant' and thought that 'every true Spiritualist' would be 'grateful for it'. But Wright had his own axe to grind: the question of money. 'The professional or paid medium,' he wrote, 'has done incalculable harm to Spiritualism.' Wright was in no doubt that it was possible for the living to communicate with the dead. 'I have experienced it,' he said, 'but the relation of my experiences would not be proof to others.' Osborn had also hit upon the subjective nature of the experience, but to dismiss it, whereas Wright stated that 'there are some things that can only be known: they cannot be proven'. Public demonstrations were worthless, he thought, mere 'thought reading or telepathy' – although if true that in itself would be quite something; but the private sittings with professional mediums were worse than worthless, they were mercenary.[13]

> One point with regard to the "demonstrations" – so called – given by professional mediums, is that their character is in proportion to the fee paid. You cannot get materialisations or the voice via the shilling medium. If you want those you must be prepared to

12 Letters, 'The Spiritualist Craze', *Sunday Times* (14 January 1917), p. 2.
13 Ibid.

pay the guinea and be admitted on the recommendation of an intermediary. If spirit return is possible – and I believe it is – why should the proof be dependent upon the payment of a guinea, or, indeed, any sum to a professional medium?

Ghosts of the *Lusitania*

The winter of 1916/1917 took its toll on the Ghost Club. Members learnt that Ionides 'had lost his only son in action'. Nineteen-year-old Theodore Alexander Ionides, a 2nd Lieutenant in the Oxfordshire and Buckinghamshire Light Infantry, had been wounded at the Battle of the Ancre in the Somme Sector on Thursday, 13 November 1916 – he died three days later. A 'vote of condolence' was passed and the secretary, Johnson, was directed to write to him, expressing their sympathy.[14]

Barrett talked about some séance experiences due to be published in a forthcoming book and Turner showed some spirit photographs – many taken in his presence – but the atmosphere must have been somewhat dampened.

Levander had been unable to attend their last meeting of 1916 and at their first in 1917 his friends learnt that he had passed away. Cassel was invited to speak about his friend and Percival, 'with deep emotion spoke also very tenderly of him, as one for whom he had the greatest regard and respect'.[15]

Crookes 'related the circumstances under which he obtained a most satisfactory spirit photograph'. He had travelled to Crewe with a certain Miss Felicia R. Scatcherd (editor of *The Asiatic Review*) and bought a 'packet of sensitized plates' on the way.

---

14 Meeting of 6 December 1916, British Library, Add. MS 52264, pp. 467–70. National Archives, 'Medal Card of Ionides, Theodore Alexander', WO 372/10/157194; and '2nd Lieutenant Theodore Alexander Ionides', WO 339/32259. Commonwealth War Graves Commission, Index No. Fr. 203, Couin British Cemetery, France. He is buried in plot VI.A.21.
15 Meeting of 3 January 1917, British Library, Add MS 52264, pp. 471–7.

Yeats had visited Mrs Leonard and 'received from the medium's control much relating to himself that was correct, and much that sounds muddled and difficult to understand, and a great deal concerning Sir Hugh Lane who had lost his life when the *Lusitania* was torpedoed. Much of this information he knew was correct [. . .] and some that was incorrect. [. . .] Sir Hugh was spoken of as passing out amidst small hills and valleys instead of rising and falling waves, etc., etc.' Unfortunately, the Ghost Club minutes are brief on the subject. Lane was to be a major preoccupation for Yeats in 1917 as he lobbied to have Lane's art collection sent to Dublin instead of London.

It was a cold winter and the 'dangerous conditions of the streets' and an 'epidemic of influenza and colds' kept many Ghosts at home. But it was not the cold nor the 'flu that kept Crookes indoors. He wrote a letter to the Secretary, who read it out at the next meeting, saying that he had become 'seriously ill' after leaving the restaurant last time and blamed it on the chef: 'he considered it would not be prudent to run the risk of again dining at the Maison Jules' and suggested that they find somewhere else. The members present had 'a long conversation' about it.[16]

The Kidwelly Mystery

'Uncanny stories' from Kidwelly in Carmarthenshire made the papers in January 1917. The *Llais Llafur* noted that that 'for the time being the war as the chief topic of conversation in the castle borough of Kidwelly has had to give place in popular interest to a series of mysterious happenings'.[17]

Strange noises disturbed the home of Mr Rippen, Kidwelly's new gas manager, shortly after the new year. Described as a 'practical,

16 Meeting of 7 February 1917, British Library, Add MS 52264, p. 477.
17 'Kidwelly Mystery: Uncanny Incidents in House', *Llais Llafur* (27 January 1917), p. 5.

level-headed business man', Mr Rippen and his wife at first ignored the noises – but the persistence and increasing insistence of mysterious knocking sounds captured the attention of the household.

The knocking sounds were heard most evenings from eight o'clock to half-past eleven. Mr Rippen could never tell whether they came from the walls, ceiling or floor. He mentioned the matter to some friends and it was decided that they should come round and help search for the cause of the disturbance. The clock had struck nine before the knocking was heard. The group made 'a complete search of the house', every room was 'carefully examined'. They looked outside as well. The attempt was in vain: 'nothing was discovered to account for the noises'.

'I am not a psychical research man in any way,' Mr Rippen told reporters, 'and I have never before had any experiences of this kind which could not be explained, but this is quite beyond me, and I cannot fathom it.'

Finally, Mr Rippen knocked back, and a conversation with the 'knocker', as it became known, unfolded. Neighbours and other townsfolk started to call round to witness the events. A simple code developed, with one knock for 'Yes' (although most times three were given) and silence for 'No', and multiple knocks to give numbers.

A 'well-known resident' in a 'responsible position in the borough' was quoted as saying: 'At the invitation of Mr Rippen, we arranged to go to his house a few nights ago. Several other friends were also present [. . .] At about 9.30 p.m. the knockings (about which, I may say, I was sceptical) began. There could be no mistake about them. They were loud and distinct, and everyone in the room heard them. The sound was a sort of muffled thud, and was repeated regularly.'[18]

One question put to 'his ghostliness' as the *South Wales Weekly Post* called it, was how many people were in the room. Seventeen knocks were counted. Afterwards, seventeen people were also counted.

'How many of the seventeen do you know?'

Six knocks.

'What is your name?'

18 ' "Ghost" at Kidwelly', *South Wales Weekly Post* (27 January 1917), p. 6.

No reply.

'Is your name Jones?'

Silence.

'Is it Thomas?'

Silence.

'Is it Morris?'

Silence.

'Is it—?'

One knock.

'I do not care to publish the name,' said the well-known person, 'as it might be connected with something that happened in Kidwelly not so long ago.'

The house was thoroughly searched, but no apparent cause for the noise could be found:

'Several of the hitherto most sceptical persons now believe that the thuds are made by supernatural hands, and that someone dead wishes to convey a message to the living.'

The well-known person said 'I came away feeling as I never did before the truth of Hamlet's dictum – "There are more things in heaven and earth, Horatio, than are dreamt of in our philosophy."'

One of those present on another occasion said that 'It would be a good thing if a member of the Psychical Research Society came to Kidwelly to investigate this extraordinary mystery.'

The knocking suddenly stopped, only to restart again 'with added distinctness'. Again questions were put to it and answered in knocks. Being the home of the gas manager, some started to wonder whether the knockings were coming from the gas pipes running from the nearby works. The *Llanelly Star* reported that an unnamed 'pronounced sceptic' believed it to be a hoax, but left after a demonstration of knockings, entirely convinced of their genuineness.[19]

19 'The Kidwelly Ghost: Another "Demonstration" Last Night', *Llanelly Star* (3 February 1917), p. 1; with further details from 'The Kidwelly Ghost: Manifestations Again Experienced', *Llais Llafur* (10 February 1917), p. 4; and 'The Kidwelly Ghost', *Llanelly Star* (10 February 1917), p. 1.

It was reported on 3 February that an account of the case had been sent to Sir Oliver Lodge, with the hope that he would investigate in person. J. Arthur Hill replied on his behalf, saying that Sir Oliver was unable to do so, but suggested that the code be further developed in order to put more complex questions to the 'knocker'.

The house itself was not the sort of house usually considered to be haunted. It was new, in fact, only four months old when Mr Rippen and his family moved there from England. It was described as being made of brick-hollow work and lay, not only close to the gas works, but also between two railway lines. Even without the knocking, it could not have been a tranquil spot.

There was also a large railway shed nearby. Workmen from the Myrnyddygarreg Railway Company arriving for late and early shifts also reported similarly unexplained knockings coming from this shed.

Eventually, the Mayor of Kidwelly himself called to investigate the matter. With him were the medical officer of health, the usual gang of 'prominent personages' and PC Fred Morris. The knocker was rather recalcitrant, however. After a time faint knocking could be heard. The health officer had some success with it, but it was the constable who made the papers with his questioning.

'Do you know me?' he asked. 'If so, give two knocks.'

There were two knocks.

'Is my name Jones?'

Silence.

'Thomas?'

Silence.

'Williams?'

Silence.

'Morris?'

One knock for 'yes'.

'How many children have I?'

Two knocks – the correct answer.

'What number is my house?'

Ten knocks – the correct answer. The people of Kidwelly generally called the constable's house 'the police station' and the number, so it was said, was not generally well known.

The policeman continued: 'How many days are there in this month?' Twenty-eight knocks – correct, for it was February.

An alphabetical code was tried out and a longer message spelt out: 'I wish my mother would come,' said the 'knocker'.

'What is my profession?'

The knocks spelt out 'police'.

On Wednesday, 14 February, a medium from Pontypridd called upon the Rippens.[20] She had three friends with her and first called on the policeman Sergeant Hodge Lewis to arrange things for them. At nine o'clock the party, including now 'a number of well-known Kidwelly gentlemen', assembled in the Rippens' house. Sitting, they formed a circle around the medium. Minutes later, the 'rapping' started up.

The lights were dimmed, leaving the room in partial darkness. The medium went into a trance and started speaking 'with a peculiar accent' unlike her own voice.

'That man,' she said, pointing to the sergeant, 'go there . . . stoop down . . . say be careful.'

Other comments (unreported) made it clear that the medium, or the voice speaking through her, was referring to a recent accident in which a young railwayman had been killed. The sergeant had been called to attend and had supervised the removal of the body. This was probably Abel John Williams, 23, run over by an engine on 11 December 1916.

She pointed to another present. 'That man . . . pay him money . . . and he signed paper.' She then described the victim's injuries 'which tallied exactly with what happened', according to the newspaper.

Someone requested the medium to ask the supposed spirit why it had come and whether it had any message. The medium, rather oddly, said that the question had been left too late and that another medium would be required 'at a cost of £5'. The reporter noted that 'the curiosity

20 'Ghost and Medium: Developments at Kidwelly', *Llanelly Star* (17 February 1917), p. 4.

of those present seemed to be considerably dampened by this £ s. d. announcement'.

The circle broke up without any further communications. The medium, perhaps thinking to take a hostage, declared that she was taking the 'spirit' home with her to Pontypridd.

The *Llanelly Star* reporter learnt details of an earlier communication 'a couple of weeks ago', when another one of those well-known local gentlemen had a conversation with the spirit using the alphabetical code.

'Are you there now?' he had asked.

Three knocks answered.

'Have you a message to give us?'

Three knocks.

'Please let us have it then,' said the gentleman, perhaps with some exasperation.

The knocks rapped out the message: 'Something. I want to say. Money hidden from the office near by gas works. In the middle of Williams' field, opposite the back garden £20.'

The next evening the message about hidden money was given again. Important new information was forthcoming, however: the treasure was buried eight yards from the gas holder. On the third evening, the sought-after treasure was now located eighteen yards from railings separating the railway from a field. The *Star* journalist made a particular point that 'It may be well to state here that no digging operations have yet been undertaken, nor are they likely to be.'

On yet 'another evening', a large group assembled and Sergeant Hodge Lewis took the lead, asking the knocker, 'Do you know me?'

Three knocks for yes.

'How long have you known me?'

Three knocks for three years.

'Can you give me my name?'

Three knocks.

'What is it?'

The knocks rapped out 'Lewis'.

'I have another name by which I am better known,' said Lewis. 'Can you give it to me?'

One knock for 'no'.

'Can you give me the name of the town that I came from to Kidwelly?'

Three knocks.

'What is it?'

The knocks spelt out 'Pembroke'.

Sergeant Lewis must have scratched his head at this point: he had come from Llanelly and had never been to Pembroke in his life.

The knocker was then quizzed on the name of the manager. It rapped out 'Rippen' and even, it was reported, got the first name of the manger and his wife (although these were not reported).

The Rippens must not have had an evening to themselves during this time. The *Llanelly Star* reported another evening session, this time involving 'a local commercial gentleman'. He had apparently taken a keen interest in the knocking phenomenon.

The commercial gentleman had devised a test. He told the assembled group that he had once given a box of fifty cigarettes to a messenger who used to call at his house. He asked one of the group to query the knocker.

'Do you know the gentleman sitting next to me?'

Three knocks for 'yes'.

'Do you remember taking messages to his house?'

Three knocks.

'Did he used to give you anything?'

Three knocks.

'What did he give you?'

The knocks spelt out 'cigeretts' (i.e., cigarettes).

'How many did he give you on one occasion? Give me a knock for each cigarette.'

Fifty knocks.

It seemed like another proof, but the commercial gentleman now announced that 'As a matter of fact, I never gave him a cigarette in my life.' The *Star* journalist made no comment.

Towards the end of the month, the *Cambria Daily Leader* reported that the Kidwelly ghost had 'turned furniture remover', with some attempt at humour, after it emerged that a chair and dress basket had apparently been thrown across one of the bedrooms. It was becoming too much for Mr Rippen and his wife. 'The premises,' the newspaper stated, 'have now been vacated for a full investigation.'[21]

The knockings were also, apparently, getting louder. What was described as 'a small committee of investigators' visited the house on a Friday night to try and find out more.[22]

The full investigation either never happened, as no news was forthcoming after this last mention on 2 March, or had already happened and referred to a visit by a group of Spiritualists on 13 February. This group was comprised of Mr and Mrs Phillip and Mr and Mrs Brabon, all from Dillwyn Street in Penrhiwceiber, and all members of the Miskin Spiritualist Society. Together with seven 'prominent residents' – note that it was always important people who were hanging about the Rippens' house – they proceeded to lay the spirit, at least until the next evening. This was dated Tuesday 13 February, but was only reported on 24 February.[23]

'We had just taken our seats when our spirit friend started knocking. We may say that it is believed that it was the spirit of a working-man who was killed by an express on the line at Kidwelly some time ago.'

Mrs Brabon was the Miskin's medium and once the knocking began, she 'allowed her spirit-guide to work' and was questioned by the group for two hours. It seems altogether unnecessary to bring in a medium when one has a communicative 'spirit' on hand that can answer questions by itself. The Miskin gang also turned up with a predetermined belief as to what the knocking was, never a good start for an investigation.

'Can you tell me who is troubling this room?'

'Yes,' answered Mrs Brabon's spirit guide, 'I will show you.'

21 'The Kidwelly Ghost: Turned Furniture Remover', *Cambria Daily Leader* (23 February 1917), p. 1.

22 'The Kidwelly Ghost', *Carmarthen Journal and South Wales Weekly Advertiser* (2 March 1917), p. 3.

23 'Kidwelly Ghost Laid? Penrhiwceiber Spiritualists' Claim', *Aberdare Leader* (24 February 1917), p. 4.

Apparently an apparition appeared, as, according to the newspaper report, 'the form of a man who was recognised by the assembly as the man who was killed by the express was shown'.

'If that is he, tell me how he died.'

'By being killed,' came the reply.

'Is there anyone in this room that knows this man?'

'Yes.' The newspaper then adds 'pointing to the station-master', but it is not clear who or what is pointing: the medium or the 'apparition'? 'That gentleman used to pay him his wages.'

The journalist wrote that details confirming the fatal accident story were allegedly given and verified 'by the man who picked up the mutilated body on the line'.

As the séance came to an end, Mr Phillips enquired of the party whether they were all convinced that it was the spirit of the man who had died in the accident who had communicated with them. They all agreed that it was and 'promised to take the spirit with them, so that it would not worry the house at the gasworks any more'. The newspaper reported that 'so far no more knocking has been heard, it is said'.

The Brabons put themselves forward to answer any questions; and they did. As the story continued into March, the Brabons countered several points made by Mr G. H. Evans, a neighbour. The Brabons were especially put out by his suggestion that their efforts to lay the ghost had failed and strongly repeated that they had succeeded. But the most serious charge was that the Spiritualists were either deceived or attempting to deceive in their representation of the matter.[24]

'I beg to say,' said Mr Brabon, 'that we are quite willing to be classed as lunatics in company with such highly scientific men as General Sir Alfred Turner, Sir Oliver Lodge, Sir Wm. Crookes, Stainton Moses, and others who firmly believe in the continuity of life and the power of communication with beings who have passed the border.'

Mr Evans wrote again to remind readers that despite the Spiritualists'

24 T. and A. Brabon, 'The Kidwelly Ghost', *Aberdare Leader* (10 March 1917), p. 8.

claiming to have taken the spirit with them, reports appeared in the press after their visit showing that it was still present.[25]

The Spiritualists had run away with themselves, developing a narrative in the face of the evidence that the knocker apparently reflected any information that was given to it, such as the messenger and the cigarettes.

The newspaper reports all tumbled over each over. It was seldom clear when events had taken place, who was present and whether subsequent reports in fact referred to the same events.

News filtered out to those fighting at the Front. Sergeant Ivor Cole, Mechanical Section, 1st Indian Army Corps, was in Mesopotamia. Writing to his father, Councillor Edmund Cole, in Kidwelly, he said, 'I hear, too, that you have a ghost at Kidwelly. You want to send him out here for us to tame him for you.'[26] On the same page, the newspaper carried news of the collapse of General Townsend's campaign 'within sight of Baghdad'. Several lords of the realm, including one of the Lyttelton clan, General Sir Neville Lyttelton, had completed their report as the Mesopotamia Committee and found the whole military campaign in Mesopotamia to have been a politically motivated blunder. The 'reckless optimism' of Sir John Nixon, Commander in Mesopotamia, was especially drawn attention to.

Professor Rajah:
'Of More Than Doubtful Repute'

Under the headline 'Tracking the Quacks' in February 1917, the *Daily Mail* noted with undisguised glee that 'satisfactory progress is being made by the Metropolitan Police in rounding up the London

---

25 *Aberdare Leader* (17 March 1917), p. 7.
26 'Kidwelly', *Carmarthen Journal* (29 June 1917), p. 3; 'Muddle in Mesopotamia: Another Deplorable Scandal', *Carmarthen Journal* (29 June 1917), p. 3.

fortune-tellers and psychists'. The police had devised a special form for 'necromancers under official review', as the newspaper put it. Details to be recorded included the usual name and address, of course, but also an account of the fees charged, the class of clients, whether business was transacted by post or in person, whether they had been mentioned in the press, any previous investigations by the police, and the nature of any instruments used (for example, crystals, cards, mirrors and even electrical apparatus).[27]

'Under the cloak of Spiritualism' the newspaper was delighted to reveal that 'male and female professors of psychic wizardry' were running 'massage and hypnotic establishments of more than doubtful repute'. One of these was 'Professor Rajah', a 'coloured mystic' and, apparently quoting his own promotional material 'the celebrated Indian phrenologist, thought-reader, physiognomist, graphologist, and nerve specialist, from Bond-street, London'. At that precise time, however, he was residing at No. 25 Dryden Street in Nottingham. Nottingham, apparently, was 'just now a happy hunting-ground for quacks of this class'.

Professor Rajah was not a Professor, nor was he called Rajah, nor was he exactly 'Indian'. Rupert Burton Smith had been born in Jamaica in 1875. He was described as a 'man of colour', 5ft 4in in height, and going by a variety of aliases, including Rupert Scott Blair, Rupert Eric Bruce Hamilton, Rupert Montmorency, Hubert Costello, and, affecting an aristocratic air, Rupert Eric Costello de Montmorency and Rupert de Montmorency, or indeed an academic one as Dr Costello, Dr Blair, Dr Mohamed, Professor Duleep, Professor Rajah, Professor Zodiac, or the fully outlandish as Zenith Zodiac.[28]

Upon arriving in a new town, he would set up in furnished apartments in an advantageous location and advertise extensively in the newspapers, by printed handbills, and using sandwich-board-men – all declaring him to be 'a Doctor, Consulting Physician, Phrenologist, Graphologist, etc.' – to draw in a mainly female clientele. He would

27 'Tracking the Quacks', *Daily Mail* (6 February 1917), p. 3.
28 *The Police Gazette*, Supplement A, vol. XI, No. 14 (4 July 1924).

prescribe medicines and induce them to have their hands read, and 'it is stated,' ran the report, 'that he has had immoral relations with many of the women who call to consult him'.

This sexual predation had also had him up in court. In 1913 serious allegations were brought against him after a young girl was charged with attempted suicide. She had been employed as a companion to Smith's wife, but 'he had ruined her', as he had others similarly in his employment. When he was arrested in 1923, he was discovered to be keeping a seventeen-year-old girl, originally engaged as a secretary, but subsequently abused.

On another occasion, he had engaged a new secretary and after finding out that she had £100 invested in Consols proposed marriage to her. He persuaded her to sell the Consols and 'invest' the money in his business, which she did, astonishingly. Once he had the cash, he told her that he was already married and that they would have to wait until he could get a divorce; but before that fictitious date came about, he suggested that as she was to become his wife it was no longer proper for her to work in his office as a secretary, and so she left his employment. Justice prevailed, however, and a solicitor was able to retrieve £80 for the defrauded young lady.

He was using the 'Professor Zodiac' alias before the war. In late 1911, he was arrested in central London for fortune-telling. Business must have been good because he was described as wearing 'a fashionable overcoat and in his gloved hands held a silk hat' as he stood in the dock of Marylebone Police Court. He had given his name as Robert Scott Blair and called himself a phrenologist 'of the Phrenological Institute'. However the police had received 'many complaints' and acting on the information from two of his clients, Annie Betts and Mary Florence Barnes, raided the premises. When Detective Inspector Tappenden entered his rooms on the Edgware Road he found Zodiac in a back room, holding a large crystal and talking to a woman, apparently giving her a 'reading'. Tappenden had him red-handed.[29]

29 'West End Palmist Sent to Prison', *London Evening News* (4 November 1911), p. 1; *The Daily News* [Perth, WA] (11 December 1911), p. 1.

'If I have been doing anything illegal,' he said, 'I shall plead guilty.' And he did.

Even then his defence tried to play the race card, complaining that 'being a black man' he had been 'singled out for prosecution, while others who were white were allowed to continue their operations with impunity'. Any criminal can complain that they have been 'singled out', simply because the others have not been caught, but it is hardly a defence.

His wife and several West End fortune-tellers were in the public gallery to watch proceedings as the magistrate Alfred Chichele Plowden heard the case. Harold Begbie described him as 'shrewd-looking, dusky skinned, with iron-grey hair easily tumbled, a short grey moustache, dark eyes, and an aquiline nose'. Begbie recalled how the court would rise at the magistrate's entrance, 'slow and majestic, with the rustling of robes'. Plowden himself seems to have been neither slow nor majestic: 'The magistrate does everything with a rush: he pushes open the door, moves swiftly to his seat, and has thrust his pince-nez on to the end of his nose, looked over his papers, and opened the register before the court has seated itself. "First applicant," he says, briskly, resting his chin in the cup of his hand and looking with corrugated brow to the witness-box.'[30]

Marylebone Police Court was a big, square, high-ceilinged room. Light poured down from the glass roof, but found little joy from the light-grey-painted walls. A line of green tiles edged with blue ran round the middle of the wall as a dado. The light found a better home reflecting from the yellow furnishings: the magistrate's bench and sounding board behind it were yellow; the benches before it were yellow; the witness box and canopy were yellow; the three large doors leading into the chamber were all yellow. Begbie thought that the dark-red curtains 'here and there about the court' added a 'mournful note of colour'. The dock was a long iron construction facing the bench; two iron rails supported by iron cross-pieces ran over the top and tin numbers were

---

30 *Daily Mail*, 16 January 1905, quoted in the *West Gippsland Gazette* [Australia] (28 March 1905), p. 4.

fixed at intervals to identify prisoners when there was a long line of them. Begbie was horrified by the dismal procession that passed through the dock, and the equally dismal crowd that came to watch, causing him to philosophise on the extent of civilisation. Here was 'the submerged life lived by the dregs of the city'. Begbie found a final heroism in Plowden as the only man to have endured this for the number of years he had 'without a nervous breakdown'. So, the scene is set, Blair stands in the iron dock; the Detective Inspector takes the witness box.

Mr Nichols, defending, asked Tappenden, 'Did you say anything about the business being profitable?'

'If anyone did, I did,' replied Tappenden, 'and I should think it is, considering that he has made about £600 in about fifteen months.'

'And that is shown in that small book, is it?' asked Nichols, attempting to imply something.

Plowden interjected, 'You see, even a little book can show a great deal.'

Tappenden added that the money received by Blair began with £2 a week, increasing to £16, £17 and finally £19, as he established himself. To put the question of money in context, a non-union worker in a munitions factory during the war might expect to earn £12 a week.[31]

'But that does not show his expenses,' argued Nichols. 'Blair [as he was then referred to] paid £60 a year in rent, and advertised extensively in the papers.' His expenses can hardly be called a good line of defence in a fraud case.

'How many people carry on this kind of business in this thoroughfare?'

'Several,' answered Tappenden.

Nichols rolled off a list of 'palmists' practising their trade in London. One of them even had an army of forty sandwich-men carrying his adverts about town. Blair, according to his defence, had repented whilst being held on remand and would give up his premises 'and while he

---

31 Harold Cox, 'The Autocracy of "Labour"', *Sunday Times* (30 September 1917), p. 5.

had been repenting in Brixton gaol other palmists had been taking coin wholesale'.

'There is,' intoned Plowden, 'more joy over one sinner that repenteth.'

Nichols was building up to his argument. He put it to the magistrate that although a plea of guilty had been entered, the accused was 'a young man' – he would have been about forty-two – who 'from his school days in the West Indies, had been told that the English always treated blacks and whites fairly', and that 'he was the only West Indian in the street where many others carried on similar businesses'.

Plowden cast a shrewd look over his pince-nez: 'If there are others, they will probably stand here on a future occasion.'

Nichols changed tack, arguing that his client did not know that he was doing anything wrong.

Plowden's sharp eyes grew shrewder: 'You have pleaded guilty to being a vulgar impostor. It stamps you as a rogue and a vagabond. You have a bad character. You have been convicted as a thief, and you have been charged with – and, I think, convicted of – trying to obtain money by fraud. This makes it extremely improbable that you did not know you were cheating those poor people to the tune of £600 in fifteen months. Very likely other people will be standing where you are standing, and if they have been doing what you have been doing, they will deserve to.'

He sentenced Blair to six weeks' imprisonment.

Towards the end of 1912, he was again arrested for fortune-telling, this time in Liverpool. He had argued that he only charged for phrenological examinations and told fortunes for free, but the court found otherwise and gave him nine months.[32]

'Rupert Eric Bruce Hamilton, alias Professor Duhleep' appeared in court in Brighton in 1914. For professing to tell fortunes he earned himself three months' hard labour. The court again heard how he had

---

32 'Scoundrel Punished. Professor Zodiac', *Illustrated Police News* (19 December 1912), pp. 12–13.

been doing this all over England, with convictions in London, Manchester and Liverpool.[33]

His marriage did not last the war. In 1915, 'Rupert Scott Blair', 'a West Indian who carried on the business of a phrenologist and palmist', was sued for divorce by his wife on grounds of 'his cruelty and adultery'. The court heard how 'a great many women came to consult him and he had seduced a great many of them'. He even 'installed several of these women as servants in his house'. One of these was a 'typist' who could not type. As to the cruelty, 'he had struck her, threatened to kill her, and thrown books at her, and had also communicated a disease to her'. His wife had been one of his early victims. Going to see him to have her fortune told, she had ended up marrying him on 23 August 1911. The divorce was granted with costs.[34]

The loss of his wife did nothing to prevent business, of course. 'Rupert Montmorency, a Hindu', next appeared in Manchester in 1916 where he was fined £10 for pretending to tell fortunes.[35]

'Rupert Montmorency', phrenologist, was back before the courts later in 1917. On 5 July he was required to appear at the Birmingham Quarter Sessions. Police had raided his rooms on the Bristol Road and found evidence that he was making about £10 a week out of his business.[36]

Montmorency seemed on this occasion to be leading his own defence, for he is stated to have asked Detective Constable Vince if he would interfere if he saw him practising as a phrenologist at a garden party in aid of charity. Vince admitted that he would not.

Mr Willes, for the prosecution, added that 'the Legislature had a tender regard for the welfare of fools. Unfortunately, a large number of people were misled into the belief that a man like the prisoner had occult powers.' Two women who appeared as police witnesses had been

33 'Gaol for Fortune-Teller', *London Standard* (27 March 1914).
34 'Suit Against a Palmist', *The Times* (1 April 1915), p. 3.
35 *Wicklow News-Letter and County Advertiser* (26 August 1916).
36 'Peeps into the Future: Prophet Meets Fate He Did Not Foresee', *Evening Despatch* (5 July 1917).

to his house and had had 'conversations with him relating principally to the future.'

Mr Willes had a punchline up his sleeve: 'The only prediction he made which was fulfilled was that at the head of his bill, "Leaving Shortly". He did leave shortly – in the company of a detective officer.' The newspaper account reports 'laughter' at this point.

However, Willes was not just out for laughs at the prisoner's expense: 'A large number of people were anxious about friends and relatives engaged on active service, and would take any means which they thought would give them information of those friends and relatives. Perhaps in normal times there would be a smaller market for a man like the prisoner.'

Montmorency was not put off his line of defence. 'If it was right at a garden party for charity,' he argued, 'it was right at other times.' He complained that 'he was placed on the same level as other offenders, yet they would not think of allowing a worker of the three-card-trick or a pickpocket to give an exhibition at a garden party'. Finally, the respectability of his profession was evinced by the fact that 'there were books on sale dealing with palmistry [palmistry and phrenology seem to have been the same with him], but none entitled, "Pockets: How to Pick Them", or "Houses: How to Burgle Them"'.

Detective Constable Vince was not to be waylaid. The prisoner, he said, had a long list of convictions for fortune-telling, fraud and theft. 'Rupert Montmorency' and all his other aliases was sentenced to twelve months' imprisonment with hard labour. He may have thought that he had been unfairly singled out, but, as the number of prosecutions shows, his case was not unique.

After being released in the summer of 1918, he seems to have simply carried on as before. He reappeared in public records for being sentenced at Hastings Sessions on 29 June 1923 to twelve months imprisonment as 'an incorrigible rogue – pretending to tell fortunes'. By now, he had amassed previous convictions for larceny, false pretences and numerous minor offences from Dublin to Portsmouth. Some particulars include purse-snatching and giving false credentials to obtain an agreement on a house. He was still 'posing as a Doctor of Science, phrenologist, nerve specialist, etc.', who 'defrauds the public by professing to tell fortunes by means of palmistry'.[37]

Yeats and the Mechanical Clairvoyant

On 7 March, Crookes, Sinnett, Ionides, Wallace, E. R. Johnson, Yeats, Gray, F. Fielding-Ould, and Withall met at Paganis Restaurant, Great Portland St – Wallace and Ionides had found a suitable replacement for Maison Jules. Sad news was announced: long-time Ghost Club members W. R. Washington Sullivan, MD, and Lt Col. Dudley Sampson had died since they last met. The President instructed the Secretary to write to their widows and express the usual sentiments. Yeats had a story to tell.[38]

Yeats had found out about David Wilson and went to visit him at St Leonards-on-Sea on 30 January 1917. He was there from two in the afternoon until midnight, and wrote up a report on Wilson's machine on 2 February.[39] Now he was at the Ghost Club, 'giving a description of the much developed psychic instrument of which mention has so frequently been made at previous meetings'.

Unfortunately, these earlier discussions were not recorded. Wilson seemed to have been working on his device because '[...] it now possessed what might be called a mechanical clairvoyant eye and a mechanical clairvoyant ear by the use of which Mr Wilson was able to receive messages from the unseen and obtain impressions on photographic plates but the instrument was only in its infancy and much more might be obtained through further development'. Yeats 'could not see the flashing of the crystal eye nor hear the signals given when

---

37 *The Police Gazette*, Supplement A, vol. XI, no. 14 (4 July 1924).
38 Meeting of 7 March 1917, British Library, Add. MS 52264, pp. 478–9.
39 John S. Kelly, *A W. B. Yeats Chronology* (Basingstoke: Palgrave Macmillan, 2003), p. 190.

Mr Wilson was receiving the communications and he wondered if anyone with greater psychic perceptions than himself with a knowledge of the code would get the same results as Mr Wilson'. It turned out that 'for financial reasons' Wilson intimated that he would have to 'discontinue the experiments'. Yeats stepped in and offered to act as fund-raiser for him, so that Wilson could 'devote his whole time to the perfection of the instrument'.

Yeats said that he was making advances in this when he heard that Wilson had been raided by the police and the machine seized as some sort of device for communicating with the Germans. Wilson was also questioned as to why he was not in the Army, and left for Switzerland.

As a note to his talk, the Secretary had written 'Yeats desires to add that he is not confident that the machine could act apart from the mediumship of Mr Wilson. The supernormal power certainly acts through it, but the independent action has to be proved.' This admission would seem to undermine any value the machine might have had.

The Secretary also noted that Yeats 'also did not intend to suggest any doubt as to Mr Wilson establishing his Swiss domicile.' There must have been some doubt, as it seems improbable that Wilson could have made it to Switzerland, lying, as it did, on the other side of war-torn France.

On 22 February, Yeats had called on Gilbert Murray at the War Office to try and get his help in recovering Wilson's machine from the police. But it was at the Omega Club in mid-March, whilst talking to T. S. Eliot, that he learnt that the police had apparently returned the 'psychic machine' – apparently Wilson had also been returned from Switzerland (assuming he actually left). Toward the end of March he was back again at Wilson's seaside home, this time with the painter and stage designer Edmund Dulac and the orientalist Edward Denison Ross, founder and director of the London School of Oriental Studies. After they left, Yeats received a message from the machine. On 4 April, he was talking about the machine to Estella Stead and this seems to be the last time he expressed any interest in it. Other concerns came to dominate Yeats's attention – he got married for one and through his new wife George's automatic writing wrote *A Vision* – and the psychic machine is heard of no more.[40]

By then Wilson himself had moved on from the New Wave Detector – he was, however, still being asked about it – and invented the Reichenbach Receiver. This was a similarly fantastical device, 'a luminous phial whose normal luminosity can be momentarily enhanced (thus producing a kind of flash) solely by an effort of the will' – it was, he said, 'superior to any electrical contrivance'.[41]

He had promised more experiments, but none were forthcoming. In a later edition of *Light*, Gow decided that 'the messages given out by the mechanism were in some cases curiously interfused with the mind of its inventor' and belittled Wilson's 'weird theories of his own'. Gow noted that Wilson 'has once more abandoned his experiments' and could not say whether he would resume them. The lack of further articles in *Light* would suggest that he did not. Others have mentioned the possibility that he was conscripted into the Army.[42]

A Widow's Suicide

Had a shot rung out, loud, abrupt? Was it blood on the mirror in the bedroom? The newspaper report was terse, the details vague. An inquest was held in Preston on 7 March 1917; Mrs Ravenhill, mother of the deceased, said that her daughter had become 'ill' that Sunday morning. When she visited her room about midday, she found her half sitting up in bed. There was 'a stained mirror on the bed'. She was holding an automatic pistol. Dr McCallum was called and had Mrs

40 Kelly, *Yeats Chronology*, pp. 191, 192. It is often reported that he first lectured to the Ghost Club on 4 April about the machine, but the Ghost Club archives record his first lecture on the subject on 7 March. W. B. Yeats, *A Vision* (Privately printed, 1925).
41 David Wilson, 'The Reichenbach Receiver', *Light* (11 August 1915), p. 252
42 'Notes by the Way', *Light* (13 October 1917), p. 321.

Ravenhill's daughter taken to Preston Infirmary. She died the next morning.[43]

Mrs Ravenhill's daughter, Margery Alice Vernon Warner, aged twenty-two, was a widow. Her husband Herbert Moline Warner had been a captain, commanding 'B' Company of the 1st Battalion, East Lancashire Regiment. Warner, then a Lieutenant, had joined the rest of the Regiment at Bucy-le-Long on 19 September, along with a new intake of eighty-three other ranks to replace casualties suffered since Le Cateau during the Great Retirement.[44]

Bucy-le-Long is on the north bank of the river Aisne, about 4.5 miles (7 km) north-east of Soissons. The Regiment was drawn up in reserve to the rest of the 11th Brigade deployed on a spur north-west of Bucy.

He would have taken part in the Divine Service held on 27 September. The men had assembled on the spur's lower slope behind Battalion HQ to hear the chaplain deliver his sermon. 'I will lift up mine eyes,' he intoned, 'unto the hills from whence cometh my help.' The soldiers eyes naturally lifted up. There above them they could make out a German aeroplane. It was spotting for artillery: what followed after was a far cry from 'help'.[45]

Back on 24 August, the reality of war still lay like a far-off thing, as far off as the Continent, for Lt Warner. Fierce fighting had already claimed many lives at Mons and the British Army was in retreat, but Lt Warner was in the Church of St James-the-Less in Plymouth exchanging rings with Miss Ravenhill, daughter of Lieutenant Colonel Ravenhill, Royal Field Artillery. It was the 1st Battalion's first war wedding. Captain Cane was Warner's best man and 'B' Company provided the honour guard. The bridegroom already had his marching orders.[46]

43 'Fate of Officer's Widow', *Daily Mail* (8 March 1917), p. 3.
44 Captain E. C. Hopkinson, *Spectamur Agendo: 1st Battalion, The East Lancashire Regiment, August and September, 1914* (Privately printed, 1926; Naval & Military Press, 2011), pp. 64–8.
45 Hopkinson, *Spectamur Agendo*, p. 64.
46 Sir Cecil Lothian Nicholson, *History of the East Lancashire Regiment in the Great War, 1914–1918* (Littlebury Bros., 1936), p. 200.

The 1st Battalion was soon on the march again, passing through St Sauveur to arrive at Campiegne at about 7 p.m. on 10 October. Here they entrained for Flanders.

Born in Sheffield on 13 January 1889, Warner had been educated at Wellington College before joining the East Lancashire Regiment as a Second Lieutenant in 1909, becoming a Lieutenant in 1911. He was part of that first wave of professional soldiers who would soon become a scarce commodity along the Western Front.

The troop train took them up towards Ypres and the Battalion deployed about 9 miles (15 km) south near Le Gheer. He would have seen action in the Battle of Armentières (19 October–2 November 1914) during the 'Race to the Sea' as each side sought to turn the northern flank of the other. As he took cover in a trench, only a few days after being promoted Captain, he was hit by shrapnel and seriously wounded. Taken to No. 2 Clearing Hospital at Bailleul the extent of his wounds could be examined: the shrapnel had pierced his lung. He died two days later on 16 November 1914. He was twenty-five years old.[47]

Mrs Ravenhill told the inquest that his young widow 'took the death of her husband very badly'. She became depressed and suffered a nervous breakdown.

'She had been in touch with Spiritualism,' continued Mrs Ravenhill, 'and that was what made her like that.'

'How long,' asked the coroner, 'had she been dealing in Spiritualism?'

'I do not know; she had been away from home for two years.'

'Did she leave any writing or anything of the kind?'

'Not for me,' said Mrs Ravenhill. 'She had written letters to her husband, but they were not sense – a sort of Spiritualist writing. They were found in her boxes.'

The newspaper report cannot convey the anguish that Mrs Ravenhill must have felt. Her next statement is given as 'added the witness', but this was a mother talking about her dead daughter: 'She often said she

47 *The Bond of Sacrifice, vol. 1, Aug–Dec 1914* (London: The Anglo-African Publishing Contractors), p. 429.

wished to join her husband. His death was an awful shock to her, and she has never been the same since.'

'When she said that,' inquired the coroner, 'had you any doubt as to her sanity?'

'Every doubt.'

The coroner gave a verdict of 'suicide while of unsound mind'.

Spiritualism was not always the comfort that it is made out to be.

Conan Doyle's Revelation

Kingsley had survived the Somme and was at Regimental Headquarters in the role of what Conan Doyle called a 'bombing officer'. His old regiment were still in the thick of the fighting. The 1st Battalion had seen action at the First Battle of the Scarpe (9–14 April) and the Third Battle of the Scarpe (3–4 May), already that year.[48]

Conan Doyle wrote to his mother, Mary Foley Doyle, known as 'the Mam', describing Kingsley's situation and his own thoughts on the matter:

> He is well in the front. I get the most cheery letters but I am naturally very anxious. I do not fear death for the boy, for since I became a convinced Spiritualist death became rather an un-caring thing, but I fear pain and mutilation very greatly. However, all things are ordained [. . .].[49]

He also told her about the bereaved parents who wrote to him for help in contacting their dead sons. He told her about one letter he had had from a mother, thanking him, adding, 'She is the 13th within my knowledge. It is indeed a most marvellous thing [. . .]'.

48 'The 1st. Bn Hampshire Regiment', http://1rhamps.com/ww1/Battalions/1stBn.html, accessed 25 July 2017.
49 Quoted in Miller, *Adventures*, pp. 368–9.

Conan Doyle knew that the Mam was set against Spiritualism. He may have been trying to convince her of its benefits, rather than rub her nose in it. But she was not the only one in the family to find Spiritualism distasteful. His sister Ida, daughter Mary and Kingsley also refrained from accepting it.

Still at the Front and writing from the Officer's Rest Room, Kingsley sent a revealing letter to his Aunt Ida in November 1917. He told her about the doubts he had concerning Spiritualism: 'however, I would not pretend to argue with Daddy on the subject'.[50]

He shared these reservations with Mary, who wrote, 'I tried to go along with it, but couldn't [. . .] These personal demonstrations of survival were to me acutely embarrassing and painful. I could not get used to the idea of contacting a loved one through someone else's body – it was all queer and uncanny to me.'[51]

Ida, for her part, thought it unlikely that spirits were 'hanging about clamouring to communicate with earth' and was unimpressed by the thought of spending eternity doing likewise. Conan Doyle in reply gave her quite a ticking-off:

Your views about the spiritland seem to me a little unreasonable [. . .] I am sorry you don't like the prospect but what you or I may like has really nothing to do with the matter. We don't like some of the conditions down here [. . .] I may be very limited but I can imagine nothing more beautiful and satisfying than the life beyond as drawn by many who have experienced it. We carry on our own wisdom, own knowledge, own art, music, architecture but all with a far wider sweep. Our bodies are at their best. We are free from physical pain. The place is beautiful. What is there so dreadfully depressing in all this?[52]

Although he had written about Spiritualism and defended Spiritualists, such as Sir Oliver Lodge, in the press, Conan Doyle had yet to come out

50 Quoted in Miller, *Adventures*, p. 369.
51 Quoted in Miller, *Adventures*, p. 369.
52 Quoted in Miller, *Adventures*, p. 369.

publicly as a committed believer.[53] To all intents and purposes this would take place at the British Artists' Gallery, Pall Mall, on 25 October 1917, when Lodge presided over a meeting of the London Spiritualists' Alliance to hear Sir Arthur Conan Doyle lecture on what he called 'The New Revelation'.[54]

'Flight of the Seers'

The *Daily Mail* had been waging what it called a 'campaign' against 'West End "seers" and fortune-tellers' and in March 1917 reported that Divisional Inspector Sanders and Detective Sergeant Hambrook of the Paddington police had closed down almost three hundred such businesses in their area alone.[55]

'Many have been arrested,' wrote Our Special Correspondent (probably Ashton again), 'and either fined or sent to prison.' The rest of the 'so-called Spiritualists' either 'took fright and vanished' or packed in the business altogether. Interestingly, the *Mail* reported that 'the serious Spiritualists' had also been moved to action: the magazine *Light*, described as 'the recognised organ of Spiritualism and the occult generally', had cancelled its page of adverts for 'Spiritist practitioners, magnetic healers, and the like', and Sir Arthur Conan Doyle had written a letter in support of the decision.

Our Special Correspondent ended on what he doubtless intended to be an ominous note: 'Meanwhile in districts beyond the Paddington area there is still a good deal of "underground" necromancy going on.'

Our Special Correspondent was back in June 1917, with a report on occult activity in Brighton – some at least, of the seers driven out of

53 Miller, *Adventures*, p. 369.
54 The meeting was reported in 'The Spirit Life', *The Times* (26 October 1917), p. 3.
55 Our Special Correspondent, 'Flight of the Seers', *Daily Mail* (13 March 1917), 3.

London appear to have fled here to become what he called 'seaside psychics':[56]

> I have met here several old occult friends with new sun-stained faces driving their trade warily. The cult of the occult in Brighton has never been more prosperous. Fortune-telling, which is only another word for Spiritualism, as the 'art' is practised nowadays, is 'booming' here if you know where to look for it.

Our Special Correspondent had dug up 'a coterie of seers': about fifty people who met at the Free Catholic and Spiritual Church, which he described as 'a guarded temple' suitably wedged in under railway arches near Preston Circus. Here, they indulged in 'the most ornate rites' in an 'atmosphere thick with incense'.

He interviewed the 'Bishop' of this establishment, a certain 'Rev.' John Partridge, describing him as a nervous man in his early twenties who smoked 'more cigarettes than he ought to'. He listened intently as Partridge told him an intriguing story.

'Yesterday afternoon,' said Partridge, 'a Portuguese gentleman came to me and complained that he had been bewitched. I was fortunately able to exorcise the demon – and the Portuguese gentleman was extravagantly grateful.' Then as if realising how this sounded, 'I should like to add that all our work is done for love and for humanity, and that we charge nothing. We have a collection at each of our services, but I do not even insist that it should be a silver collection!' Silver was in reference to the colour of the coins, meaning that he would take old coppers as well. The Correspondent evidently attended one of his 'rites', for he describes seeing him arrayed in 'rich Sarum vestments, with cope and alb complete', although the journalist was not impressed by the effect: 'he gives me the impression of a glorified choir-boy', he wrote. He observed that the congregation was mostly composed of women.

Despite the Correspondent's allusion to 'sun-stained faces', Brighton in 1917 was not the Brighton of old, not quite the seaside resort that it

56 Our Special Correspondent, 'Seaside Psychics', *Daily Mail* (2 June 1917), p. 5.

had been. The social psychologist and pacifist Caroline Playne was there for a weekend:

> There the legless soldiers are sent for treatment. A Lady said at first you were horrified when you saw four or five men who had lost a leg. Now that every part of town, the front and the piers has swarms of such men getting about on crutches, you have got to the stage of talking about it all quite naturally.[57]

The Correspondent wondered why a young, apparently healthy man was wearing white robes in Brighton instead of wearing a khaki uniform at the Front. He had been classified 'Army Reserve W, C3' – 'so he told me', as if to suggest some doubt on the matter. Class W Reserve had been created in June 1916 by Army Order 203/16 for 'all those soldiers whose services are deemed to be more valuable to the country in civil rather than military employment'; C3 was a medical grading, meaning that he was only fit for sedentary work.[58]

The journalist pressed him on the point. 'Supposing you are called up for military service in the midst of this work?'

According to the account, Partridge lit another cigarette before answering. 'Then I suppose it will be all up!' he said, 'with a sigh'.

An old photograph from around 1910 shows the interior of the church, apparently, on Campbell Road. Rows of wooden chairs face an altar fairly crammed with candles, with flower pots and greenery liberally scattered about. Strange orbs dangle from the rafters.[59]

57 Caroline Playne, *Britain Holds On, 1917, 1918* (London: Allen & Unwin, 1933), pp. 76–7.

58 http://www.1914-1918.net/reserve.htm, accessed 17 July 2017; 'British Army Medical Categories 1914', http://www.epsomandewellhistoryexplorer. org.uk/MedicalCategories.html., accessed 17 July 2017.

59 http://www.sussex-opc.org/index.php?p=295&k=1272&t=Church, accessed 17 July 2017.

The Survival of the Dead

In June 1917, the *Strand Magazine* published an article by Sir Oliver Lodge: 'How I Became Convinced of the Survival of the Dead'. The magazine held a public debate in its pages on the validity of Lodge's arguments, asking 'Is Sir Oliver Lodge Right?' Conan Doyle wrote the piece for 'Yes'; Edward Clodd represented 'No'. The *Strand* was home turf for Conan Doyle and he had the advantage.

Conan Doyle described his transformation from sceptic to believer, forced by the evidence into 'amazed and reluctant reconsideration'. Clodd's main attack concentrated on Spiritualism's charlatans, 'a pack of sorry rascals of both sexes, some of whom have been committed to prison and rogues and vagabonds'. But he had something to say about the so-called spirits, as well, whose only contribution was 'nauseating, frivolous, mischievous, spurious drivel'.[60]

There could be little warning that mention of a book on Spiritualism written by a moderately well-known psychiatrist would blow up into a wonderful scandal involving the creator of Sherlock Holmes, the man behind Thorpeness holiday village and Oscar Wilde's former lover.

It was a testament to how well known Lodge was that, when a book criticising him was published, a note appeared in *The Sunday Times*. 'Sir Oliver Lodge Attacked' ran the headline on 29 July 1917. Dr Charles Mercier, described as 'an expert on mental diseases and logic', had launched 'a fierce attack' in his book *Spiritualism and Sir Oliver Lodge*. *The Sunday Times* was happy to publish a particularly virulent, but pointedly polite, paragraph:[61]

---

60 Quoted in Miller, *Adventures*, p. 368.
61 'Sir Oliver Lodge Attacked', *Sunday Times* (29 July 1917), p. 4; Charles Mercier, *Spiritualism and Sir Oliver Lodge* (London: Mental Culture Enterprise, 1917), later republished by Watts & Co., in 1919.

That Sir Oliver Lodge is a man who works at scientific objects, and works at them successfully, is, of course, beyond all question; but there is all the difference between a man who works at scientific subjects and a scientific man. It is no disparagement to Sir Oliver Lodge to repudiate any claim he may make, or that may be made for him, to authority outside matters of electricity. Up to the present, nothing whatever that is wonderful has been performed by Sir Oliver Lodge's mediums that has not been exceeded in marvellousness by Messrs Maskelyne and Devant. Up to the present the professors of electricity and spectrum analysis and psychology and history have shut their eyes and opened their mouths, and swallowed any trash the mediums liked to present them with.[62]

Mercier made a valid point; Lodge's scientific reputation tended to spill over into areas in which he had no training, no expertise and, frequently, no clue. But he also slipped up. The fact that magicians might be able to recreate an event such as a séance does not prove that all séances are created by magicians. It is a point of logic of which he should have been well aware: we will come back to logic below. Similarly, today's sceptics, particularly the 'Amazing Randi', continue to make the same argument. This is not to say that mediums are not fraudsters, but simply that a different and better argument has to be made. *The Sunday Times* piece ended by saying that 'some sort of reply from Sir Oliver Lodge would seem inevitable'.

The first letters in response to *The Sunday Times* article were not from Lodge. Someone calling himself 'M. A. Cantab' of Jarvis Brook in Sussex – Jarvis Brook, incidentally, is a village near (now in) Conan Doyle's village of Crowborough – made the sensible and logical point that if Lodge must keep to electricity, then Mercier must stick to logic and psychology. 'Perhaps,' mused M. A. Cantab, 'he has studied logic to such purpose that his logical faculty has become impaired? It

62 The newspaper assembled this passage from Mercier, *Spiritualism*, pp. 15, 16 and 20.

would appear so.' However, one might argue that he did stick to psychology.[63]

'Who is Dr Mercier?' asked M. A. Cantab, with irritation. M. A. Cantab thought he was a nincompoop, but Charles Arthur Mercier (1851–1919), MD, FRCP, FRCS, was a leading psychiatrist of the day as, among other things, Consulting Physician for Mental Diseases at Charing Cross Hospital and a past president of the Medico-Psychological Association. He later wrote a scathing satire on Spiritualism called *Spirit Experiences* (1919), shortly before his death.

As to the question of magic, M. A. Cantab thought Dr Mercier's point 'almost too silly to be worth answering', but answer he did: 'The records of séances in *Raymond* do not partake of the marvellous in the sense of the Great Trunk Trick.'

M. A. Cantab ended by berating Mercier for not keeping an open mind. Was M. A. Cantab Sir Arthur Conan Doyle? Cantab is short for Cantabrigiensis, indicating that his degree was from Cambridge. Conan Doyle studied at Edinburgh University. However, William Stainton Moses (1839–1892) had frequently used the pseudonym 'M. A. Oxon', i.e., a graduate of Oxford University, and it may be that 'M. A. Cantab' was a play on that – a familiar reference for any Spiritualist of the period. Conan Doyle's house, Windlesham Manor, was only a stone's throw from Jarvis Brook, so near in fact that the address can hardly have been a coincidence. 'Jarvis Brook' could have meant Crowborough and hence Conan Doyle to anyone 'in the know'.

The next correspondent, B. A. Cochrane of Ossington Street, London, gave his name not a degree, and threw Mercier's words back in his face in a brief riposte. Dr Mercier had forgotten, he argued, that magicians produced their effects with concealed mechanical devices, whereas 'mediumistic marvels are produced in a room without any such appliances', although he overlooks that such tricks as were employed by Almira Brockway, for example, required no elaborate machinery. Whatever the merits of these arguments and

63 M. A. Cantab, 'Spiritualism and Sir Oliver Lodge', *Sunday Times* (5 August 1917), p. 2.

counter-arguments, the editor of *The Sunday Times* was no doubt happy to keep blowing on the embers of controversy.[64]

When Lodge did reply, the newspaper was delighted that 'for weeks past now we have been receiving correspondence almost embarrassing in its volume and conflict of opinion upon the claims Sir Oliver Lodge makes'. Lodge and Mercier had already been arguing the toss in the pages of the *Medical Press*, a point Lodge refers to, but now they had a national platform and the attention of the better part of the reading public not currently enduring the monstrosities of modern warfare.[65]

'Though disinclined to spend much time in controversy,' began Lodge, 'I must respond to the Editor's invitation to reply to Dr Charles Mercier's attack and the correspondence thereby evoked.' With such ponderous solemnity, the duel was accepted.

With a pompous prelude to introduce the reader to the great debate that had already been fought in the august *Medical Press*, Lodge delivered his first riposte. Mercier was 'a novice', whereas Lodge had the mighty authority of the SPR gathered round him like robes of imperial purple:

> He is a novice in the inquiry which we have been conducting for so long; he says he was unacquainted with the subject till he read my book, and as he cannot accept our results, he considers that we of the Society for Psychical Research must be a lot of gullible fools, and does not hesitate to say so.

Mercier had not attacked the SPR, so it is interesting that Lodge should seek to bolster his own position by dragging them into it. It would also suggest that Lodge saw himself as entirely aligned with and perhaps representative of the Society.

64 B. A. Cochrane, 'Spiritualism and Sir Oliver Lodge', *Sunday Times* (5 August 1917), p. 2.
65 Oliver Lodge, 'Proofs of Spiritualism', *Sunday Times* (23 September 1917), pp. 6, 12.

Lodge tried to pack Mercier into an even smaller box: 'I am not acquainted with any work of Dr Mercier's in science, but I take it for granted that he is a distinguished alienist, and I agree with his statement that "exclusive devotion to any study, or to any walk of life, inevitably tends to narrowness and to inability to judge correctly of matters outside the scope of daily work".'

Lodge filled several columns in the newspaper in this vein, countering Mercier's arguments, but mostly countering Mercier's character and judgement. In reply, he was quite as smug as Mercier.

The magicians, of course, did not miss a trick. In the same paper there was an advert for 'Maskelyne's Mysteries' at St George's Hall, everyday at 3 and 8 p.m., where the audience would see 'Spiritualism outdone'. According to a quoted press review, it was 'a cure for depression'.

Debate raged into the next week, with A. P. Sinnett notably joining the fray, comparing Mercier to the 'Philosophic Chicken' in *Rhymes of Science*, who rejects the idea that he could have come from an egg:[66]

For I'm a chicken that you can't deceive;
What I can't understand I won't believe!

Surprisingly, the mild-looking, mystical Sinnett excelled at character assassination. He argued that humans who refuse to believe had fewer excuses than chickens because they had the power to learn to read and write and could, therefore, have acquainted themselves with the earliest scientific investigations conducted into Spiritualism by the Dialectical Society and others, and so 'might have been guarded from making themselves ridiculous'.

Picking up on Lodge's 'novice' put-down, Sinnett obliged readers by informing them that 'I have been immersed in super-physical experiences for more than fifty years'. Sinnett then proceeded to give a long account of the many wonders he had witnessed in the séance room.

66 A. P. Sinnett, 'Our Touch with "the Other Side"', *Sunday Times* (30 September 1917), p. 5.

He began by mentioning one of his earliest experiences, forty years ago, with 'the lady then sometimes called "the Empress of physical mediums"'. He describes the séance room, empty except for a round table and some chairs, the single window shuttered and screwed down by himself, the single door, which if opened would have immediately given itself away with a flood of light. Sitting here in the dark with the others he felt himself 'splashed and brushed with something'. When they turned up the light they discovered 'branches of trees wet with the drizzling rain outside – more than one man could have carried in his arms' covering the floor. With this he fell into the opposite argument to Mercier. Where Mercier thought that if it could be reproduced by stage magicians then it must be a trick, Sinnett believed that if he could see no evidence of stage magic then none had been used. He would not have seen evidence of stage magic at Maskelyne's Mysteries, either.

Sinnett resented Lodge's success, however. *Raymond*, he argued, was 'only interesting because of its author's splendid claims to respect as a man of science'. He had already mentioned one of his own books – *In the Next World* (1914) – before he said 'many better books of the same kind are available, though their authors may be undistinguished'. By the end of the war, *Raymond* would become something of a literary genre, with so many others in similar vein, such as *Private Dowding, Thy Son Liveth* and *Rupert Lives!*[67]

In the same issue, Sir Arthur Conan Doyle (under his real name and giving his real address this time) wrote in to complain about Mercier's mention of him and point out that Mercier was 'by his own admission, very ill-read upon the subject'. He then listed the many eminent scientists who had been convinced by the evidence of

---

67 Wellesley Tudor-Pole, *Private Dowding: A Plain Record of the After-Death Experiences of a Soldier Killed in Battle* (New York: Dodd, Mead & Co., 1919); Grace Duffie Boylan, *Thy Son Liveth: Messages from a Soldier to His Mother* (Boston: Little, Brown & Co., 1919); L. Kelway Bamber, *Claude's Book* (New York: Henry Holt & Co., 1919) and *Claude's Second Book* (New York: Henry Holt & Co., 1920); 'His Mother', *Grenadier Rolf* (London: Kingsley Press, 1920); Walter Wyn, *Rupert Lives!* (London: Kingsley Press, 1923); Lilian Walbrook, *The Case of Lester Coltman* (London: Hutchinson & Co., 1924).

Spiritualism: 'very many men of the front rank of science – men like Lombroso, Flammarion, William James, Crookes, Wallace, Charles Richet, Sir William Barrett, and others'. Conan Doyle particularly disliked Mercier's tone: 'the want of all restraint and all manners in his book'. Again the charge of novice was raised: 'He has no right at all to impute evil motives or to make clumsy ridicule of men who have devoted many more years to this study than he has months.'

Poor Mercier got quite a drubbing and few wrote in his defence. When the magician David Devant wrote in criticism of Lodge it was only to say that he was not 'the late David Devant' as Lodge had written, but still very much alive. He thought Lodge had meant to do him harm by the statement, rather than having made a simple mistake. It was in fact Devant's colleague, the elder Maskelyne, who had died in May that year.[68]

Mercier had a more staunch defender in the shape of Glencairn Stuart Ogilvie of Sizewell Hall, Suffolk, barrister, playwright, architect and creator of the fantasy holiday village of Thorpeness. Ogilvie asserted that 'While always clamouring for "the open mind", it is a significant fact that the Occultists never satisfy sane scepticism by scientific methods.' No proof had been offered in contradiction of Mercier's contentions, he said, hence the phenomena of Spiritualism were 'merely subjective hallucinations produced either by pernicious auto-excitation or hetero-suggestion'. Ogilvie linked the rise of Spiritualism with current conditions 'of great mental and physical strain' and saw its effect as entirely pernicious: 'the cult revives, impostors flourish, insanity increases, and *the sum total of the National will-power is, pro tanto, decreased*' (italics in the original).

Another letter printed under the heading of 'Uninteresting Spooks' by 'Oc. Sedet' made the entirely facetious and inaccurate remark that Spiritualism was best avoided because one invariably ended up in contact with boring relatives – 'I don't want to talk to my grandmother, still less to an aunt, who married my father's brother, survived him, and left all her property to *her* family' – rather than 'Moses, or Alexander, or

68 'A Modern Magician', *Daily Telegraph* (19 May 1917), p. 7.

Micawber'. Many Spiritualists were in fact in supposed contact with the spirits of the great and the good, and they generally, with their sermon-ising and pontificating, tended to be the most uninteresting of the bunch. He also wanted to know how it was that the first medium found out 'that darkness, a round table, an endless chain of hands, and prob-ably other conditions, were essential for a spirit to manifest itself'.

The writer Samuel Waddington was similarly unimpressed by what he saw as the general absurdity of the afterlife described by Lodge. 'We must not take Sir O. Lodge too seriously,' he wrote, because we cannot seriously believe that, as he states in *Raymond*, the afterlife is filled with houses made of 'emanations from the earth', white robes from 'decayed worsted', and that cigars and whiskey sodas are provided for those who enjoyed them in life.

Unexpectedly, there was also a letter from Alfred Bruce Douglas. Lord Douglas had been, as might be recalled, Oscar Wilde's lover and the one who urged Wilde to bring a lawsuit against his own father, the Marquess of Queensbury, for calling Wilde a 'somdomite' (i.e., sodo-mite), which backfired and led to Wilde's arrest and conviction as a homosexual in 1895. After the trial Douglas had fled for the Continent, but he was back in Britain, staying at Shelley's Folly, the poet Percy Bysshe Shelley's former home in Lewes – the then current owner, Lord Monk Bretton, had rented it to his mother, the Marchioness of Queensbury in 1915.[69] Douglas had by now repudiated Wilde and his own poetic stance as one of the Uranians, and thrown himself upon the mercy of the Church. His letter was published under the title of 'The Catholic Attitude', as if Douglas was their spokesman. He took Lodge's side against Mercier, but also castigated Lodge for ignoring the Catholic Church upon the matter.

Douglas summed up Mercier's main contention as 'supernatural things, like miracles, "don't happen", and anyone who says they do must be a gullible fool'. Lodge, he thought, had 'little difficulty in expos-ing the absurdity of Dr Mercier's crude attempts at throwing ridicule on all people who do not deliberately shut themselves up in an armour

69 Ross Clark, 'A Peerless Prospect', *The Telegraph* (24 March 2004).

of impenetrable materialism'; and he threw it back in Mercier's face: 'there is nobody in the world so gullible and so easily discomfited as your materialist'. Douglas agreed with Lodge's scorn of Mercier's 'cocksureness' as a 'novice', but took Lodge to task because 'his own attitude towards the Catholic Church is just as temerarious and just as astonishing'. The whole business of Spiritualism, according to Douglas, belonged rightfully to the theologian and it was a staggering oversight not to take theological opinion into account in such matters.

Douglas had a tentative connection with the SPR: his sister was married to SPR Council member St George William Lane Fox-Pitt. But his conversion to Catholicism was an attempt to expunge the guilt of his past and the more ferociously he defended it, the more ferociously he revealed how much guilt there was.

That Sunday there were two columns of letters printed under the heading 'Proofs of Spiritualism'. One was from Mercier himself with the intriguing heading of 'Is Dr Mercier Converted?'[70]

Of course, Mercier had to begin on a pompous note. 'I predicted that Sir Oliver Lodge would not answer me,' he wrote, 'and he has not answered me.' The long reply he gave to Mercier was dismissed as talking round the subject. He complained about Lodge's personal criticisms and tried to dodge the accusations of being a novice and all-round humbug by calling them 'quite irrelevant' and 'red herrings'. However, he had to deal with them. On being biased against the very possibility of the supernatural, he said 'but I am not prejudiced against miracles'. On being a novice he had to concede, but wrote that 'want of experience may be mended'. And mending it he was: 'I have lately been investigating some phenomena that appear to be miraculous' and was 'quite ready to admit miracles when there really is evidence for them'. He went even further to say 'such evidence I think I have found' and intended to publish his results 'as soon as the state of the paper market and of the printing trade permits'.

70 Chas. Mercier, et al., 'Proofs of Spiritualism', *Sunday Times* (30 September 1917), p. 2.

The Conversion of Dr Mercier

His 'evidence' was published in the form of *Spirit Experiences* in 1919. For the price of ninepence the reader could learn of the 'Conversion of a Sceptic!' and marvel at the 'startling and astonishing experiences of a seeker after truth'.

The book begins with what appears to be a humble apology:

When a man makes a mistake, and finds that he has made a mistake, I think he ought to acknowledge it. At any rate, when he has made assertions and published them in a book, a book advertised, reviewed, and widely circulated, and when he subsequently finds these assertions unwarrantable, it is his duty to correct them. [. . .] It is this duty that I am discharging in the present publication.[71]

However, that is not what he is doing at all.

I thought, rashly and hastily, that the experience of a lifetime spent in investigating the mind in health and diseases should give me a certain competence in investigating intelligences, discarnate as well as incarnate. I assumed too readily that evidence of this order was susceptible of examination by the same logical canons as evidence of any other order, and that, as a trained logician, I might rely upon conclusions arrived at by strict logical methods.[72]

How could anyone have questioned the great doctor and master logician? Mercier's professional pride had been dented, if not knocked over

71 Charles Mercier, *Spirit Experiences* (London: Watts & Co, 1919), p. 3.
72 Mercier, *Spirit Experiences*, p. 4.

and trodden on, by the correspondence in *The Times*. He had not been converted as *The Times* thought; even then he had been laying the groundwork for his response. Now, he was out for revenge.

The book ostensibly follows Mercier's investigation of 'Thought-transference' between 'two young ladies'. After an 'innocent and amusing pursuit of what are called "parlour games", including – and he is determined to tell us – 'Consequences, Puss in the corner, Beggar my neighbour, Spellikins, and other recreations', he suggested an experiment in telepathy disguised as another game. Quite deliberately it is the worst experiment in telepathy ever devised, offering all sorts of opportunity for cheating and collusion, and, of course, proving nothing, except that all such experiments in telepathy were flawed. He quoted Lodge throughout to try and show how absurd his arguments are and, generally, how gullible he is.

One of his best jokes is built around the sound of 'mysterious' raps heard when he separates the two girls in two different rooms. When he asks 'Are you ready?' he hears three loud raps on the wall separating him from one of the girls. 'At first I naturally supposed,' he writes, 'that these sounds were made by the thought of the object struggling to make its way through the brick wall.' But revised this notion when he realised that three raps 'constitute a well-known spirit signal, and are used by the spirits to convey the meaning that is expressed in the House of Commons by the familiar formula, "The answer is in the affirmative."' The punchline cannot fail to raise a weak smile from the reader:

> I may here remark in parenthesis how greatly superior the spirit language is to that of us poor mortals who have not yet passed over. A spirit is able to convey in three raps an answer that cannot be conveyed by a Member of Parliament in fewer than eleven syllables. Why, I ask, should not Ministers adopt the far better method of the spirit world, and, when an affirmative answer is to be given, signify the same by giving three knocks on the table before them?[73]

73 Mercier, *Spirit Experiences*, p. 14.

He admits that this was a digression, but excuses himself on the grounds that Sir Oliver Lodge frequently does the same, noting with false wonder 'how strongly intercourse with spirits tends to the introduction of seemingly irrelevant digressions into a narrative'. There are pages and pages of this sort of stuff. Needless to say the two telepathic girls have thoroughly pulled the wool over the eyes of Mercier's parody of a psychical researcher, pulled his other leg and attached the bells to it themselves.

Mercier then investigates the 'famous' (read fabricated) medium Mrs Bacca of Chicago, 'a city famous for the manufacture of wooden nutmegs, worm-eaten ancient furniture, artificial eggs, unqualified practitioners in law and medicine, and other ingenious products of the highest civilization'. Her spirit control is called 'Mrs Shegessdit', whom he directly compares to Leanora Piper's control 'Dr Phinuit' as being of the same class. Mrs Bacca is of course a great confidence trickster and has soon fooled the investigator into thinking that she has miraculous powers.[74]

He manages to offend Mrs Shegessdit and she goes off in a huff, but another spirit called Hodgkins takes her place. Hodgkins is 'the spirit of a fellow-student of mine' explained Mercier, who had been 'a bit of rip' in life. 'Hodgkins' would, of course, put someone like Lodge in mind of Richard Hodgson (1855–1905), one of the founder members of the Society for Psychical Research. Although he had exposed many fraudulent mediums, Hodgson believed that Leonora Piper – one of Mercier's particular targets – was genuine and after his death allegedly returned to communicate through her.[75]

Mercier puts many (im)pertinent questions to Hodgkins, based on Lodge's revelations from *Raymond*:[76]

'What are your houses built of?' asked Mercier.

'Fire-brick,' came Hodgkins' reply.

74 Mercier, *Spirit Experiences*, p. 25.
75 Mercier, *Spirit Experiences*, p. 30.
76 Mercier, *Spirit Experiences*, pp. 33, 34.

Houses in the afterlife according to Lodge were made of eman-ations, leading Mercier to ask, 'Why fire-brick?'

'You'll know when you come down here, old thing.'

'Do you get whisky and cigars? Sir Oliver Lodge says you do.'

'Whisky! My Gad, I haven't tasted whisky for forty-two years.' He had been dead for forty-two years. 'What wouldn't I give for a B. and S.'

The spirit of Hodgkins taps him for a sovereign before he departs.

'But how shall I get it to you?'

'Give it to Mrs Bacca,' says the spirit.

Mrs Bacca comes out of her trance to interject 'I will have nothing to do with it' before again becoming apparently unconscious.

'You hear what Mrs Bacca says?'

'Well,' said Hodgkins, 'put it somewhere near her.'

Mercier puts it on the table next to the medium and Hodgkins is carried off back to the spirit world with a cry of 'Take your damned pitchfork out of my back!' Mercier admits to being so upset by the inci-dent that he went off to 'the cellaret to get just a little whisky to calm my nerves'. When he got back he was astonished to find, or rather not to find, the sovereign. It had vanished and *Not one vestige of the coin was ever seen again* (italics in the original): 'If this is not veridical, I should like to know what is.'[77]

He visits another medium, a Mrs Lambnard, to try and get his sover-eign back from Hodgkins. One of Mrs Lambnard's spirit controls is a child called Googoo who only talks in baby language. Lambnard and Googoo are, of course, a spoof on Mrs Leonard and Feda. But Hodgkins will only appear on the pledge of a further two sovereigns – 'You needn't pay him,' advises Googoo – so Mercier puts them down on the table. Hodgkins promises to show himself for a fiver. Mercier gets him down to another three sovereigns, plus half a crown for Googoo. Mercier puts the lot down on the table, but resolves to keep his eye on the pile of coins. Presently, Googoo calls out, 'Look behind 'oo!' Mercier turns in his seat and sees 'a wavering light' in the corner of the room. A shadow appears against the light: 'It never became very distinct, but it was

77 Mercier, *Spirit Experiences*, p. 35.

distinct enough for me to recognize the portrait of a good-looking middle-aged man, about forty, I should say, with black hair and beard.' Mercier 'was dumbfounded': Hodgkins had been in his early twenties when he died, and had sandy-coloured hair and a broken nose, all in complete contrast to his current configuration. Hodgkins has a lively answer for these objections, but the image suddenly disappears as the questions mount, leaving his voice to call out 'So long. Many thanks for the fiver.' Of course, when Mercier turns back to the table the money has gone. He and the medium hunt the room for the money, 'but it was nowhere to be found'. What is more, the séance had run into another hour and he had to hand over a further two guineas to the medium.[78]

The book ends with Mercier recounting his experiences to a magistrate after being unwittingly gulled by a pair of conmen on the train to London. When his story is finished, the magistrate asks him 'Pray, sir, does your mother know you are out?'

It is possible that Dr Mercier had spent too long studying insanity to remain free of it himself, for his fifty-four-page spoof was as pointless as it was bizarre except as a poetic monument to sour grapes. Dr Mercier had made some valid points in his criticism of *Raymond*, but now a perverse and simply annoying spirit revealed itself in his character. An argument that Mercier could not win by rational argument, he tries to win by satire. *Spirit Experiences* was the last book Dr Mercier wrote and he surely enjoyed many of his own jokes – he certainly got the last laugh.

Cruff on the Road to Flanders

Cruff made the most of his time at Sandhurst, passing out twelfth out of 350 in April 1917. When Winifred saw him next he was 'looking very well and sunburned, very tall and slender and gallant, wearing a big sword and his stars on his shoulders'. As she flung her arms around

78 Mercier, *Spirit Experiences*, p. 42.

his neck and he stooped to kiss her, one of the stars scratched her arm, drawing blood. She thought it a lucky omen: 'his first blood and may it be his last'. There is a picture of him in uniform sitting on the lawn at the family home of Cadoxton, still looking like a schoolboy whose trousers are not quite long enough. On 1 May, he was gazetted as a 2nd Lieutenant in the Welsh Guards. 'I feel so agonized about his future,' confided Winifred in her diary.[79]

After another brief spell at home, Cruff was sent for further training at Tadworth Camp in Surrey. Like a city under canvas, the camp would hold eight thousand men at its peak. Here, they would learn trench warfare, gas drills, throw grenades and practise shooting. For Cruff there was further training in London: a Lewis machine-gun course at Chelsea Barracks in June and a 'bombing course' at Southfields in July.[80]

While in London there were also the allures of the Berkeley, where he ran up a £7 bill on lunches, dinners and champagne. Winifred accidentally found out about it and gave him a roasting. Afterwards, he had 'swimming eyes' and, perhaps feeling guilty, she took him to Gunter's Tea Shop in Berkeley Square for an ice, as they had in days gone by. Nevertheless, Cruff still went out for dinner that evening with a Guard's chum, Paul Llewellyn, getting back after one in the morning, Llewellyn still in tow, having missed his train. 'I received Llewellyn cordially,' she wrote in her diary, 'and said nothing.'[81]

Later that month there was his first London ball, organised by his friend Geoffrey Crawshay, the Regimental Adjutant. This time, 'dancing with young ladies of fashion', she could only envy 'how good it must be to be young, heart-whole, rich, strong and healthy'. Shortly after, he was home on draft leave: last stop before the Front.[82]

Winifred had already written to the Wilkinson Sword Company about what she called a 'body shield' and they went up to London

---

79 Tennant, *Between Two Worlds*, pp. 213, 214.
80 Tennant, *Between Two Worlds*, p. 217; Letter of Christopher Tennant to Winifred, 13 June 1917, in Lodge, *Christopher*, p. 209.
81 Tennant, *Between Two Worlds*, p. 218
82 Tennant, *Between Two Worlds*, p. 220.

together to get supplies and try on a 'steel-plate lined service tunic'. This was 'Wilkinson's Safety Service Jacket' made of steel plates one and a half inches by one inch sewn inside the jacket's lining. Winifred had seen just such a jacket that had saved the life of another officer; although the jacket's cloth had been blown away, the officer had escaped with only a wound on his arm (where there was no protection). The mother of writer Dennis Wheatley also bought one for her son.[83]

Winifred saw her son off from Waterloo station, with the Welsh Guards singing 'Aberystwyth', 'Men of Harlech' and 'Land of My Fathers'. 'I shed no tear while he was with me,' she later wrote in her diary, 'but smiled to the last, though my heart was bursting.'[84]

Something Strange About Thiepval

One day in August 1917, the official war artist William Orpen found an interesting scene near the trenches at Thiepval, now behind the British lines after the fierce fighting of autumn 1916. His driver Gordon Howlett was half a mile off with the car, leaving Orpen quite alone. The last time he had been at the Somme, it was a sodden mess of mud, blood and melancholy, an 'abomination of desolation'. Now, he found it transformed: 'the dreary, dismal mud was baked white and pure – dazzling white' where 'white daisies, red poppies and a blue flower, great masses of them, stretched for miles and miles', and the air was full of white butterflies and blue dragonflies. 'It was,' he wrote, 'like an enchanted land; but in the place of fairies there were thousands of little white crosses'. He set up his easel and started to paint 'the remains of a Britisher and a Boche – just skulls, bones, garments'.[85]

83 Tennant, *Between Two Worlds*, p. 222; Lewis-Stempel, *Six Weeks*, unpaginated.
84 Tennant, *Between Two Worlds*, p. 223; Lodge, *Christopher*, p. 226.
85 William Orpen, *An Onlooker in France, 1917–1919* (London: Williams and Norgate, 1921), pp. 39–40.

> When I had been working about a couple of hours I felt strange. I cannot say even now what I felt. Afraid? Of what? The sun shone fiercely. There was not a breath of air. Perhaps it was that – a touch of the sun. So I stopped painting and went and sat on the trunk of a blown-up tree close by, when suddenly I was thrown on the back of my head on the ground. My heavy easel was upset, and one of the skulls went through the canvas.

Orpen got to his feet and mulled it over. He decided to keep on working and nothing further happened. He met his friend, the French artist Joffroy, later that evening and told him about the skulls, particularly how one had an interesting crack in it. Joffroy wanted to see it for himself and make a study of it, so Orpen took him up the next day and left him at the spot whilst he went to paint at Thiepval Wood, about half a mile away. He came back with lunch later and found the Frenchman lying down some way off from the skulls. He said that he felt ill from the smell of decomposition. Orpen pointed out that there was no smell. 'But didn't you see one has an eye still?' asked Joffroy. Orpen knew that neither skull had an eye between them. 'There must have been something strange about the place,' he concluded.

His painting of the two skulls at Thiepval is now in the Imperial War Museum, London. Orpen also painted SPR member Arthur Balfour, although more on account of his political reputation than his parapsychological interests.[86]

A Vision in Bermondsey

A hundred years after the tragedy of the First World War began, the Society for Psychical Research was still receiving reports of possibly paranormal phenomena in connection with it. On 18 May 2014, in my

---

86 Imperial War Museum, catalogue no. Art.IWM ART 2377.

capacity as editor of the SPR's magazine, I received an email from Dr Zofia Weaver on behalf of the Society's grand-sounding Spontaneous Cases Committee, forwarding a message received via the SPR website with the subject 'First World War Paranormal Experience'. In it were the barest details about a visionary experience, possibly of the type known as a 'crisis apparition', in connection with a soldier killed in the war. Intrigued, I contacted the sender and elicited a fuller though still far from complete picture; nonetheless, it gives us an important insight into the experience of the war and, surprisingly at this late date, is a previously unreported case, as far as I am aware.[87]

The case was reported by a relative, the granddaughter, of the percipient named as Caroline Lee, née Hickling (1891–1983). The correspondent, who wished to remain anonymous, had first heard the story from her grandmother at the age of around eleven years sometime in the 1970s. As she recalled, she was sitting in her grandmother's kitchen having tea and biscuits when, 'out of the blue', her grandmother told her that she had had a 'vision of her brother while she was working at Peek Freans'. James Peek and George Hender Frean had founded Peek, Frean and Co. in Bermondsey in 1857, which continued baking biscuits there until the brand was discontinued in 1989. The respondent added that 'it must have been the biscuits that reminded her'. The respondent's mother (the grandmother's daughter) was also there and 'nodded in sympathy'.

On another occasion while visiting her grandmother after school, the granddaughter asked what the vision had looked like. The grandmother replied that 'the vision was of his head and shoulders and it was very clear'. She asked if it was scary, but the grandmother said 'no, it wasn't'. After a telephone conversation between the correspondent and her mother in respect of my enquiries, she was able to later add the detail that the vision had 'appeared in a "flash"'.

87 Personal communication, 26 May 2014 to 2 June 2014, name withheld on request; published as Leo Ruickbie, 'A Vision in Bermondsey, 1917: A Previously Unreported First World War Anomalous Experience', *Paranormal Review*, 71 (July 2014), pp. 28–9.

When the percipient returned home to Mile End later that day 'her father was standing at the gate with a telegram in his hand'. This contained the tragic news that her twenty-eight-year-old brother John Hickling, Private 204107 of 'D' Company, 1st Battalion, Royal Fusiliers (City of London Regiment), had been killed in action. The date given was Thursday, 26 August 1917. Caroline told her father of the vision, but she told neither her daughter nor granddaughter what his reaction had been. She had also told the other girls at the factory on their tea break, but again we have no idea what their reaction was.

The correspondent also sent me two photographs. One of her grandmother sitting with a friend at the Peek, Frean & Co. factory. Both are in white uniforms with white caps, reclining in deckchairs for the photograph. The other is of a smart young man in a suit holding a bicycle – her great uncle – a somewhat puzzled expression on his face. Then think of that iconic photograph 'Field of Mud' by Lieutenant William Rider-Rider of a lone soldier making his way across the shattered, shell-shocked landscape of Passchendaele. Stumps of trees like broken limbs form ragged exclamations. Water lies in the shell holes as if the earth had welled up with tears. This was where he was heading.

Under the heading 'Private', the name 'Hickling, J.' is inscribed on the Menin Gate Memorial in Ypres, West Flanders, Belgium.[88] The memorial bears the names of over fifty-four thousand British and Commonwealth soldiers who fought and died during the five campaigns in the Ypres salient and whose final remains have never been identified. From this information we can reconstruct that John must have been listed as missing, presumed killed in action, during the Third Battle of Ypres, the infamous 'Passchendaele', most probably on the first day of the Battle of Langemarck fought from 16 to 18 August.

Although the correspondent initially thought that Caroline had not had any another anomalous experiences, she learnt from her mother

88 International Wargraves Photography Project, 'Private John Hickling', http://www.findagrave.com/cgi-bin/fg.cgi?page=gr&GRid=12052389 (15 October 2005), accessed 23 June 2014.

she had had another visionary-type experience in the late 1920s: 'My mum also told me that nan nearly lost her life and saw her own funeral.' The correspondent also said that she herself had had what she called 'unusual/paranormal experiences'. Commenting on her grandmother's vision, she said 'Looking back now, I think nan's brother was communicating with her so she would not forget him.'

It is important to note that the percipient had the 'vision' on the day the telegram was received. This means that her brother must have been killed some time earlier and hence prior to the 'vision'. This means that it does not fit the conditions of the true crisis apparition. In addition, only officer's next of kin were informed by telegram, the next of kin of other ranks received a standard letter by post: Army Form B104-82 for notification of death; B104-83 for those listed as missing. Sir Oliver Lodge learnt of his son's death by telegram three days after the event. We might assume a letter would take longer than a telegram, but it is generally impossible to determine how much longer, or indeed how long either would take.[89]

Assuming the veracity of the experience and taking into account the time lag between the official notification and the actual death, the 'vision' could also bear interpretation as an instance of telepathic communication between the father, who had received the telegram first, and his daughter. At this late date it is impossible to ascertain further particulars, but the case remains a poignant reminder of the tragedy of war and the way in which non-combatants could be affected by distant events on the front line.

Cruff 'to the Dark Tower Came'

'I feel like Childe Roland,' wrote Cruff from Flanders, almost on the eve of battle, 'and when I have won the Dark Tower – across all this

89 Lodge, *Raymond*, p. 72.

waste and desolate battlefield – I shall return, please God, to the "haven where I would be".'[90]

After Cruff had left Waterloo for Southampton, Winifred 'took refuge', as she put it, in St Faith's Chapel, Westminster Abbey. Alone in the darkness she found there, she could let out the tears she had been holding back. Then, 'Margaret Verrall came and spoke to me, assuring safety and that he would return': 'This war,' said Verrall, 'is not going to cut short his career.' This vision or voice told her to have faith and trust in 'the constant powerful protection which would be over him'.

The train took Cruff and his friends and fellow officers – Lieut. Ralph Walter Hargreaves ('such a nice fellow', according to Winifred), Lieut. R. G. de B. Devereux, 2nd Lieut. Thomas Harry Basil Webb (an old school-friend from Winchester and heir to the Baronetcy of Llwynarthan), 2nd Lieut. Charles Penfold Ballard and 2nd Lieut. Paul Llewellyn – to Southampton and there he boarded a ship captured from the Germans. They left at nightfall and Cruff slept on deck. Cruff and Hargreaves were in charge of the draft, about 150 men, while the others travelled separately.[91]

On 10 August, he arrived at the Welsh Guards' base camp at Harfleur, near Havre, and found it be much like Tadworth. He shared a tent with Hargreaves and took trips into Havre with Llewellyn, practising his French in the cafés. In between the café visits, there was still more training to be done, this time with real poison gas, according to his letters.[92] Like the other officers, Cruff also had a soldier-servant. This was Private Ernie Hobbs of Cardiff, 'a fair, strong, very clean, cheerful Welshman', according to Winifred. Cruff found him 'very efficient'.[93]

Before the end of the month he was arranging to spend his leave in Paris with Webb, three days before mid-September, possibly even as early as 4 September. Webb was going to stay at the Ritz – Cruff thought that he would probably join him. He wrote to his mother and they

90 Lodge, *Christopher*, p. 246; quoting from Robert Browning, 'Childe Roland to the Dark Tower Came', in *Men and Women* (1855).
91 Tennant, *Between Two Worlds*, p. 224; Lodge, *Christopher*, p. 228.
92 Lodge, *Christopher*, pp. 229–30.
93 Tennant, *Between Two Worlds*, p. 223; Lodge, *Christopher*, p. 228.

made plans for her to meet him there. But there was still the matter of a war to be fought.[94]

There were rumours in camp that the Kaiser thought the war would be over in three weeks and large notices were prominently positioned warning against spies. The war machine did not believe in rumours and on 15 August Cruff and his men entrained for the 1st Battalion and the Front. Llewellyn was left behind with 'some sort of fever'.[95]

'Do not be anxious or worried,' Cruff wrote to his mother, 'I know I shall return safe to you.' He promised to take care of himself and 'come through everything all right'.[96]

They stopped at Rouen *en route* and Cruff visited the Cathedral – 'most lovely' – and bumped into Betty Haggard, Captain Haggard's widow. Sir Oliver Lodge wrote that Cruff 'had spent many happy days with Mrs Haggard before her marriage, at the home of her parents in the Vale of Neath'. The train was waiting, however, and they had little time to renew their friendship.

The journey continued. Cruff rode partway up front in the engine, talking to the driver and watching the French, then Belgian countryside roll by. By 18 August they arrived at a reinforcement camp – Petworth Camp, Proven, in Flanders. They were to relieve the 2nd Battalion, The Scots Guards, near Elverdinghe to the left of Langemark in the Ypres salient (to the north-west of Ypres itself). From here they could hear the guns at the Front and were bothered by German aeroplanes dropping the occasional bomb. At night it was 'a wonderful sight' to see the enemy bombers caught in the beams of searchlights, shrapnel shells bursting all around.[97]

Cruff must have read *Raymond* because he used a line from the book to give an indication of the Battalion's location to his father:

94 Lodge, *Christopher*, p. 252; Tennant, *Between Two Worlds*, p. 226.
95 Lodge, *Christopher*, pp. 229, 236.
96 Lodge, *Christopher*, p. 231.
97 C. H. Dudley Ward, *History of the Welsh Guards* (London: John Murray, 1920), pp. 158–9; Lodge, *Christopher*, p. 236.

I may not tell you where we shall be when we go up into the line; I do not know really where we shall go to. Last time we were up north of blank and south of blank! and north-west of somewhere else – where the Germans were very pressing.[98]

'Where the Germans were very pressing' was used by Raymond to tell his family that he was at Ypres. At the time, the Third Battle of Ypres (Passchendaele; 31 July to 10 November 1917) was underway. Ypres, Passchendaele – the names ring out like the death knells of hope, but there was still time for cricket. Ballard picked up a limp after a bad tackle at football.[99]

Angels of Peace

'Have you seen the angels?' According to the *Grays and Tilbury Gazette* on 18 August 1917 this was the question everybody was asking in and around the town of Grays on the Thames Estuary. The newspaper had heard conflicting accounts, but the main points were that strange visions had been seen in the sky from the Thames beaches on the evenings of Tuesday and Wednesday that week.[100]

The variety of accounts was impressive: two seated figures with the word 'peace' between them fading into a rainbow; three angels with roses in their hair; or three seated angels chained together. There was talk of the Angels of Mons, but the paper insisted that these were 'harbingers of peace'. The newspaper confirmed that there had been a rainbow on Tuesday evening and speculated whether these 'Riverside Apparitions' were not some meteorological phenomenon, such as the *aurora borealis* or *rayons de crépuscule*, possibly exaggerated by children.

---

98 Lodge, *Christopher*, p. 234.
99 Lodge, *Christopher*, pp. 234–5, 238–9; Lodge, *Raymond*, p. 17.
100 Quoted in James Hayward, *Myths and Legends of the First World War*, pp. 60–1.

The paper reported that 'numerous mothers agreed that they had heard tales of "angels" from their children'. A final account from a female resident of Globe Terrace was published the following week:

> I don't know about any angels, but I saw a wonderful cloud. We were out with my landlady and the children, and were looking at the rainbow. Then I saw a white cloud a little distance away. It was shaped just like a woman. It quite unnerved me. My husband is away in the army and I thought it meant something over the water. I couldn't sleep for thinking of it. It was a wonderful thing. I've never seen a cloud like it before and don't want to again.[101]

'A Very Quiet Part of the Line'

Nineteen-year-old Cruff was given command of No. 4 Platoon, The Prince of Wales's Company: 'a good lot of men, but one has to be strict with them'. Training continued with hand-grenade practice, bayonet fighting, musketry and gas drill. There were requests home for various things: a new fountain pen, medium nib, to replace the one he had lost; a 'platoon roll book' to record the names of his men; and Winifred sent things she thought would be useful, such as scissors, photographs of home and a book of poetry. Cruff always placed the photographs near his bed at night.[102]

Soon the time for moving up to the Front came. They took the train again, but covered the last part of the journey in cattle trucks and on foot. Now they entered the landscape of destruction: 'farmhouses half demolished and churches with part of the tower blown off', and ruined

101 *Grays and Tilbury Gazette* (25 August 1915) quoted in Hayward, *Myths and Legends*, p. 61. My father, William Ruickbie, saw an 'angel'-shaped cloud in the south of France shortly after the death of my mother on 27 April 2017. Knowing my interest in the Angels of Mons, he sent me a photograph.
102 Lodge, *Christopher*, pp. 237, 262; Adam L. Gowans (ed.), *The Hundred Best Poems (Lyrical) in the English Language* (Glasgow: Gowans & Gray, 1904).

trees reduced to skeletons and stumps. The occasional German shell reached out to them, but still bursting a mile off. They reached their own artillery positions as 'a tremendous bombardment [. . .] like continuous thunder' was underway. Cruff thought it 'all very wonderful'.[103]

At Bleuet Farm, they made camp in a field of thistles, the officers three to a tent and the men in bivouacs, a simple sheet pegged down over a frame. Breakfast of bacon and eggs was served from seven to nine; lunch at one; tea from four to five; and dinner with white wine and soda at eight – eating from tin plates and drinking from mugs. They had brought their mascot with them, a tame jackdaw from the last camp; so tame, 'you can pick him up'. The *Daily News* was delivered only a day late. 'This whole business,' he wrote in a letter to his mother, 'seems often to me just a dream.' Yet despite this growing sense of unreality and the physical distance from the world he had once known, he felt closer to his mother: 'we are close together in the spirit, you and I'. He felt that their minds were in contact and so strong was the sensation that 'I feel you so near to me that when I open my eyes I expect almost to see you before me.'[104]

'We are going to a very quiet part of the line, I hear,' wrote Cruff to his mother on 31 August. 'I feel very philosophical about danger,' he added, 'and I have the conviction that I shall return to you safe.' His kit was packed up in two sandbags and taken to Company HQ by mule. Cruff and the 1st Battalion marched off as the light faded.[105]

They marched for 2 miles (3 km) on the road before turning off on to duckboards and tramped 'for miles past shell holes' with 'nothing but mud to be seen and trees stripped of branches'. Cruff walked at the head of his column, talking to his orderly and fellow Welshman, Private William Rees, about Wales. After 9 miles (14 km), their guide brought them to their new position: an old German trench, which 'really faces the wrong way'. It was breached in several places and German shells gave him a baptism of mud. His billet was a concrete blockhouse. As

103 Lodge, *Christopher*, pp. 240–1.
104 Dudley Ward, *History*, p. 158; Lodge, *Christopher*, pp. 243–4, 248.
105 Lodge, Christopher, p. 250.

candles were lit, he saw the effects of another officer, wounded earlier that day, still laid out like a scene from the *Marie Celeste*.[106]

'The men are all splendid,' Cruff wrote, 'and nobody is the least bit afraid.' Cruff especially displayed the *sang-froid* required of an officer: 'he was always cheerful,' wrote Webb, 'and very cool under fire'; in the words of Rees, 'he didn't know what fear was'.[107]

He inspected the line – described by Dudley Ward as a series of scattered shell-hole posts – under cover of dark, going out across No Man's Land to reach the outlying machine-gun posts. 'This No Man's Land,' wrote Rees, 'was strewn with dead – groups of them lying here and there.' During the day, they kept their heads down owing to German snipers. The reputation this stretch of the Front had had for being a quiet spot was no more and 'it became an absolute hell', according to Rees.[108]

Cruff expected to be at the Front for four days and was looking forward to his Paris leave. But then news came that the Military Permit Office would not allow Winifred out to visit him: only wives of officers were allowed. Webb, who had been expecting to meet his father, was similarly disappointed.[109]

As it was, he only spent two days and three nights in the old German trench. Smoking cigarettes together in Ballard's dug-out at midnight on 2 September, Cruff told him how disappointed he was not to be able to meet his mother in Paris, but as he walked him back to his own dug-out, Ballard could not help but notice how 'unusually bright and cheerful' Cruff was. Ballard, commanding No. 10 Platoon and half of No. 9, was Cruff's neighbour on the line, his own dug-out only about fifteen yards away. They would visit each other once or twice a day. 'He often told me,' Ballard wrote later, 'he loved the Welsh Guards'; and to Webb he had said that he was 'having the best time of his life'. Cruff was due

106 Lodge, *Christopher*, pp. 250–1.
107 Lodge, *Christopher*, pp. 250–1. Letter of T. H. B. Webb to Winifred, 13 September 1917, in Lodge, *Christopher*, p. 269; Rees quoted in Lodge, ibid., p. 275.
108 Dudley Ward, *History*, p. 158; Rees quoted in Lodge, ibid., p. 275.
109 Lodge, *Christopher*, p. 252.

to report back to Company HQ in the morning and then take his leave.[110]

Before he left he had time for one last letter. 'By the time you get this,' he wrote sometime on 2 September to his mother, 'you will know I am through all right.' He folded it up and put it in his pocket. At about 3 a.m, 3 September, the relieving officer, 2nd Lieut. Bob Bonsor came into Cruff's dug-out and, surprised to see him, said 'For God's sake, Tennant, get off quickly. There's a fearful bombardment going on, and it's going to get worse.'[111]

'I don't mind the shells,' replied Cruff, 'what I object to is the snipers.'

In Cadoxton, Winifred was still asleep, dreaming. 'I dreamed incessantly,' she wrote in her diary, 'and in the early morning dreamed of receiving a long telegram saying he was well.' But she woke full of anxiety.[112]

Cruff set off with Hobbs carrying his kit and Rees carrying Cruff's rifle, as well as his own, 'over shell holes and through thick mud' with 'shells falling all the time'. After ten minutes they made it to Captain Arthur Gibbs at Company HQ about two hundred yards behind the front line. Cruff talked to his captain before setting off again at about 3.30 a.m. with Hobbs and another man, Private J. Lewis, who knew the way down to Battalion HQ. They were still making their way along the duckboard track when 'suddenly they opened a barrage just where we were', recalled Hobbs.[113]

Cruff called out, 'Oh, Hobbs, I'm hit in the eye!'

Back in Company HQ, Rees had only just finished taking his equipment off when Lewis staggered in, 'pouring with blood' in Rees's

110 Letter of C. P. Ballard to Winifred, dated (incorrectly) 6 August 1917, in Lodge, *Christopher*, pp. 261–2. Letter of T. H. B. Webb to Winifred, 13 September 1917, in Lodge, *Christopher*, p. 269.
111 Lodge, *Christopher*, p. 252; quotations from an account by Rees in Lodge, ibid., p. 277.
112 Tennant, *Between Two Worlds*, p. 227.
113 Letter of Pte Hobbs to Winifred, 18 September 1917, in Lodge, *Christopher*, p. 273.

words. All he said was that an officer had been hit. Lewis had been hit in both legs and had already lost a lot of blood. After delivering his message he collapsed in a dead faint. Despite the continuing bombardment, the stretcher bearers headed off at once and, with an ominous feeling, Rees joined them.[114]

They found Cruff lying in a shell hole, Hobbs tending him. Rees reckoned that only five or six minutes had passed, but Cruff was already dead. After talking to the medical officer, Captain Gibbs could write to Cruff's mother and say, 'I am certain he never suffered at all.' Hobbs, only a foot or so away from Cruff when the shell struck, was somewhat knocked about, but otherwise unhurt.

The last letter he wrote was found upon his body. 'Just one of those bits of bad luck which go to make this business of war,' wrote Webb.[115] Cruff was buried on 4 September at Canada Farm, 6 miles (10 km) north-east of Poperinghe. Still in the line, few of his friends could be there. For devotion to duty – he had been wounded in seven or eight different places – Pte Lewis was awarded the Military Medal.[116]

Winifred described herself as 'a ghost among shadows' as she waited for news. The days were 'so long, so interminable'. Finally, at 20.15 on 6 September, the telephone rang: a trunk call from Cardiff. A man's voice read out the telegram, not from Cruff as she had hoped, but from the Army Council: 'Deeply regret 2nd Lieutenant G. C. S. Tennant, 1st Battalion Welsh Guards, killed in action [. . .]' He was buried close to Raymond Asquith.

Of the five other young officers who left Waterloo Station with Cruff, only two survived the war and neither of them unscathed. During an unsupported attack to take the village of Gonnelieu to the south of Gouzeaucourt on 1 December 1917, 'a perfect hurricane of machine-gun fire' mowed down 248 out of the 370 men sent over the top. Among

---

114 Letter of Cpt Arthur Gibbs to Winifred, 5 September 1917, in Lodge, *Christopher*, p. 256; Rees quoted in Lodge, ibid., p. 275.
115 Letter of T. H. B. Webb to Winifred, 13 September 1917, in Lodge, *Christopher*, p. 269.
116 Letter of A. Gibbs to Winifred, 5 September 1917, in Lodge, *Christopher*, pp. 256–7.

the dead were Hargreaves and Webb. Among the wounded was Devereux: he recovered, but his fighting days were over. Llewellyn was seriously wounded leading a raiding party on 10 March 1918 and the German bombardment that followed the attack killed Ballard as he sat at the door of his dug-out watching the fireworks.[117]

Oliver Lodge published *Christopher: A Study in Human Personality* in 1918, with letters and various accounts of his life. Following on from *Raymond*, one might have expected a similar book, with a similar message, but Lodge gave no hint of what had happened after Cruff's death.

'The Haven Where He Would Be'

'He had won his Dark Tower,' wrote Winifred of Cruff, 'and has woken up to find himself in the haven where he would be.' Winifred recorded her grief in her diary in restrained but intimate detail. It still affects one, reading it today. However, Winifred had one consolation: Spiritualism. She felt that her role was to give him strength through her love and forbearance and she felt sure that he must be in good company. 'He has Daphne, Fred and Margaret Verrall,' she wrote on the day she heard the news of his death – Daphne was the daughter she had lost in 1908 to influenza, Fred was Frederic Myers. When she had to explain the matter to her surviving children, she told Alexander ('Zanga'): 'death was only a door one stepped through, leaving the body behind'.[118]

Despite her fortitude, Winifred was having difficulty coming to terms with the loss of Cruff. Echoing Cruff's sense of unreality at the Front, she wrote that 'Sometimes it seems to me as if it could not be true'. Cruff was constantly in her thoughts. Every night she would go into his old room 'to tuck him up', as she put it. Letters from friends,

117 Dudley Ward, *History*, pp. 186–7, 200; Lodge, *Christopher*, p. 226.
118 Tennant, *Between Two Worlds*, pp. 227, 228.

family and well-wishers began to arrive and she began working on a memoir.[119]

In this state of grief and intense concentration upon Cruff, she had her first supernatural experience involving him. As she was falling asleep on Tuesday night, 11 September, 'he was *there*, beside me [. . .] It was *himself*.'[120]

On Sunday, 23 September, at a time when she felt 'drowned by sadness', she attempted automatic writing. Messages, first from Myers, then Cruff and finally Margaret Verrall, came through. It was, she said, 'the first script I have had since he passed over'.[121]

When she went up to London in November to arrange for a memorial plaque for Cruff, she had time to call on Gerald Balfour's sister, Lady Edith Lyttelton, at 21 College Street. They drew the curtains against the afternoon light and, with a red lamp to illuminate proceedings, attempted to communicate with the spirits through table tilting. 'Cruff speaking,' she later wrote in her diary, but remained sceptical. She confessed that she could not tell whether it was genuinely Cruff's personality communicating or simply unconscious movements of the sitters creating the communication.[122]

Afterwards they talked about the SPR. Winifred found that Edith shared her views on the current strategy: she 'utterly rebels against the methods of the group'. These methods were the system of anonymisation and distribution that they tried to enforce across the Automatists to provide more scientifically credible data. But Winifred and Edith had gone beyond the point of needing proof themselves and in their enthusiasm did not think that they needed to provide it to anyone else. Winifred complained of 'the endless scripts' and wanted 'new methods, new light', deriding 'Gerald and Aunt Nora' (Balfour and Mrs Sidgwick) as 'hidebound'. Later that week, Winifred dined with Edith and Sir Oliver, where they had a 'great talk regarding SPR-ical things'.

---

119 Tennant, *Between Two Worlds*, p. 229.
120 Tennant, *Between Two Worlds*, p. 229.
121 Tennant, *Between Two Worlds*, p. 231.
122 10 November 1917, Tennant, *Between Two Worlds*, p. 238.

Edith was now in Winifred's eyes a 'loveable creature' and together they planned a revolt.[123]

On Sunday, Winifred visited a certain Mrs Robinson at 6 Stanhope Terrace, described as a 'table medium'. Still seeking for signs of Cruff in the afterlife, she nevertheless found the séance 'unpleasant'. She noted some hits – she being identified as 'W' and the words 'Oh Mother' that seemed typical of Cruff – but she could not avoid the fact that much of it was far off the mark. 'A sort of travesty,' she called it, although she was sure no cheating had taken place, and 'repulsive' in comparison to her own automatic writing communications with Cruff. Winifred did not give up on mediums and through Sir Oliver, she would later be introduced to Gladys Leonard – posing as a 'Mrs Myra' – and report 'Cruff certainly there'.[124]

Back at Cadoxton Lodge, she met the bereaved father of Ewart Williams, who 'had seen his boy as in a vision'. Mrs Byrne, whose son Francis had been posted as missing at Gallipoli since August 1915, told her how she had heard loud knocks one night, which she took as an omen of death: it was the night Cruff died. Then, she had had a vision of Francis and felt sure that he was dead, although he said to her 'You think I am dead, Mam, but I am not'. Mrs Byrne believed that this visitation was somehow Cruff's doing.[125]

Winifred's SPR rebellion was mirrored by changes in her relationships at this time. After Cruff's death, a distance had grown between her and Gerald – 'hidebound' Gerald – and she began to describe him in unflattering terms. In contrast, her increasing involvement with Sir Oliver led her to Mrs Leonard and resulted in Sir Oliver taking charge of her Cruff memoir and publishing it under his own name, apparently at the direction of Myers from the Beyond.

123 Tennant, *Between Two Worlds*, pp. 238, 239.
124 Tennant, *Between Two Worlds*, pp. 239, 246.
125 Tennant, *Between Two Worlds*, pp. 240–1.

Does Death End All?

Dr Mercier's name was still being mentioned in *The Times* into October 1917. Sir William Barrett, billed prominently as 'Ex-President of the Society for Psychical Research' had contributed a two-part article 'Does Death End All? The Value of Psychical Research'.[126] Barrett included him with Edward Clodd in the phrase 'distinguished sceptics', but dismissed them both as 'being satisfied with their agnosticism' and enjoying 'sitting in the seat of the scornful'. For Barrett, the 'converging lines of carefully sifted evidence have, after prolonged inquiry, convinced me and many others of the continuity of human life when stripped of its present "muddy vestures of decay"'. Barrett assured readers that he always welcomed 'instructive criticism' but had no time for 'ill-informed strictures' and 'personal attacks'; and 'as regards Dr Mercier's amusing critiques, I fancy he will agree with me that it would spoil their fun if they were taken too seriously'. Mercier had recently been 'amusing' in the *British Medical Journal* in connection with C. G. Jung's newly published *Psychology of the Unconscious*.

Barrett then launched on the usual defence that great discoveries in science have often provoked censure from the scientific establishment and had a string of fine quotations from eminent individuals that a mind must be always kept open even if it required wooden wedges to do so. He was quite sure on the matter of telepathy, 'now widely taken as an accepted fact', and by implication the carpers must stop their carping.

His most interesting comment is almost by the way:

How widespread and keen is the interest in this subject at the present time your columns bear witness. So do the numerous pathetic letters I receive from complete strangers. 'May a

126 'Does Death End All?', *Sunday Times* (14 October 1917), p. 5.

broken-hearted mother,' writes one, 'venture to write to you and ask if you could help her to get into touch, even for a moment, with a dearly-loved son recently killed in France?' 'All is gone for me,' writes another, 'in the death of my beloved husband, except a splendid memory of an heroic life lived and died for God and his country . . . Oh! The agony of desolation in life without him. How little the suffering of a poor stricken soul appears to affect the great scheme of things, which seem ruthlessly to pursue some unknown end.' And so on in many other letters, from lives made desolate by the insane madness of Prussian militarism.

Barrett thought Christianity had failed to provide the consolation it promised, but this failing had given risen to the 'special value of psychical research':

It teaches us that the physical plane is not the whole of Nature, nor is it, as so many think, that aspect of the Universe which alone concerns us, and alone is open to investigation.

He held back from throwing the baby Jesus out with the religious bathwater. People were 'tired of the shibboleths of sects, the pretensions of priestcraft, and of forms and ceremonies which have lost their spiritual significance'. Psychical research had bridged the crevasse of materialism to find a spiritual reality beyond, but religion still held the keys to the Kingdom of Heaven.

He had his caveats, however, and reminded the reader that Spiritualism was not always reliable. Communications might be 'due to subconscious fabrication by the medium' or be 'inventions of mischievous spirits' – with the latter we are back with Brockway defending herself so miserably in court. But he made no apology for his position, nor any scientific argument, for that matter, that death did not end all. Notice was already given that next Sunday the newspaper would print an article on 'Psychical Research and Religion' by the Revd R. J. Campbell.

Barrett described an experiment with a Ouija board in which, to rule out fraud, the sitters had been blindfolded and after which Barrett had quietly placed a sufficiently large and opaque screen over their hands, so that even if they could see through their blindfolds they would not be able to see their hands and thus the messages spelt out. Sir Charles Edward Fryer, Superintending Inspector of the Board of Agriculture and Fisheries, queried how such complicated arrangements could be made without impeding the whole operation. Notwithstanding the evident problems, Barrett described some of the evidence obtained with these precautions in place:[127]

> In one of these blindfold sittings a remarkable message from Sir Hugh Lane came. The *Lusitania* had just been torpedoed, but nobody in Ireland knew that he was on board, still less that he had been drowned.

Sir Hugh Lane (1875–1915) was an Irish art collector who had created the world's first public gallery of modern art in 1908 in the form of Dublin's Municipal Gallery of Modern Art. Grant Richards wrote in response to Barrett's claims, pointing out that Sir Hugh's name appeared in the papers as the news of the sinking broke and that, at any rate, his intention to return from America must have been known among his friends and associates. This was probably the publisher and writer Grant Richards (1872–1948), who had once worked under W. T. Stead at the *Review of Reviews*.[128]

---

127 'Does Death End All?' [Pt 1] *Sunday Times* (7 October 1917); additional details on Fryer from *The London Gazette* (3 June 1915), p. 5325.
128 Grant Richards, et al. 'The Unseen World', *Sunday Times* (14 October 1917), p. 2; 'Grant Richards', https://www.doaks.org/resources/bliss-tyler-correspondence/annotations/grant-richards, accessed 22 July 2017.

'A Dead Soldier's Message'

On 22 September, somewhere in Bolton, Lancashire, a young woman sat down to write a letter. She was probably in her twenties, although her age was not given, and had only written the word 'Dear' at the top of the sheet of paper when she fell into a strange sleep.

When she woke up, she found that she had finished writing the letter. The pen was still in her hand. But the handwriting was different. It looked like her brother's, who was at that time believed to be in Flanders. It read:

> Mother, – I was left to die on the battlefield at ¼ to three in after-noon, on Thursday, shot through the stomach by a sniper. Tell Annie [his wife] 5s is in my inner pocket, and photos and a wallet. Ask for my things from the War Office, and leave rest to God. Albert.

Albert had died on 20 September, but official news of this did not reach his next of kin until 9 October.

Motivated by Barrett's article, A. W. Orr of Chorlton-on-Medlock, Manchester, wrote in to the newspaper with this account of apparent afterlife communication from the dead soldier. He knew both Albert's sister and mother, and could 'vouch for their respectability and credibility'. They were both 'sensitives or "mediums"; all the family are Spiritualists'. Orr added that one of Albert's comrades, who was there when he was hit, had written to his mother with a full account, although we only learn that he had dragged him into a shell-hole.

Unfortunately, there were not enough details given to be able to check any of this story; however, some traces of A. W. Orr still remain. He must have had a long-standing interest in psychical research. Two letters from him were published in the SPR's *Phantasms of the Living* in 1886. Both letters concerned a veridical dream case known to his father.

He was later involved in founding the Britten Memorial Institute and Library in Manchester in 1900, intending it to be 'a school for prophets' after the work of the Spiritualist Emma Hardinge Britten. The library had over three thousand volumes, many of them coming from Sir Arthur Conan Doyle. Orr served as Secretary of this organisation until 1922.[129]

The obituary for Emma Britten's sister, Margaret Floyd Wilkinson, appeared in *The Two Worlds* in 1912, mentioning Orr as having been present at the funeral. A small newspaper notice at the time tells us that he was Margaret's executor, full name William Arthur Wellesley Orr, a 'gentleman of independent means'.[130] Emil Mattiesen described him as President of the Manchester Society for Psychical Research.[131] These few details show that he was directly involved in Spiritualism himself.

Oliver Lodge forwarded a letter he had received from the Army Chaplain H. G. White in France as material to the subject under discussion:

Dear Sir, – I have just read a reply by yourself to Dr Mercier, under the heading 'Proofs of Spiritualism', in *The Sunday Times* (September 23). With regard to a statement of Dr Mercier, which you quote as follows:– 'As a medical man of many years' residence in medical institutions, I am sure I have seen many more dying people than Sir Oliver Lodge has, and I have never yet witnessed a look of ecstasy on the face of a dying person.' It

129 Gurney, Myers, Podmore, *Phantasms of the Living*, vol. II (London: SPR and Trübner and Co., 1886), p. 393; *Enc. Occultism and Parapsychology*; 'Britten Memorial Museum and Library', *The Pioneer*, vol. 3, no. 4 (August 2016), p. 119.
130 http://ehbritten.blogspot.de/2011/06/1912-death-of-margaret-floyd-wilkinson.html, accessed 22 July 2017.
131 There was also a Revd Arthur Wellesley Orr, MA, curate of St Giles, Pontefract in 1911 (*London Standard*, 13 March 1911, p. 10), but I am not entirely sure that they are the same person. Although it would be surprising to find two individuals with the same unusual name living at the same time, the other Orr is never referred to as Revd.

may be of interest to you to know that, some days ago, I was standing by the bed of a soldier who was dying, and just before he passed away he suddenly raised his hand, and his face lit up with such a look of joy that one could hardly use any other word than ecstasy to describe it. The Sister who had been attending him had placed a screen round his bed to screen him off from the other wounded soldiers, and I could see no cause for his sudden look of joy. He had almost ceased to breathe, and for some minutes had not answered or responded in any way when I spoke to him. Then, suddenly, came this wonderful radiant look of joy; he appeared to look right past me, as if suddenly recognising someone. I cannot account for it in any way, but that a dying man can have a look of ecstasy on his face I know is true.[132]

The Ghost of Nurse Cavell

When the war came to London, Cheiro left town. It was a Monday afternoon, 8 October, and 'we were in the middle of an air-raid in the worst days of the war'. He recalled the 'Boom! Boom! of the guns protecting London' and the 'Crash! Crash! of splinters of shells falling on the roofs'. Poor Cheiro: 'we had had little rest for the four previous nights and were beginning to feel the strain on our nerves'; or he may have felt the heat of the *Daily Mail*'s campaign against London's fortune-tellers. He and his wife decided to take the train to their country house. By a happy coincidence a medium friend of theirs telephoned – she too was feeling the strain – so they took her, he did not say whom, with them; and added a few more friends to make a party.[133]

132 Oliver Lodge, et al., 'The Unseen World', *Sunday Times* (28 October 1917), p. 2.
133 Cheiro, *True Ghost Stories*, pp. 125–39.

Soon they were all far away from the inconsiderate reminders of the war and 'in the quiet of the country soon forgot the nerve-racking experiences of the previous nights'. To say thank you, the medium offered to put on a séance, in fact, a whole series of them, just as we knew she had to. They were, said Cheiro, 'in some ways the most remarkable that I ever experienced'. It was only to be expected. Even before dinner was served, roses levitated out of a vase on the dining table and were distributed round their dinner places, according to Cheiro, who was sitting with the others by the open window, enjoying the scent of flowers wafting in from the garden and the birds' evening chorus.

After dinner they went upstairs to a room reserved for their séances, taking the roses with them as a sign from the spirit world. They sat themselves in a circle and waited. They did not have to wait long before 'a curious floating light' appeared and introduced itself.

'I am Edith Cavell,' said the light, 'or you will know me better as Nurse Cavell who was, as of course you have read, executed in Brussels.' Edith Cavell had been executed by the Germans two years previously for helping wounded allied soldiers to escape German-occupied Belgium.[134]

Cheiro expressed his sympathies, adding, 'Why do you come to me, Nurse, of all people in this world?'

It turned out that she and Cheiro had a mutual friend, some doctor whose name Cheiro did not reveal. She could not appear to him directly as he was too sceptically minded, but wanted Cheiro to convey her love to him and his wife when he saw him tomorrow. Cheiro was taken aback: he had no reason to suppose that the doctor would believe him, or that he would see him tomorrow.

'You will see him tomorrow at 9 o'clock in the morning,' she answered, 'standing at the foot of your bed.'

Cheiro must have blinked at the information, but he agreed to her request to pass on her love. Cavell had more to say. Since passing over she had been re-united with old friends and even met von Bissing, whom she claimed was mostly responsible for her death.

134 Cheiro, *True Ghost Stories*, pp. 130, 132.

'I went forward and held out my hands to him,' the light said. 'At first he kept his head down and would not look at me, but now he understands and we are quite good friends.'

'I am only sorry now I did not take Dr —'s advice, as I would have been more use to our poor men, but I knew well the risk I ran, and the end was not a surprise to me.'

The doctor was a confirmed disbeliever in Spiritualism, so Cavell gave Cheiro a piece of information that was sure to convince him: the reason he was given one of his names by his mother. She whispered it in Cheiro's ear. The séance continued and a good more was said that Cheiro preferred not to publish because of its personal character.

Cheiro went to bed convinced that 'Cavell' had been wrong on one point. It was entirely unlikely that the doctor would be standing at his bedside tomorrow morning.

Cheiro woke the next morning 'with a start' – he was not feeling well, but 'queer and quite dizzy'. There was something wrong with his throat. He could not swallow and could hardly speak. He called the doctor; of course, it was *the* doctor. There was nothing much wrong with his throat: 'some form of temporary paralysis' said the doctor. As the clock struck nine that morning Cheiro realised that Cavell's improbable prediction had been fulfilled.

'Doctor,' he gasped, 'Edith Cavell was speaking here last night. Nurse Cavell, I mean. She wanted me to tell you . . .'

'What! What!' interrupted the doctor. 'Have you gone mad?'

'No, doctor, I am as sane as you are,' said Cheiro calmly, putting aside such strange afflictions as temporary paralysis of the throat. 'I swear what I am saying is the absolute truth. Nurse Cavell, speaking last night, asked me to tell you. She wants you to come here tonight – she wants to speak to you herself – she wants to . . .'

'Enough! My good man, don't talk such nonsense,' said the doctor, putting his hand on Cheiro's head 'as if to calm me', thought Cheiro; but Cheiro continued.

'. . . that it would be next to impossible to get you to believe my story.' Cheiro gave his secret information and the doctor was astounded into agreeing to come back that evening for the next séance.

The séance as Cheiro reported it was not of any great interest. The doctor came, sat by the medium to keep an eye on her and out of the medium the voice calling itself 'Cavell' talked some more. Anything that might have been evidential was not printed because of its personal nature, but Cheiro assured his readers that his editor had seen Cheiro's notes on the séances, signed by all who were present, including the doctor. Cavell repeated that she had forgiven her persecutors and gave the good doctor her message – the usual Spiritualist message – that 'the soul side of life goes on after the death of the material body'. A flower from a vase on a table near a window supposedly floated across and was laid on the doctor's hand.

Cheiro collected celebrities, such as Kitchener, so it was not surprising that he should be delighted to add Edith Cavell to his list, but neither of them were his greatest catch.

'I Weep for My People'

'Cavell' came back to Cheiro's country house on 11 October. She prattled on in her usual way. One interesting detail let slip concerned a relative of Cheiro's who had been killed in the trenches 'a few months previously', but Cheiro gave no name. It was part of this Cavell's character to add that 'I help the German soldiers that pass over just as willingly as I do our own men'.[135]

Cavell was rather rudely interrupted on this occasion by a new voice, deeper and masculine, speaking like some prophet of old:

> Oh, men of the world, how little you understand the things that are around you. Even insects have more instinct than you have. The angle-worm provides for its food more than you do, and the blind ant stores up provision for the winter. But you men fight and kill one another in the name of civilisation.

135 Cheiro, *True Ghost Stories*, p. 144–9.

Then another voice was heard, 'a very different voice to the previous one', speaking slowly and with emphasis:

> Pray for my country. Pray for my people. England has many dark days before her. I weep for my people – for the people of England. I was called 'Edward, the Peace-maker'.

One of the sitters asked, 'Do you mean Edward the VII?'

'Yes, I am Edward the VII — pray for England and for the British Empire.'

Cheiro described the voice as 'turning towards me':

> I am indebted to you, sir, for having told me the exact date of my death even to the month and the day, when I first met you many years before it occurred. Your warning made a deep impression on my mind, and through it I made preparations which I might otherwise have left till perhaps too late.

Cheiro had met the King when he was still the Prince of Wales at Lady Arthur Paget's house in 1891. The séance continued with the spirits singing along with a cylinder recording of *The Tales of Hoffmann*, with the famous dead soprano Nordica joining in – she was another old friend of Cheiro's. After the séance, Cheiro reported that a crowd had gathered outside the house, attracted by the singing. When they entreated him to request an encore from the singer, Cheiro found himself with a difficult situation to explain. 'I could only say that the singer had left,' he said.

When the war had encroached too much upon Cheiro's world he had fled the danger and recreated his Spiritualist haven elsewhere. Like most supposed communications from beyond, the spirit revealed nothing of any interest. There were personal details, no doubt interesting to the persons involved, but Cheiro kept the lid on these. What was left was simply the usual refrain that there was an afterlife, but he played with trump cards: his séance spirits – 'ghosts that are bidden' as he called them – were top drawer.

Cheiro was a popular occultist and so was generally ignored by the Society for Psychical Research. There were no attempts to verify his supposed abilities, no reports on his claims. Nor were significant proponents of Spiritualism much impressed: Lodge and Conan Doyle took little notice of him, for example. Despite that popularity, he is also largely ignored today by historians re-examining the war years. Yet Cheiro was an influential member of his society and, even if everything he ever said is unsubstantiated, he played a significant role in promoting supernatural interpretations of the events breaking over Europe.

Dennis Wheatley and 'Something Malevolent'

After admitting to the Westminster Dragoons that he could not ride a horse, Dennis Wheatley took a commission in the Royal Field Artillery. In March 1917, he was attached for duty to 'C' Battery, No. 6 Reserve Brigade, at Biscot Camp, Luton. On 8 August 1917, with the rank of lieutenant, he was on his way to France, wearing his armoured tunic.[136]

After a hard time at Passchendaele, his division had been pulled out from the Ypres sector to what was then a quiet part of the line at Cambrai in early November. He and his fellow officers pitched their tents in a walled garden belonging to a ruined château previously used as a field hospital by the Germans. Thinking that they would be resting there throughout the winter, they started work building more permanent and warmer structures. Two bricklayers were set with building a mess and Wheatley decided to build 'a little lean-to house with a fireplace in it'.[137]

---

136 'Medal Card of Wheatley, Dennis', National Archives, Kew, WO 372/21/101780; Dennis Wheatley, *Officer and Temporary Gentleman, 1914–1919* (London: Hutchinson, 1978).

137 Dennis Wheatley, *The Devil And All His Works* (London: Peerage, 1983 [1971]), pp. 266–7.

Busy about his duties during the day, he could only work at night. He had a full moon to see by and a stack of bricks, salvaged and cleaned by his servant, to build with. He would usually start after dinner and work until after midnight. One evening, after laying and levelling bricks for about three hours, a strange feeling came over him.

He was mixing mortar and humming to himself when he had the distinct sense that someone was behind him. He swung round. No one was there. By now his brother officers would be long asleep – in the moonlight he could see their tents some way off. He turned back to his mortar. Almost immediately, he felt again 'a presence menacing me from behind'. Again he turned round, and again no one was there.

One more row of bricks, he decided. He worked on, but 'my whole being told me that something malevolent was about to strike me down from behind'. He dropped his tools and ran back to his tent in panic. 'I have no doubt,' he wrote later, 'that I was threatened by an elemental.' According to Wheatley, every thought creates a thought-form: the good ones give strength to one's guardian angel; the bad ones become elementals that 'build up etheric bodies'.

During his time in the walled garden, Wheatley shared a tent with a certain Lieutenant Pickett. Pickett's sister was dying and he was allowed compassionate leave to visit her. When he returned to the Front, he had a curious story to tell Wheatley. Pickett had been at his sister's bedside when she died. Her last words had been 'Hello, Daddy'; and then in surprise, 'Why, Jean – you here, too? Jean, a French officer, was the husband of another sister. He was also at the Front, but at the time believed to be alive and well. Two days after Pickett's sister died, they had news of Jean's death. He had been killed in action only two hours before his sister-in-law passed away. At least, that is the story as Wheatley told it. A few weeks later, he was in the Battle of Cambrai.[138]

138 Wheatley, *The Devil*, p. 291.

The Case of Captain Russell

'Daddy is dead,' said the three-year-old boy, Dicky, sitting up suddenly on the bed.[139]

His mother, Elizabeth, sitting by his side, stopped her sewing, 'Oh no, dear, he's not and I expect he'll come back to us some day.'

'No he won't,' said the boy, becoming flushed and on the verge of tears, 'Dicky knows he's dead.'

'No, dear,' said Elizabeth, 'I don't think he is.'

'No, no,' the boy persisted, 'Dick knows it.'

Elizabeth decided not to contradict him further, he was so emphatic.

She told her sister, Mary Holt, about it shortly afterwards. She recalled the incident quite clearly; however, 'even then it never occurred to us that the child's words were true'.

Elizabeth's husband, Edward Stanley Russell, was a Captain in the 1st Battalion, the Herefordshire Regiment, and then fighting in British Palestine. But as Elizabeth noted, 'we had got to look upon my husband's safety as a foregone conclusion, for he had been through Gallipoli, El Arish and the first battle of Gaza without a scratch'. The First Battle of Gaza had been the Egyptian Expeditionary Force's unsuccessful attempt to take the city from the Turks. The British suffered some four thousand casualties – killed, wounded and missing. For his part, Captain Russell had been awarded the Military Cross.

Before the war, Russell had trained for the Nonconformist Ministry and had been first Assistant Minister and then co-Pastor of Ullet Road Church in Liverpool. After marrying Elizabeth in 1913, he had devoted more time towards literary pursuits. In September of 1914, he enlisted as a private in the Liverpool 'Pals' Battalion before receiving a

139 'L. 1217. Veridical Impression. Child Percipient', *JSPR* (June 1918), pp. 193–6.

commission in the 1st Herefordshires. He wrote poetry whilst in uniform, earning a place among the 'war poets' – a collection was due to be published.[140]

Neither Elizabeth nor her sister could recall the exact date of Dicky's outburst, but thought that it was probably on 8 or 9 November. On 16 November they received news that Capt. Russell had been killed near Beersheba in the Battle of Khuweilſeh, aged thirty-four. Public announcement was made in *The Times* on 20 November.

The Editor of the SPR's *Journal*, Helen Salter, noted that the collection of the evidence was not perfect, but concluded that it was genuine. She also compared the case to several documented earlier in *Phantasms of the Living*. The case was catalogued as 'L. 1217. Veridical Premonition. Child Percipient'. Elizabeth Russell joined the SPR.[141]

The Folkestone Poltergeist

Wednesday, 22 November 1917, seventy-three-year-old Sir William F. Barrett, Fellow of the Royal Society and all the rest of it, was crouching in a hole in the ground, the candlelight illuminating his breath as it condensed in the chilly air. He could hear Mr Thomas Hesketh, Managing Engineer of the Folkestone Electricity Supply Co., and his secretary, outside, shuffling about and talking in low tones. He could hear Mr Rolfe the builder and his sixteen-year-old apprentice Penfold

---

140 Arthur St John Adcock, *For Remembrance: Soldier Poets Who have Fallen in the War* (London: Hodder and Stoughton, c.1920), pp. 101–2; *Supplement to the London Gazette* (8 March 1915), p. 2360. Both a Memoir by Rev. Arnold H. Lewis and selection of poems were said to have been in preparation, but neither were published. His papers are preserved at Harris Manchester College, Oxford, MS Russell 1, including poems, a novel and Lewis's unpublished biography (parts of which dealing with the war have been given to the Imperial War Museum).

141 'New Members and Associates', *JSPR* (February–March 1918), p. 132.

going about their work. He tried to ignore all of them. He was waiting for the supernatural.[142]

He was in what he called a 'dugout' then being built on the orders of Mr H. P. Jacques, JP and Chairman of the Urban District Council, in the garden of his house Enbrook Manor, Cheriton, then a village near Folkestone, now in Folkestone. The Manor was close to the huge military camp at Shorncliffe, a staging area for troops heading for the Western Front. On 25 May, German Gotha G.IV heavy bombers had bombed the camp, killing British, Canadian and American soldiers. Then the Gothas had bombed Folkestone, Sandgate and Cheriton, killing civilians – the windows of Enbrook Manor had been blown in by one blast. Mr Jacques was now taking precautions.[143]

Barrett was not thinking about Gothas, he was thinking about the 'remarkable and inexplicable disturbances' that Hesketh had told him about the day before in London. Rocks had been thrown about by unseen hands, the brickwork damaged and in one instance, blood had been drawn from Rolfe's hand. Hesketh believed that 'possibly some supernormal force was evidencing itself' and said as much to Barrett. In 1911, Barrett had addressed the SPR on the subject of 'Poltergeists Old and New'; now he felt on the verge of capturing the newest of them all.[144]

After an hour, he gave up. He climbed back up to Hesketh and his secretary. He was disappointed and admitted as much, but such was the fickle nature of poltergeists. With the secretary as stenographer, he set about collecting witness statements.

142 My account is based on the original notes at Cambridge University Library, SPR.MS/Journal Vol. XVIII–XIX 1917–1920, as well as the printed version, Sir W. F. Barrett and Thos. Hesketh, 'The Folkestone Poltergeist', *JSPR* (April–May 1918), pp. 155–83 and 'Correspondence', *JSPR*, (June 1918), pp. 196–7.
143 Details of the raid, http://www.iancastlezeppelin.co.uk/25-may-1917-2/4593795816, accessed 26 June 2018.
144 Published as W. F. Barrett, 'Poltergeists Old and New', *Proceedings of the SPR*, vol. XXV (1911).

'The beginning,' explained Fred Penfold the builder's lad, 'was when the hole was first dug, when sand began to drop to the bottom. Mr Rolfe accused me of pushing it down the hole, and after a second lot dropped on him, and a stone, I assured him that I had not touched it.'

Private Edward Firth Cummins of 'D' Squadron, Canadian Light Horse, then billeted with Rolfe, thought Rolfe had 'bats in his belfry' when he told him about what had been going on, but when he went to see for himself witnessed stones and large rocks being thrown down the steps although no one was there to do it. Miss Thomas, Jacques's cook of fifteen years, had seen bricks 'jump about'. Jacques himself had had stones thrown at the back of the dugout door as he closed it. A brick had even hovered over Rolfe's head, among the many other amazing things he stated had occurred. Mr W. H. Stephens, Military Tailor, had a look in and got hit behind the ear with a small stone, but he managed to catch young Fred in the act of throwing some sand. Fred then confessed to having done it all. Despite this, the other witnesses all swore that the boy could not have been responsible for every occurrence, either due to his location at the time or the weight of the object in question.

A Lieutenant Colonel Todhunter popped up and theorised that the phenomena were caused by natural gas. Reporting to Sir Boverton Redwood, Bart, DTI, of His Majesty's Petroleum Executive, Mr E. H. Cunningham Craig and Major A. de Boissiere of the British West Indies Regiment went to investigate the gas theory. Cunningham Craig thought the stories had become exaggerated and recommended that Jacques keep his new dugout well ventilated against any build-up of gases.

Barrett considered Stephens 'hasty and ill informed' and discounted the gas theory. Although Barrett believed in poltergeists, he did not say one way or the other what he thought of the Folkestone Poltergeist. He ended his report to the SPR with a general appeal to science and a specific one not to take the evidence piecemeal but as a whole, but he tried to present the facts of the case as he had recorded them, rather than force an explanation.

Before the month was up, Sir Arthur Conan Doyle had also appeared on the scene, sat in the dugout and interviewed witnesses. Sir William Barrett, he pointed out, 'had seen nothing' and 'his stay was a short one', whereas Conan Doyle himself 'made four visits of about two hours each', but also had to confess that he 'got nothing direct'. He thought Hesketh was 'a man of high education and intelligence', believed all the witnesses, dismissed all the sceptics and was certain strange forces were at work. He left the last word to Hesketh, quoting a letter from him in which he theorised that Rolfe was an unconscious physical medium.

By December the newspapers had got hold of the story and headlines talked of ' "Spooks" at Cheriton', 'Mystic Forces in a Dug Out' and 'Stones that Fly'. However, the *Folkestone Herald* conceded: 'that it is no ordinary fairytale may be gathered from the fact that such eminent men as Sir Conan Doyle and Sir William Fletcher Barrett, Ex-President of the Psychical Research Society, have been called into consultation'. The *Daily Mail* was similarly impressed by the 'careful investigations' of Conan Doyle and Barrett.[145]

Barrett mentioned the case to his fellow SPR members at a private meeting on 22 November, only hours after his initial investigation, but his report on the case was not published until the April–May issue of the Society's *Journal*, which was only available to members and a smattering of subscribed libraries. Conan Doyle publicised his version of the case in *The New Revelation* published on 29 April 1918. Conan Doyle's book went through many reprintings – four UK editions and one US edition in 1918 alone – and would have been the main source of information on the case for most people.[146]

---

145 ' "Spooks" at Cheriton', *Folkestone Herald* (1 December 1917); 'Stones that Fly', *Daily Mail* (3 December 1917), p. 5.
146 Arthur Conan Doyle, *The New Revelation* (London: Hodder & Stoughton, 1918).

A Message from Bim

'When danger was greatest,' wrote a soldier who had served under him, 'his smile was loveliest.' Cruff's school-friend Edward Wyndham 'Bim' Tennant went straight from Winchester to the Army on the outbreak of war, during what his mother called the 'the days of the Singing Armies': 'Armies that went singing through the streets, with crowds running beside them, and the air rang with cheers'. He was commissioned into the 4th Battalion, the Grenadier Guards, with the distinction of being, at seventeen, the youngest Wykehamist to go to war and, with a flair for versifying, became one of the war poets. He, too, had his lucky charms: four photographs of his mother and 'my little medal of the Blessed Virgin' that he carried into battle. He was shot dead by an enemy sniper on 22 September 1916 during the Battle of the Somme – the King wrote a personal letter of condolence to his parents, Lord and Lady Glenconner.[147]

The first recorded communication through Mrs Leonard is for April 1917, but the wording of it would imply that it was not the first communication received. The method used was generally the so-called book-test: the spirit's message would be given on a certain line on a certain page in a certain book. The book-test often involved George Heremon Wyndham, the son of Lady Glenconner's brother Colonel Guy Percy Wyndham. Commissioned as a 2nd Lieutenant in the Devonshire Regiment, attached to the 2nd Battalion, Northumberland Fusiliers, he had been killed in action on 24 March 1915. In the first message, Mrs Leonard's spirit control 'Feda' says 'Bim has brought George again.'[148]

147 Pamela, Lady Glenconner, *Edward Wyndham Tennant: A Memoir* (London: John Lane, 1919), pp. 119, 235, 241. For his poems, see *Worple Flit and Other Poems* (Oxford: Blackwell, 1916). He is buried at Guillemont Road Cemetery, Guillemont, France, at I.B.18.
148 Pamela, Lady Glenconner, *The Earthen Vessel* (London: John Lane, 1921), p. 21.

However, it was at a sitting of 17 December 1917 that the family received what they considered to be the most convincing demonstration of Bim's surviving personality in the afterlife. Mrs Leonard would stay at another house nearby and make her way to the Glenconners' home, Wilsford Manor in Salisbury. There, in the drawing room, she would go into trance and let Feda come forth.[149]

> Bim now wants to send a message to his Father. This book is particularly for his Father; underline that, he says. It is the ninth book on the third shelf counting from left to right in the book-case on the right of the door in the drawing-room, as you enter; take the title, and look at page 37.

They found the book and took it out. It was *Trees* by J. Harvey Kelman, part of a series called 'Shown to the Children' published by Jack of Edinburgh. At the bottom of page 36, continuing onto page 37, they read:

> Sometimes you will see curious marks in the wood; these are caused by a tunnelling beetle, very injurious to the trees [. . .]

The family immediately recognised the reference. Before the war, Lord Glenconner was deeply interested in forestry – even visiting Germany to learn their superior system of arboriculture – and during family walks in their woodlands would frequently point out the dangers posed by 'the beetle' to the trees. Lady Glenconner quotes him on the subject:

> You see all those quirks – those sudden bends in the new growth? Those show the beetle has got at them. You wouldn't see the damage to the young trees as I do; it's the greatest pest we have to deal with.

It became an in-joke. During their walks, Bim would whisper to his mother, 'See if we get through this wood without hearing about the

149 Glenconner, *Earthen Vessel*, pp. 58–9.

beetle.' Whenever his father was despondent, Bim would say 'All the woods have got the beetle.'

Lady Glenconner argued that the book-tests overcame explanations based on fraud, coincidence or telepathy because they involved places and information unknown to the medium and sometimes unknown to the intended recipient of the message. The book-tests, she argued, 'provide a strong argument in favour of the continuity of personality beyond the grave'.[150]

Shortly after the book-test addressed to him, Lord Glenconner joined the SPR. Lady Glenconner published the results of twenty-seven of these book-tests as *The Earthen Vessel* in 1921, including the misses as well as the hits to give a balanced account.

'Beware of the Ginger Girl'

One winter evening, two Army lieutenants made their way up a deserted Brompton Road in London, the collars of their trenchcoats turned up against the wind. They turned off into Lancelot Place and went into the Dak Bungalow, described as an 'Oriental Restaurant'.[151]

True to its description, the restaurant was decorated with oriental wall hangings inside. The lieutenants introduced themselves to the proprietress Miss Louise Hutchinson, saying that another officer had recommended her on account of her psychic powers.

'I must close the shutters because of the police,' she said, before beginning. The officers sat down and she examined the palms of their hands for signs of the future. They would both be wounded again, she said; and one of them in particular should 'beware of the ginger girl'.

Afterwards they each handed her a £1 note.

150 Glenconner, *Earthen Vessel*, p. viii.
151 'Psychic Powers', *The Times* (28 December 1917), p. 3.

'That's too much,' she said, keeping one of the notes and handing back 8s 6d – 'that's all the change I have.' She promised to get charms for them and have them blessed.

The next time she saw the two officers was in Westminster Police Court on 27 December 1917. They were police officers – not Army – and had Hutchinson up before the magistrate Charles King Francis on the charge of pretending to tell fortunes.

Mr Percy Handcock, for the defence, argued that Mr Barker, prosecuting for the Commissioner of Police, had failed to prove that Hutchinson had intended to deceive. The defendant believed that she had psychic powers.

Giving evidence, Hutchinson said that she was the daughter of a late Judge of the Bengal Presidency (not named in the report), trying to demonstrate respectability. She had, she said, been interested in 'psychic research' since childhood. She claimed that she never asked for money for her readings. She had taken pity on the two supposed officers when they called and 'tried to cheer them up'. They then 'pressed her to take money against her principles'. They also asked her 'to buy them medals or blessed charms'. They paid for these with a £1 note and she was going to send them the change.

Mr Barker added that the charms cost thruppence each.

She flatly denied closing the shutters because of the police or having made any reference to the police at all.

Handcock called his witnesses – 'principally women' noted the newspaper – to testify to their belief in the defendant's psychic ability. The only one to be named was the grand-sounding Lady Muir Mackenzie[152] – surely the same Lady Muir-Mackenzie who was involved with the International Club for Psychical Research. She had known the defendant for about a year and was 'much interested in her psychic

---

152 This could have been one of several women. Sir Robert Smythe Muir Mackenzie of Devline, 4th Baronet, had four children and of the three girls, two were then alive: Cecily (d. 1961) and Sophia (d. 1966); or it could have been his son's wife; Sir Robert Cecil Muir Mackenzie had married Kate Brenda Blowde, née Jones in 1914. The 4th Baronet's wife Anne had died in 1908.

powers'. When Hutchinson opened 'her tea shop', Muir Mackenzie gave her a present of Egyptian and oriental tapestries.

'Had the defendant carried on an extensive business?' asked Francis.

'The defendant has been under suspicion for twelve months,' reported Detective Inspector Bedford, adding that 'there had been several complaints. She had been very astute, only, as a rule, dealing with those who furnished personal introductions.'

Francis had made up his mind: 'there must be a conviction, but thought it was not one of those cases from which serious harm had resulted'. Hutchinson was fined £10, with 10 guineas costs.

1918

'On No Account To Curtail Her Holiday'

....

When the Council of the SPR gathered at 20 Hanover Square on Thursday, 31 January 1918, many of the old familiar faces were there. In the chair was the cross-correspondences fanatic J. G. Piddington, presiding over W. W. Baggally, the Rt Hon. Gerald Balfour, Sir William Barrett, the Revd M. A. Bayfield, St. G. Lane Fox Pitt, and Mrs Henry Sidgwick; also Mrs Salter, Editor, and Miss Isabel Newton, Secretary. One of their first acts was deciding to re-elect Dr L. P. Jacks as President. H. Arthur Smith, for many years the Society's Honorary Secretary, was forced by ill health to retire – J. G. Piddington stepped into the breach.[1]

In the Council Chamber at 20 Hanover Square, they listened to Miss Radclyffe-Hall give a paper on 'A Series of Sittings with Mrs Leonard' that she had undertaken with her lover Una Troubidge in 1917.[2] The SPR would consider its principal research in 1918 – conducted as a Society – to be the investigation of what it called the 'trance-phenomena' of Mrs Leonard. For three months Mrs Leonard made herself available exclusively to the Society. Only appointments made through the Society were granted and on the condition that an official recorder from the Society was always present.[3] Another case to dominate the pages of its *Journal* in 1918 was that of the Folkestone poltergeist as investigated by Sir William Barrett and Thomas Hesketh, who had also joined the Society.[4]

The investigation of Mrs Leonard would seem like a different country, a different time. Apart from some references to Zeppelin

---

1 'Meetings of the Council', *JSPR* (February–March 1918), p. 133.
2 First as papers presented to General Meetings of the Society on — and 22 March 1918, and then published.
3 'Report of the Council for the Year 1918', JSPR (February–March 1919), p. 19.
4 W. F. Barrett and W. F. Hesketh, 'The Folkestone Poltergeist', *JSPR*, 18 (1917–1918), pp. 155–82; Correspondence (*JSPR*, June 1918, pp. 196–7).

raids in Radclyffe-Hall and Troubridge's notes, one would hardly think that a war was being waged. Reading the accounts, now, creates a strange dissonance, knowing all that we know. But it was not just the SPR that seemed cosseted and divorced from the Front, soldiers on leave, such as Robert Graves, remarked on it as well. Trance phenomena were not just restricted to mediums. And in the end, what was there really to say about Mrs Leonard? Even she could not decide whether Feda was an independent spirit or some aspect of her own personality. Despite the endless book-tests, they never got past square one.

Just as the SPR had not seen the beginning of the war, it did not see its end – although retrospectively, there would be signs of that, too. Instead, the Council had to debate the pressing needs of a country still at war. The Ministry of Munitions had requested the release of printers' metals to sell to the government to save the higher costs of importing the needed metal. The SPR's Council had received news of this through their printers and decided to sell most of the stereotype plates of back issues of the *Proceedings*, perhaps to become bombs, bullets or bayonets.[5]

When Helen arrived at 20 Hanover Square one morning in April, she was surprised to find the premises vacant. Miss Newton had been suffering from ill health for some time and had finally relented to taking a holiday. This she knew, but she was surprised to find no sign of Shirley Thatcher, Assistant Secretary. Instead, 'I arrived at the Office one morning to get the news that Mrs Thatcher's husband had been killed at the Front and she would not be coming to work.' Lt George Robin Thatcher had been in charge of 'M' Anti-Aircraft Battery and died of wounds on 1 April 1918, aged thirty. At some point in the war he had been awarded the Military Cross; he would now get a granite stone in Bac-du-Sud British Cemetery, Bailleulval, Pas de Calais, France, the burial place for the 7th, 20th and 43rd Casualty Clearing Stations behind the front lines at Arras.[6]

---

5 *JSPR*, vol. 18 (April–May 1918), p. 154.
6 [Helen Salter] *Proc. SPR*, pt 178, p. 58; Commonwealth War Graves Commission website www.cwgc.org, accessed 28 March 2018.

Helen did not record her reaction to this news, nor do we have details from anyone else. Helen did, however, write to Newton to tell her the sad news, insisting that she could manage the office single-handedly and that Newton 'was on no account to curtail her holiday'. It was characteristic of her that she came back to work the next day.

The White Cavalry

The following account of what occurred between the months of April and August, 1918, I can personally vouch for as being true.

Captain Cecil Wightwick Haywood was an intelligence officer responsible for a sector of the Front between Ballieul and Béthune in Northern France. He had made his headquarters in Béthune – 'a very good position strategically' – then about 3 miles (5 km) from the forward trenches across the La Bassée Canal, according to his description.

'It was,' said the Captain, 'an anxious time for Great Britain. The British troops had been in the trenches fighting for weeks without rest or relief owing to the fact that reserves were practically exhausted.' On 11 April 1918, Field Marshal Sir Douglas Haig had issued a special order to all ranks, the famous 'Backs to the Wall' order, demanding that 'Every position must be held to the last man.'[7] The Germans had launched a spring offensive – codenamed 'Michael', the patron saint of soldiers – to smash the Allies before fresh American troops could be deployed against them.

It was in such a mood of desperation that Captain Haywood welcomed the news of the impending arrival of a Portuguese force to relieve the British. They had already landed in early March and were on their way.

7 'Special Order of the Day by Field-Marshal Sir Douglas Haig [. . .]', dated 11 April 1918. Haig's original MS version of the order is held by the British Library, London, Add MS 45416. It was reprinted in many British newspapers on 13 April.

However, the Captain described his position in the worst terms. 'Owing to the vigorous enemy action,' he said, 'the line from La Bassée to Lens and Arras was left in a "pocket" which was liable to be "hemmed in" at any moment, with all the troops, ammunition, arms and equipment it contained.'

According to the Captain, there was a real fear that the Germans could break through and reach Paris before the American reinforcements could be trained and fielded. Consequently, 'the whole British nation was called to prayer', the US President had exhorted his people to do likewise, indeed, a 'united prayer went up from all the English-speaking peoples' – they had remembered the Angels of Mons and were seeking another such miracle; forgetting that the Germans were Christians, too, and believed that they had just as much right to fickle Jehovah's favours.

When they did arrive, the Portuguese came in for heavy shelling 'practically blotting them out wholesale'. Although the Captain and his staff were three or so miles behind the lines, the intensity of the bombardment was such that it 'literally shook the ground and dazed us'. A few Portuguese survivors 'came staggering through Béthune' and the Captain learnt that their destruction had left a breach in the line through which the Germans were now advancing. British troops followed after: their flank had been turned.

German shells were now falling directly on Béthune and the situation looked grim. Then the shelling stopped.

'Fritz has gone balmy, Sir,' said Haywood's Sergeant, 'what in the world is he peppering the naked ground for?'

Following his gaze, the Captain could see the German shells bursting on an empty piece of high ground outside of the town. The explosions were assisted by concentrated bursts from massed machine guns.

'We stood looking in astonishment,' recalled the Captain. 'I can't think,' he replied to his Sergeant. 'Get along down to the canal and see what is happening there.' Curiosity got the better of him and Haywood followed shortly after to see for himself 'as there were obviously no troops within sight against whom the Germans could be directing their fire'.

As Captain Haywood picked his way across the rubble of Béthune, the German guns fell silent. Coming out of the ruined town, he saw his Sergeant and some men standing on the rim of a crater, waving their helmets.

'Fritz is retiring!' shouted the Sergeant. Haywood joined him and could see in the distance:

Outlined on the slight rise by the La Bassée village, and as far as we could see, was a dense line of German troops, who a short time before had commenced a forward movement to victory, in mass formation. This line suddenly halted, and, as we watched, we saw it break! Before our astonished eyes, that well drilled and seemingly victorious army broke up into groups of frightened men who were fleeing from us, throwing down their arms, haversacks, rifles, coats and anything which might impede their flight.

The British were able to capture some German prisoners and his Sergeant brought him two German officers. The senior officer made the following statement:

The order had been given to advance in mass formation, and our troops were marching behind us singing their way to victory; when Friedrich my lieutenant here said: 'Herr Kapitan, just look at that open ground behind Béthune, there is a brigade of cavalry coming up through the smoke drifting across it. They must be mad, these English, to advance against such a force as ours in the open. I suppose they must be cavalry of one of their Colonial forces, for see, they are all in white uniform and are mounted on white horses.'

'Strange,' said Haywood, 'I never heard of the English having any white-uniformed cavalry, whether Colonial or not. They have all been fighting on foot for several years past, and anyway, they wear khaki, not white.' The German officer continued:

We saw the shells bursting amongst the horses and their riders, all of whom came forward at a quiet walk trot, in parade ground formation, each man and horse in his exact place. Shortly afterwards, our machine guns opened a heavy fire, raking the advancing cavalry with a dense hail of lead. But they came quietly forward, though the shells were bursting amongst them with intensified fury, and not a single man or horse fell. Steadily they advanced, clear in the shining sunlight; and a few paces in front of them rode their Leader, a fine figure of a man, whose hair, like spun gold, shone in an aura round his bare head. By his side was a great sword, but his hands lay quietly holding his horse's reins, as his huge white charger bore him proudly forward.

Fear overcame the German officer and he fled, 'and around me were hundreds of terrified men, whimpering like children, throwing away their arms and accoutrements in order not to have their movements impeded, all running'.

'That is all I have to tell you,' said the officer, 'We are beaten. The German army is broken. There may be fighting, but we have lost the war. We are beaten, by the White Cavalry. I cannot understand.'

Haywood said that he interrogated other prisoners and heard the same story, but his astonishment remained:

At least two of us could swear that we saw no cavalry in action, here or elsewhere, at that particular time. Neither did any of us see so much as a single white horse either with or without a rider. But it was not necessary for us to do so, the evidence of their presence had to come from the enemy.

Had the Angels of Mons returned? The story of the white cavalry has been printed and reprinted in many sources, none of them contemporary with the events described. The earliest version I could find, and from which I have quoted above, was a pamphlet printed in 1936 by the British Israel Prayer League in Vancouver, British Columbia, apparently itself a reprint of an earlier 1935 edition.[8] There was a Cecil Wightwick Haywood in the British Army, but according to the surviving records, he was a lieutenant in the 'East African Somali' and 'East African Intelligence Department'.[9]

The 16 October 1918 issue of *The Sketch* noted that 'Miss Joan Bankes, only daughter of Mr and Mrs Jerome Bankes, is engaged to Mr Cecil Wightwick Haywood, eldest son of Lieutenant-Colonel Haywood'.[10] This must have been Lt Col. A. H. W. Haywood, CMG, CBE, DSO, of the 2nd Battalion, The Nigeria Regiment, who captured Susa in the early months of the war.[11] A 'Mr C. W. Haywood' is mentioned as having made a journey along a Somali trade route from Kismayu to Wajheir c.1913 and the name 'Cecil Wightwick Haywood' appears again in the 1920s as the Attorney General of Kenya.[12]

The African connection is well established, so we might think it doubtful that he was also serving on the Western Front in France. The appearance of the story at the juncture of another crisis for the British people – the Second World War – from an intelligence officer might suggest a different set of circumstances.

8 Cecil Wightwick Haywood, *How God Won the War* (Vancouver: British Israel Prayer League, 1936).

9 'Medal Card of Cecil Wightwick Haywood', National Archives, WO 372/9/110315.

10 'On the Home Front: Royalty and Other Personalities', *The Sketch*, issue 1342, vol. 104 (16 October 1918), p. 63.

11 Brig.-Gen. E. Howard Gorges, *The Great War in West Africa* (London: Hutchinson & Co., 1930), p. 279; Col. A. Haywood and Brig. F. A. S. Clarke, *The History of the Royal West African Frontier Force* (Aldershot: Gale & Polden, 1964), p. 319.

12 C. W. Haywood, 'The Lorian Swamp', *Geographical Journal* (May 1913); I. N. Dracopoli, FRGS, *Through Jubaland to the Lorian Swamp* (London: Seeley, Service & Co., 1914). E.g., in the *Kenya Gazette*, vol. 27, no. 1008 (22 April 1925), p. 320.

We Lost Our Only Son in France

Conan Doyle was a firm believer in the power of photography to capture the supernatural. He quoted one example relating to the war several times, obviously deeply impressed by it. This was a letter from Mr R. S. Hipwood of Sunderland, for whom the war had brought both tragedy and hope:

> We lost our only son in France, August 27, 1918. Being a good amateur photographer I was curious about the photos that had been taken by the Crewe Circle. We took our own plate with us, and I put the plate in the dark slide myself and put my name on it. We exposed two plates in the camera and got a well-recognized photo. Even my nine-year-old grandson could tell who the extra was, without anyone saying anything to him. Having a thorough knowledge of photography, I can vouch for the veracity of the photograph in every particular. I claim the print which I send you to be an ordinary photograph of myself and Mrs. Hipwood, with the extra of my son, R. W. Hipwood, 13th Welsh Regiment, killed in France in the great advance in August, 1918. I tender to our friends at Crewe our unbounded confidence in their work.[13]

There was no '13th Welsh Regiment' as such: Hipwood must have been in the 13th Battalion, The Welsh Regiment, known as 2nd Rhonnda. The Regiment was renamed The Welch Regiment in 1920 before being amalgamated with the South Wales Borderers in 1969 to form the Royal Regiment of Wales.

Records show that there was a Richard William Hipwood, son of

13 Sir Arthur Conan Doyle, *The Case for Spirit Photography* (New York: George H. Doran, 1923), p. 129.

Richard and Mary Hipwood, enlisted as a Private, no. 31499, in the 13th Battalion, The Welsh Regiment, who was killed in France on 27 August 1918. Born in Barrow-in-Furness, he enlisted in Sunderland and died of wounds, aged twenty-three. He is buried at Contalmaison Château Cemetery, France.[14]

The Crewe Circle was a well known Spiritualist group, taking its name from the town in Cheshire where they met. Its founder was William Hope (1863–1933), a pioneer of 'spirit photography', producing such images from 1905 onwards. William Crookes had been convinced by a photograph supposedly showing his dead wife taken by Hope in 1906. Conan Doyle was also a firm believer; he refused to concede the Society for Psychical Research's resolute proof of fraud when it investigated Hope in 1922.

Hope's – and the Crewe Circle's – method was double exposure. Hope would expose photographs of the sitter and the alleged spirit – itself another photograph – on the same plate and develop a composite image. It seems simple to us now, but in the early days of photography, such effects were little known and could appear convincing. The Circle's additional trick was to allow, even encourage, sitters to bring their own photographic plates. These, of course, would be substituted with the prepared plates.

Undoubtedly, there was a Richard Hipwood. Undoubtedly, his father visited the Crewe Circle for proof of his survival. Undoubtedly, the resulting photograph was a fake.

14 Roland Riddell, 'Notes on Names from 1914–1918', for the North East War Memorials Project, http://www.newmp.org.we/detail.php?contentId=8722, accessed 9 May 2017; 'Book of Remembrance 1914–1918', Donnison School Heritage and Education Centre, Church Walk, Sunderland.

The Anxious Soldier

Conan Doyle had a similar case from Mr W. T. Waters of Tunbridge Wells. Waters, like many others, visited mediums, and one of those he visited was the well-known J. J. Vango, probably in July 1918.[15] Born in London on 12 February 1861, Vango started practising as a medium in 1879 and continued up until 1936. He had been involved in William Stead's 'Julia's Bureau', opened on 24 April 1909.[16] In Waters's own words:

> In July last I had a sitting with Mr. J. J. Vango, in the course of which the control suddenly told me that there was standing by me a young soldier who was most anxious that I should take a message to his mother and sister who live in this town. I replied that I did not know any soldier near to me who had passed over. However, the lad would not be put off, and as my own friends seemed to stand aside to enable him to speak, I promised to endeavour to carry out his wishes.
>
> At once came an exact description which enabled me instantly to recognize in this soldier lad the son of an acquaintance of my family. He told me certain things by which I was made doubly certain that it was he and no other, and he then gave me his message of comfort and assurance to his mother and sister (his father had died when he was a baby), who, for over two years, had been uncertain as to his fate, as he had been posted as 'missing'. He described how he had been badly wounded and captured by the Germans in a retreat, and that he had died about a week

15 First published in *Light* in 1919, reference to 'July last' would suggest that the event occurred in July 1918.
16 'Morse & Vango', The Pioneer, vol. 2, no. 5 (September 2015), pp. 143–6; see also John Lewis, 'The Mediumship of J. J. Vango' (1913), an eight-page pamphlet.

afterwards, and he implored me to tell his dear ones that he was often with them, and that the only bar to his complete happiness was the witnessing of his mother's great grief and his inability to make himself known. I fully intended to keep my promise, but knowing that the lad's people favoured the High Church party and would most likely be absolutely sceptical, I was puzzled how to convey the message, as I felt they would only think that my own loss had affected my brain. I ventured to approach his aunt, but what I told her only called forth the remark : 'It cannot be,' and I therefore decided to await an opportunity of speaking to his mother direct.

Before this looked-for opportunity came, a young lady of this town, having lost her mother about two years ago, and hearing from my daughter that I was investigating these matters, called to see me, and I lent her my books. One of these books is 'Rupert Lives', with which she was particularly struck, and she eventually arranged a sitting with Miss McCreadie, through whom she received such convincing testimony that she is now a firm believer. During this sitting, the soldier boy who came to me came to her also. He repeated the same description that I had received, mentioned in addition his name – Charlie – and begged her to give a message to his mother and sister – the selfsame message which I had failed to give. So anxious was he in the matter, that at the close of the sitting he came again and implored her not to fail him.

Now, these events happened at different dates – July and September – the same message exactly being given through different mediums to different persons, and yet people tell us it is all a myth and that mediums simply read our thoughts.

When my friend told me of her experience I at once asked her to go with me to the lad's mother, and I am pleased to state that this double message convinced both his mother and his sister, and that his aunt is almost brought to the truth if not quite.[17]

17 Conan Doyle, *History of Spiritualism*, vol. II, pp. 337–9.

Miss McCreadie was another well-known medium of the time: even Field Marshal Douglas Haig had been to see her (in 1906), more to please his sister Henrietta, and received advice from the spirit world on how to establish the Territorial Army.[18]

'The Greatest Revelation for Two Thousand Years'

Kingsley was in St Thomas's Hospital, London, fighting with pneumonia for his life. He died on 28 October 1918. His father was on a lecture tour and on his way to a meeting in Nottingham when the news reached him: a telegram from Mary.

As he sat in his room at the Victoria Station Hotel before the lecture, he wrote to his brother Innes: 'I can hardly realise it and am stunned by the news.'[19] The hall in Nottingham was full and more crowded outside. He was urged to cancel. Conan Doyle went on with the show – 'Kingsley would wish it so' – but 'It was,' he said, 'a severe trial and test.'[20]

Back in London, he gave an interview to the *Evening News* on 30 October.[21] At first he was reluctant to talk, not because his son had just died, but because experience had taught him that the subject was seldom discussed with reverence: 'it is one that must be discussed with reverence when men are dying in battle and the hearts of their survivors are pining for some revelation that the link is not broken'.

'We have that revelation,' said Conan Doyle. 'I have been on this quest for thirty years, and I say that we have the revelation and we must carry it throughout the country as the new religion.'

18 Gary Mead, *The Good Soldier: The Biography of Douglas Haig* (London: Atlantic Books, 2007), unpaginated digital edition.
19 Quoted in Miller, *Adventures*, p. 375.
20 Quoted in Miller, *Adventures*, p. 375.
21 Reproduced as 'Sir A. Conan Doyle and His Son', *Daily Mail* (31 October 1918), p. 3.

'It is,' he continued, 'the greatest revelation for two thousand years. Religion has hopelessly broken down – I mean by that formal religion. Lutheranism has given us these Prussian devils on the one hand, and on the other, Roman Catholicism has given us the Bavarian. [. . .] The Prussian who puts on a military belt with the motto "Gott mit uns" imagines he has something there: and there is nothing.'

It is remarkable that Conan Doyle chose to ascribe German militarism to 'Lutheranism' (not Protestantism) and Roman Catholicism. The Church of England must have been a different kettle of fish. Even so, 'we must add to religion,' he argued. 'We must add something now that the war has shown us the breakdown of formal religion, when millions of men and women are looking as they never have done before for a sign and a consolation.'

He had a growing body of evidence to add credence to his claims. 'Some time ago I said I knew of thirteen mothers – thirteen – who were receiving direct messages from sons who had passed away. Doubt was expressed – gentle doubt – by a newspaper, which asked, "Who are the mothers?" What are their names?" Well, I know thirty mothers now who are receiving these messages.'

For Conan Doyle, however, even thirty mothers were not as convincing as one British officer: 'I have had a letter from a British Corps Commander who lost his son, assuring me that they are in communication. Here you have a warrior, a responsible, hard-fighting, level-headed British soldier – not the long-haired visionary, the caricature, who stands in the mind of flippant, uninformed people as the type of Spiritualist.'

Conan Doyle found an eager and serious audience for his message, despite those 'flippant, uninformed people': 'I find the most intense earnestness everywhere among the audiences.'

Conan Doyle added that he took no fees for his lectures, nor otherwise made any money out of them. It was the constant refrain of the Spiritualist: if it was done for free, then it was done only for good; overlooking the fact that Conan Doyle was comfortably well off. He did, however, end by plugging his latest book, *The New Revelation*.

When asked about the death of his son, Conan Doyle could not yet discuss such a personal loss, but acknowledging that others also had lost their sons, said, 'A mother, a father, firm in the new revelation, knows that the one who departed is no farther away than you who sit in a chair a yard away.'

It was clear that Conan Doyle's belief in Spiritualism was a great comfort to him in this hour of darkness, and it was a conviction made more concrete, more pressing by loss, to continue preaching the New Revelation.

The next day he was in Leeds. The *Daily Mail* printed a short notice of his address to a large audience of the 'Spiritualist Society': 'At a time of world-wide mourning Spiritualism afforded a satisfaction which no creed-bound religion could supply.'

One of Conan Doyle's chief satisfactions was a message from Kingsley, sceptical in life, but now praising his father's 'Christ-like message'.[22]

At another séance, Kingsley would materialise and, laying a hand on his father's shoulder, tell him he was happy.[23] The medium was Evan Powell, a Welshman working as a coal merchant in Devonshire. According to Conan Doyle, Powell always insisted on being tied up during séances 'for his own protection, since he cannot be responsible for his own movements when he is in a trance'. Conan Doyle thought him to have 'the widest endowment of spiritual gifts of any medium at present in England'.[24]

On 7 September 1919, Conan Doyle, Jean and two others held a séance with Powell. After searching his pockets they tied him to a chair and put out the lights:

Then came a voice in the darkness, a whispered voice, saying 'Jean, it is I.' I heard the word 'Father'. I said 'Dear boy, is that you?' I had then a sense of a face very near my own, and of breathing. Then the clear voice came with an intensity and note very distinctive of my son, 'Forgive me!' I told him eagerly that I

22 Quoted in Miller, *Adventures*, p. 377.
23 Miller, *Adventures*, p. 382.
24 Conan Doyle, *History of Spiritualism*, vol. II, pp. 209, 210.

had no grievance of any kind. A large, strong hand then rested upon my head, it was gently bent forward. And I felt and heard a kiss just above my brow. 'Tell me, dear, are you happy?' I cried. There was silence, and I feared he was gone. Then on a sighing note came the words, 'Yes I am so happy.' A moment afterwards another gentle voice, claiming to be that of my wife's mother, recently deceased, was heard in front of us. We could not have recognised the voice as we could the other. A few loving words were said, and then a small warm hand patted both our cheeks with a little gesture which was full of affection. Such were my experiences.[25]

The sensation of breath and the warm hand should have alerted Conan Doyle to something being amiss. What lungs do the dead have? What need of air? What heart pumps blood round the shadow of a corpse?

He would later write to *The Times* saying, 'I can solemnly declare that, using an unpaid medium, I have beyond all question or doubt spoken face to face with my son, my brother, my nephew by marriage, and several other close friends since their death. On each occasion there were six or more witnesses.'[26]

Over the next year, from the death of Kingsley to October 1919, Conan Doyle would give fifty lectures across the country, speaking to about a hundred thousand people by his own calculation.[27] His lectures alternated between a spirit photography slide show, screening the usual dubious double exposures, and a philosophical lecture, essentially a summary of *The New Revelation*.

He would bring out another book on Spiritualism in August 1919, *The Vital Message*. Here he transformed the war from the great tragedy that it was into something with 'inner reason' intended to 'shake mankind loose from gossip and pink teas, and sword-worship, and

25 *The Two Worlds Christmas Supplement* (19 December 1919).
26 Letter to *The Times*, January 1920, quoted in Miller, *Adventures*, p. 382.
27 Miller, *Adventures*, p. 379.

Saturday night drunks, and self-seeking politics and theological quibbles – to wake them up'.[28]

The decadence of the roaring Twenties and the Weimar Republic, and the re-run of Europe's great tragedy in the form of the Second World War put paid to such bunkum, but I have had the same beliefs repeated to me by Spiritualists in the twenty-first century. It was an attempt to find meaning in the madness – an understandable attempt – but there was no meaning, no 'inner reason'.

Death Conquers All

Conan Doyle was in London on 11 November 1918, staying in what he called a 'staid' hotel, when at 11 o'clock a well-dressed woman spun through the revolving doors, waltzed around the entrance hall with a flag in each hand, and exited, all without saying a word. Conan Doyle rushed out after her and in the streets 'the news was everywhere at once'.

He headed down to Buckingham Palace. Crowds were gathering. A girl was standing on top of a vehicle conducting the singing 'as if she was some angel in tweeds just dropped from a cloud'. But he was disgusted to see 'a hard-faced civilian' drinking straight from a bottle of whisky. It was a time for prayer he thought – and waltzing and singing at a pinch – and uncharitably wished that the crowd would lynch the man.

Only two weeks before, on 28 October 1918, his son Kingsley, also in London, had died of pneumonia. He had a right to be uncharitable.

His brother Innes, having, like Kingsley, served in and survived the terrible war, also died of pneumonia in February 1919. 'He was called,' wrote Conan Doyle, 'and he went like the hero he was.'

It is still repeated that Conan Doyle became a Spiritualist because of his personal losses during the war, but he was a Spiritualist before that and Spiritualism helped carry him through, whatever we may think of it. Yet it is also true that the loss of his eldest son and younger

28 Quoted in Miller, *Adventures*, p. 377

brother made him throw himself wholeheartedly into missionising Spiritualism. Both Kingsley and Innes would come back to him: at a séance a voice told him 'I am a spirit. I am Innes. I am your brother.' His mother and nephew Oscar Hornung, too. With pride he noted that in three years he had travelled 55,000 miles (88,500 km) and spoken to a quarter of a million people in the name of Spiritualism.

The Meaning of Angels

The Society for Psychical Research was deeply affected by the conflict in practical terms: membership declined, income declined, the volunteer workforce declined. Like many another organisation, it saw its members called to the Front, some never to return. In the membership book for the period there are several entries with the words 'killed in action', poignantly written in the column headed 'Date of Resignation'. Familial ties radiated out beyond such entries, so that at every level of the Society, someone was affected by loss from the presidents and former presidents, such as Sir Oliver Lodge, to the office staff and appointees, Shirley Thatcher and Helen Verrall.

But the Society had had a Good War. It had weathered the storm. It had conducted serious research. It had even emerged somewhat renewed with a higher membership, increased sales of its publications and a handful of cases that seemed to offer a glimpse of a reality beyond. At the end of the First World War, it could report an 'increase of interest in the Society's work'. After a drop to a low point of 1,085 members in 1916, the Society had come out of the war with 1,215 – three more members than in 1914 – and membership would continue to grow into 1919, giving a total of 1,305 members.[29]

29 'Report of the Council for the Year 1918', *JSPR* (February–March 1919), p. 18; Leo Ruickbie, 'A Report on "The Society for Psychical Research and the First World War" Research Project', paper given at the Annual Conference of the Society for Psychical Research, University of Leeds, 4 September 2016.

Why, then, were there complaints among members that there had not been more spontaneous cases? As we have seen there was an abundance of cases. An answer as to why the SPR should come to this conclusion is provided by the example of Professor Charles Richet.[30] He appealed directly to soldiers for their accounts and he received them, hundreds of them. The SPR, at that time, appealed, if it appealed at all, only to its own membership and received only a fraction of what it might have found. The aloof attitudes of Schiller and Murray set the tone for a general reluctance to get involved with the beliefs and stories of the great unwashed. Even after the war, knowing what Richet had discovered, prominent members of the SPR continued their strange obsession with the cross-correspondences – the revelations of 'The Plan' give some reason for this.

The cross-correspondences, as interpreted, had created, for some, certainty in the afterlife and certainty in an SPR of deceased members – the Upstairs Committee – working to change the world of the living. The coterie of leading members of the SPR became something like a secret cult, with supernatural schemes, sordid sex and a lovechild at the centre of it. The Plan, such as it was, came to nought. A boy was born – the 'Wise One' – but he did not become the world saviour. Augustus Henry Serocold Coombe-Tennant, the natural child of Winifred and Gerald Balfour, instead went on to have a distinguished military career during the Second World War, first as an officer in the Welsh Guards and then as a Special Operations Executive (SOE) commando on Operation Jedburgh, being awarded the Military Cross and Croix de Guerre. After the war, he worked for MI6. He finally retired from the world to become a monk, changing his name to Joseph, and died in 1989 at Downside Abbey. He only learnt of the Plan later in life and, even then, may not have been told all of it.[31]

During the First World War, there had been such a wide range of phenomena reported, from traditional hauntings to remote viewing to

30 'Premonitions and Other Strange Experiences in France During the Great War', edited by Cesar de Vesme, trans. H. A. Dallas, *JASPR*, vol. 15 (1921), pp. 16–28.
31 Roy, *Eager Dead*, p. xvi; 'Obituary of Dom Joseph Coombe-Tennant', *The Times* (14 November 1989).

astonishing coincidences and, of course, angelic interventions. Some people, although not having any paranormal experiences themselves, became the paranormal experiences of others, such as Rupert Brooke with Aelfrida Tillyard. The Angels of Mons had become a defining narrative of the war, so hotly debated throughout 1915, that when someone chose not to believe it on logical grounds he had to acknowledge that such doubt could be 'very unpatriotic'.[32] Whatever the ultimate reality of these events, their impact was widely felt; some understood this power, some possibly tried to manipulate it, everyone was affected by it.

Although, as President of the SPR, Dr Schiller had dismissed the plethora of predictions apparently forewarning of the war, the SPR would later discover its own predictions in the voluminous cross-correspondences, too late, though, to be of practical use. However, taking these prophecies out of their surroundings makes them seem prescient, but it would be a selective use of the evidence. Other, less mystical, voices were also warning of war. In an interview for *The San Francisco Chronicle* in September 1909, the managing director of *The Times*, the noted journalist Charles Frederic Moberly Bell, gave a grim but accurate forecast:

> I do not think there is any doubt that there will be a war between
> Great Britain and Germany before long. The situation is very much
> as a French writer pictured that between France and Germany
> before the Franco-German War, when he said the two countries
> were like two railway trains rushing together on a single track.[33]

He added that the war would come within five years – and it did – but he claimed no supernatural powers. The idea of war was 'in the air' so to speak.

Whether mediums had been in contact with the dead or not, through their reputed communications the Spiritualists had created a fantasy war that went beyond the personal drama of momentary contact

32 'The Legend of Mons', *Light* (15 May 1915), p. 251.
33 Quoted in 'A Woman of No Importance' [Mrs Stuart Menzies], *Memories Discreet and Indiscreet* (New York: E.P. Dutton, 1917), p.220.

between deceased and bereaved. Instead of being a senseless conflict, started by chance, invoked through the unthinking logic of treaties and prolonged by pigheadedness, this was a war fought for meaning of the highest order, a grand battle between the forces of good and evil. Even the casualties of this war were saved: the dead lived on and found peace and meaning again, even friendship with their enemies in a Christian-influenced wonderland beyond reality. It must have been immensely comforting to religious sensibilities to believe that all differences were resolved, just as much as it was personally comforting to the bereaved to learn that the deceased lived on in a better place.

The similarities between the combatants demanded this extreme differentiation. Here were countries ruled by members of the same royal houses, countries inhabited by the same peoples, divided only by the artificialities of nationality. Recall the football match between Tommy and Kraut that first Christmas, those calls across the trenches reminding the British that 'we are all Anglo-Saxons' and the poignant fellow-feeling of arch-warrior Ernst Jünger.

It has always been a mystery why the Second World War did not produce the same effect on the spiritual feelings of the nation as the First. Here may be a reason. The fight against the political ideology of Nazism provided the extreme differentiation that was lacking during the First and hence provided by the Church and Spiritualism.

Although Spiritualism had already enjoyed widespread popularity since emerging in the middle of the nineteenth century, its popularity was dramatically enhanced by the involvement of well-known authority figures – such as Sir Oliver Lodge and Sir Arthur Conan Doyle – who could command respect and a large audience, but also, through their own involvement and losses in the war, enjoin with the commonality of experience and especially the experience of suffering. Looking at the well-established mechanisms of influence, such proponents of Spiritualism brought several key factors to bear: liking – people genu-inely liked them; authority – granted through their work and public recognition, such as the awarding of knighthoods; and social proof – they shared in a widespread experience and used this abundance of personal accounts to further their views.

Spiritualism served a sociological function by providing a meaning that both justified the conflict and ameliorated personal loss. Furthermore, it was promoted by powerful influencers using the social media of their day – print and the public platform – to their utmost advantage.

A central difficulty for Spiritualism was the question of what the dead should do. All of life is largely about the sustaining of life. In our entertainment-dominated culture we too often forget this, but family, the daily bread and shelter are what life is about. The dead have no need to procreate since the living will provide the next generation of the dead. The dead have no need to eat since they have no bodies. The dead have no need of shelter since there is nothing to shelter from. What should they do? Previous Christian ideas of the deceased forming heavenly choirs to sing the praises of God, if they were not roasting in hell or languishing in purgatory, no longer had any currency even in a still predominantly Christian country. Instead, Spiritualists created an idealised place. For Lodge this had touches of the gentleman's club with Raymond's whisky and cigars, but even here he joined the majority of Spiritualist accounts in describing an everlasting Sunday School in which the dead morally improved themselves through suitable study in order to progress through the ranks of the afterworld or be sent to help the living. Like all idealised pictures of a supposed afterworld, it sounded immensely boring.

In the post-war Spiritualist literature there is also the sense that the afterlife functions as a reconciliation committee. Edith Cavell meets von Bissing, for example, and they become 'quite good friends'. Those who had lost most – their lives – nevertheless find it possible to forgive, or are forgiven. This represents, of course, the wishes of those writing such stuff. Through their privileged revelations the Spiritualists were mending the wounds of the recent, still burning past. They expressed Christian sentiment where the established Christian Church had preached the victory of one at the cost of the other's destruction. The Church as an established institution had easily, intentionally, and perhaps already, become politicised in the service of the State.

The Angels of Mons was the perfect example of a paranormal event that could be conscripted by the Church – and was. The revelations of Lodge and Conan Doyle, on the other hand, were more than bordering on forbidden necromancy and could never be condoned by the official Creed.

The overriding question is whether the Spiritualists did this consciously. It would appear that they did not. Through automatic writing and trance communication they expressed the wishes of the unconscious – perhaps wishes that could not be expressed otherwise. The experience of Spiritualism was a collective dream representing a collective desire. The repression of 'good' sentiments in a period of societal warlikeness found expression in the mouths (or pens) of autohypnotic subjects.

Whilst we might think that we have the answer, in the midst of such slaughter how could we deny anyone the smallest iota of solace? And even then, not everything can always be explained away.

The maidservant's remote viewing and little Dicky's foreknowledge of his father's death are obviously not of the same type as the séance-room gatherings; and could anyone doubt the experiences of Vera Pownall, so well documented by the Society for Psychical Research? I have in my collection some 'lucky' coins dating from the First World War and sometimes turn one or other over in my fingers and think of Joe Cassells of the Black Watch and his 'lucky' half-franc piece, or Private Shore of the Machine Gun Corps and his silver shilling, and wonder, like Rupert Brooke, of the time when we will 'see, no longer blinded by our eyes'.

Index

INDEX

Elmslie, R. C. 95
Emden 137
Empress of physical mediums 332
England 10, 13, 24–5
    declaration of war 47
ethereal vibrations 111–13
Evan-Thomas, Admiral 244
Evans, G. H. 308–9
Eve 168
Evening News (newspaper) 61, 80, 204, 207, 216, 394
Evening Post (newspaper) 14
Eves, Private 58
evil 76–7, 401

Fairclough Smith, Mrs 107
Faunus message 175–7, 181–2, 185
Feda/Freda (spirit control) 183–9, 199–202, 339, 375–6
Feilding, Everard 21, 22, 43, 102, 133
Feilding, Rudolph, 8th Earl of Denbigh 21
Ferenczi, Sandor 104
Ferguson, John 40–1
Festing, Major Michael Wogan 26
Festubert 167
Fielding-Ould, Dr Robert 43, 105
Fielding-Ould, F. 317
First World War 65–6, 102–3
    1914 1–95
    1915 97–223
    1916 225–82
    1917 283–379
    1918 381–404
    Autumn Offensive 153, 177
    as battle between good and evil 44–5
    and the battle of Heligoland Bight 65–6, 107, 108, 110, 237
    build up to 24
    and the Conan Doyles 25–6
    and Dogger Bank 107–10, 237, 246
    and Gallipoli 11, 119, 120, 121, 122–3, 164, 221–2, 266, 357, 370
    and the Great Retirement 61, 62, 206, 270, 320
    and Jutland 237–53, 255, 256
    and Loos 162, 177, 178, 267, 269, 278
    and the *Lusitania* (cruise liner) 70, 134–44
    and Marne 214
    outbreak 14, 18, 19–20, 23, 38–9, 45–53, 67, 72–3, 133, 214
    prediction 3–11, 7, 16, 53–6, 401
    and the 'Race to the Sea' 73, 124–5, 321
    see also Mons; Somme; Ypres
Fisher, Charles 277
Flammarion, Camille 298, 333
Flanders 116, 118, 191, 321, 361
Fleming, John M. 29
Fletcher, Eric 116, 128–9, 145, 147, 150, 152, 180–1
Folkestone Herald (newspaper) 374
Folkestone poltergeist 371–4, 383
Forbes, Alec 26
Forbes Phillips 220

Ford, Ford Maddox 69
Foreign Office 18
Forman, Henry James 6, 10
Fortnightly Review 24
fortune-tellers/fortune-telling 310, 312, 314–15, 324, 363, 377–9
Fox-Pitt, St George William Lane 21–2, 335, 383
Frameries 60, 62
Frampton, Walter 279, 294
France 4, 10, 50, 68, 69, 70, 72, 73, 90–1, 115, 123, 149, 263, 272, 401
Frances, Lady 38
Francis I 81, 154
Francis, Charles King 278, 279, 293, 294, 378–9
Franz Ferdinand, Archduke 4, 9, 149
Fraser, Lovat 10–11
Frean, George Hender 344
Free Catholic and Spiritual Church 325
Freeman, Arthur Samuel 167–8, 169–70
French, Field Marshall Sir John 56, 60
French army 50, 63, 70, 155
    Fifth Army 56, 60
    and Mons 59
    Third Army 265
French, the 125, 145–6, 177, 223, 267
Freud, Sigmund 40, 104, 133, 297
Friend, Edwin William 133–5, 137–40, 141, 142–4
Friend, Faith 143–4
Friend, Marjorie 133, 134, 142–4
Front 80, 88, 91–3, 101, 115–17, 124, 144, 147, 152, 154, 158, 165, 178–9, 187, 193, 206, 266, 277, 279, 289, 309, 322–3, 326, 342, 348, 350–2, 355, 384, 385, 399
    see also Western Front
Frothingham, Thomas 108
fruitarianism 168–9
Fryer, Sir Charles Edward 360
Fullerton, George Stuart 132, 134
'Fums Up' 162–3

G-194 (German destroyer) 64
Gallipoli 11, 119, 120, 121, 122–3, 164, 221–2, 266, 357, 370
Gambetta, Léon 158
Garibaldi 47
gas
    natural gas phenomena 373
    poison gas attacks 125–7, 146, 223, 347
Gaufridi, Louis 297
Gemini 17
George, St 53, 61, 62, 205
George V 53, 119, 168, 375
German aeroplanes 348
German Army 51
    1st Army 51, 59
    2nd Army 51
    3rd Army 51
    IX Corps 59
    mobilisation 149
German artillery 116, 117–18, 122–3, 128, 165, 179
German Empire 3, 9, 173
German General Staff 105

409